PHARMACEUTICAL BIOTECHNOLOGY

FUNDAMENTALS AND APPLICATIONS

PHARMACEUTICAL BIOTECHNOLOGY

FUNDAMENTALS AND APPLICATIONS

Dr. CHANDRAKANT KOKARE

Professor and Head (Pharmaceutics)

Sinhgad Technical Education Society,
SINHGAD INSTITUTE OF PHARMACY,
Narhe, Pune - 411041, INDIA

N1661

PHARMACEUTICAL BIOTECHNOLOGY

ISBN NO. 978-81-85790-68-8

First Edition	:	October, 2007
Third Edition	:	September, 2013
©	:	Author

The text of this publication, or any part thereof, should not be reproduced or transmitted in any form or stored in any computer storage system or device for distribution including photocopy, recording, taping or information retrieval system or reproduced on any disc, tape, perforated media or other information storage device etc., without the written permission of Authors with whom the rights are reserved. Breach of this condition is liable for legal action.

Every effort has been made to avoid errors or omissions in this publication. In spite of this, errors may have crept in. Any mistake, error or discrepancy so noted and shall be brought to our notice shall be taken care of in the next edition. It is notified that neither the publisher nor the authors or seller shall be responsible for any damage or loss of action to any one, of any kind, in any manner, therefrom.

Published By :
NIRALI PRAKASHAN
Abhyudaya Pragati, 1312, Shivaji Nagar,
Off J.M. Road, PUNE – 411005
Tel - (020) 25512336/37/39, Fax - (020) 25511379
Email : niralipune@pragationline.com

Printed By :
Repro Knowledgecast Limited,
Thane

DISTRIBUTION CENTRES
PUNE

Nirali Prakashan
119, Budhwar Peth, Jogeshwari Mandir Lane
Pune 411002, Maharashtra
Tel : (020) 2445 2044, 66022708, Fax : (020) 2445 1538
Email : bookorder@pragationline.com

Nirali Prakashan
S. No. 28/27, Dhyari,
Near Pari Company, Pune 411041
Tel : (020) 24690204 Fax : (020) 24690316
Email : dhyari@pragationline.com
bookorder@pragationline.com

MUMBAI
Nirali Prakashan
385, S.V.P. Road, Rasdhara Co-op. Hsg. Society Ltd.,
Girgaum, Mumbai 400004, Maharashtra
Tel : (022) 2385 6339 / 2386 9976, Fax : (022) 2386 9976
Email : niralimumbai@pragationline.com

DISTRIBUTION BRANCHES

NAGPUR
Pratibha Book Distributors
Above Maratha Mandir, Shop No. 3, First Floor,
Rani Jhanshi Square, Sitabuldi, Nagpur 440012,
Maharashtra, Tel : (0712) 254 7129

BENGALURU
Pragati Book House
House No. 1, Sanjeevappa Lane, Avenue Road Cross,
Opp. Rice Church, Bengaluru – 560002.
Tel : (080) 64513344, 64513355,
Mob : 9880582331, 9845021552
Email:bharatsavla@yahoo.com

JALGAON
Nirali Prakashan
34, V. V. Golani Market, Navi Peth, Jalgaon 425001,
Maharashtra, Tel : (0257) 222 0395
Mob : 94234 91860

KOLHAPUR
Nirali Prakashan
New Mahadvar Road,
Kedar Plaza, 1st Floor Opp. IDBI Bank
Kolhapur 416 012, Maharashtra. Mob : 9855046155

CHENNAI
Pragati Books
9/1, Montieth Road, Behind Taas Mahal, Egmore,
Chennai 600008 Tamil Nadu, Tel : (044) 6518 3535,
Mob : 94440 01782 / 98450 21552 / 98805 82331, Email : bharatsavla@yahoo.com

RETAIL OUTLETS
PUNE

Pragati Book Centre
157, Budhwar Peth, Opp. Ratan Talkies,
Pune 411002, Maharashtra
Tel : (020) 2445 8887 / 6602 2707, Fax : (020) 2445 8887

Pragati Book Centre
Amber Chamber, 28/A, Budhwar Peth,
Appa Balwant Chowk, Pune : 411002, Maharashtra,
Tel : (020) 20240335 / 66281669
Email : pbcpune@pragationline.com

Pragati Book Centre
676/B, Budhwar Peth, Opp. Jogeshwari Mandir,
Pune 411002, Maharashtra
Tel : (020) 6601 7784 / 6602 0855

PBC Book Sellers & Stationers
152, Budhwar Peth, Pune 411002, Maharashtra
Tel : (020) 2445 2254 / 6609 2463

MUMBAI
Pragati Book Corner
Indira Niwas, 111 - A, Bhavani Shankar Road, Dadar (W), Mumbai 400028, Maharashtra
Tel : (022) 2422 3526 / 6662 5254, Email : pbcmumbai@pragationline.com

www.pragationline.com   info@pragationline.com

Dedicated to

My Family Members

FOREWORD

It is my privilege to write the foreword for the book entitled **'PHARMACEUTICAL BIOTECHNOLOGY- FUNDAMENTALS AND APPLICATIONS'** has been written by **Dr. Chandrakant Kokare**.

Biotechnology is a fast developing science and I think there is wide scope for its further development, especially in pharmaceutical industries. This is so because of the relevance of biotechnology in pharmaceutical industry particularly in the area of microbial bioconversion of drugs, fermentation, development of new drugs by rDNA technology, applications of genetic engineering, production of bioactive molecules, storage and preservation of drugs, and testing of pharmaceuticals.

This book contains basic aspects and applications for biotechnology techniques based on the syllabus of the courses conducted by various Indian Universities. Biotechnology is the subject being taught at degree level in B. Pharm., B. Sc. (Biotechnology), B. Tech., M. Sc. (Microbiology and Biotechnology) and medical sciences. The concepts have been elaborated through different chapters, including historical aspects, applications of microbes in pharmaceuticals, fermentation technology, genetics, plant cell culture and animal biotechnology etc. The book is unique, concise and an up to date source offering students an innovative, adoptive and valuable presentation on the subject. The concepts applied to pharmaceutical biotechnology have been illustrated and compiled with current examples. The central theme has been carefully projected with the help of neat diagrams, figures and schematics. This book will fulfill the needs of undergraduate and post-graduate students of pharmacy and science. I am also sure that industrial biotechnologist engaged in the production and processing of microbial products would also find this book useful in their respective fields.

Dr. Kokare has rich experience of teaching and research in Pharmaceutical Microbiology and Biotechnology. I wish all the success for his present venture.

Dr. B. P. KAPADNIS
Professor and Head,
Department of Microbiology
University of Pune
Pune 411 007, India

PREFACE OF THIRD EDITION

The knowledge of biotechnology has expanded a lot in recent years. This subject has been included in the syllabus of almost all colleges and universities both at under-graduate and post-graduate levels. Pharmaceutical Biotechnology is related to development of new strains for pharmaceuticals, fermentation technology, recombinant technology, enzyme immobilization, developments of transgenic plants and animals and production of new molecules by biotransformation.

This 'PHARMACEUTICAL BIOTECHNOLOGY- FUNDAMENTALS AND APPLICATIONS' book has been written by taking into consideration to cover all parts as general biotechnology, rDNA technology, industrial microbiology, plant tissue culture and animal biotechnology. While framing these different chapters, care has been taken to cover the prescribed syllabus of Indian Universities for B. Pharm. and some part of B. Sc. (Biotechnology), M. Sc. (Microbiology and Biotechnology), B. M. Tech. and Medical sciences at degree level. The book is designed to use for third year B. Pharm. students (Pharmaceutical Biotechnology) and final year students for Gate and other competitive examination. Many Indian Universities in the country have started conducting a part of undergraduate examination in multiple choice questions. All the chapters in the present book are followed by short answer, long answer, multiple choice, match the following and fill in the blank questions.

The realization of the need for this book and great response from the students and professors encouraged me to upgrade the previous edition. All chapters are revised by addition of new development in biotechnology. The book is a simple, handy, comprehensive and profusely illustrated digest on Pharmaceutical Biotechnology with special stress on the requirement of undergraduates. It is also hoped that it will serve as a useful resource for teachers of Pharmaceutical Microbiology and Biotechnology and post graduate students.

I express my sincere thanks to all my teachers, faculty members and students for their kind help, motivation and valuable guidance in writing this book.

Readers are requested to write any shortcomings in this edition and give me valuable suggestions for the improvement of this book for the next edition.

5th September, 2013

Dr. Chandrakant Kokare

kokare71@rediffmail.com

PREFACE OF FIRST EDITION

The knowledge of biotechnology has expanded a lot in recent years. This subject has been included in the syllabus of almost all colleges and universities both at under-graduate and post-graduate levels. Pharmaceutical Biotechnology is related to development of new strains for pharmaceuticals, industrial technology, recombinant technology, enzyme immobilization, developments of transgenic plants and animals and production of new molecules by biotransformation.

This 'PHARMACEUTICAL BIOTECHNOLOGY- FUNDAMENTALS AND APPLICATIONS' book has been written by taking into consideration to cover all parts as general biotechnology, rDNA technology, industrial microbiology, plant tissue culture and animal biotechnology. While framing these 13 chapters, care has been taken to cover the prescribed syllabus of Indian Universities for B. Pharm. and some part of B. Sc. (Biotechnology), M. Sc. (Microbiology and Biotechnology), B. M. Tech. and Medical sciences at degree level. The book is designed to use for third year B. Pharm. students (Pharmaceutical Biotechnology) and final year students for Gate and other competitive examination. Many Indian Universities in the country have started conducting a part of undergraduate examination in multiple choice questions. All the chapters in the present book are followed by short answer, long answer, multiple choice, match the following and fill in the blank questions.

The realization of the need for this book and great response from the students and professors for my previous book on Pharmaceutical Microbiology and Biotechnology encouraged me to upgrade the previous edition and produce new separate book on Pharmaceutical Biotechnology. All chapters are revised by addition of new development in biotechnology. The book is a simple, handy, comprehensive and profusely illustrated digest on Pharmaceutical Biotechnology with special stress on the requirement of undergraduates. It is also hoped that it will serve as a useful resource for teachers of Pharmaceutical Microbiology and Biotechnology and post graduate students.

Readers are requested to write any shortcomings in this edition and give me valuable suggestions for the improvement of this book for the next edition.

21st October, 2007

Dr. Chandrakant Kokare
kokare71@rediffmail.com

CONTENTS

1. Biotechnology: Scope and Importance .... 1.1 – 1.10
2. Development of Industrial Strains .... 2.1 – 2.14
3. Fermentation Process .... 3.1 – 3.22
4. Down Stream Process and Biological Waste Treatment .... 4.1 – 4.10
5. Production of Pharmaceuticals .... 5.1 – 5.20
6. Microbial Biotransformation .... 6.1 – 6.14
7. Introduction to Genetics .... 7.1 – 7.22
8. DNA Replication, Transcription and Translation .... 8.1 – 8.20
9. Genetic Recombination (Gene Transfer) .... 9.1 – 9.10
10. Recombinant DNA Technology (Gene Cloning) .... 10.1 – 10.22
11. Techniques of Genetic Engineering .... 11.1 – 11.20
12. Blotting Techniques and Gel Electrophoresis .... 12.1 – 12.14
13. Healthcare Biotechnology .... 13.1 – 13.10
14. Blood and Blood Products .... 14.1 – 14.20
15. Surgical Dressings, Ligatures and Sutures .... 15.1 – 15.18
16. Enzyme Technology .... 16.1 – 16.26
17. Plant Tissue Culture .... 17.1 – 17.30
18. Transgenic Plants .... 18.1 – 18.10
19. Animal Tissue Culture .... 19.1 – 19.16
20. Biotechnology and Ethics .... 120.1 – 20.8

APPENDICES

Appendix-I : Answers For MCQS .... AI.1 – AI.2
Appendix-II : Bibliography .... AII.1 – AII.4
Index .... I.1 – I.4

•••

CHAPTER 1

BIOTECHNOLOGY: SCOPE AND IMPORTANCE

CONTENTS

INTRODUCTION
APPLIED BRANCHES OF BIOTECHNOLOGY
MILESTONES IN BIOTECHNOLOGY
SCOPE AND APPLICATIONS OF BIOTECHNOLOGY

1.1 INTRODUCTION

Biotechnology has created many opportunities for the benefit of mankind and in the understanding of the fundamental life processes. The term biotechnology was introduced in 1917 by a Hungarian engineer, **Karl Ereky**. He used the term for large-scale production of pigs by using sugar beets as the source of food. According to Ereky, all types of work are biotechnology by which products are produced from raw materials using living organisms. Traditional Biotechnology that led to the development of processes for producing products like yogurt, Vinegar, alcohol, wine and cheese. The modern biotechnology embraces all the genetic manipulations and the improvement made in the old or traditional biotechnological processes. Modern biotechnology has offered opportunities to produce more nutritious and better tasting foods, higher crop yields and plants that are naturally protected from disease and insects.

Biotechnology is one of the world's fastest growing and most rapidly changing technology. During the end of 20th century biotechnology emerged as a new discipline of biology integrating with technology. Biotechnology is the application of scientific and engineering principles to the processing of materials by biological agents (microorganisms, plant and animal cell) to provide goods and services. The **Spinks Report** (1980) defined biotechnology as the application of biological organisms, system or processes to the manufacturing and service industries. Biotechnology can be represented as a mixture of various biological sciences for better services in the field of pharmaceuticals such as microbiology, biochemistry, biophysics, cell biology, genetics, molecular biology, engineering technology etc.

1.2 APPLIED BRANCHES OF BIOTECHNOLOGY

Biotechnology has given to humans several useful products by using microbes, plant, animals and their metabolic machinery. Recombinant DNA technology has made it possible to engineer microbes, plants and animals such that they have novel capabilities.

The main applied branches of biotechnology are classified as follows:

(i) **Agriculture Biotechnology:** It deals with a group of scientific techniques, including genetic engineering which are used to create, improve or modify plants and animals. It develops new techniques for the production of high yielding and pest and disease resistant plants by using concepts of mutagenesis and rDNA technology.

(ii) **Pharmaceutical Biotechnology:** Pharmaceutical biotechnology is a major branch of biotechnology. It include production of therapeutic proteins and hormones, fermentation products like antibiotics, vaccines or drugs, production control using biosensors, drug design using the receptor hypothesis, standardization of chemotherapeutic agents and diagnostic aids using the gene cloning technology, recombinant DNA technology, enzyme immobilization etc.

(iii) **Medical Biotechnology:** The area of medical biotechnology which utilizes diagnostic kits for detection of different diseases. e.g. AIDS detection kits, glucose measuring kits etc. and rapid detection kits for autoimmune diseases, cancers, infectious diseases, genetic disorders, based on specificity of monoclonal antibodies are now available in the market. The production of artificial organs (e.g. liver, kidney) as an option or replacement alternative for vital organs lost due to accidents or birth disorders is an emerging field in medicine.

(iv) **Environmental Biotechnology:** The destruction of wastes from industrial, urban or other sources by the use of specific microorganisms is the major application of environmental biotechnology. Biological treatment methods have played a significant role in improving the human environment by converting complex-organic matter from waste into simple forms. Bioremediation is an emerging technology and offers significant potential for cost effective, environmentally acceptable treatment of contaminated waters and soils. Waste can also be converted to biofuel to run generators. Microbes can be induced to produce enzymes needed to convert plant and vegetable materials into building blocks for biodegradable plastics

(v) **Engineering Biotechnology:** The utilization of genetically modified strains for chemical synthesis and utilization of biotech based enzyme sensors for chemical process monitoring are mainly included in engineering biotechnology.

(vi) **Textile Biotechnology:** The application of biotechnology to the textile industry involves the use of natural and recombinant enzymes obtained from specific microbial cells. These enzymes are used at different stages of textile manufacturing to get high quality and cheaper clothes. Biotechnology also plays a major role with respect to waste treatment by the use of enzymes to remove colour dye and effluent treatment for heavy metals in the textile industry.

(vii) **Mining and Metal Biotechnology:** Biotechnology principles applied in the mining and metal industry includes, bio-degradation, passive bioremediation and bioleaching of ores from sulfides, bio-concentration of metals from solutions, metal reduction, phosphate bioprocessing, cyanide degradation, coal processing etc. It helps in metal extraction with low cost-recovery.

(viii) **Leather Biotechnology:** In the leather industry microbial enzymes have played a major role in the improvement of the quality of leather. Enzyme immobilization has offered automation of the technology and cost effective treatment of leather. Acid active enzymes (protease and lipase) are used to treat partially processed substances such as tanned leather and pickled skin to make the substrate more consistent.

The basic areas and applied branches of biotechnology are shown in Figure 1.1.

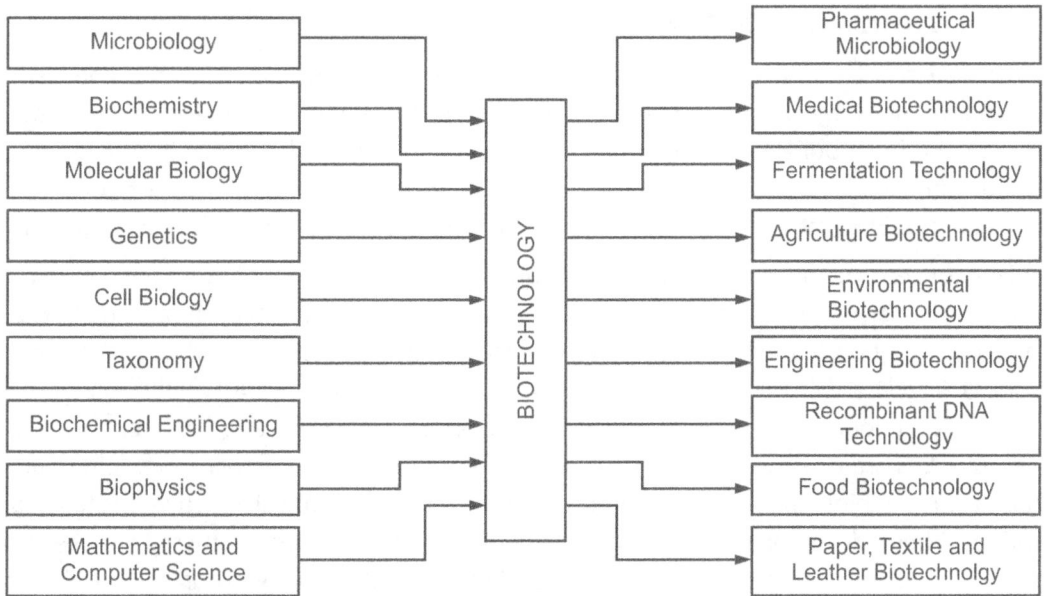

Fig. 1.1: Basic areas and applied branches of Biotechnology

A series of derived terms have been coined to identify several branches of biotechnology. **Bioinformatics** is an interdisciplinary field which addresses biological problems using computational techniques, and makes the rapid organization and analysis of biological data. The field may also be referred to as **computational biology,** and it is defined as, "conceptualizing biology in terms of molecules and then applying informatics techniques to understand and organize the information associated with these molecules." Bioinformatics plays a key role in various areas, such as genomics and proteomics, and forms a key component in the biotechnology, molecular biology and pharmaceutical sciences. **Blue biotechnology** is a term that has been used to describe the marine and aquatic applications of biotechnology. **Green biotechnology** is biotechnology applied to agricultural processes. The designing of transgenic plants to grow under specific environments in the presence or absence of chemicals is the example of green biotechnology. **Red biotechnology** is applied to medical processes. The designing of organisms to produce new active molecules such as antibiotics, and the engineering of genetic cures through genetic manipulation are the examples of red biotechnology. **White biotechnology**, also known as industrial biotechnology, is biotechnology applied to industrial processes. The designing of an organism to produce active chemicals which are useful for industry such as enzymes and proteins are the examples of white biotechnology. The investment and economic output of all of these types of applied biotechnologies is termed as **bioeconomy**.

1.3 MILESTONES IN BIOTECHNOLOGY

In the late 19th century, many discoveries and developments were made to gene birth of molecular biology by biochemists, geneticists and cell biologists. The term biotechnology was described in a bulletin of the Bureau of Biotechnology published in 1920. The articles in this bulletin described the different roles of microbes in leather industry, pest control and fermentations. The historical developments in biotechnology are summarized in Table 1.1.

The concept of molecular biology, microbiology, and biotechnology has changed the scenario of pharmaceutical developments. The advancements in recombinant (rDNA) and monoclonal antibody technology have led to developments of new drug molecules. Products developed from the basis of genetic engineering are recombinant soluble CD_4, tissue plasminogen, erythropoietin, colony stimulating factors etc. Different types of diagnostic kits are developed by using monoclonal antibodies. The most developing field in pharmaceutical biotechnology is the production of therapeutically active proteins and peptides. These drugs have been extensively utilized in replacement therapies where the patient is unable to produce the required protein (e.g. insulin). Many drugs and vaccines are developed by using basic concepts of biotechnology. Genomics, pharmacogenomics, proteomics, gene therapy, gene cloning and tissue engineering are the present focus of biotechnology.

Table 1.1: Historical development in biotechnology

Development	Year
Pasteur proposes that microbes that cause fermentation	1857
Discovery of genetic basis of heredity by **Gregor Mendel**	1860
Fleming discovers chromation, i. e. chromosomes	1879
The first cancer causing virus is discovered by Rous.	1911
Microbes are used to treat sewage for the first time in Manchester, England.	1914
Development of fermentations process for acetone and n-butanol by **Chain Weizmann**	1916
Discovery of penicillin by **Alexander Fleming**	1929
Discovery of streptomycin by **Selman Waksman**	1943
DNA is proven to carry genetic information.	1944
Elucidation of double helical structure of DNA by **Francis Crick** and **James Walson**	1953
Mechanism of DNA replication was studied in *E .coli* by **Meseleson** and **Stahl**.	1958
Determination of genetic code by **Nirenberg** and **Mathaei**	1961
DNA transformation into *E.coli*	1970
Discovery of restriction enzymes	1971
Preparation of monoclonal antibodies using hybridoma cells by **Cesar Milstein** and **George Kohler**	1975
Sequencing of DNA by **Sanger** and **Coulson**	1975
Genetically engineered microorganisms can be patented(US Supreme Court)	1980
Development of Gene Bank	1982
Discovery of PCR	1985
Development of human genome project	1990
Complete sequencing of yeast genome	1996
Dolly (sheep), first cloned animal	1998
Maintenance of human stem cells in culture	1998
Human genome, the first mammalian genome sequenced	2001

Some major advancements in the field of pharmaceuticals in the last few decades have come forth as a result of extensive research and development in biotechnology. Human Insulin (Humulin) is the first pharmaceutical product derived from DNA technology which was discovered by Genetech and Eli Lilly and Company in 1882 and this product has been approved by US FDA. Recent advances in genetics, immune system, recombinant DNA, hybridomas and monoclonal antibiotics have led to a rapid increase in the number of biotechnological products (Table 1.2) for human use. In 1988, only five proteins from genetically engineered cells had been approved as drugs by the United States Food and Drug Administration (FDA), but this number would skyrocket to over 125 by the end of the 1990s. There was tremendous progress in agricultural field since the market introduction of the genetically engineered Flavr Savr tomato in 1994. Ernst and Young reported that in 1998, 30% of the U.S. soybean crop was expected to be from genetically engineered seeds.

Table 1.2: Important biotechnology drugs and vaccines

Generic name	Product name	Name of company	Year of discovery
Human insulin	Humulin	Eli Lilly	1982
Sometrem	Protropin	Genetech	1985
Digoxin Immune Fab	Digibind	Burroughs Wellcome	1986
Interferon -α - 2a	Roferon –A	Hoffmann – La- Roche	1986
Interferon -α - 2b	Intron- A	Schering- Plough	1986
Hepatitis – B-vaccine	Recombivax HB	Merk	1986
Somatotropin	Humatrope	Eli Lilly	1987
Heamophilus –B-conjugate Vaccine	Hib. Titer	Praxis Biologics	1988
Hepatitis – B-vaccine	Engerix-B	SmithKline Beecham	1989
Interferon – y-Ib	Actimmune	Genetech	1990
Sargramostim	Leukin	Immunex	1991

1.4 SCOPE AND APPLICATIONS OF BIOTECHNOLOGY

Biotechnology is the applied science and has made many advances in different fields. Pharmaceutical biotechnology is based on the production of antibiotics, vaccines, therapeutic proteins, hormones, vitamins and other pharmaceuticals. It also includes targeted drug delivery system, standardization of chemotherapeutic agents, production control using biosensors, enzyme immobilization, gene cloning technology, monoclonal antibodies etc. Fields of medical biotechnology, agriculture biotechnology, environmental biotechnology and marine biotechnology are linked with pharmaceutical biotechnology. Major developments are taken place in the field of pharmaceuticals in the last few decades because of extensive research and advancement in the field of biotechnology, biochemistry, organic chemistry, pharmacology and new drug delivery systems.

Recombinant DNA technology: The recombinant DNA technology is appreciated as a milestone in development of pharmaceutical biotechnology. Different products are prepared by genetic engineering such as human insulin, erythropoietins, tumour necrosis factors, monoclonal antibodies, clotting factor, tissue plasminogen activator, interleukins, interferons, antitrypsin etc. The production of human insulin by recombinant DNA techniques was an early goal for the pharmaceutical industry. This technique has been used to produce number of natural proteins, vaccines and enzymes. Various diagnostic kits have been developed such as tumour kits, pregnancy testing, ovarian cancer detecting test, immunoradiometric assay kits etc.

Gene therapy: Inserting a missing gene or replacing a defective one in human cells is an important outcome of gene therapy. This technique uses a harmless virus to carry the missing a new gene into the appropriate chromosome. Gene therapy has been used to treat patients with adenosine deaminase (ADA) deficiency, a cause of severe combined immunodeficiency disease (SICD), in which cells of immune system are missing or inactive. Spliceosome-mediated RNA trans-splicing (SMaRT) is a new technology for gene therapy that exploits the expressed genetic differences between normal and diseased cells. This technology may be applied to a wide range of diseases that involve the expression of unique or mutated genes. Cystic fibrosis, duchenne muscular dystrophy (DMD), spinal muscular atropy (SMA) diseases are easily treated by SMaRT gene therapy.

Molecular markers: The last decade has seen great advances in the development of molecular biological reagents, robotics, arraying techniques, assay detection technologies and faster computers. This has made it possible to embrace comprehensive monitoring of complex biomolecular events at reasonable costs. The use of microarrays and other technologies has provided the ability to monitor the expression of essentially the whole genome in the form of individual mRNA levels for a wide variety of situations and settings. This has opened the door to use of molecular profiling or multi-variant biomarker strategies for every step in the drug discovery and development process. The use of large complex sets of genomic biomarkers, generally in the form of microarrays used to monitor the expression of large set of genes. It is used in the identification and validation of drug targets. Polymerase chain reaction (PCR), is also being used to more quickly and accurately identify the presence of infections such as AIDS, Chlamydias and other microbial diseases.

Criminal forensic: DNA fingerprinting is the process of cross matching two strands of DNA. In criminal investigations, DNA from samples of hair, body fluids or skin at a crime scene is compared with those obtained from the suspects. It uses highly developed technologies with scientific evidence to investigate criminal cases involving robbery, kidnapping, rape, murder or identification of any missing relatives in any calamity. It has become one of the most powerful and widely known applications of biotechnology today.

Monoclonal antibody: Antibodies are glycoproteins that can be made to specifically target the immunizing agent. They are invaluable for *in-vitro* and *in-vivo* diagnostic applications. They are also being used to detect allergies, anaemias and heart diseases. Monoclonal antibody diagnostic kits are available for drug assays, blood typing and infectious diseases such as hepatitis, gonorrhoea, syphilis, streptococcal infections, AIDs etc. The most important utilization of the hybridoma technology is the target oriented therapy so as to attain cell specific delivery of drugs for cancer, HIV etc.

Genetically engineered vaccine: The first genetically engineered vaccine was approved in US in 1986 for hepatitis B. Genetic engineering allows large scale production of the protein components of a virus. Many vaccines are under development for production of humans against influenza, rabies, hepatitis, herpes simplex, poliomyelitis etc.

Plant tissue culture: Plant tissue culture is the technique of growing plant cells, tissues and organs in an artificially prepared medium under aseptic conditions. This technique has many applications for production of secondary metabolites. Many natural products are prepared by plant tissue culture such as vincristine, vinblastine, opium alkaloids, digitalis glycosides etc. Plant cells are also used in the process of biotransformation. It has potential for bioconversion of steroids, alkaloids, tannins etc. The method of immobilized plant cells has been found very effective for the production of secondary metabolites. Animal cell culture deals with the study of organs, tissues or individual cells in vitro. Antibodies, enzymes, hormones, cytokines etc. are produced by animal cell culture techniques.

Genetically engineering plants: Genetically engineering plants are also poised to produce vaccines. A few hundred acres of genetically engineered banana plantation can provide enough vaccine to immunize 120 million children every year that need to be protected against common diseases. *Bacillus thuringiensis* produce proteins that kill certain insects such as lepidopterans (tobacco budworm, armyworm), coleopterans (beetles) and dipterans (flies, mosquitoes). *B. thuringiensis* forms protein crystals during a particular phase of their growth. These crystals contain a toxic insecticidal protein. The Bt toxin protein exist as inactive protoxins but once an insect ingest the inactive toxin, it is converted into an active form of toxin due to the alkaline pH of the gut which solubilise the crystals. The activated toxin binds to the surface of midgut epithelial cells and create pores that cause cell swelling and eventually cause death of the insect. Bt toxin gene has been cloned from the bacteria and been expressed in plants to provide resistance to insects without the need for insecticides

Genetically engineered animals: One of the future sources of cheap protein-drugs in the coming years, would be genetically engineered animals who would secrete these drugs in their milk. They will be available at a cost of three or more times lower than the current cost. Animals that have had their DNA manipulated to possess and express an extra (foreign) gene are known as transgenic animals. Transgenic rats, rabbits, pigs, sheep, cows and fish have been produced, although over 95 per cent of all existing transgenic animals are mice. Transgenic animals can be specifically designed to allow the study of how genes are regulated, and how they affect the normal functions of the body. Many transgenic animals are designed to increase our understanding of how genes contribute to the development of disease. These are specially made to serve as models for human diseases such as cancer, cystic fibrosis, rheumatoid arthritis and Alzheimer's so that investigation of new treatments for diseases is made possible. Transgenic animals that produce useful biological products can be created by the introduction of the portion of DNA which codes for a particular product such as human protein (a-1-antitrypsin) used to treat emphysema. In 1997, the first transgenic cow, **Rosie,** produced human protein-enriched milk. The milk contained the human alpha-lactalbumin and was nutritionally a more balanced product for human babies than natural cow-milk. Transgenic mice are being developed for use in testing the safety of vaccines before they are used on humans. Transgenic mice are being used to test the safety of the polio vaccine. Transgenic animals are made that carry genes which make them more sensitive to toxic substances than non-transgenic animals. Toxicity testing in such animals will allow to obtain results in less time.

Pharmacogenomics: Pharmacogenomics is the study of how the genetic inheritance of an individual affects his/her body's response to drugs. The term is derived from the root of the word "pharmacology" and the word "genomics". The vision of pharmacogenomics is to be able to design and produce drugs that are adapted to each person's genetic makeup. Using pharmacogenomics, pharmaceutical companies can create drugs based on the proteins, enzymes and RNA molecules that are associated with specific genes and diseases. These tailor-made drugs not only to maximize therapeutic effects but also to decrease damage to nearby healthy cells. The discovery of potential therapies will be made easier using genome targets. Genes have been associated with numerous diseases and disorders. With modern biotechnology, these genes can be used as targets for the development of effective new therapies, which could significantly shorten the drug discovery process.

Bioinformatics: Bioinformatics is an emerging interdisciplinary area of science and technology encompassing a systematic development and application of IT solutions to handle biological information by addressing biological data collection and warehousing, data mining, database searches, analyses and interpretation, modeling and product design. Being an interface between modern biology and informatics it involves discovery, development and implementation of computational algorithms and software tools that facilitate an understanding of the biological processes with the goal to serve primarily agriculture and healthcare sectors with several spinoffs. In the pharmaceutical sector, it can be used to reduce the time and cost involved in drug discovery process particularly for third world diseases, to custom design drugs and to develop personalized medicine. Computer-aided drug design (CADD) is a specialized discipline that uses computational methods to simulate drug-receptor interactions. CADD methods are heavily dependent on bioinformatics tools, applications and databases.

Human Genome Project (HGP): The Human Genome Project (HGP) is an attempt to map completely the entire spectrum of genetic materials that can be found in all human beings. It is used to determine the complete sequence of the DNA from a typical human cell and it provides information and resources to understand some of the critical differences that make us individuals and that often contribute to diseases. Technology and resources promoted by the Human Genome Project are starting to have profound impacts on biomedical research and promise to revolutionize the wider spectrum of biological research and clinical medicine. It is expected that the development in biotechnology will lead to a new scientific revolution that could change the lives and future of the people.

QUESTIONS

(A) Short answer questions:
1. Define:
   (i) Biotechnology
   (ii) Recombinant DNA technology
2. Explain in short different branches of biotechnology.
3. Write full form of GEAC. What is its use?
4. What are the various approaches to treat DNA deficiency disease?
5. What is gene therapy?
6. Why insecticidal protein present in *B. thuringiensis* does not kill bacteria?
7. What is the most common application of PCR?

(B) Long answer questions:
1. Explain in detail scope and applications of Biotechnology.
2. Write in short 'historical developments in biotechnology'.
3. Write advantages and disadvantages of production of genetically modified crops
4. How can biotechnology be useful in agriculture? Explain with examples.
5. Explain in detail importance of Biotechnology in Pharmaceutical Sciences.

(C) Multiple choice questions:
1. The double helical structure of DNA is discovered by _____ .
   (a) **Crick** and **Walson**
   (b) **Meselesson** and **Stahl**
   (c) **Milstein** and **Kohler**
   (d) **Sanger** and **Coulson**
2. Which one of the following is the first rDNA product?
   (a) Interleukins
   (b) Leptin
   (c) Tissue of plasminogen activator
   (d) Insulin
3. The enzyme not used in genetic engineering
   (a) Ligase
   (b) Polymerase
   (c) Phosphatase
   (d) Lipase
4. Fermentation technique was introduced by-----
   (a) **Paul Ehrlich**
   (b) **Louis Pasteur**
   (c) **Robert Koch**
   (d) **A. Fleming**
5. Pencillin was discovered by-----
   (a) **Paul Ehrlich**
   (b) **Louis Pasteur**
   (c) **Milstein** and **Kohler**
   (d) **A. Fleming**
6. Who is said to be founder of modern genetics
   (a) **Charles Darwin**
   (b) **Gregor Mendel**
   (c) **Robert Koch**
   (d) **August Weismann**

(D) Match the following:

A	B
(a) Human insulin (Humulin)	(i) Merk
(b) Hepatitis B-vaccine (Recombivax HB)	(ii) Immunex
(c) Sometrem (Protropin)	(iii) Eli Lilly
(d) Sargramostim (Leukin)	(iv) Genetech

(E) Fill in the blanks:
1. _____ is the technique of growing plant cells, tissues and organs in an artificially prepared medium under aseptic conditions.
2. Mechanism of DNA replication was studied in *E. coli* by _____ in 1958.

■■■

CHAPTER 2
DEVELOPMENT OF INDUSTRIAL STRAINS

CONTENTS
> INTRODUCTION
> ISOLATION OF CULTURES
> SCREENING OF INDUSTRIAL IMPORTANT MICROBES
>> Primary screening
>> Secondary screening
> STRAIN IMPROVEMENT METHODS
>> Mutation
>> DNA transfer techniques

INTRODUCTION

Industrial microbiology is the field of microbiological sciences concerned with the use of microorganisms in industrial processes. Most important for the success of any fermentation industry is to isolate new strains which produce new active metabolites and in larger amounts. Isolation of microorganisms from the environment is the first step in screening for natural products. It is possible to isolate many different microorganisms by enrichment techniques. However, for industrial isolation and screening, such enrichment techniques usually require more time, labour and money.

The discovery of novel natural products is possible if we use different approaches such as desired product characteristics and process development, and ecophysiological methods of isolation and screening. The different microbial types can be isolated from natural sources such as soil, water, plants, animals etc.

ISOLATION OF CULTURES

Industrially important strains can be isolated from different natural sources. Samples are collected from natural sources to isolate bacteria, fungi, actinomycetes or other microorganisms. All samples should be collected aseptically, with the aid of sterile spatulas, forceps, scalpels, gloves and plastic bottles. Samples should be representative of all sites e.g. soil type, marine sand, sediment and mud, plant surface and parts, rhizosphere plane and zone or water column. It should be labeled with a full description and date of collection. Seasonal and temporal aspects may be considered for the collection of samples. Actinomycetes population may decrease after a heavy rainfall. Samples should be collected from soil and water several inches deep because the surface contains lot of dust particles. Water samples may be collected from estuaries, lakes, marine environments, streams etc. Once the samples are brought into the laboratory, they should be examined immediately and stored at $4^\circ C$ in the refrigerator.

The following techniques are used for the isolation of microorganisms.

1. **Media and ecological parameters:** Incorporation of natural extracts and environmental biophysical parameters into media can affect the number and variety of microorganisms isolated in the laboratory. Some agar media contain extracts at concentrations of 10 to 50% of the total liquid volume. Infusions and extracts are usually prepared from soils, muds, leaves, roots, rocks, compost, barks etc. Some agar media are prepared by addition of multiple carbon and nitrogen sources or complex natural carbon-nitrogen sources, such as chitin, cellulose or pectin.

2. **Non-selective isolation from soil:** Standard dilution spread plate technique may be used to isolate microorganisms from soil. Soil sample (1/5/10 gm) is mixed with 99 ml of sterile saline solution and shaken at 100 to 150 rpm for 25 to 30 min. The soil suspension is serially diluted in the appropriate sterile diluent and 0.1 ml volume of diluents is spread onto the agar plates (spread plate techniques). For the isolation of actinomycetes, all samples (sediment, mud or soil) are air dried in sterile Petri plates at room temperature for 6 to 10 days. Plates are incubated upside down at 25 to $30^\circ C$ for 5 to 10 days. The incubation temperature may depend on the original soil temperature and types of microorganisms. All plates should be examined every 2 days for new colony formation.

3. **Selective enrichment:** Selective enrichments are designed to enhance isolation of one or more species over the other species. Antibiotics such as penicillin, streptomycin, chloramphenicol, cycloheximide, chlorotetracycline, polymyxin are incorporated in the media for isolation of specific groups of actinomycetes and fungi. Preheat treatment is one of the important technique mainly used for isolation of actinomycetes. Soil samples may be treated at 40 to $120^\circ C$ for 2 hour to 30 days and then used for isolation of heat-resistant actinomycetes. A combination of pretreatment with a suitable selective medium is necessary for the efficient isolation of certain genera. The selective isolation of bacteria may be performed by addition of specific or desired enzyme systems such as chitin, cellulose, pectin, amino acids, metals and antibiotic precursors in the media.

4. **Isolation from plant material:** Plant parts such as flowers, leaves, stems and roots are mainly used for isolation of bacteria, fungi and actinomycetes. Parts of plants are cut with a sterile scalpel or scissor in a laminar flow hood or clean room. A sample (1/2/5 gm) of plant materials is placed in a flask containing appropriate diluent. The flask is shaken at room temperature for 20 to 30 min (150 rpm). Sample (1 ml) is withdrawn and serially diluted. Three to four dilutions are spread onto plates containing plant isolation agars.

5. **Isolation from water:** Water (50/100 ml) sample is filtered through a 0.22 μm membrane filter. The membrane is gently scraped with a wide mouth 2 ml sterile pipette. The suspension is transferred to 9 ml of diluent and vortexed for 5 to 10 min. The sample is serially diluted and spread on selective media for isolation of actinomycetes, bacteria and fungi. Pretreatment of water samples may enhance the number of actinomycetes. Microbial species may be isolated from water samples by centrifugation. 'Rhodococcus' and 'Micromonospora' species are selectively isolated by heating water samples at 55°C for 6 min. *Actinoplanes* species are isolated from flowing water on water agar plates made with filtered lake water or chitin agar and by incorporating 0.1% (w/v) potassium tellurite.

Colonies are picked with a flamed wire loop or sterile L-shaped needle or a sterile wooden stick and transferred to appropriate agars or replica plated for screening. All isolates are properly maintained and preserved to ensure genetic stability and high titer. Flow sheet for isolation of marine actinomycetes is shown in Figure 2.1.

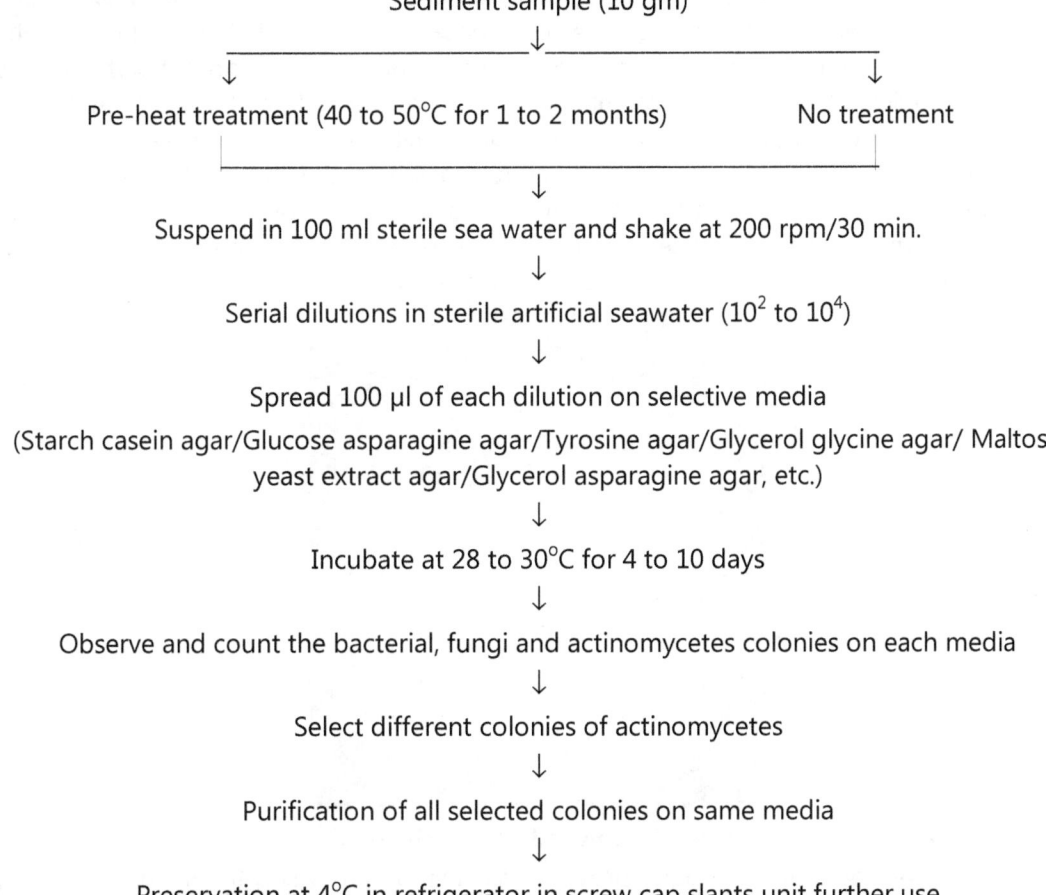

Fig. 2.1: Flow sheet for isolation of marine actinomycetes from sediments

SCREENING OF INDUSTRIAL IMPORTANT MICROBES

Screening may be defined as the use of selective procedures for isolation of high-yielding species from natural sources, such as soil, water, plants and animals containing a heterogeneous large microbial population. Screening techniques are mainly classified as primary screening and secondary screening.

Primary screening:

Primary screening consists of some preliminary tests required to isolate microbial species exhibiting bioactive property. These tests are performed for isolation of microorganisms capable of producing antibiotics, organic acids, enzymes and vitamins. Some of the techniques used for primary screening are described as follows:

1. **Crowded plate technique:** The crowded plate technique is the simplest screening technique used for isolation of antibiotic producing microorganisms. Soil or other sources of microorganisms are diluted in sterile saline solution and then spread on nutrient agar plates by using the spread plate technique. The agar plates having 300 or more colonies per plate are selected because they are helpful in locating the colonies producing antibiotic activity. Microorganisms producing antibiotic activity are indicated by a zone of inhibition around the colony (Fig. 2.2). Antibiotic producing colonies are subcultured by using similar medium. All active colonies are purified by streak plate technique, before making stock cultures. It is necessary to carry on further testing to confirm antibiotic activity associated with a micro-organism because the zone of inhibition can be occurred by other causes such as acid production by the microorganism which can alter pH of the medium thus inhibiting growth of other organisms nearby.

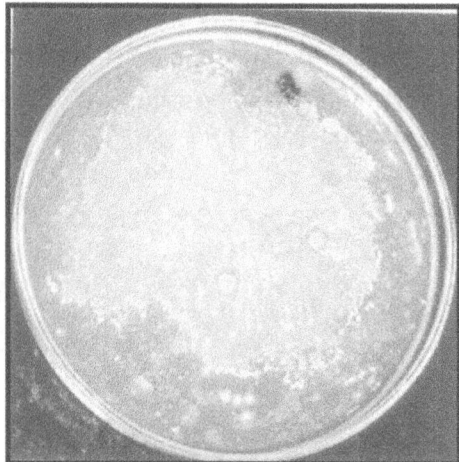

Fig. 2.2: Crowded plate technique

The crowded plate technique provides information regarding the inhibitory activity of a colony against unknown microorganisms. It is necessary to confirm activity against specific microorganisms. Therefore, the crowded plate technique has been modified by introducing a 'test-organism'. Dilutions of soil or other sources are spread on the surface of agar plates so that isolated colonies are developed (approx. 50 to 200/plate). After development of well isolated growth, test organism suspension is spread on same agar plate. The plates are again incubated for the growth of test microorganisms. The formation of inhibitory zones around certain colonies indicates their antimicrobial activity. Antibiotic producing colonies are again isolated and purified before preservation and further testing.

2. **Accidental contamination method:** In these techniques, plates are further incubated for study of growth characteristics of newly isolated microbes. These plates are accidentally contaminated by environmental microorganisms. If these contaminated plates are further incubated for 2 to 5 days then the isolated microbes (those having antimicrobial activity) show a zone of inhibition against the colonies (Fig. 2.3).

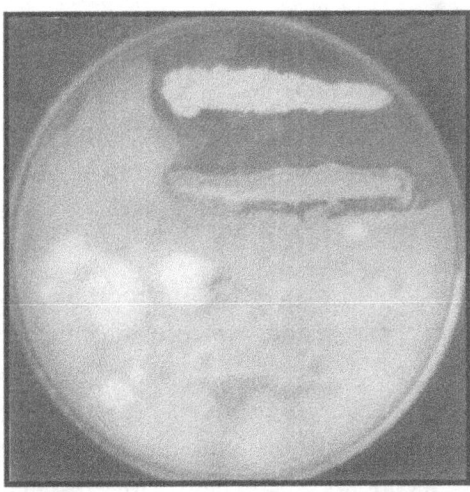

Fig. 2.3: Actinomycetes species shows zone of inhibition against contaminated fungi

3. **Enrichment culture technique:** In this method, medium composition or incubation conditions are adjusted that favour the growth of desired microorganisms. Undesired microorganisms are not developed because they do not find suitable growth conditions. It is necessary to screen microbial sources in order to find microorganisms capable of utilizing specific carbon and nitrogen sources. Soil samples are usually heated at 80 to 100°C for 10 to 20 minutes for isolation of actinomycetes, fungi and other spore carrying microorganisms. This spore carrying species are mainly isolated for production of antibiotics, enzymes and other bioactive metabolites. Preheat treatment kills vegetative cells but spores are unaffected.

Heat treated samples are diluted and spread onto the surface of nutrient agar containing casein at pH 10 to 12. The colonies surrounded by a clear zone are isolated, purified and then subcultured. This clear zone indicates that the particular species excrete alkaline protease which degrades casein.

4. **Indicator dye method:** The pH indicating dyes mainly employed for detecting microorganisms are capable of producing organic acids or amines e.g. neutral red, bromothymol blue etc. These pH indicating dyes are added into the poorly buffered nutrient agar media which undergoes colour changes according to its pH. The change in the colour of a dye in the vicinity of the colony suggests the capability of cells to produce organic acids or amines. The production of organic acids may be detected by the addition of calcium carbonate in the medium. Acid production is indicated by a cleared zone of dissolved calcium carbonate around the colony.

5. **Auxanography:** This technique is largely employed for detecting microorganisms capable of synthesizing extracellular vitamins, amino acids or other growth stimulating metabolites. Dilutions of soil are applied to agar plates which produce well isolated colonies. Another agar plate contains the test organism. The agar layer of the first plate is aseptically transferred on the surface of the second plate containing the test organism. Vitamins and amino acids producing colonies present (in soil) on the surface of the first layer of agar can diffuse in the lower layer of agar. The zone of stimulated growth (zone of exhibition) of the test organism near the colonies indicates that these colonies may produce vitamins and amino acids. The isolated active colonies are purified, sub-cultured and re-tested for metabolites.

Secondary screening:

Primary screening allows the isolation of microorganisms that possess important industrial applications. This technique does not provide much information related to the fermentation process, production or yield potential of the isolated new microorganisms. Secondary screening helps in detection of useful microorganisms in fermentation processes and the discarding of those lacking industrial potential. It is necessary to know the following points associated with secondary screening for isolation, standardisation and characterisation of new bioactive producing microorganisms.

(i) Secondary screening is very useful for separation of new microbial cultures that have real industrial applications from isolates obtained in primary screening.

(ii) It provides information about whether the microorganisms are producing new chemical compounds or not. This may be confirmed by comparison with known compounds using thin layer, paper or other chromatographic techniques.

(iii) It helps in providing information regarding the product yield of newly isolated microorganisms. This information is very useful in selecting specific cultures for the final fermentation process.

(iv) Secondary screening reveals that the pH, temperature, aeration or other critical requirements associated with bioactive microorganisms for the growth of particular microbes and for the formation of new chemical products. It may give an idea whether specific medium constituents are missing or some constituents may produce toxic effects on the growth of microorganisms.

(v) The screening techniques detect the genetic instability of isolated new microbial species. Many microbial species may lose their capability for maximum production of active components by the process of mutation or recombination.

(vi) Physical, chemical and biological properties of a product are determined by secondary screening. It gives an idea about chemical stability of products and solubility of products in various organic solvents.

(vii) It reveals whether a product produced from fermentation occurs in the culture broth in more than one chemical form. Two or more different bioactive compounds also produced by a single fermentation.

(viii) It provides information about new products. The product may have a simple, complex or macromolecular structure.

(ix) Many fermentation products (mainly antibiotics) are tested for toxicity to animal, plant or human beings. These techniques give information about toxicity of products which are mainly used for therapeutic purposes.

(x) It reveals whether microorganisms are able to chemically alter or destroy their own fermentation products. The microbial cultures may produce adaptive enzymes that destroy the usefulness of the product. They may produce a 'racemase' enzyme that change the L-configuration of an amino acid product to a mixture of the D and L-isomers.

Thus, secondary screening gives answers to many questions that arise during the isolation of bioactive molecules from natural sources. Secondary screening is mainly performed on agar plates, in flasks or small scale fermenter containing liquid media or, by a combination of these approaches.

Streptomyces species are mainly considered for an understanding of the sequence of events during a screening programme. *Streptomyces* is a well known genus for production of antibiotics, enzymes and other active molecules mainly isolated from soil, water and other natural sources. All primarily isolated species are screened for antibiotic production on agar media. Species exhibiting antimicrobial activity are subjected to an initial secondary screening. A simple 'giant colony technique' is used to determine initial 'inhibition spectrum' for the antibiotics produced by each *Streptomyces* species (Fig. 2.4). The *Streptomyces* isolates are inoculated on starch casein agar or any other suitable agar media as a straight line and incubated at 28 to 30°C for 5 to 7 days. After proper growth, different test microorganisms such as *Staphylococcus aureus, Escherichia coli, Bacillus subtilis, Pseudomonas aeruginosa, Aspergillus niger, Aspergillus fumigatus, Candida albicans, Penicillium* species and *Cryptococcus* species are cross-streaked at right angles to the border of the actinomycetes. Plates are further incubated at 35-37°C for 24 to 48 hours if test organism is bacteria and at 25-28°C for 3 to 4 days for fungal test organism. After incubation, growth inhibitory zones for each test microorganism are measured in millimeters. *Streptomyces* species that have produced antibiotics with interesting microbial inhibition spectra are retained for further testing.

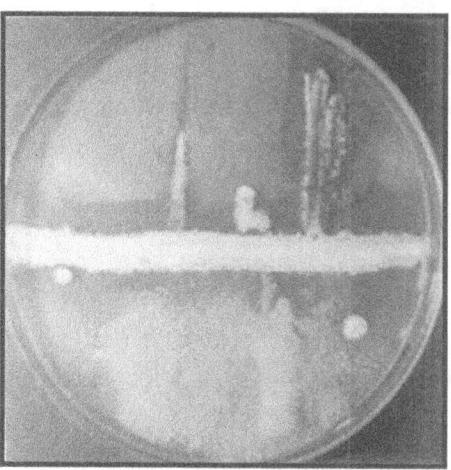

Fig. 2.4: Giant-colony technique

Antimicrobial screening is carried out by using liquid media in flasks. These broth studies give more information than which can be obtained on agar media. It is advisable to use the cylinder plate method (Fig. 2.5) and cup-plate method (Fig. 2.6) to determine exact amounts of antibiotic present in isolated culture fluids. Actinomycetes isolates are studied by using different liquid media in Erlenmeyer flasks provided with baffles. The media are sterilised and inoculated with one of the *Streptomyces* species to be tested. The flasks are shaken at a constant temperature, usually near room temperature by keeping them on a mechanical shaker. Streptomycetes growth and antibiotic production are better in aerated flasks than the stationary ones. In some cases (e.g. polyene antibiotics), the antibiotic activity is present not in the culture fluid but within the mycelium of *Strep*tomyces species (intracellular). Thus, such cases require special extraction procedures for recovering antibiotics from the mycelium. In the present discussion, we have considered only those species that produce antibiotics in the culture fluids (extracellular). Samples are withdrawn at regular intervals under aseptic conditions for analysis.

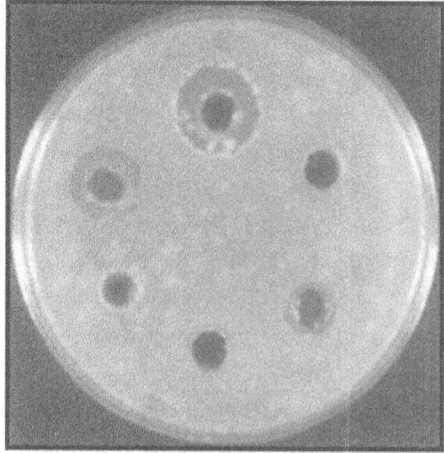

Fig. 2.5: Cylinder plate method

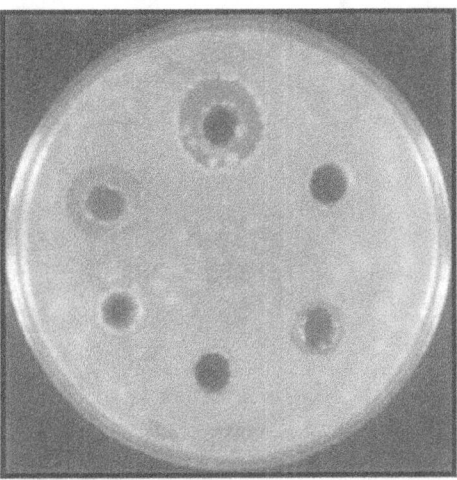

Fig. 2.6: Cup-plate method

The samples are checked for the presence of contamination by microscopic observation and by addition of inoculum into the medium. The pH value of the sample is also determined for proper growth of the *Streptomyces* species during antibiotic production. The culture samples are adjusted to a pH value near neutrality and assayed for antibiotic production against a sensitive test microorganism. These techniques give information about the best medium and growth phase for antibiotic production. Samples are analysed by paper or thin-layer chromatography to determine the antibiotic is similar to previously known antibiotics or whether there is more than one antibiotic present in the culture broth (Fig. 2.7). It is also important to compare the microbial inhibition spectrum of the liquid and agar grown *Streptomyces* species and expand the spectrum by using viruses and carcinoma agents. The solubility of the antibiotic in various organic solvents is determined by solvent extraction of culture filtrate. The antibiotic is purified by column chromatography and the structure is determined by IR, NMR, mass and elemental analysis. Purified antibiotic material is tested for toxicity in mice or other laboratory animals. It is also tested for adverse effects on plant, animal or human beings.

Some isolated species of *Streptomyces* may not produce valuable new antibiotics and such species are discarded. Further studies are required that yield additional information about fermentation media, microbial species and the antibiotic. Similar techniques are employed for the isolation of new strains from natural sources for production of different bioactive molecules. For the enhancement of antibiotic yields, different strain improvement techniques are used.

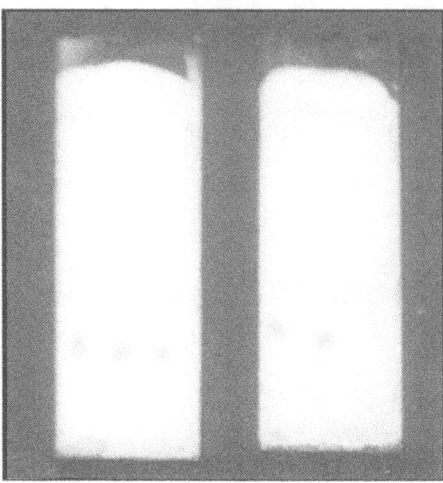

Fig. 2.7: Thin layer chromatography

STRAIN IMPROVEMENT METHODS

Strain improvement is one of the essential steps in fermentation for obtaining the highest possible yield and is economical. This mainly depends upon the efficiency of the production strain involved in the fermentation process. Active microbial strains obtained by primary and secondary screening are not so efficient as can be used in fermentation processes. Therefore, such strains require improvement for production of high yield compounds. Main objectives for strain improvement are:

(i) To obtain highly stable and infection resistant strains.

(ii) To produce high yield strains that make the process more economical.

(iii) To obtain a strain which is resistant to medium constituents and can tolerate low oxygen tension.

(iv) To obtain a morphologically favourable strain.

(v) Easy removal of all undesirable constituents from the bioactive strain.

Microbial strain improvement can be achieved by mutation and DNA transfer techniques.

Mutation:

Microbial cells change their own characteristics by natural cell division. These strains are called mutants. The factors which are responsible for the changes are called mutagens and the process is called mutation. Mutagenic agents are UV-radiation, X-rays, gamma rays, cobalt 60, nitrogen mustard, ethidium bromide, 5-bromouracil, nalidixic acid etc. (For details please refer to Chapter 6). General protocol for mutation techniques is given in Figure 2.8. These mutants are mainly grouped into two categories such as auxotrophic mutants and mutants resistant to analogues.

Isolation of strains from natural sources
↓
Primary and secondary screening for bioactive strains
↓
Select different types of bioactive strains
↓
Mutagen treatment (UV, X-rays, ^{60}CO, NTG etc.).
↓
Check the activity
↓
Select higher yielding strains
↓
Large-scale testing
↓
Highest yielding strain
↓
Production

Fig. 2.8: General method for mutation

Microorganisms cannot synthesize excess metabolites overlimiting the cells requirements because cells have some regulatory mechanisms that control the synthesis of metabolites. Suppression of these regulatory mechanisms is necessary to develop the strains to produce higher yields of the required metabolities. Specific mutants are developed which have lost the ability to synthesize one of the end product capable of feedback inhibition or feedback repression. Feedback inhibition means over accumulation of the end product which inhibits the activity or strength of the enzyme catalysing the reaction. Feedback repression means over accumulation of the end product which inhibits the synthesis of the enzyme catalysing the reaction. This may be explained by considering a situation where two end products (X and Y) are produced by branched biosynthetic pathway from substrate 'A' as shown in Figure 2.9.

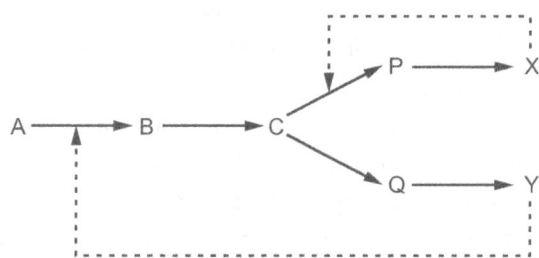

Fig. 2.9: Regulatory system of enzymes involved in biosynthetic pathway

The product 'Y' (primary metabolite) can show a feedback inhibition on its own production by inhibition of the enzyme catalysing the reaction for formation of 'B' from 'A'. Product 'X' can show an inhibition of the enzyme catalysing the reaction 'C' and 'P'.

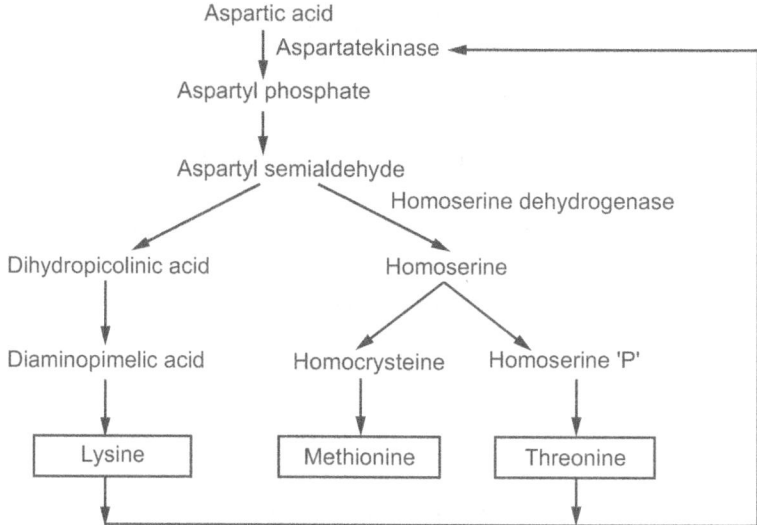

Fig. 2.10: Control of lysine production (primary metabolite) in *Corynebacterium glutamicum*

Corynebacterium glutamicum and *Brevibacterium flavum* produces an important amino acid (lysine) as a primary metabolite. These organisms also produce some other amino-acids like threonine and methionine. The pathway (Fig. 2.10) is subject to feedback inhibition by a mixture of lysine and threonine controlling the activity of aspartate kinase. When these two amino acids are over accumulated as a end product then their synthesis is inhibited by inhibiting enzyme activity. This type of control is termed an 'absolute feedback inhibition'. Isolation of specific mutants can help for avoiding the inhibition of the enzyme activity. This isolated mutant cannot catalyse the conversion of aspartic semialdehyde to homoserine and therefore, prevents the formation of threonine and methionine. A mutant is able to grow in homoserine supplemented medium and the organism is called 'homoserine auxotroph'. This nutritionally deficient mutant is cultured in a medium with low concentration of threonine and methionine to support growth but not enough threonine concentration to co-operate with lysine in inhibition of asparate kinase activity. Therefore, lysine production increases from *Corynebacterium glutamicum*.

Moulds, actinomycetes and spore forming bacteria mainly produce secondary metabolites (e.g. antibiotics) in the process of fermentation. The techniques for isolation of mutants overproducing secondary metabolites are more difficult because very less information is available for control of production. The yield of an antibiotic also depends on various types of genes, so it is difficult to find individual mutations that can increase the yield from bioactive strains. The media composition and environmental conditions also strongly influence the production of antibiotics. Various genetically improved strains have been developed through mutation to increase yields (Fig. 2.11). The isolated culture is treated with a mutagen and then mutant colonies are tested for activity.

Spore suspension of isolate (e.g. *Penicillium chrysogenium*)
↓ Mutagenic treatment
(UV, X-rays, NTG, ^{60}Co)
Survivors of mutation grown on agar medium
↓
Select the specific colonies (150 to 200 colonies) and suspend separately in saline water
↓
Each cultures are again inoculated into liquid medium for inoculum development
↓
Each inoculum is inoculated into production medium
↓
Best antibiotic producers are identified (10 to 12 colonies)
retested, maintained as the stock cultures and remutated

Fig. 2.11: Strain improvement technique for isolates which produces secondary metabolites

DNA transfer techniques:

Different DNA transfer techniques are used for obtaining high-yielding strains. These techniques are performed by transferring all or part of the DNA to the recipient microbial cell from the donor cell (For details, please refer Chapter 8). Bacterial recombination occurs whenever new gene arrangements are formed through exchange, elimination or insertion of DNA. Recombination has been applied for the production of various industrial strains.

The techniques used for the transfer of genetic material are listed as follows:

(i)   Transformation
(ii) Transduction
(iii) Conjugation
(iv) Parasexuality
(v)   Protoplast fusion

QUESTIONS

(A) Short answer questions:

1. What is Industrial Microbiology?
2. List different strain improvement techniques.
3. Comment "Crowded plate technique is the simplest primary screening technique for isolation of antibiotic producing strains".

(B) Long answer questions:

1. Explain different techniques used for strain improvement.
2. How will you screen microbial cultures from soil for production of antibiotics?
3. Explain techniques used for isolation of microbial cultures from natural sources.

(C) Multiple choice questions:

1. Secondary screening is carried out by following technique for production of antibiotic except _____
   - (a) Cup plate method
   - (b) Cylinder plate method
   - (c) Giant colony method
   - (d) Crowded plate method

2. *Corynebacterium glutamicum* produces an amino acid as a primary metabolite which is _____
   - (a) Lysine
   - (b) Threonine
   - (c) Methionine
   - (d) All of the above

3. The DNA transfer technique mainly used for improvement of strains is _____
   - (a) Protoplast fusion
   - (b) Transformation
   - (c) Conjugation
   - (d) All of the above.

(D) Match the following:

A		B	
(a)	Crowded plant technique	(i)	DNA transfer
(b)	Cup plate method	(ii)	Strain improvement
(c)	Mutation	(iii)	Secondary screening
(d)	Transduction	(iv)	Primary screening

(E) Fill in the blanks:

(i) Halophilic microorganisms generally occur in _____.

(ii) _____ plating method is used for selection of cloned variants in genetic engineering.

■■■

CHAPTER 3

FERMENTATION PROCESS

CONTENTS

    INTRODUCTION

    KINETICS FOR CELL GROWTH

    INOCULUM DEVELOPMENT

    FERMENTATION MEDIA

    FERMENTER

        Types of Fermenter

        Design of Fermenter

INTRODUCTION

Fermentation may be defined as the process of growing microorganisms in a nutrient media by maintaining physicochemical conditions and thereby converting feed in to a desired end product. Fermentation is a biochemical reaction in which micro-organisms serve as biocatalysts. Microorganisms are designed to produce different pharmaceuticals such as antibiotics, enzymes, amino acids, insulin, vitamins etc. A list of major industrial products prepared from fermentation is given in Table 3.1. Microorganisms useful in fermentation are bacteria, actinomycetes, viruses and fungi. The vessels or containers in which fermentation processes are carried out are called fermenters. A fermenter is frequently confused with a bioreactor. Fermenters are mainly used for growth of prokaryotic cells such as bacteria, actinomycetes etc. and bioreactors are used for growth of eukaryotic cells such as insects mammalian cells etc. Fermenters also differ from bioreactors in their parts such as agitators and mixers. The selection of a good medium is very important to the success of an industrial fermentation. The medium supplies nutrients for cell growth and biosynthesis of fermentation products. The fermenter is designed and operated for production of different pharmaceuticals under conditions of constant temperature, pH, dissolved oxygen and substrate concentration. The complete fermentation process is represented in Figure 3.1.

Table 3.1: Major fermentation products

Group	Product	Producing micro-organism
Antibiotics	Penicillin	*Penicillium chrysogenum*
	Streptomycin	*Streptomyces griseus*
	Chlorampenicol	*Streptomyces venezuelae*
	Polymyxin	*Bacillus polymyxa*
Enzymes	Amylases	*Aspergillus oryzae*
	Proteases	*Bacillus* species
	Lipases	*Saccharomycess lipolytica*
Amino acids	L-lysine	*Corynebacterium glutamicium*
	Glutamic acid	*Corynebacterium glutamicium*
Polysaccharides	Dextran	*Leuconostic mesenteroids*
	Xanthan gum	*Xanthomones compestris.*
Vitamins	Riboflavin	*Ashbya gossypi*
	Vitamin B_{12}	*Pseudomonas dentrificans*
Industrial chemicals	Ethanol (from glucose)	*Saccharomyces cerevisiae*
	Citric acid	*Aspergillus niger*
	Lactic acid	*Lactobacillus delbrueckii*
Food and beverages	Beer or bread	*Saccharomyces cerevisiae*
	Cheese	*Streptococcus* species.

KINETICS FOR CELLS GROWTH

Kinetics for cell growth is necessary to the understanding of kinetics of microbial, plant and animal cell growth for designing a specific fermenter and to study different metabolite products. Cell production kinetics revolves around the cell growth rate and it is affected by various physicochemical conditions.

Batch culture: In a batch culture, nutrients are added in the fermentation for single time only and growth continues until the particular nutrients are exhausted.

When a micro-organism is added into a medium which supports its growth, the culture passes through a number of stages in the batch process (Fig. 3.2) A typical growth curve is obtained after addition of microbial culture and it passes through lag, acceleration, log, stationary, accelerated death, exponential death and survival phase.

Lag phase is the period of adaptation to new conditions before growth. Transition from lag phase to exponential growth phase is interrupted by an acceleration phase. In the exponential phase, cell size increases and it divides into two and the cycle continues. Under optimum conditions, the growth rate in this phase is most rapid. The period of maximum growth rate is known as log or exponential phase and the time required to complete cell division is called generation time. In the log phase, many microbial cells produce different metabolites as a result of every generating metabolism (e.g. lactic acid, ethanol) or compounds required for cell synthesis (e.g. Amino acids, proteins, vitamins etc.). Such products are called primary metabolites. Growth rate in log phase is expressed as follows.

$$\frac{dx}{dt} = \mu x \qquad \ldots (1)$$

where
$\frac{dx}{dt}$ = Population growth rate
μ = Specific growth rate (h^{-1})
x = Cell concentration (g dm^{-3})
t = Time of incubation (h)

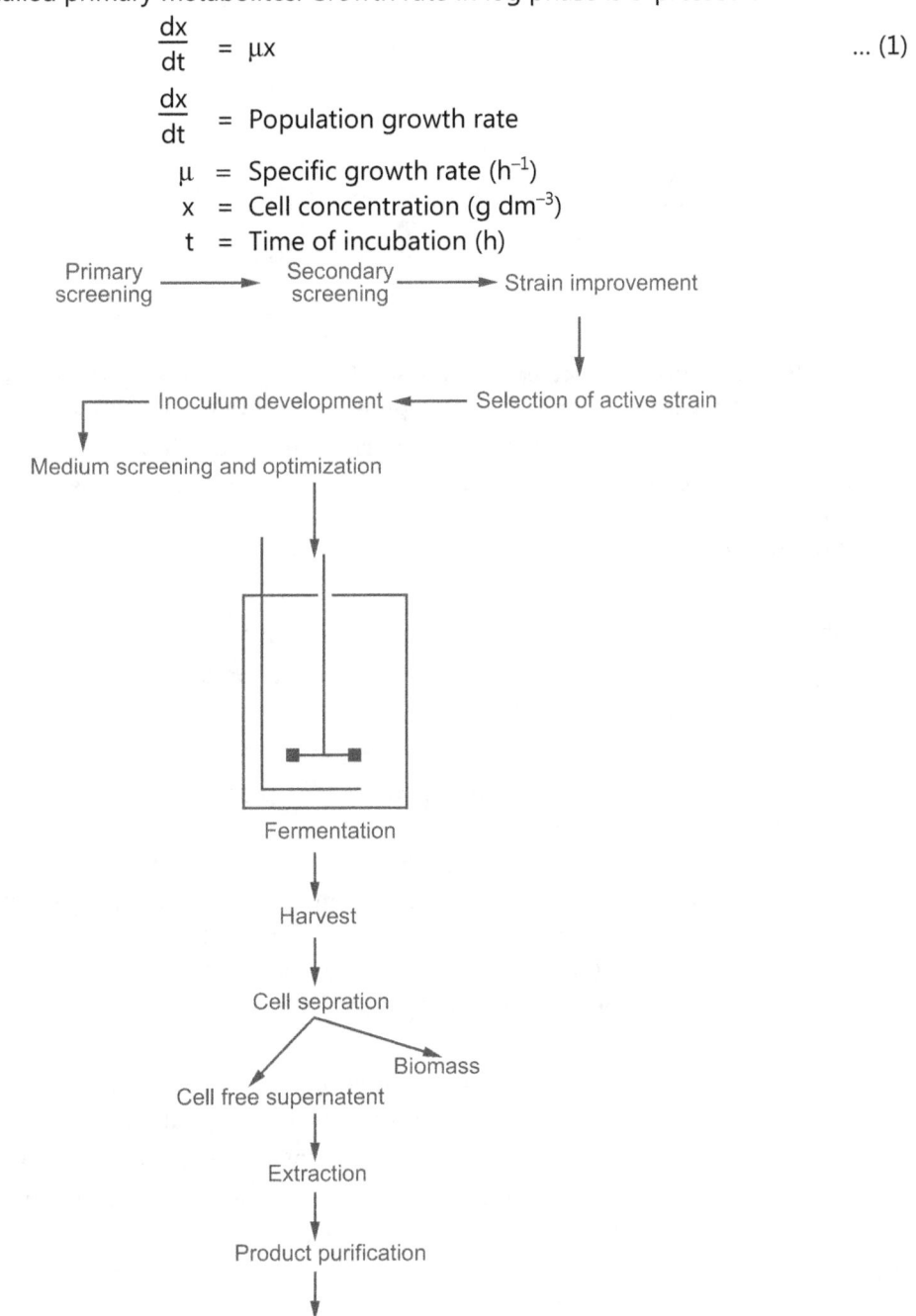

Fig. 3.1: Flow sheet of typical fermentation process

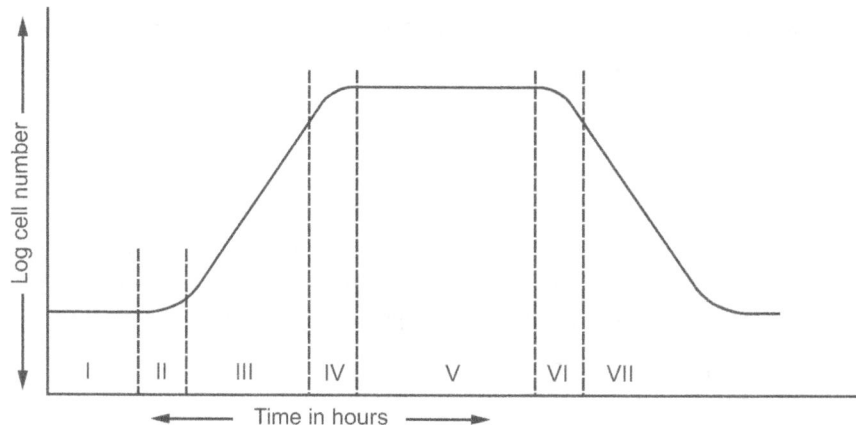

(I) Lag phase, (II) Acceleration phase, (III) Log phase, (IV) Stationary phase,
(V) Accelerated death phase, (VI) Exponential death phase (VII) Survival phase

Fig. 3.2: Growth curve of a bacterial culture (Batch fermentation)

As the time increases, growth rate of the population also increases but growth of the cell remains constant.

Integration of eq. (1) ... (2)

$$x_t = x_0 e^{\mu t} \quad \text{... (3)}$$

where x_t = cell concentration at time 't'
x_0 = cell concentration at time 'o'

Taking the logarithm of eq. (2) ... (4)

$$\ln x_t = \ln x_0 + \mu t \quad \text{... (5)}$$

Logarithm of the cell concentration against time plot gives a straight line and its slope is the specific growth rate (μ)

The environmental conditions in the batch culture are continuously changing and the micro-organisms are affected by the changing cultural conditions. The growth rate of micro-organisms decreases because of reduction of nutrients or accumulation of toxins. The growth rate decreases and reaches the stationary phase. The biomass concentration at the stationary phase is determined by following equation.

$$x = Y \cdot S_R \quad \text{... (6)}$$

where x = Cell concentration
Y = Yield factor for the limiting nutrient.
S_R = Original nutrient concentration in the medium.

The term 'Y' represents measure of efficiency of a cell in converting nutrients into biomass. The biomass at a particular time during fermentation is given by the following equation.

$$x = Y(S_R - s) \quad \text{... (7)}$$

where s = Nutrient concentration at particular time in the fermentation.

Thus, Y is represented by the following equation.

$$Y = \frac{x}{S_R - s} \quad \ldots (8)$$

Many microbial cells produce bioactive molecules during the period of deceleration and the stationary phase. These compounds are called as secondary metabolites (e.g. Antibiotics).

Continuous culture:

The growth rate and physiological conditions of microorganisms can be maintained by using a process of continuous culture (chemostat). The fresh medium is added continuously at an appropriate rate and the vessel is fitted with an overflow device so that the culture is displaced by the incoming fresh medium. The dilution rate is the ratio of inflowing amount of medium to the volume of the culture.

Thus,

$$D = F/V \quad \ldots (9)$$

where,
- D = Dilution rate (h^{-1})
- F = Flow rate (dm^3/h)
- V = Volume (dm^3)

The change in cell concentration of cells at a particular time period is expressed by the following equation.

$$\frac{dx}{dt} = \text{growth} - \text{output}$$

OR

$$\frac{dx}{dt} = \mu x - Dx \quad \ldots (10)$$

In the process of continuous culture technique, the output is balanced by growth and hence,

$$\mu x = Dx$$
$$\mu = D$$

Therefore, $\frac{dx}{dt} = D$

In the steady state conditions, the system is controlled by the flow of medium through the dilution rate. The relationship between specific growth rate (μ) and residual limiting substrate concentration was described by Monod (1942)

$$\mu = \frac{\mu_{max} \bar{S}}{K_s + \bar{S}} \quad \ldots (11)$$

where
- K_s - Limiting substrate concentration
- $\bar{S}$ - Steady state residual concentration in the medium

From eq. (10), we know that

$$\mu = D$$

$$D = \frac{\mu_{max} \bar{S}}{K_s + \bar{S}} \quad \ldots (12)$$

The biomass concentration in the chemostat is determined by the following equation.

$$X = Y(S_R - \bar{S}) \quad \ldots (13)$$

where

X = Steady state biomass concentration

S_R = Original nutrient concentration in the incoming medium

Fed-batch culture:

Fed-batch culture is the intermediate between batch and continuous culture. Nutrient substrates are fed continuously with fresh medium without removal of culture fluid. The volume of fed-batch culture system increases with time. The total amount of biomass in the vessel increases but the biomass concentration is maintained constant. The system appears as a steady state. The dilution rate decreases with time as per the following equation.

$$D = \frac{F}{V_o + F_t}$$

where

D = Dilution rate

F = Flow rate

V_o = Initial volume of culture.

F_t = Time from the onset of fed-batch.

Growth rate decreases with time and the system is not in a genuine steady state but may be called as a quasi-steady state. The growth rate may be maintained constant by increasing the flow rate exponentially using a computer controlled system.

INOCULUM DEVELOPMENT

The microbial cells are required to inoculate large quantities of production medium in a larger fermenter. A single loopful of culture can not meet the requirement of complete fermentation. Hence, inoculum is prepared as a stepwise sequence employing increasing volume of media (Fig. 3.3). The fermenter can be inoculated with a large quantity of actively growing microbial cells. The size of the inoculum is normally between 1 to 10 percent by volume. The chemical composition of the inoculum medium may be different from the production medium. The main objective of inoculum medium is to produce active biomass of cells and that of production medium is to produce the required fermentation product. The inoculum must be available as actively growing cells and must be free from contaminants.

Microbial cells must pass through many generations during inoculum production. It is possible for microbial cells to undergo mutation during inoculum development. Mutation does not poses a serious problem if the strain used in fermentation is not a mutant. These cells mutation is generally infrequent and if occurs it does not interfere with the growth of non-mutated cells. It becomes a serious problem if mutated strain is used for the fermentation process. These mutated strains have high frequency of the occurrence of a back mutation. This may be overcome by employing media and incubation conditions which tend to select the growth of the mutant strain.

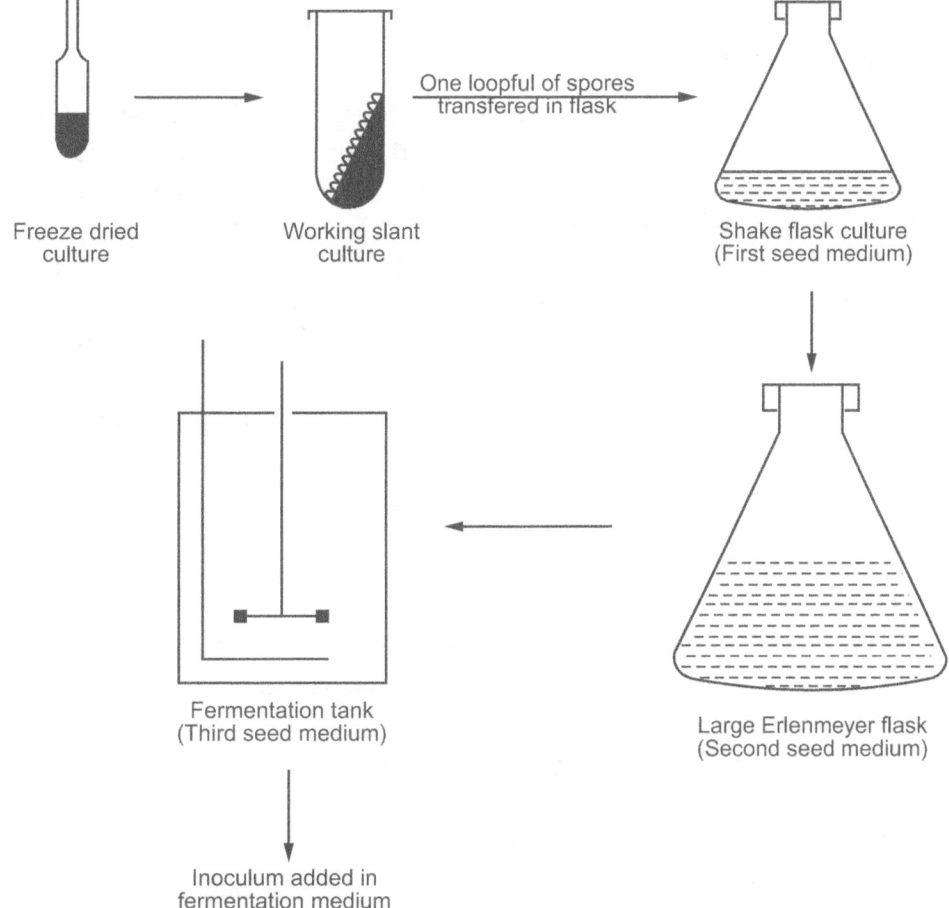

Fig. 3.3: Inoculum development technique of spore forming micro-organisms

Industrially important micro-organisms are filamentous and are capable of producing spores (fungi, actinomycetes, bacteria). The initiation of growth in the liquid inoculum media depends upon the nature of micro-organisms. Bacterial cells or spores are suspended in a sterile diluents for transfer in the liquid inoculcum medium. *Clostridium* species often require heat treatment to induce germination of spores. Spores of fungi and actinomycetes are germinated by using special medium. Then these germinated spores are transferred to the normal inoculum medium. One example of inoculum development technique is given in Figure 3.3. The preparation of spore suspensions (e.g. actinomycetes) is done by adding a suitable diluent to sporulated agar growth. The spores must be loosened from the surface with a sterile wire loop. It is also required to add a non-toxic wetting agent (e.g. sodium lauryl sulfonate) in the diluent to make the distribution of spores uniform in the dilution fluid. In contrast, some stationary fungal fermentation (e.g. *Aspergillus niger* citric acid fermentation) require the spores to be floated on the surface of the liquid medium. In case of poorly sporulating fungi or actinomycetes, fragmented hyphae are transferred to the broth medium.

FERMENTATION MEDIA

The choice of a good medium is very important for the success of industrial fermentation. All microorganisms require water and sources of nitrogen, carbon, mineral elements, vitamins amino acids etc. for growth. The microbial cells also require different growth factors, precursors of fermentation products, dissolved gases, buffers, antifoaming agents for the synthesis of specific fermentation products. One of the major problems for the fermentation industry is to design a suitable production medium. This is only done by a trial and error method. The ideal characteristics of fermentation medium should meet the following criteria.

- Production of the maximum yield of product or biomass in short duration.
- A minimum yield of undersized other products.
- A simple, suitable chemical composition of production medium.
- Free from any toxic effect on culture or product.
- Low cost, good quality and easily available.
- Raw materials required for production medium are easily available at a low cost.
- Most suitable for production process such as agitation, extraction, purification, waste treatment etc.
- Production medium must be suitable for adjustment pH, consistency and composition.
- Inhibition or slowing of the growth of contaminating micro-organisms.
- Allowing the proper growth and maintenance of the genetic stability of active microorganisms.
- Foaming must be minimum.
- Media components must not interfere with the extraction and purification of desired product.

The composition of a fermentation medium may be simple or complex depending on the particular micro-organism, its nutritional needs and the product required. A synthetic medium contains known components and these media components are easily redesigned to increase possible yield of the product. Foaming is not a problem of fermentation which contains synthetic media because these media do not contain any high molecular weight peptides and proteins. The purification of fermentation products is also simple with the synthetic media. The synthetic media may be expensive because of the high cost of pure ingredients and the yields obtained from these media are low. Crude or non-synthetic medium mainly produce higher yield of fermentation products. Crude medium mainly contains soyabean meal, black strap molasses and corn steep liquor as a source of carbon and nitrogen.

Carbon sources:

The common carbon sources used in pharmaceutical fermentation processes are glucose, fructose, sucrose, molasses, hydrolyzed starch, organic acids, hydrocarbons plant oils etc. Beet and cane molasses are the concentrated syrups formed in the sugar-refining process as by-products of sugar industry. Blackstrap molasses is the cheapest and most useful sugar source for industrial fermentation. In addition to sucrose, blackstrap molasses also contain small amounts of complex polysaccharides and invert sugars. Glucose, sucrose and fructose are more expensive as compared to molasses but it gives more clean medium. Complex starch-containing substrates such as cornmeal are widely used in secondary metabolite fermentation. Plant oils are a rich source of carbon than carbohydrates.

Cellulose material are complex carbohydrates made up of repeating units of β-glucose. Sulfite waste liquor is the spent sulfite liquor obtained from the paper-pulping industry. It is a dilute sugar solution having approximately 2% sugar content. Hexoses (D-glucose, D-galactose, D-mannose) and pentoses (D-xylose, L-arabinose) are mainly present in sulfite waste liquor as monosaccharides.

Nitrogen sources:

The most common nitrogen sources are yeast extract, peptone, ammonia, distillers solubles, soyabean meal, corn steep liquor, fish meal, cottonseed meal etc. Distillers solubles are prepared from fermented grain or maize by distillation using alcohol. Effluent is concentrated to reach the solid content 35% w/v (evaporator syrup). This syrup is then dried to yield 'distillers solubles'. It is used as a production medium and it supplies nitrogen with many accessory food factors. Corn-steep liquor is the water extract by-product resulting from the steeping of corn during the production of starch, gluten and other corn products. The spent steep waters are concentrated to approximately 50% solids and this concentrate is called corn-steep liquor. It was first extensively used in fermentation media for the production of penicillin. Corn-steep liquor mainly contains lactic acid, amino acids, glucose, salts and vitamins. Soyabean meal is the components left after deoiling of soyabean seeds and it contains approximately 8% w/v nitrogen.

Buffers:

Buffers are generally added in the production medium for their buffering capacity. During microbial growth in the fermentation, pH may be changed by acidic or alkaline products. Decarboxylation of organic acids among the medium constituents may raise the pH and deamination of strongly basic organic amines lower the pH of fermentation media. Calcium carbonate is generally added in fermentation media to provide neutralization of acidic fermentation products. Media containing proteins, peptides and amino acids posses good buffer capacity in the pH range near neutrality.

Antifoaming agent:

Fermentation media containing proteins or peptides can produce foam in the process of agitation and aeration. Proteolytic bacteria mainly produce high levels of foam. If this foam is not controlled, it may rise in the head space of the tank. This condition is mainly responsible for causing contamination of the fermenter. In high levels of foam, medium may be forced out from the tank as foam. Therefore, antifoam agents are added in the media to control the foam. These antifoam agents can lower the surface tension and decrease the stability of the foam bubbles. Two types of antifoam agents are commonly used in fermentation i.e. crude organic materials and inert antifoams. Antifoams made from crude organic materials are sterilized separately and then added in the fermentation. Corn oil, soyabean oil, lavd oil, octadecanol and other fatty acids are commonly used as antifoam agents. These antifoam agents may be toxic or lower the pH of media or provide specific nutrients to cultures. Silicon compounds are mainly used as inert antifoam agents. These agents are not utilized by the micro-organisms and they are also nontoxic.

Minerals:

Most fermentation process requires minerals for the growth of micro-organisms. Minerals such as potassium, phosphorus, sulfur, copper, chloride, cobalt, iron, manganese and zinc are frequently added in the media. These compounds are mainly present in complex nitrogen or carbon sources.

Precursors:

Precursors are added prior to or simultaneously with the fermentation. These substances are used to increase the yield or improve the quality of the product. Phenylacetic acid is added in the fermentation medium of penicillin G and inorganic cobalt in the medium of vitamin B_{12} as a precursor.

All fermentation media are generally sterilized by boiling or passing steam through the medium or steam under pressure i. e. autoclaving. In a small -scale laboratory fermenter, the medium is directly placed in the fermenter and then the fermenter is sterilized by autoclave. Large- scale medium is sterilized by passing it through heated retention tubes containing steam jet heaters. The medium constituents at double to triple strength are mixed with water in a mixing tank. The final medium is then passed through retention tubes and heat exchangers. Retention tubes contain steam jet heaters that inject high pressure steam into the medium to sterilize it. The rate of passage of steam is adjusted to provide proper sterilization without over cooking. Sterilizing synthetic media requires less time than the crude media. Media containing vitamins and enzymes cannot be sterilized by the heat method. These sensitive components are sterilized separately by a bacteriological filter and then added into the sterilized media.

FERMENTER

The industrial microorganisms require to grow in a large vessel containing considerable quantities of nutrient media by maintaining favorable conditions. These containers are called as fermenters. These fermenters provide optimum growth and metabolism to microbial strains for production of the desired product. The term 'bioreactor' is often used synonymously for fermenter. Generally, fermenters are used for growth of prokaryotic cells such as bacteria, actinomycetes etc., while bioreactors are used for growth of eukaryotic cells such as insect, mammalian cells etc. The design of the fermenter depends upon the purpose for which it is to be used. An ideal fermenter should possess the following characteristics.

(i) It should provide the best possible growth conditions to industrial strains.

(ii) It must make some provision for the control of contaminating microorganisms during fermentation.

(iii) It should have the provision and control over various operations like pH, temperature, agitation, aeration etc. It may have facilities for monitoring all conditions.

(iv) The fermenter should provide all aseptic conditions at the time of sample withdrawal and addition of inoculum.

(v) The fermenter vessels must be strong enough to withstand the pressures and toxicity of media.

(vi) Fermenter must have the facility of incorporation of sterile air and stirring.

(vii) It should provide all facilities for intermittent addition of antifoam agents, alkali or acid and other nutrients.

(viii) Fermenter should have additional inoculum, seed or media tanks.

(ix) It should be designed in such a way that it consumes less power, has less evaporation, can be used for long periods of operation and has proper sampling facilities.

(x) It should have the facility for complete removal of broth from the tank and should be easy to clean.

Types of fermenter:

Fermenters are available in various sizes and their sizes are defined on the total volume capacity of the fermenter. According to size, fermenters are classified as follows.

(i) Small laboratory and research fermenter: 1 to 50 litre.

(ii) Pilot plant fermenter: 50 to 1000 litre

(iii) Large size industrial production scale fermenter: more than 1000 litre.

Small scale fermenters are autoclavable while large scale fermenters are sterilized by in-situ sterilization. The small laboratory fermenters are designed to provide varying conditions for the growth of micro-organisms and are adjusted to provide similiar growth conditions mainly found in the largest industrial production tanks. Broadly, the fermenters are also classified as submerged fermenters and surface fermenters (Fig. 3.4)

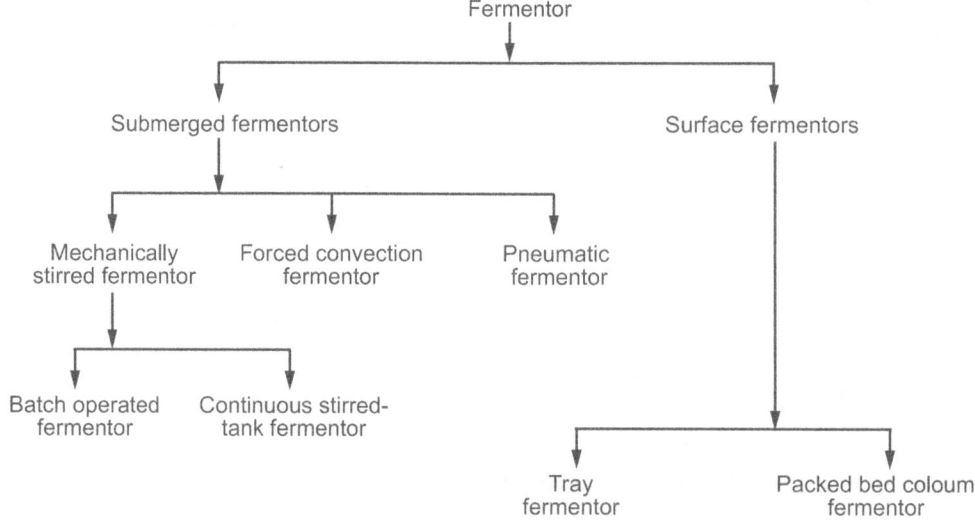

Fig. 3.4: Types of fermenters

(I) Submerged fermenters:

In submerged fermenters (suspended-growth system), the micro-organisms are dispersed in nutrient medium (liquid) at maintained environmental conditions. On the basis of mechanism of agitation, fermenters are further classified as follows.

1. Mechanically stirred fermenters: These fermenters are equipped with a mechanical agitator so as to maintain homogencity and rapid dispersion and mixing of materials. Mechanically stirred fermenters are stirred tank fermenter, stirred multistage fermenter (continuous process), paddle wheel reactor and stirred loop reactor. Stirred tank fermenter is the most applicable fermenter in fermentation industry for the batch process.

The main advantage of this fermenter is the flexibility in design and is used in the range of 1 litre to 100 ton capacity sizes. The agitators consist of one or more impellers mounted on a shaft. Different types of blades are used according to the requirements. It is rotated with the help of an electric motor. A basic computer controlled stirred tank fermenter is shown in Figure 3.5.

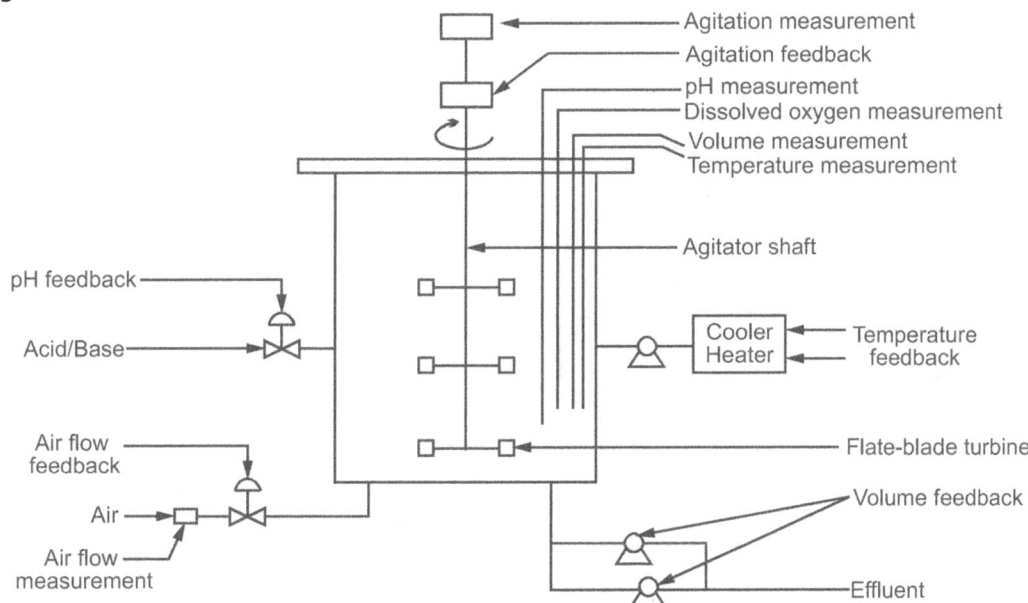

Fig. 3.5: A computer controlled stirred-tank batch fermenter

A continuous stirred-tank fermenter (CSTF) is basically the same as a batch fermenter. However, in addition of feed and overflow devices, steady-state condition can be achieved by 'chemostatic' or 'turbidostatic' principles. In continuous fermentation, fresh medium is added continuously in the fermentation vessel and in other end medium is withdrawn for recovery of fermentation products. A continuous fermenter can be conducted in various techniques. It can be performed as a 'single stage' in which single fermenter is inoculated and then kept in continuous operation by balancing the input and output culture media [Fig. 3.6 (a)]. In a 'recycle' continuous fermentation, a portion of the withdrawn culture or residual unused substrate plus the withdrawn culture is recycled to the fermentation vessel [Fig. 3.6. (b)]. The 'multiple-stage' continuous fermentation, involves two or more stages with the fermenters being operated in sequence [Fig. 3.6 (c)].

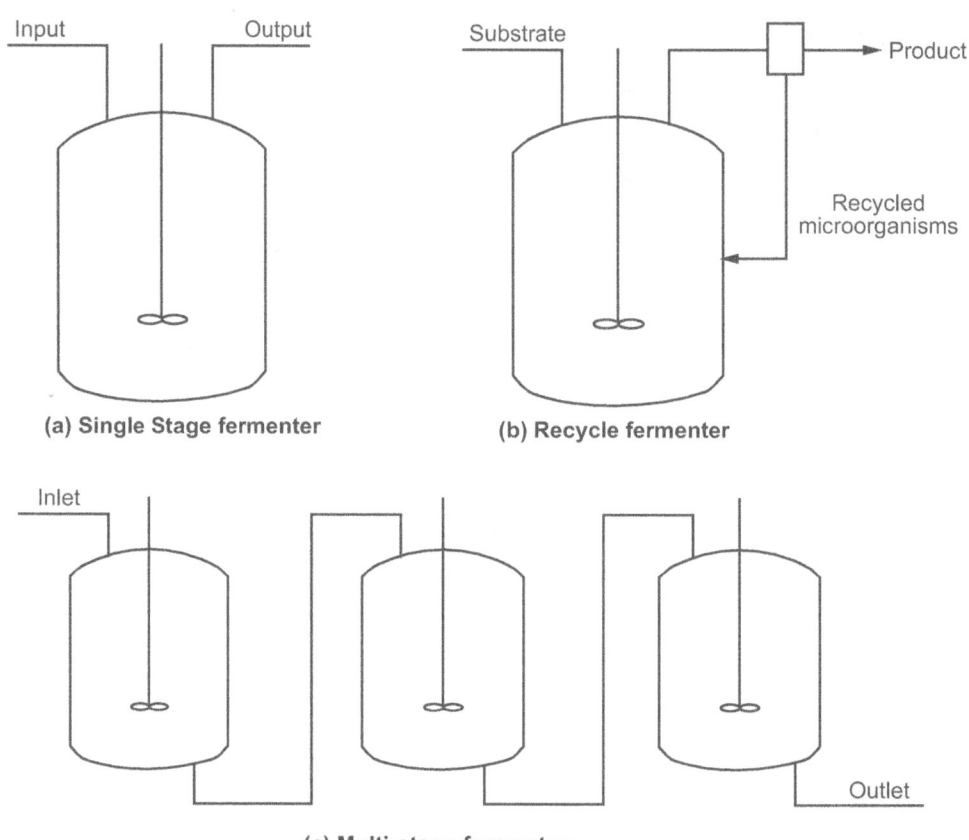

Fig. 3.6: Types of continuous fermentation

Advantages of batch fermentation:

- Less risk of contamination or cell mutation because of short growth period.
- More flexibility with different product and biological systems.
- Process is more economical and simple.
- Raw material conversion level is more.

Disadvantages of batch fermentation:

- Low productivity due to the time required for sterilizing, filling, cooling, emptying, cleaning etc.
- More expenses are required for subcultures for inoculation, labour and process control.
- More focus on instrumentation due to frequent sterilization
- Larger industrial hygiene risks due to potential contact with pathogenic micro-organisms.

Advantages of continuous fermentation:
- Less labor expense due to automation of fermentation process.
- Less toxicity risks to operator by any toxins producing by micro-organisms.
- High yield and good quality product due to invariable operating parameters and automation of the process.
- Less stress on fermenter as sterilization is not very frequent.

Disadvantages of continuous fermentation:
- Uniformity in media quality is necessary to ensure that the process remains continuous.
- Higher investment cost in control and automation equipment.
- More risk of contamination and cell mutation.
- Slight variation only is possible in the continuous process.

2. Forced convection fermenters: In forced convection fermenters, the agitation is affected by using a pump, instead of a mechanical stirrer. 'Loop fermenter' and deep jet fermenter are available involving liquid movement and gas entertainer. In the loop fermenter, gas distribution device is a subsidiary vessel, where a liquid saturated with gas is circulated by forced convection into the fermenter vessel. In deep jet fermenter, gas is entertained into a high power jet of liquid into the liquid of the fermenter. Two different types of forced convection fermenters are available i.e. gas-lift or air-lift fermenter and bubble column or sparged tank fermenter. Different forced convection fermenters are shown in Figure 3.7 and Figure 3.8.

Air-lift fermenters are classified as draught tube or internal loop fermenter and external loop fermenter. In the gas-lift fermenters, internal liquid circulation in the vessel is achieved by sparging the vessel with gas. Fluid volume of the vessel is divided into two interconnected zones by draught tube. Air is typically fed through a sparger ring into the bottom of a central draught tube that controls the circulation of air and the medium. The airlift external-loop reactor system is used for circulation of direct air and liquid throughout the vessel. This system consists of a riser and an external down comer, which are connected at the bottom and the top respectively. The injected air at the bottom of the riser creates gas bubbles that rise through the fermentation tank and the heavier solution descends through the down comer. The external-loop airlift reach system has some advantages as compared to standard airlifts (Internal-loop reactors). These are:

- Easy measurement and control in the riser and the down comer.
- Efficient temperature control and heat-transfer.
- Low friction with an optimal hydraulic diameter for riser and down comer.
- Specific residence time in the individual section.

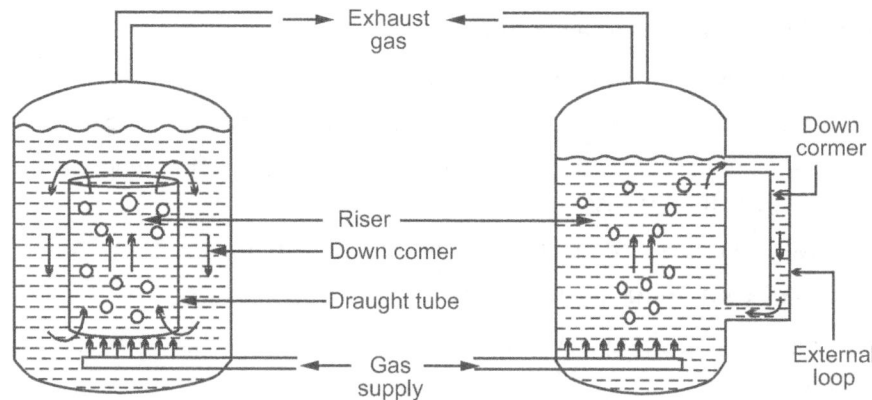

(a) Draught-tube or internal loop air-lift bioreactor

(b) External-loop air-lift bioreactor

Fig. 3.7: Air-lift bioreactors

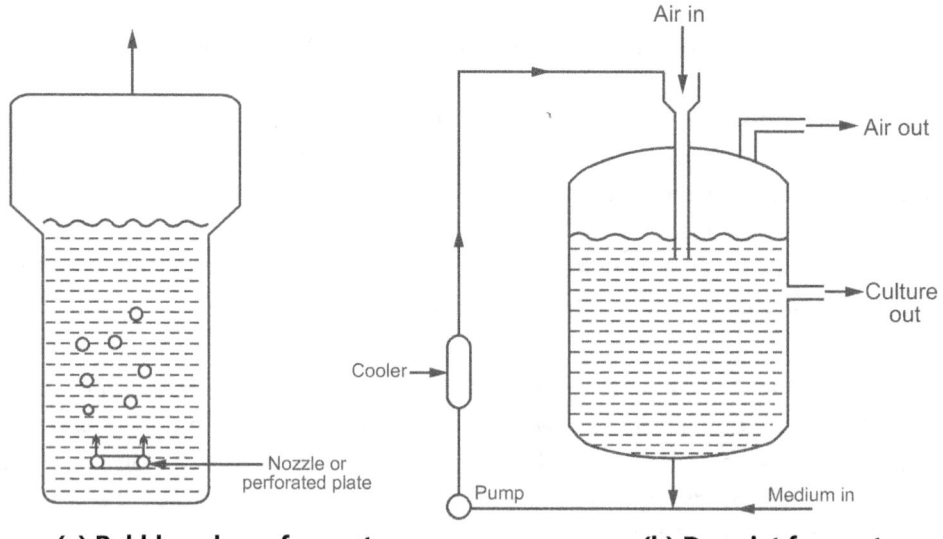

(a) Bubble-column fermenter

(b) Deep jet fermenter

Fig. 3.8: Types of fermenters

Bubble column reactor is a cylindrical column, in which the gas is sparged at the bottom through nozzles on a perforated or porous distributor plates. The gas bubbles rise through the liquid in the vessel and may be redispersed by a succession of horizontal perforated baffle plates. Temperature controls are maintained by the temperature jacket or the internal coils.

Air-lift fermenters provide many advantages as compare to the standard fermenter.
- High flexibility, less shear rate.
- Controlled flow and efficient mixing.
- Simple design without any moving parts like agitator.
- Easy maintenance, less risk of defects and easy sterilization.

- Specific defined residence time for all phases.
- Large volume tanks, possible specific interfacial contact-area with low energy input.
- Higher mass-transfer due to enhanced oxygen solubility achieved in larger tank with greater pressure.

3. Pneumatic fermenter: Fluidized bed bioreactor is an example of pneumatic bioreactor used in fermentation involving fluid with suspended particulate biocatalyst (enzyme) or cell particles or microbial flocs (Fig. 3.9). The cell particles are fluidized with up-coming stream of liquids. Top part of the fluidized fermenter is expanded to reduce superficial velocity of fluidized bed. Solids set easily in setting zone and then dropped into fluidized zone.

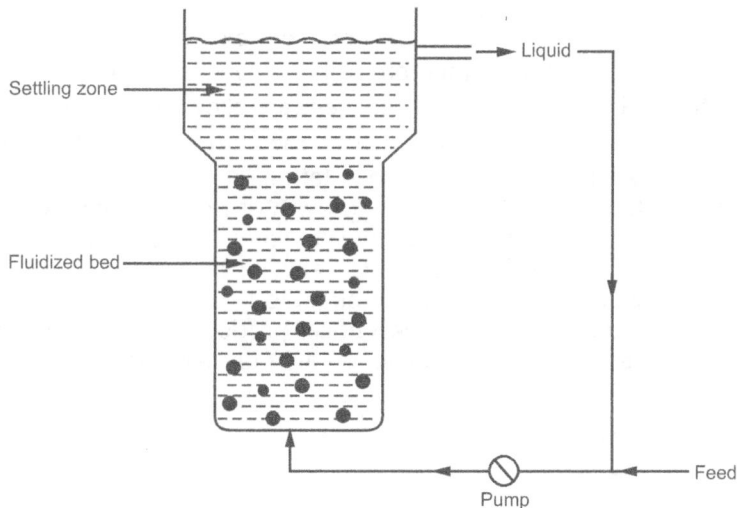

Fig. 3.9: Fluidized bed bioreactor

(II) Surface fermenters:

Microbial cells are cultured on the surface layer of the nutrient medium (solid/ liquid) held in a dish or a tray and is generally called as surface culture system or supported growth system. This technique is commonly used for production of citric acid from *Aspergillus niger* and nicotanic acid from *Aspergillus terrus*. Microbial films can be developed on the surfaces of suitable packing medium. This may be in the form of a fixed bed, stones or plastic sheets. This system is commonly used in biological waste water treatment. Packed bed column fermenter and tray fermenter are the example of surface fermenters.

1. **Packed bed column fermenter:** This is type of surface culture bioreactor in which solid particles form the packed bed on which enzymes are immobilized. A liquid nutrient is allowed to flow continuously through the packed bed. Metabolic products are released in the fluid and removed in the outflow (Fig. 3.10). When the film of micro-organisms is formed on the surface of packing material then this is called is film bioreactor.

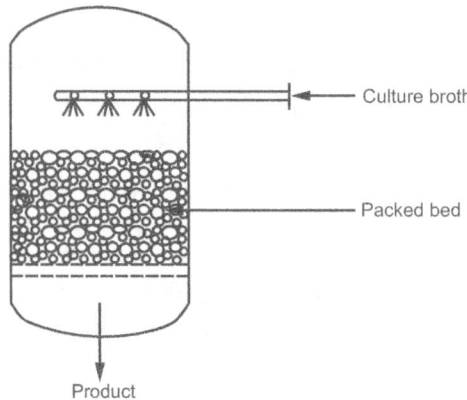

Fig. 3.10: Packed bed fermenter

2. **Tray fermenter:** In tray fermenter, solid as well as liquid media are used for fermentation. If liquid medium is used, cells are allowed to float easily and to make the process continuous (Fig. 3.11). If solid medium is used for tray fermenter then the process is called as solid state fermentation.

Solid state fermentation is defined as the growth of microorganisms (mainly fungi) on moist solid materials in the absence of free-flowing water. These processes have been used for the production of antibiotics, alkaloids, enzymes, organic acids, and also for bioremediation of hazardous compounds, biological detoxification of agro-industrial residues, nutritional enrichment, biopharmaceutical products etc. Solid state fermentation (SSF) has become a more attractive alternative to liquid fermentation for many productions.

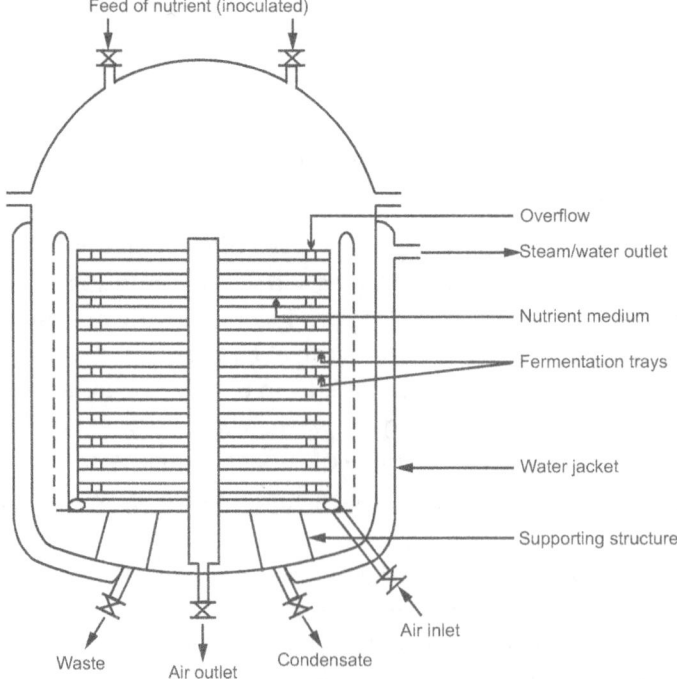

Fig. 3.11: Tray fermenter as a continuous process

Advantages of solid state fermentation:

- Solid state fermentation produce higher yields than submerged liquid fermentation.
- The possibilities of contamination by bacteria and yeast are very less because of low availability of water.
- All natural habitats for fungi are easily maintained in solid state fermentation.
- Culture media are very simple and it provides all the nutrients for growth of micro-organisms
- Simple design of fermenter and low energy requirements.
- Small reactors are used due to concentrated nature of the substrate.
- Low moisture availability may favor the production of specific compounds.
- Inoculations with spores (fungi) facilitate its uniform dispersion through the medium.

Disadvantages of solid state fermentation:

- The solid nature of the substrate causes problems in the monitoring of the process parameters (pH, moisture content, substrate and oxygen concentration).
- Agitation and biomass determination is very difficult.
- Solid state fermentation is only suitable for microorganisms that can grow at low moisture levels.
- The substrates require pre-treatment such as size reduction, homogenisation, chemical or enzymatic hydrolysis, vapours treatment etc.
- Possibility of contamination by different types of undesirable fungi.
- Aeration may be difficult due to high level of solid contents.
- Spores have larger lag times due to need for germination and also require more cultivation times.
- Products obtained by leaching of fermented solids are often viscous.

Design of fermenter:

Fermenter is a system consisting of different types of equipments to provide microbial growth by controlling environmental conditions. A typical fermenter consists of three parts such as the culture vessel, associated supply and environmental systems and measurement and control system. The various designing aspects required to be considered in constructing a ideal fermenter for production of pharmaceuticals are:

- Provide operation free from contamination.
- Adequate mixing and aeration.
- Maintain specific temperature and pH.
- Access points for inoculation and sampling.
- Non-toxic to microorganisms and safety.

- Minimize liquid loss from the fermenter.
- Monitoring and control of dissolved oxygen.
- Allow feeding of nutrient solution and reagent.
- Suitability for wide range of microbial cultures.
- Minimal use of labour and finances.
- Cheapest materials and smooth internal surfaces for vessel.

The fermenter is made up of stainless steel or borosilicate glass. They are non-corrosive, non-toxic and easily cleanable. The head plates provide parts for nutrient medium probes, gas input and waste product removal. Head plates and other accessories are fitted to the vessel by making use of gaskets, lip-seal and silicon rubber o-rings. Aeration and agitation are achieved by using stirrers, baffles, agitators (impeller), paddles and aeration system (sparger). Agitation and aeration system is one of the major requirements of aerobic fermentation.

Measurement and control of environmental conditions and biological variable is called fermentation monitoring. The process monitoring parameters are listed in Table 3.2. New developments in digital electronics have permitted a high level of monitoring and control of fermentation processes. The computer can be a vital instrument for process optimization and control.

Table 3.2: Controlled parameters and monitoring devices in fermentation

Sr. No	Process control	Monitoring device
1.	Air flow (0 to 6 lit/ min)	Flow meter
2.	Water flow	Rota meter.
3.	Temperature (8 to 60° C)	Thermometer/ thermistor/ thermocouple
4.	pH (2 to 12)	pH meter
5.	Agitator speed (0 to 1000 rpm)	Tachometer
6.	Pressure (2000 m bar)	Pressure gauze.
7.	DO_2 (0 to 100 %)	DO_2 analyzer
8.	Power input	Vom, target
9.	Foam	Foam, sensing and control unit.
10.	Rheology	Tube or cone-plate viscometer
11.	Cell concentration	Gravimetric dry weight or turbidimetry.
12.	State of culture	Enzyme probes, substrate concentration.
13.	Gas analysis	CO_2 analyzers, gas chromatography.
14.	Redox potential	DO_2 analyzer, DCO_2 analyzer, Polarographic probes, Galvanic probes.

QUESTIONS

(A) Short answer questions:
1. Draw a neat labelled diagram of a fermenter.
2. How will you regulate concentration of gases in fermentation?
3. What are secondary metabolites?
4. Draw a complete typical flow sheet of fermentation process.
5. Write advantages and disadvantages of air-lift fermenter.
6. Differentiate between internal loop air-lift fermenter and external loop airlift fermenter.

(B) Long answer questions:
1. Discuss the different factors for designing of a fermenter.
2. Explain in detail 'cell growth kinetics' for the process of fermentation.
3. How will you develop inoculum of spores forming microorganisms for fermentation process?
4. List different types of fermenters. Explain any one surface fermenter.
5. Write a short note on:
    (a) Continuous fermentation
    (c) Fluidized bed bioreactor
6. How will you monitor and control different parameters in fermentation?
7. What is submerged fermentation? Explain any one submerged fermenter.

(C) Multiple choice questions:
1. Air-lift bioreactors contain draught tube which is situated in to the fermenter.
    (a) Internal   (b) External
    (c) Both of the above   (d) None of the above
2. External loop reactor system is a type of _____ fermenter.
    (a) Air-lift   (b) Stirred-tank
    (c) Tray   (d) Packed-bed
3. Sparger is used in fermenter for a addition of _____ .
    (a) Antifoaming agent   (b) Antimicrobial agent
    (c) Sterile medium   (d) Sterile air
4. The size of the inoculum is normally _____ % added into a production tank.
    (a) 0.1 – 1   (b) 1 – 10
    (c) 10 – 20   (c) 20 – 30
5. Antibiotics are mainly produced by microorganisms in _____ phase.
    (a) Lag   (b) Log
    (c) Stationary (d) Death

(D) Match the following:

Column 'A'	Column 'B'
(a) Bubble-column fermenter	(i) Draught tube
(b) Air lift fermenter	(ii) Continuous process
(c) Tray fermenter	(iii) Nozzle or perforated plate
(d) Fluidized bed fermenter	(iv) Settling and bed zone.

(E) Fill in the blanks:

1. The most commonly used microorganism in alcoholic fermentation is _____.
2. The important substrate for large scale production of commercial yeast is _____.

CHAPTER 4

DOWN STREAM PROCESS AND BIOLOGICAL WASTE TREATMENT

CONTENTS
- INTRODUCTION
- DOWN STREAM PROCESSES
  - Pre-Treatment
  - Separation
  - Concentration
  - Purification
  - Formulation
- BIOLOGICAL WASTE TREATMENT
  - Physical Method
  - Chemical Method
  - Biological Method

INTRODUCTION

Isolation or separation of biological active agent from a cell culture supernatant is one of critical part of the manufacturing biotech products. Design and scale-up are two important stages of downstream process. Separating the impurities from the product requires a series of purification steps (process design) and bringing the product in final stage as per specification. After purification, formulation and sterilization are performed on the bulk product in order to obtain final product. Scale-up is the term used to describe a number of processes employed in converting laboratory procedure into the pilot plant, economical and industrial process. The main objective of scale-up is to produce a product of high quality at a less price.

Fermentation utilizes different types of raw materials that may be converted into a variety of products. Fermentation industry produces varying amount and wide range of waste materials. The waste includes salts and organic matters from spent media, cell contents, waste waters, traces of solvents, acids, alkalis, etc. Environmental Pollution Control Act does not permit disposal of wastes without any treatment. If the fermentation process employs plant or animal pathogens, the waste is required to be sterilized before its treatment. All wastes are treated in municipal sewage treatment plant or in its own effluent treatment plant. Industrial wastes mainly contain organic components and it oxidize completely into carbon dioxide and water.

DOWN STREAM PROCESSES

Harvesting, purification and final processing of fermentation product in suitable dosage form for its intended use after completion of fermentation is called down stream processing. Stages of product recovery from fermentation broth are shown in Fig. 4.1.

The down stream process, involves three major stages i.e. separation of cells from fermentation broth, isolation of impure product and purification and final processing of product. The product formed by fermentation can be intra-cellular or extra-cellular and heat stable or sensitive. Hence, downstream process is designed by considering many factors to achieve pure isolated product with least cost. The selection of specific processes depends on the following factors.

- Product location - extra-cellular/intra-cellular.
- Product sensitivity.
- Concentration of product or possible yield.
- Properties and use of product.
- Acceptable standards of purity.
- Possible impurities.
- Economy of process and market price of product.

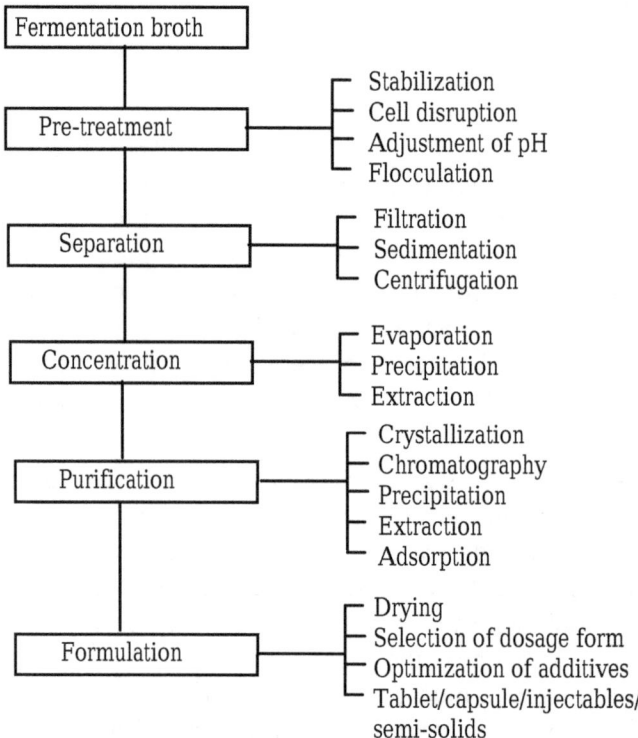

Fig. 4.1: Stages of down stream processing

Pre-treatment:

Fermentation broth contains microbial cells, cell fragments, soluble and insoluble medium components alongwith the active product. Pre-treatment is given to fermentation broth to change viscosity of medium, biomass size and interaction between particles. Synthetic polymers, cellulosic polycations and inorganic salts are added into broth as a flocculating agent. These agents can lead to agglomeration of individual cell particles into large flocs, facilitating separation by centrifugation. When product is intra-cellular, some methods (Fig. 4.2) are used to disintegrate the cell to release the intra-cellular product.

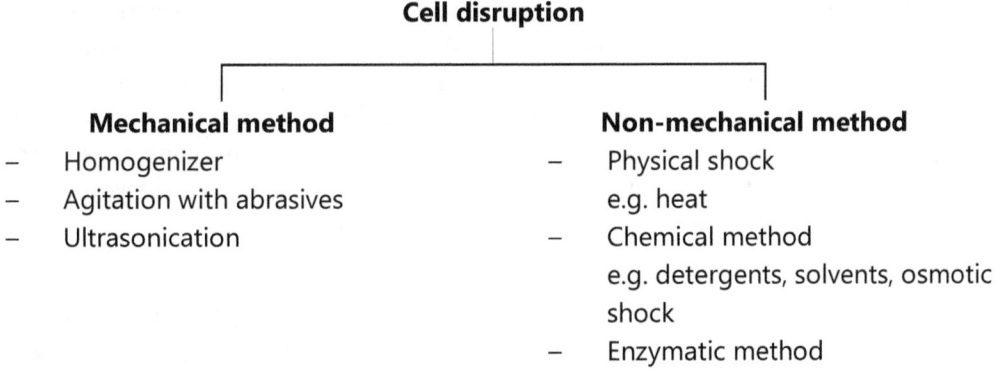

Fig. 4.2: Cell disruption methods

Separation:

The cells after cell disruption for intra-cellular products and without cell disruption for extra-cellular products are separated by centrifugation or filtration. Filtration retains large particles as a cake and allows passage of liquid through the filter. Flow of liquid through filter medium is dependent on area of filter, pore size of filter and flow resistances by the cake formed on filter medium. Cellulose, glass, ceramics, synthetic membranes, synthetic fibers, cloth, metal, etc. are used as filter media. When filtration is not a satisfactory method to remove micro-organisms, centrifugation can be employed. Different types of centrifuges are available with varying r.p.m. (Fig. 4.3).

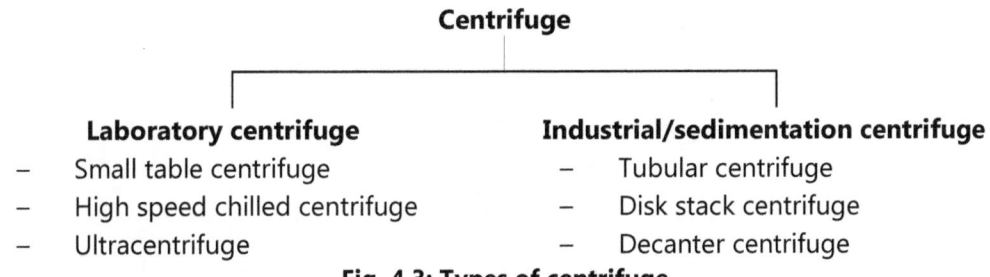

Fig. 4.3: Types of centrifuge

Concentration:

After separation of microbial cells, broth is fractionated or extracted by using different techniques of extraction, evaporation and precipitation. Evaporation is simple but energy consuming process mainly for removal of water. Falling film evaporators, forced film evaporators, plate evaporators and centrifugal forced film evaporators are commonly used for concentration of solvents.

In the product recovery process, precipitation is carried out to enrich and concentrate the product in one step. Precipitation technique is commonly used for recovery of product as well as to separate the impurities. Precipitation is achieved by external agents such as acids and bases (to change the pH); organic solvents like chilled acetone, ethanol, methanol (to change in dielectric properties); salts like ammonium or sodium sulfate (recovery of proteins), non-ionic polymers like polyethylene glycol (PEG), polyelectrolytes and protein binding dyes. Extraction is commonly applied in a large scale fermentations for concentration and purification. Solubility and polarity of the product plays a major role in the selection of solvent for extraction. Multistage extraction or counter-current extraction is also employed with high extraction yield. Mixer settlers, column and centrifugal extractors are commonly used for the extraction. Solvents used for extraction are expensive. Hence, all solvents are recovered and re-circulated in extraction process.

Purification:

The crude product obtained by concentration is then purified by fractional precipitation, crystallization and chromatographical techniques. Crystallization is used especially in the recovery of acids, solvents and in purification of various compounds. The crystals obtained by crystallization are separated by filtration, redissolved in a suitable solvent and then re-crystallized to assure the removal of all impurities. Chromatographic techniques are commonly used in isolation and purification of fermentation product. The components are distributed between a stationary phase and a mobile phase. Stationary phase is a packed column of uniformly sized particles equilibrated with suitable solvent, while mobile phase is solvent which moves in this packed column (Fig. 4.4).

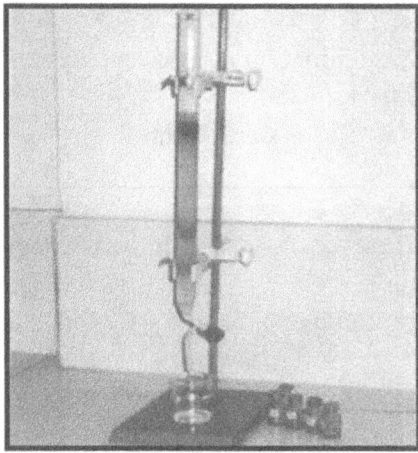

Fig. 4.4: Column chromatography

The mixture to be separated is packed into a column followed by mobile phase. Adsorption chromatography, ion-exchange chromatography, gel-filtration chromatography, affinity chromatography, reverse phase chromatography and high performance liquid chromatography are the commonly used techniques for purification of proteins and pharmaceuticals. Purity of products are continuously confirmed by paper and thin-layer chromatography (Fig. 4.5).

Different types of paper chromatography are used for checking the purity of isolated product such as ascending paper chromatography, descending paper chromatography and circular paper chromatography.

Formulation:

Antibiotics, proteins and enzymes are formulated as a solution, suspension or as dry powders. Stabilizers such as ammonium sulphate salt, sorbitol, glycerol, PEG, etc. are added in these preparations. Depending on dosage form, different other additives are also added in the final formulation e.g. diluents, lubricating agent, suspending agent, emulsifying agent, colouring agent etc. Drying is the most essential step mainly for protein products. Contact dryers (e.g. drum dryer), convection dryers (e.g. spray dryer, fluidized dryer) and radiation dryer (freeze dryer) are commonly used for drying the final product. The antibiotics are packed in sterile vials as a powder or suspension for parenteral or oral use. They may be formulated as film coated tablet.

Fig. 4.5: Thin-layer chromatography

Estimation of the fermentation products is necessary during drying in down stream processing and at the end of the process. Gravimetry, spectrophotometry, specific gravity, optical density, packed cell volume, total viable count, measurements of cell components, counting chambers and chromatography are the common methods used for estimation of fermentation products.

Quality control of fermentation products is done during the process and the finished final product. During down stream processing, the efficiency of the unit operations is determined by product evaluation at each step. Quality assurance or quality control tests for fermentation products include sterility testing, pyrogen testing, toxicity testing, allergy testing, microbiological assays and carcinogenicity testing. It must satisfy all government standards before being marketed.

BIOLOGICAL WASTE TREATMENT

Industrial wastes should be adequately treated before disposal in a receiving water course because it reduces the spread of pathogenic micro-organisms, prevents pollution and contamination, avoidance of health and aesthetic hazards, prevents objectionable odours, colours and tastes, maintain the oxygen balance, etc.

The level of decomposable organic matter present in industrial waste waters is measured in terms of 'Biochemical or Biological Oxygen Demand' (BOD) or 'Chemical Oxygen Demand' (COD). Biological oxygen demand measures the quantity of oxygen consumed during the biological decomposition of organic matter (oxidation) in one litre of waste water during a specified time (usually five days). Chemical Oxygen Demand determines the milligrams of oxygen consumed per litre of waste water during the oxidation of the organic matter by hot acidified dichromate. Biological Oxygen Demand and Chemical Oxygen Demand determination can be employed at any stage in the treatment of industrial or municipal wastes so as to ascertain the efficiency of the treatment. Industrial sewage contains both organic and inorganic compounds. The nature and amount of compounds depend upon the type of product and nature of the process involved in industry. Organic matter are readily degraded by micro-organisms due to a high content of sugars, proteins, urea, amino acids, amines, etc. Organic components in the sewage serve as food for micro-organisms. These micro-organisms oxidize the industrial wastes in presence of oxygen. If the organic content of the industrial wastes is high, the oxygen requirement is also more for oxidation of organic content.

Organic matter of industrial waste + oxygen $\xrightarrow{\text{Microorganisms}}$ New micro-organisms + H_2O + CO_2 + treated sewage.

Industrial waste treatment methods:

Industrial wastes are treated by different methods. The selection of method is dependent upon the cost of the plant, quantity and nature of wastes, sanitary requirement of health department etc. Treatment methods are classified as follows:

- **Physical Method:**

  It is employed to remove suspended solids by using sedimentation tanks. Sedimentation tanks are circular or rectangular continuous flow tanks operating at retention time of 6 to 12 hours. It can remove upto 60 to 70% of suspended solids and 30 to 40% of BOD load.

- **Chemical Method:**

  Chemical treatment is done by flocculation or co-agglutination. Aluminium sulphate (alum), calcium hydroxide (lime), ferric sulphate and polyelectrolytes are often used as coagulant and added into the effluent mixed tank. Suspended matter is precipitated and settled in the tank to form sludge.

- **Biological Method:**
    It involves use of microorganisms for decomposition of substances. Various biological treatment methods are classified in Fig. 4.6.

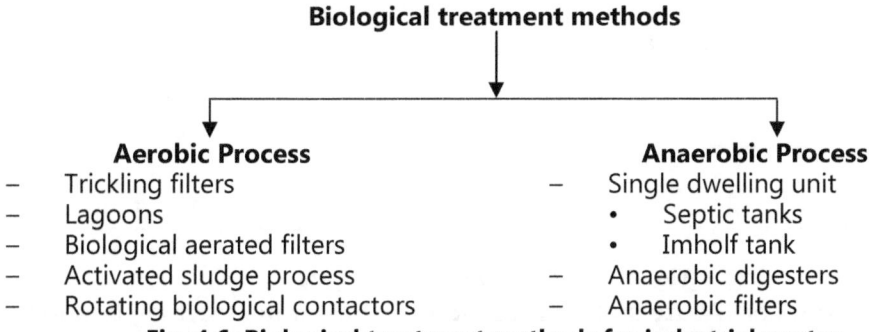

Fig. 4.6: Biological treatment methods for industrial wastes

A **Trickling filter** consists of a bed of coarse pieces of stone, gravel and related substances. Individual rocks being two to four inches in diameter and the depth of the bed being approximately six to ten feet. This leaves many open spaces in the bed for penetration of air. Waste waters are sprayed over the rock bed continuously from nozzles located on a horizontal rotating arm (Fig. 4.7).

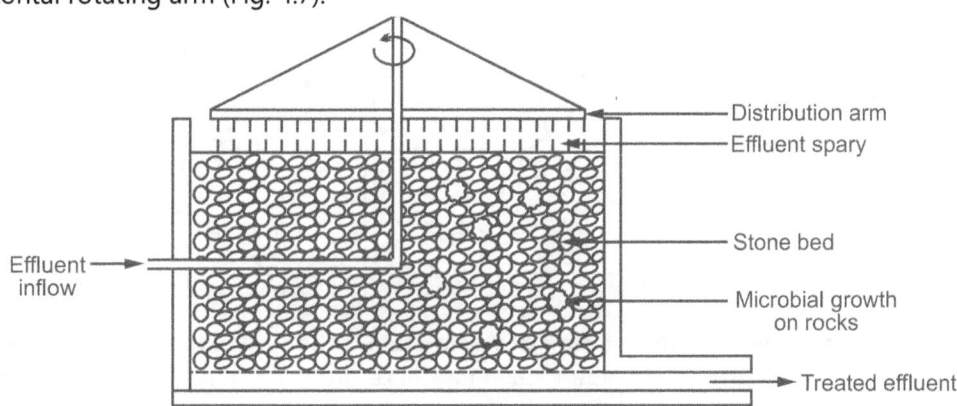

Fig. 4.7: Trickling filter

Waste water may be pre-aerated before spraying, although some aeration occurs during spraying. Micro-organisms such as bacteria, fungi, algae and protozoa become attached to the surface of the rocks. The large surface area permits close contact between flowing air, effluent and biologically active growth, which converts organic materials into simple form. The effluent waters are passed slowly through a final settling tank to remove the sloughed microbial cells and other debris before the waters are chlorinated and discharged into a stream.

The **Activated sludge process** is a highly efficient system for the aerobic biological treatment of industrial wastes. The process is based on vigorous aeration of sewage. This practice of vigorous aeration causes the fine particles to clump into flocs. Such flocs are allowed to settle (Fig. 4.8) and then added to fresh sewage that is vigorously aerated. The process is repeated and most of the sludge is recycled from the sedimentation tank to the aeration tank.

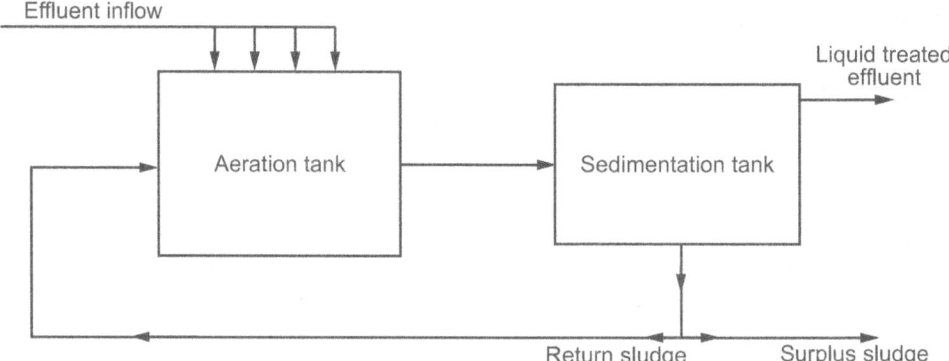

Fig. 4.8: Activated sludge process

'Oxidation pond' or **'Waste stabilization pond'** is one of the most important method of sewage treatment in hot climates. It is also called 'Lagoons'. Lagoonization is a natural process of sewage purification because oxidation of putrescible matter occurs through symbiotic action of algae and aerobic bacteria present in the effluent (4.9).

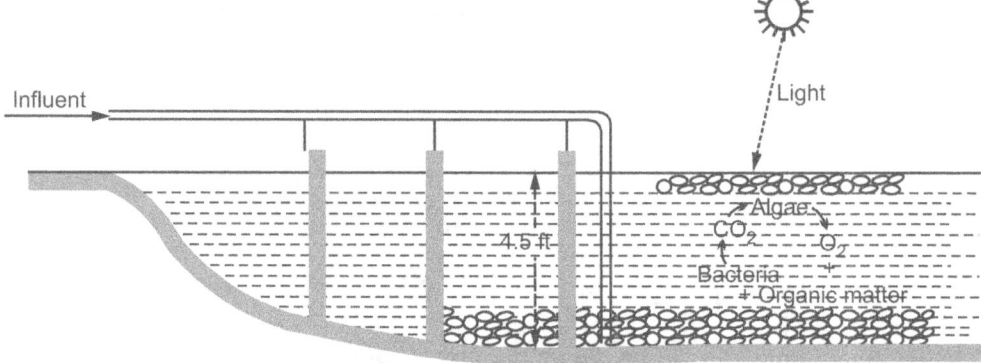

Fig. 4.9: Diagrammatic representation of waste-stabilization pond method or lagoons

In the presence of light and oxygen, bacteria utilize organic matter to convert into CO_2 to algae, which will be utilized as a source of energy by photosynthesis and as nutrients. Oxygen is again helpful in multiplication of aerobic bacteria.

$$6\ CO_2 + 12\ H_2O \xrightarrow{\text{Algae/light}} \underset{\text{glucose}}{C_6H_{12}O_6} + 6\ H_2O + 6O_2$$

Septic and Imholf tanks (Fig. 4.10) are anaerobic digestion chambers used for decomposition of simple or complex organic materials to simple organic molecules and fermentation gases. These tanks are small, rectangular sited below ground level. The sewage enters into the first tank, where particles settle at the bottom (1 to 3 days), to form the sludge and are digested under anaerobic conditions. A thick crust of scum is formed at the surface which makes the system anaerobic. Solids not settled in the first tank are settled in the second tank. The sludge accumulated is removed once in every 1 to 5 years. The Imholf tank works as a septic tank but differ in its larger size and physical design.

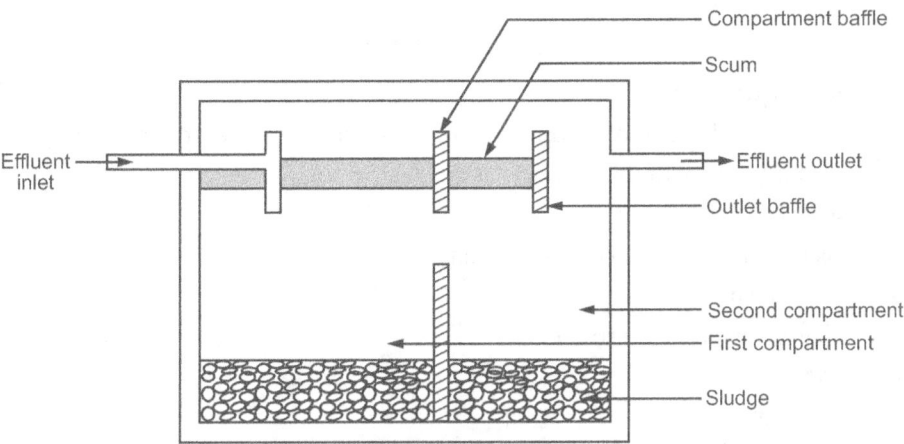

Fig. 4.10: Septic tank

The complete effluent treatment plant of an antibiotic manufacturing industry is shown as a flow sheet in Fig. 4.11.

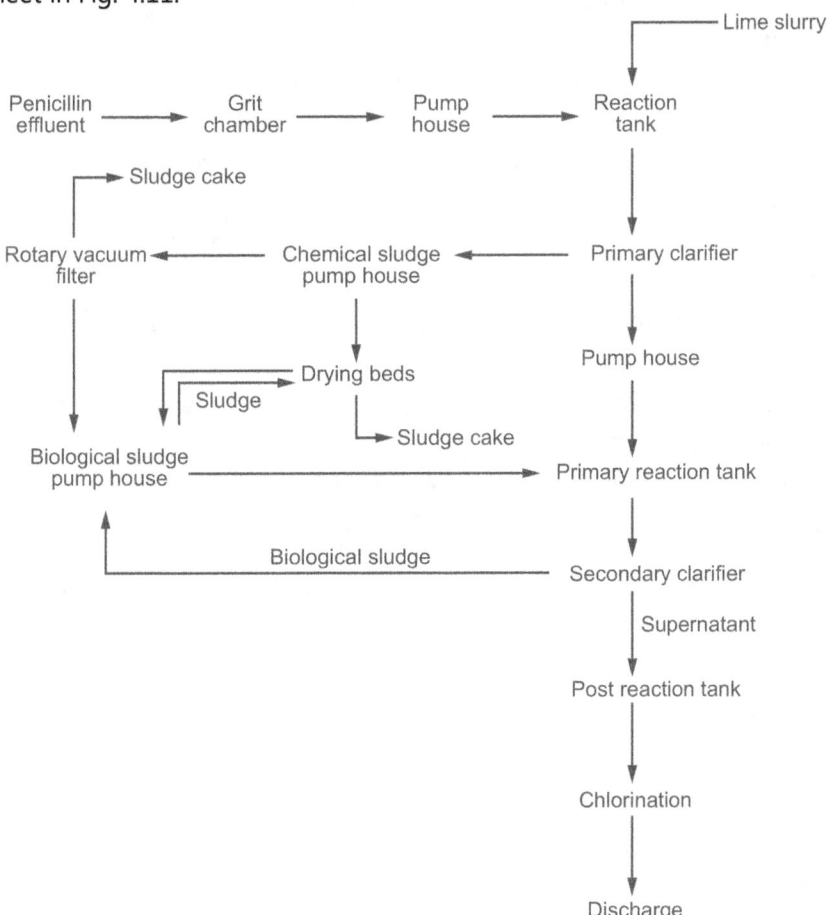

Fig. 4.11: Flow sheet of effluent treatment plant of an antibiotic manufacturing industry

QUESTIONS

(A) Short answer questions:
1. Write the role of chromatographic techniques in down stream processing.
2. Explain different techniques used for cell disruption.

(B) Long answer questions:
1. What is downstream processing? Explain.
2. Write a short note on:
   (a) Biological waste treatment
   (b) Trickling filter

(C) Multiple choice questions:
1. Factor affecting on cake resistance in filtration is _____
   (a) Temperature (b) pH
   (c) Types of micro-organisms (d) All of the above
2. Cell disruption follows _____ kinetics.
   (a) Zero order (b) First order
   (c) Second order (d) None of the above
3. _____ is the anaerobic method used for treatment of wastes.
   (a) Trickling filter (b) Lagoons
   (c) Septic tank (d) All of the above.

(D) Fill in the blanks:
1. The most commonly used chemical disinfectant for treatment of municipal water is _____.
2. Genetically engineered strain of _____ used in biodegradation of several pollutants, also called as 'superbug'.
3. Chemical Oxygen Demand determines the milligrams of _____ consumed per litre of waste water during the oxidation of the organic matter

■■■

CHAPTER 5

PRODUCTION OF PHARMACEUTICALS

CONTENTS

    INTRODUCTION

    PENICILLIN

    STREPTOMYCIN

    TETRACYCLINE

    VITAMIN B_2

    VITAMIN B_{12}

    DEXTRAN

INTRODUCTION

Production of antibiotics, vitamins, enzymes and alcoholic products is the main aim of the fermentation industry. Most pharmaceuticals are produced by the process of fermentation using specific microbial strains. Interest in utilization of antibiotics for therapy began in 1929 when **Alexander Fleming** found that a mould *Penicillium* had an effect against *Staphylococcus aureus*. Penicillin was the first antibiotic commercially produced from the *Penicillium* species by the process of fermentation. Its use in treatment of infections, led to the invention of thousands of antibiotics. These antibiotics are mainly produced from fungi, actinomycetes and bacteria. These substances have wide applications in medical, veterinary and agriculture practices.

PENICILLIN

Production of penicillin began in the United States (1941) by surface culture fermentation of *Penicillium notatum*. During World War II, penicillin producing fungi were studied extensively to increase yields of penicillin. Now a day, penicillin is produced from *Penicillium chrysogenum* by submerged culture techniques. Morphology of *Penicillum* species is shown in Fig. 5.1. Penicillin is effective against Gram-positive bacteria and also some large viruses and *Rickettsia*. Penicillin is a genèric term applied to an entire group of antibiotics.

(5.1)

The penicillin nucleus contains two amino acids, L-cysteine and D-valine (Fig. 5.2) which are closely related in structure. Penicillins are N-acyl derivatives of 6-aminopenicillanic acid (6-APA). By adding side chains to the penicillin nucleus, new penicillins are synthesized (Fig. 5.3). The semisynthetic penicillins are prepared from 6-aminopenicillanic acid (6-APA). Acylation of the 6-APA is easily and efficiently brought about by chemical reactions (Fig. 5.4) Different derivatives of semisynthetic penicillin are shown in Fig. 5.5.

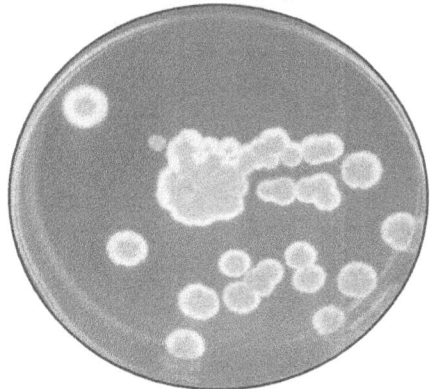

Fig. 5.1: *Penicillium* species

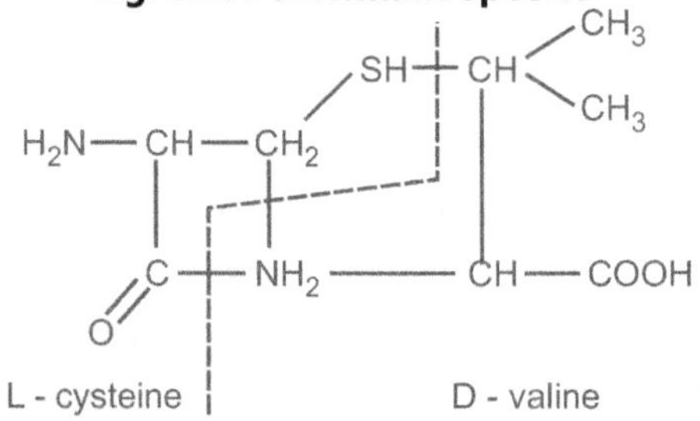

Fig. 5.2: Penicillin molecule showing component amino acids L-cysteine and D-valine

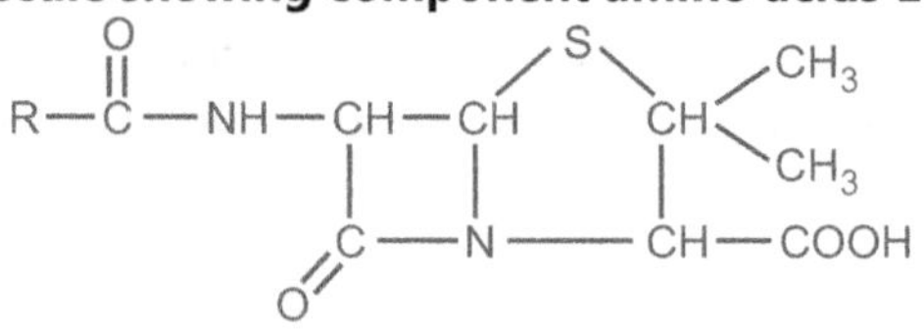

R   — $C_6H_5CH_2$– Penicillin G (Benzyl penicillin)
R   — $HOC_6H_4CH_2$– Penicillin X (Hydroxy benzyl penicillin)
R   — $C_6H_5OCH_2$– Penicillin V (Phenoxy methyl penicillin)
R   — $CH_3CH_2CH=CHCH_2$– Penicillin F (2-Pentenyl penicillin)
R   — $CH_3(CH_2)_3CH$– Dihydropenicillin F (n-Pentyl penicillin)
R   — $CH_3(CH_2)_5CH_2$– Penicillin K (n-Heptyl penicillin)

Fig. 5.3: Types of penicillin

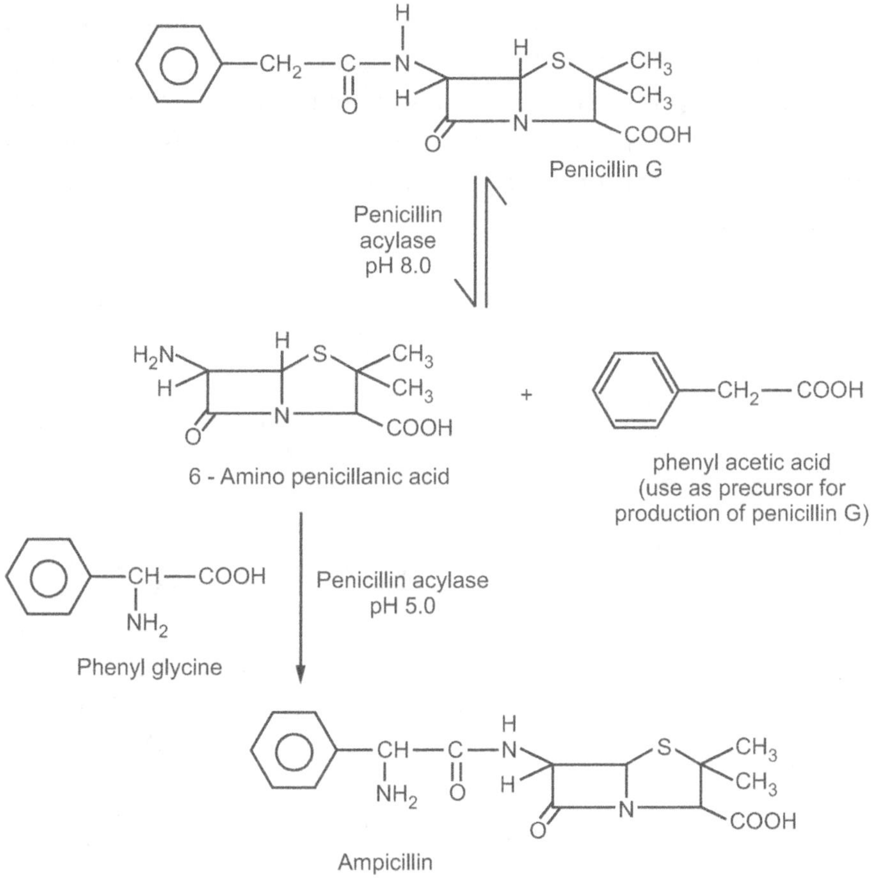

Fig. 5.4: Preparation of semisynthetic penicillin (ampicillin) from 6-aminopenicillanic acid

Inoculum development:

The selected strain of *Penicillium chrysogenum* is maintained in the form of a master culture and preserved by lyophilization, or by fixing the spores in sterilized soils and mixtures. For inoculum preparation, spores from working solid cultures are suspended in water. These spores are added in flasks containing nutrient solution and incubated for 4 to 6 days at 25°C. The resulting spores are used directly to inoculate inoculum tank. The inoculum tanks are incubated for 48 hours with agitation and aeration to grow more mycelium. The resulting inoculum is used for a production tank or it is added to a second or even third-stage inoculum tank to produce more inoculum for large-scale fementation.

Production media:

The exact composition of penicillin production media used in the industry for production of penicillin is unknown. These media are considered to be trade secrets of that particular fermentation industry. A typical medium described by **Jackson** (1958) contains fermentable carbohydrates, such as corn steep liquor solids (3.5%), lactose (3.5%) and glucose (1%); potassium dihydrogen phosphate (0.4%), calcium carbonate (1%), edible oil (0.4%), and penicillin precursor. The pH of this medium after sterilization is 5.5 to 6.0. Inoculum media are similar to production media except that lactose and precursors are not added in the inoculum media. These media compositions may be slightly changed to increase yields and meet economic changes.

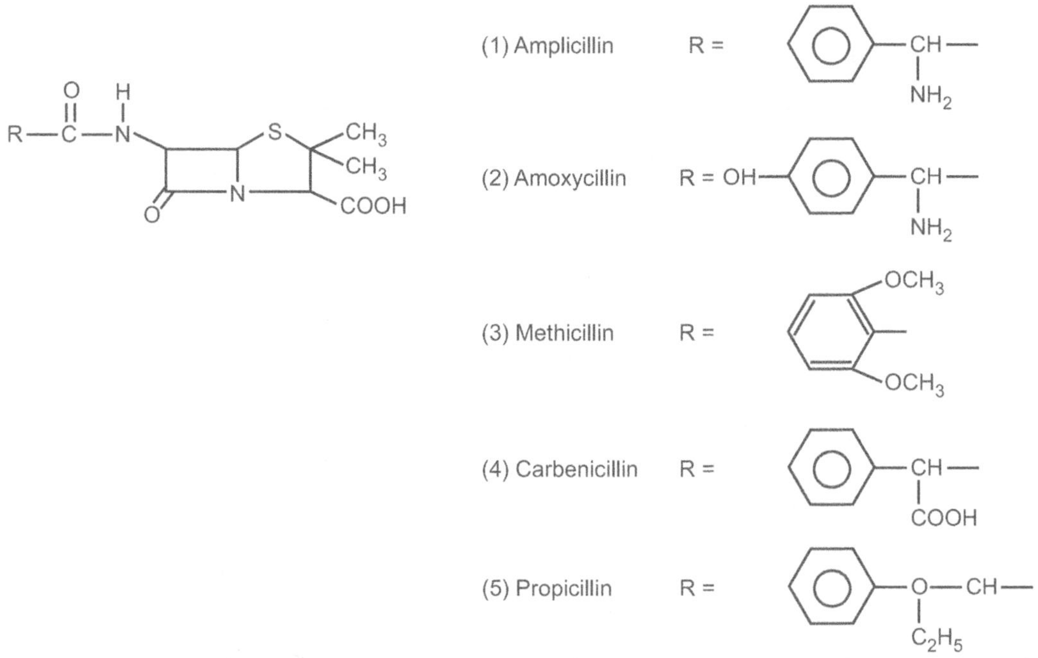

Fig. 5.5: Chemical structures of important semisynthetic penicillins

Fermentation:

The media are placed in a fermentation vessel, sterilized and inoculated with a suspension of *Penicillium chrysogenum* (inoculum). A flow sheet for large scale production of penicillin is shown in Fig. 5.6. The fermentation vessel is equipped with devices which allow continuous addition of nutrients, acids/bases to maintain the pH (7 to 7.4) and cooling coils to maintain the temperature (24°C).

The mycelium grows rapidly by utilizing organic nitrogen compounds and lactic acid as a source of carbon. Ammonia is liberated by deamination of the amino acids of the corn steep liquor and pH rises. Ammonia is actively assimilated and maintains the pH. Active penicillin production is associated with this phase of lactose and ammonia utilization (Fig. 5.7). Maximum antibiotics are produced within 4 to 5 days.

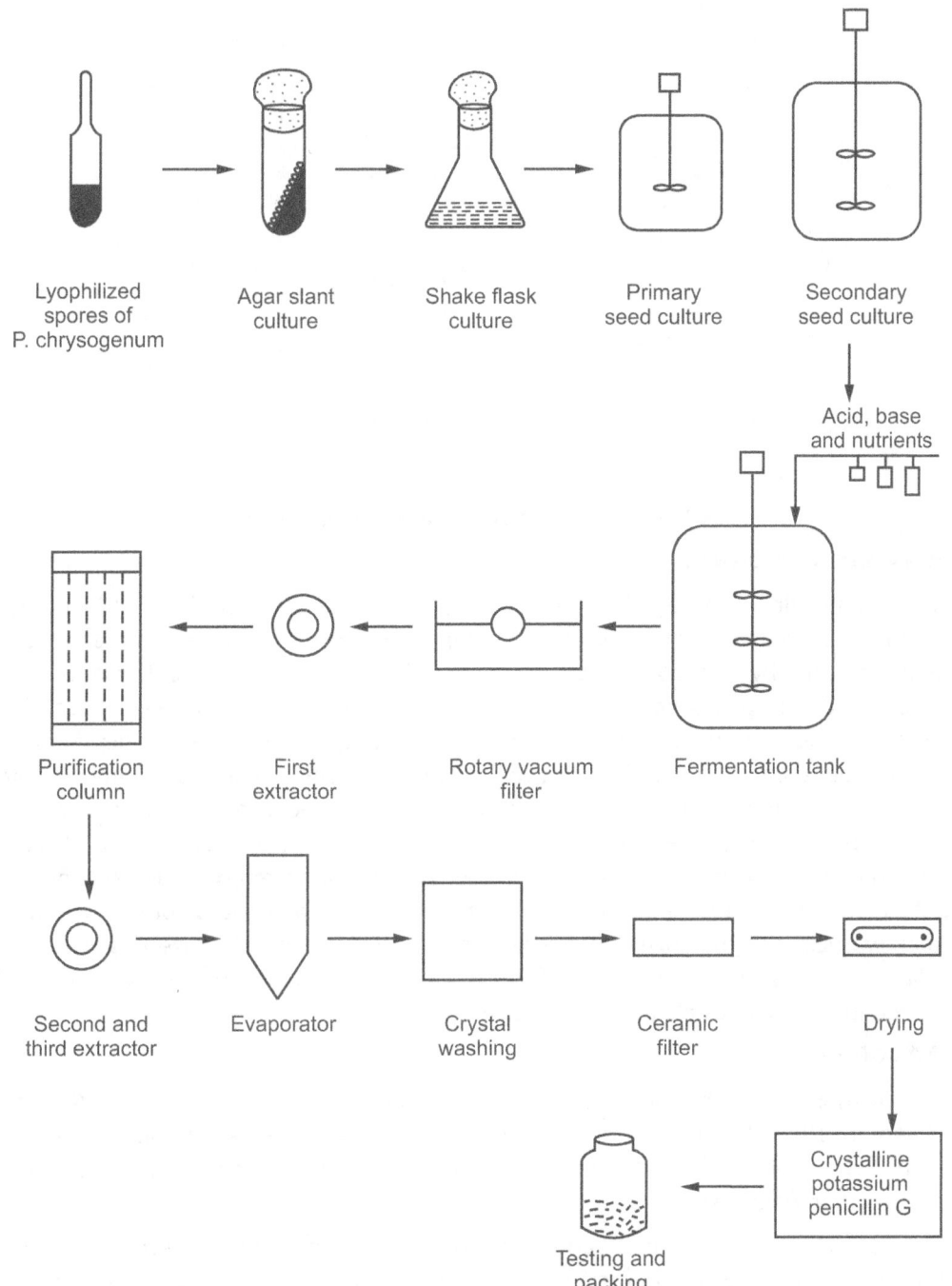

Fig. 5.6: Flow sheet for large scale production of penicillin

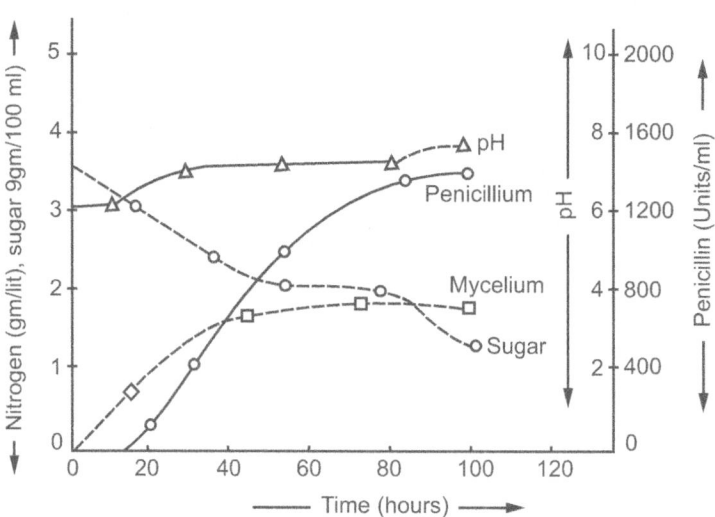

Fig. 5.7: Events in batch fermentation of penicillin

Recovery and purification:

A schematic flow diagram for the recovery of potassium penicillin G (down stream process) is incorporated in Fig. 5.6. The first step in the recovery process is the removal of mycelium or cells by filtration (rotary vacuum filter) or centrifugation. These stages are carried out under aseptic conditions, to avoid contamination of the filtrate with penicillinase producing microorganisms (*Bacillus* species) which may cause loss of antibiotics. Penicillin is extracted under controlled conditions of temperature, pH and sterility to minimize chemical and enzymatic degradation. It is extracted in the form of acid into amyl acetate, methyl isobutyl ketone or butyl acetate in a counter-current solvent extractor at pH 2.5 to 3.0. A penicillin containing solvent is treated with active charcoal to remove pigments and other impurities. The charcoal is separated from the extract on a precoated rotary vacuum filter and then washed with the solvent. Penicillin from the solvent is crystallized by the addition of sodium or potassium hydroxide to form its salt. The end product of penicillin is then crystallized into sodium or potassium penicillin.

STREPTOMYCIN

Streptomycin was the first aminoglycoside antibiotic, discovered by **Selman A Waksman** in 1944 that is very active against Gram-negative as well as Gram-positive organisms. The main use is for treatment of tuberculosis due to their strong activity against *Mycobacterium tuberculosis*.

Streptomycin was the first antibiotic produced from the *Streptomyces* genera (actinomycetes) from *Streptomyces griseus*. One of the antibiotic producing strain of *Streptomyces* species is shown in Fig. 5.8. Streptomycin and dihydrostreptomycin are basic compounds and they are usually prepared as salts. Streptomycin at high dosages may produce neurotoxic reactions. Hence, chemical reduction of streptomycin to dihydrostreptomycin (Fig. 5.9) decreases this neurotoxicity.

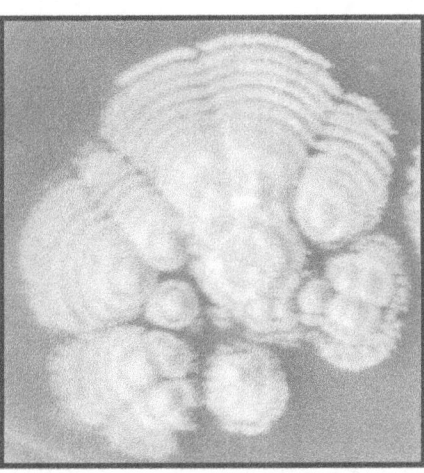

Fig. 5.8: *Streptomyces* species

Different strains are used for production of streptomycin and other derivatives (Table 5.1). Production yield was increased by the process of mutation and by culture media optimization. Production media includes sources of carbon and nitrogen and some essential materials. Glucose, fructose, galactose, xylose, mannitol, lactose, starch, dextrin or glycine can be used as sources of carbon and peptone, meat extract, glycogen, soyabean meal, corn-steep liquor, casein hydrolysate or nitrates are employed as source of nitrogen. Growth stimulating compounds (factor A, phenylacetic acid) antioxidants (agar or sodium sulphite), mineral salts and vegetable or mineral oils are often added in the fermentor. Merck's media (glucose + soybean extract + NaCl), Schartz media (glucose + peptone + meat extract + NaCl) and Rake and Donovik's media (glucose + soyabean extract + NaCl) are commonly used for the commercial production of streptomycin. **Hockenhull** (1963) described a typical industrial medium containing glucose (2.5%), soyabean meal (4%), distillers dried soluble (0.5%) and sodium chloride (0.25%).

Table 5.1: Strains used for production of streptomycin and other derivatives.

Antibiotic	Producer strain
Streptomycin	*Streptomyces griseus, S. rameus, S. bikiniensis, S. erythrochromogenus*
Dihydrostreptomycin	*S. humidus*
Hydroxystreptomycin	*S. grisecarneus, S. subrutilus*

Production:

Flow sheet for production of streptomycin is shown in Fig. 5.10. Streptomycin yield in fermentation respond strongly to aeration and agitation. The optimum fermentation temperature is in the range of 25 to 30°C and the optimum pH ranges is 7 to 8. The fermentation lasts approximately 5 to 7 days (Fig. 5.11) and the fermentation passes through three phases.

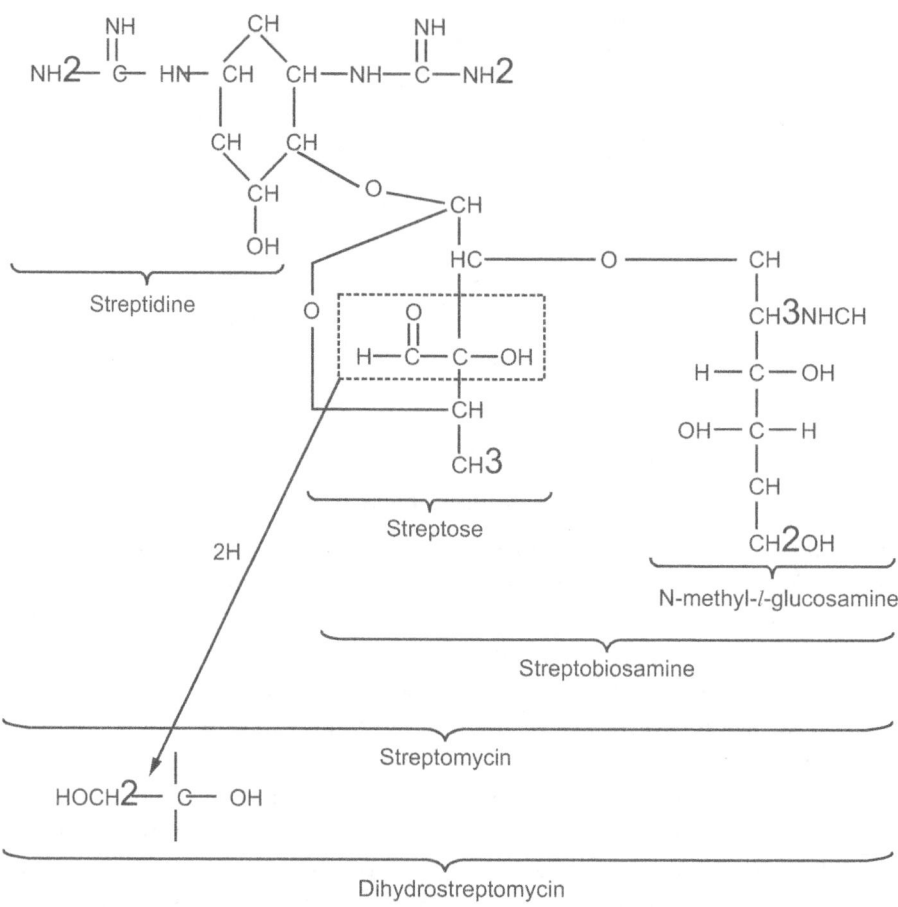

Fig. 5.9: Structure of streptomycin and dihydrostreptomycin

Phase (I): The first phase (1 to 2 days) of streptomycin fermentation consists of mycelial growth. The proteolytic activity of *Streptomyces griseus* releases ammonia to the medium from the soyabean meal and the pH rises to about 7.6 due to the production of ammonia. Glucose of the medium is slowly utilized with slight production of streptomycin.

Phase (II): In this phase (1 to 3 days) production of streptomycin increases at a faster rate without growth of any new mycelium. Large quantities of glucose and oxygen are required and ammonia is utilized. The pH remains fairly constant in the range of 7.4 to 7.8.

Phase (III): In the last phase, sugar has been depleted from the medium and reduces the streptomycin production. The cells are lysed which then release ammonia and rapid increase in pH. The streptomycin is isolated before the third phase.

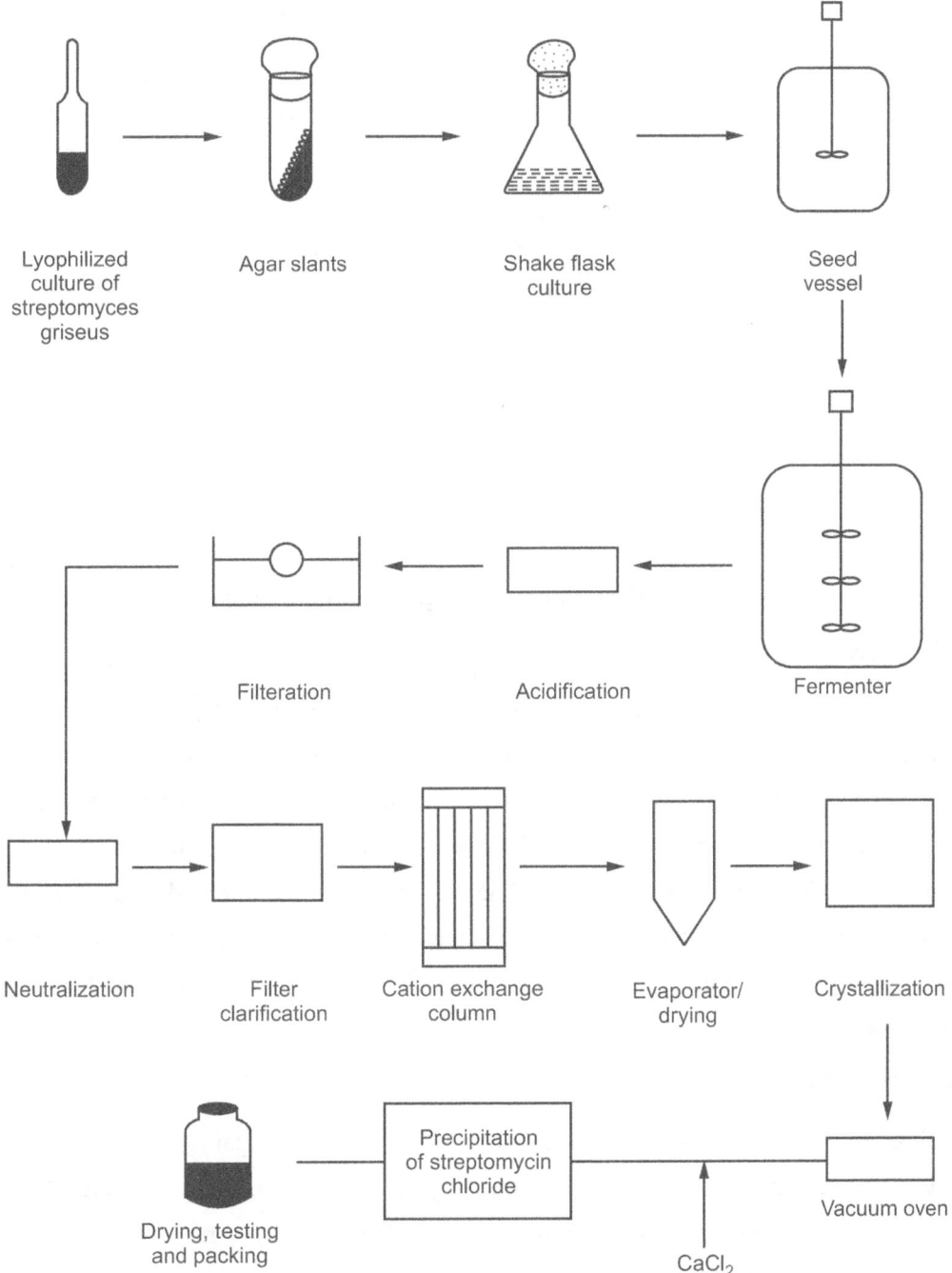

Fig. 5.10: Flow sheet of streptomycin production

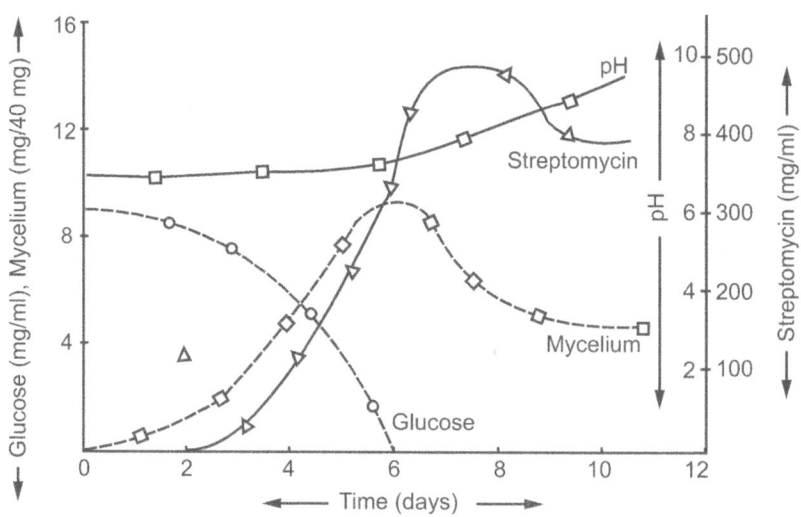

Fig. 5.11: Time course of streptomycin production

Product recovery:

Streptomycin is recovered by different methods depending on the particular fermentation industry. The fermentation broth is acidified, filtered and neutralized. It is then passed through a column containing a cation exchange resin to absorb the streptomycin from the broth. The column is washed with water and the streptomycin diluted with hydrochloric acid before concentration. The streptomycin is dissolved in methanol and filtered. Acetone is added to the filtrate to precipitate the antibiotic. Finally, the precipitate is washed with acetone and dissolved in methanol for preparation as a pure streptomycin calcium chloride complex.

TETRACYCLINE

Tetracyclines are broad-spectrum antibiotics mainly active against Gram-positive and Gram-negative bacteria, rickettsia and some large viruses. There antibiotics are produced mainly by *Streptomyces aureofaciens* and *Streptomyces rimosus*. Aureomycin (*chlortetracycline*) is discovered by **Duggar** (1948) which was produced by fermentation of *Streptomyces aureofaciens*. Oxytetracyline was produced by fermentation of *Streptomyces rimosus*. The structures of tetracyclines are shown in Fig. 5.12.

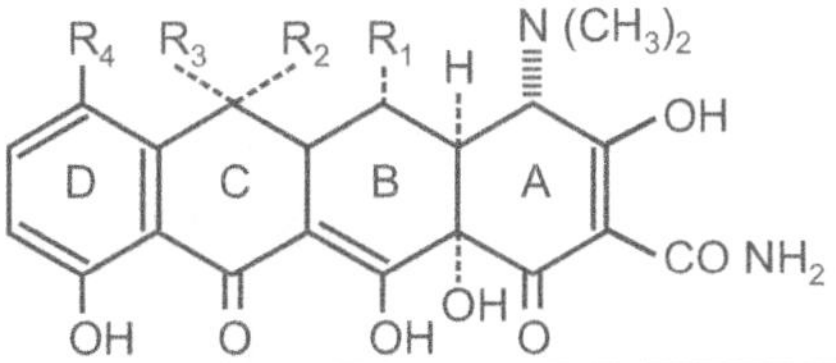

Name	R_1	R_2	R_3	R_4
Tetracycline	H	OH	CH_3	H
Oxytetracycline	OH	OH	CH_3	H
Chlortetracycline	H	OH	CH_3	Cl
Doxycycline	OH	H	CH_3	H
Demeclocycline	H	OH	H	Cl
Methacycline	OH	H	CH_3	H
Minocycline	H	H	H	$N(CH_3)_2$

Fig. 5.12: Chemistry of tetracyclines

Streptomyces aureofaciens ATCC 13908-13911 and NCI B-9114 are used for industrial production of tetracycline. The stock cultures are maintained for longer periods in the form of lyophilized spores or at liquid nitrogen temperature as spore stock. Tetracycline antibiotic yield can be improved by mutagens like UV light, X-rays, γ-radiation, ethylene amine and nitrogen mustards, alone or in combinations.

Inoculum development:

The medium used for inoculum development contains carbohydrate (sucrose and maltose)- 2.5%, corn-steep liquor – 1.7%, calcium carbonate – 1%, $(NH_4)_2SO_4$ – 0.2% and other inorganic salts and minerals. The composition of inoculation media is made similar to the fermentation media to ensure short lag phase. The different steps in the inoculum development of tetracycline production are shown in Fig. 5.13. The culture is monitored for temperature, pH, residual sugar, carbon dioxide, biomass etc. Optimum yield is obtained from medium containing inoculum for 24 hours.

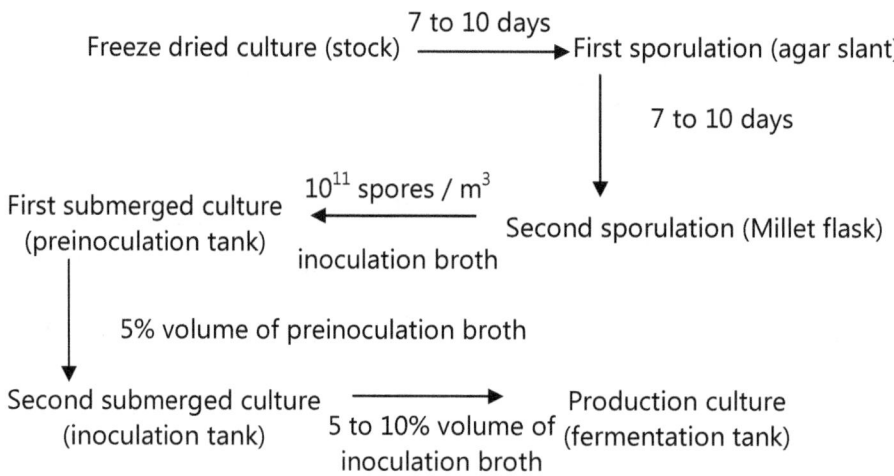

Fig. 5.13: Inoculum preparation for tetracycline fermentation

Fermentation:

Tetracyclines are obtained by submerged culture technique. A typical medium for production of tetracycline by fermentation contains carbon sources (e.g. sucrose, dextrose, corn starch, vegetable oils), nitrogen sources (e.g. corn-steep liquor, soybean meal, peanut meal) and inorganic salts ($MgSO_4$, $ZnSO_4$, $NaCl$ etc). Lactose and saccharose are not used by *Streptomyces* species. Animal and vegetable oils are used as antifoaming agents as well as carbon sources. Calcium carbonate helps in maintaining pH and also binds with antibiotics. Hence, it prevents from product accumulation and inhibition of product formation. The fermentation is conducted at 28 to 30°C, pH 6 to 6.5 and aeration level of 0.5 to 0.8 volume of air per volume of liquid per minute. The fermentation process may be batch or semi-continuous type. The yield of antibiotic depends upon pH, age of the inoculum and composition of the medium. Aeration of the culture is also very important for the biosynthesis of antibiotic.

Product recovery:

Tetracycline is obtained from the filtrate of the acidic medium by adsorption on diatomaceous earth or activated charcoal. It is precipitated in the form of salts with metals of alkaline earth. Extraction is carried from the broth with 1-butanol or in addition of a carrier i.e. quaternary ammonium compounds. Tetracycline forms complex salt with divalent Ca^{2+} and Mg^{2+}. It is purified by crystallization as salts or bases from boiling solvents like lower alcohols, ketones etc.

VITAMIN B₂ (RIBOFLAVIN)

Riboflavin is an important vitamin required by man and animals. **Kuhn, Gyorgy** and **Wagner Jauregg** in 1933 isolated riboflavin from whey of milk. It was first isolated from milk and then prepared by fermentation in 1935. It is also present in other foods as flavoproteins which contain the prosthetic group flavin mononucleotide (FMN) or flavin adenine dinucleotide (FAD). Chemically, riboflavin is an alloxazine derivative which consists of a pteridine ring condensed to a benzene ring. The side chain consists of a C_5-polyhydroxyl group (Fig. 5.14). Riboflavin is prepared by a fermentation process as well as by a synthetic method. It is produced by a number of microorganisms including bacteria *(Clostridium butyricum, Clostridium acetobutylicum, Clostridium felsineum, Mycobacterium smegmatis, Aerobacter aerogenes)*, yeast *(Candida arborea, Candida flareri, Saccharomyces* species) and yeast like fungi, ascomycetes *(Ereomothecium ashbyii, Ashbya gossypii)*.

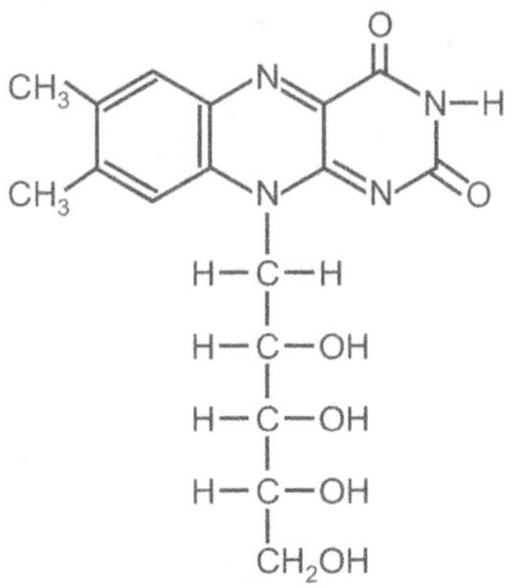

Fig. 5.14: Structure of riboflavin

Fermentation process:

The hyphae of *Ashbya gossypii* can produce large amount of riboflavin. Carbon sources (glucose, sucrose, maltose), Nitrogen sources (peptone, corn-steep liquor) and other nutrients are used to produce maximum yield of riboflavin. Production medium is prepared according to the type of microorganisms to be used for the fermentation process.

Inoculum is prepared from slants or spores of particular cultures. After one or two flask stages, further inoculum is prepared through one or two small fermentation tanks.

Glucose, corn steep liquor, soybean and glycine are most suitable for production of vitamin B₂, from *Ashbya gossypii*. Flow diagram for production of riboflavin is shown in Fig. 5.15. A laboratory culture of *Ashbya gossypii* is inoculated into a sterilized medium containing the required ingredients. The fermentation is carried out at 28°C temperature and at pH 6.8 for 4 to 5 days under aerobic conditions. The excess aeration is not suitable for growth of cells because it inhibits mycelia production and reduces the yield.

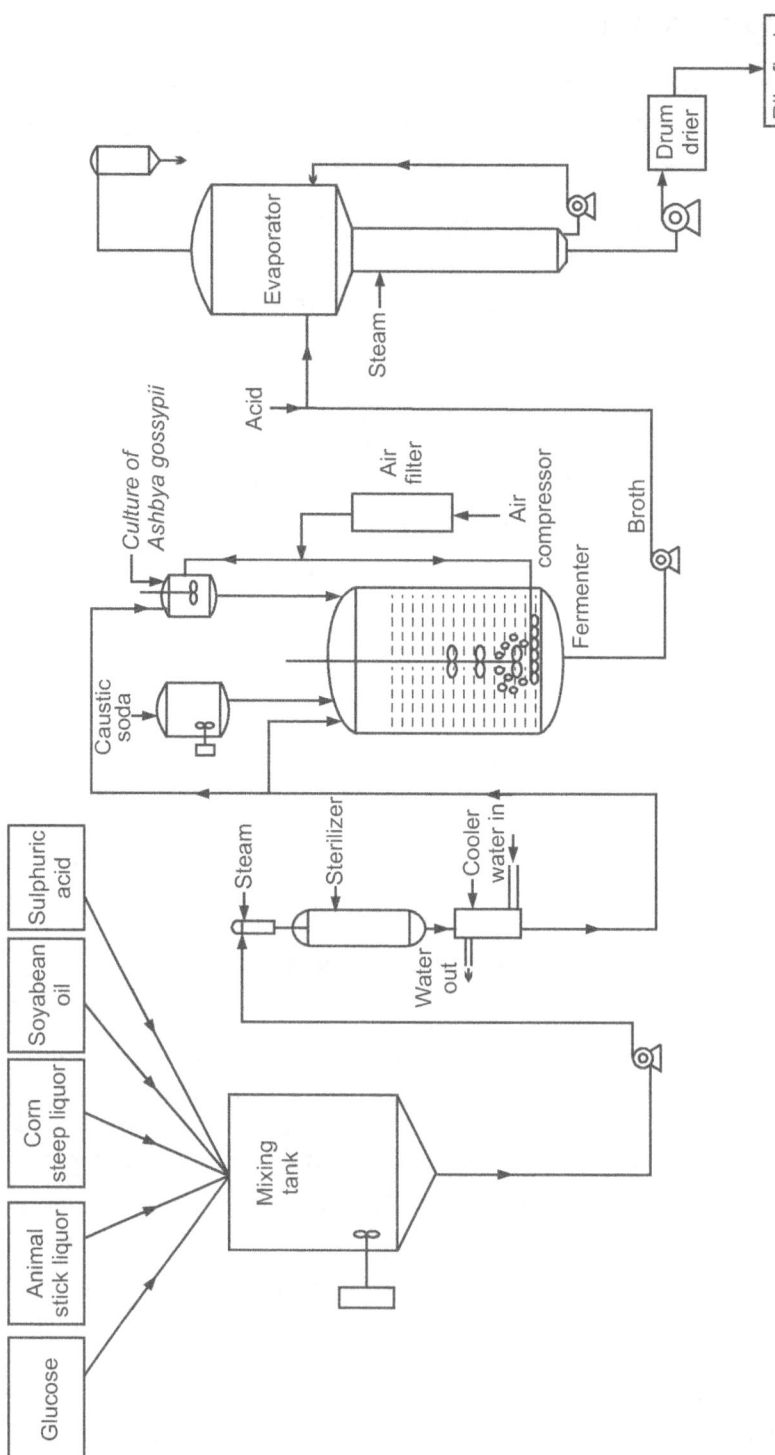

Fig. 5.15: Flow diagram for production of riboflavin

An aeration rate at 0.25 to 0.30 volumes of air per volume of medium per minute is satisfactory for maximum yield. The fermentation progresses through four phases.

(a) **First phase:** It is the initial rapid growth phase of *Ashbya gossypii*. In this phase, glucose is utilized and decreases the pH due to accumulation of pyruvic acid.

(b) **Second phase:** In the phase, sporulation occurs and this phase is called as production phase. Ammonia in the medium accumulates (deaminase activity) and increases the pH.

(c) **Third phase:** The third phase is characterized by the synthesis of cell bound riboflavin in the form of flavin adenine dinucleotide (FAD) and flavin mononucleotide (FMN). This phase is accompanied by rapid increase in catalase activity and subsequently cytochromes disappear.

(d) **Fourth phase:** The free riboflavin is released into the medium due to autolysis of the cells.

Recovery of riboflavin:

The riboflavin is present in solution as well as bound form to the mycelium. Acetone, petroleum, ether and butanol are used for extraction of riboflavin from fermentation broth. It is precipitated by using reducing agents as hydro sulphite and finely divided diatomaceous earth.

VITAMIN B_{12}

Vitamin B_{12} is a water-soluble vitamin, commonly known as cobalamin. It is an important dietary component for normal growth in human beings and animals. **Ricke E. L.** and **Smith L.** (1948) isolated small amount of active material from liver and crystallized it as vitamin B_{12} which was active in the treatment of pernicious anemia.

Vitamin B_{12} is one of the largest and the most complex molecule. The main part in the structure of vitamin B_{12} is porphyrin ring containing cobalt as the central element. The cyanide (CN) group, hydroxyl group (– OH) or nitrite group (– NO_2) attached to the cobalt is called cyanocobalamin (vitamin B_{12}), hydroxocobalamin and nitritocobalamin respectively. The structure of vitamin B_{12} is shown in Fig. 5.16.

Vitamin B_{12} is produced by bacteria and actinomycetes (Table 5.2). *Streptomyces olivaceus, Pseudomonas denitrificans, Propionibacterium shermanii* and *Propionibacterium freudenreichii* are mainly used for commercial production of vitamin B_{12}. Generally, vitamin B_{12} is prepared by the submerged culture process. Production of vitamin B_{12} from *Streptomyces olivaceus* have been discussed here.

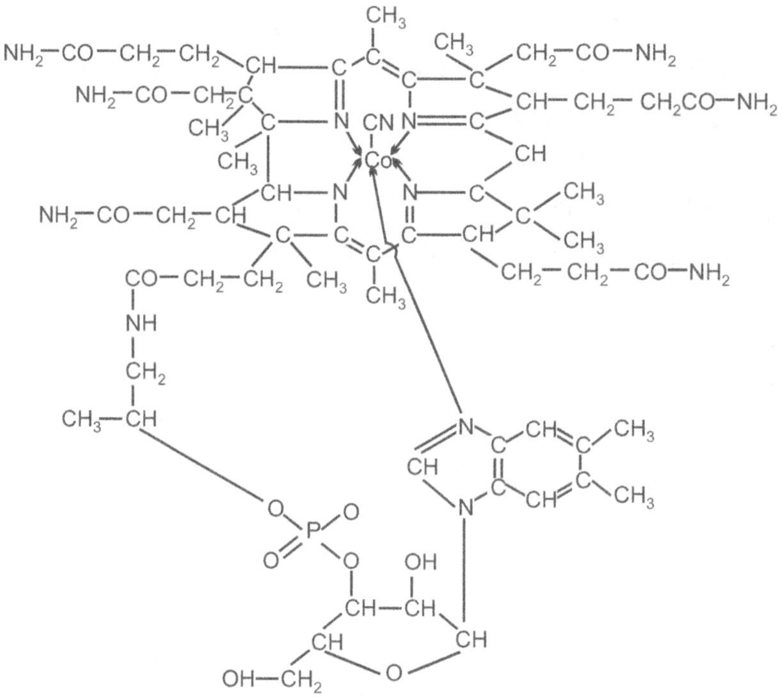

Fig. 5.16: Structure of vitamin B_{12}

Table 5.2: Vitamin B_{12} producing microbial species

Microbial group	Species
Actinomycetes	*Streptomyces olivaceus, Nocardia* species, *Streptomyces albidoflavus, S. antibioticus, S. aureofacieus, S. griseus, S. roseochromogenus.*
Bacteria	*Pseudomonas denitrificans, Aerobacter aerogenes, Bacillus subtilis, Bacillus megaterium, Propionibacterium Shermanii, Propionibacterium freudenreichii, Clostridium butyricum, Flavobacterium acetylicum, Flavobacterium flavescens, Lactobacillus arabinosus, Mycobacterium smegmatis, Serratia marcescens, Proteus vulgaris, Streptococcus faecalis*

Preparation of inoculum:

Pure culture of *Streptomyces olivaceus* is inoculated in inoculum medium contained in Erlenmeyer flasks. Bennett's broth [yeast extract (0.1%), beef extract (0.1%) , glucose (1%) and enzymatic hydrolysate of casein (0.25%)] is employed for development of inoculum. Flasks are kept on the mechanical shaker during incubation for the aeration. These flask cultures are used to inoculate the large amount of inoculum media. The required amount of inoculum (5% of the volume of production medium) is prepared by successive transfers.

Fermentation:

The culture of *Streptomyces olivaceus* is grown with aeration at 28°C in a nutritionally rich crude medium. Distiller's soluble (4%), dextrose (1%) and calcium carbonate (0.5%) are mainly present in typical production medium used in production of vitamin B_{12}. Cobalt chloride ($COCl_2 \cdot 6H_2O$) at approximately 2 to 10 ppm is added to this medium as a precursor. The flow diagram for the production of vitamin B_{12} by *Streptomyces olivaceus* is shown in Fig. 5.17. The pH of the medium is adjusted to 7 to 7.5 before sterilization and may

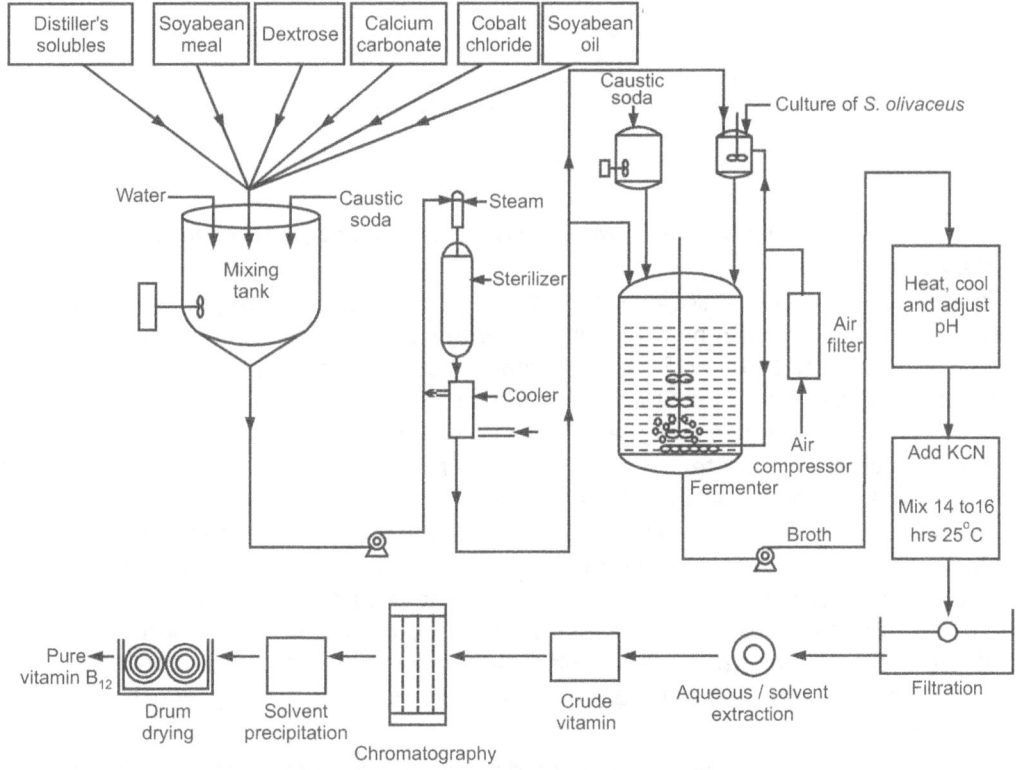

Fig. 5.17: Flow diagram for production of vitamin B_{12}

or may not be controlled during fermentation. In the first 24 hours, pH of fermentation is reduced due to rapid sugar consumption and again pH increases after 48 to 96 hours due to lysis of mycelium. The change in pH, sugar and production of vitamin B_{12} during a typical fermentation process is shown in Fig. 5.18. A correct rate of aeration and speed of agitation are required for proper growth of microbial strains. The optimum rate of aeration is about 0.5 volume air/volume medium/minute. Soyabean oil, corn oil, lard oil etc. are used as antifoaming agents to suppress the foam formation.

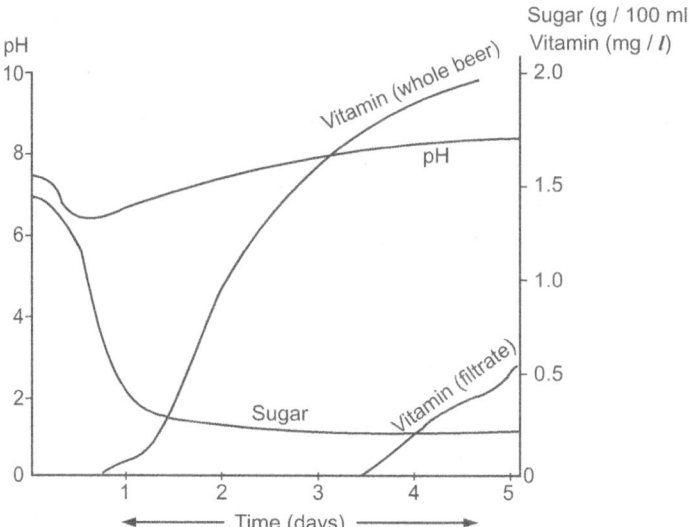

Fig. 5.18: Changes in medium during vitamin B_{12} production

Recovery of vitamin B_{12}:

Vitamin B_{12} is mainly associated with the mycelium of *Streptomyces* species. Most of cobalamin is recovered with the mycelium by centrifuging or filtering the whole beer after 3 to 4 days. Concentrated vitamin B_{12} is also obtained by reducing the pH of the beer to 5 with sulfuric acid and heating the mixture to boiling. Sodium sulfite (100 ppm) may be added in the mixture for the protection of vitamin. The medium is filtered to remove mycelium and then the filtrate broth is treated with cyanide to convert cobalamin to cyanocobalamin. The adsorption of the cyanocabalamin from the solution is done by using activated charcoal, fuller's earth, bentonite etc. Finally, elution of cyanocobalamin is performed by using an aqueous solution of materials ranging from organic bases to hydrochloric acid. Single step extraction into an organic solvent or counter-current extraction and product purification is carried out by the process of precipitation. Chromatography on alumina and final crystallization from ethanol-acetone is performed. The final product is drum-dried or spray-dried. The vitamin B_{12} content may vary from 10 to 30 mg/l in the final product.

DEXTRAN

Dextran is the long chain polymer of dextrose (D-glucose), used as a substrate for plasma. They are slender molecules of unbranched chain of glucose units joined by 1 : 6 glucosidic linkages or highly branched polymers consisting of short chains (Fig. 5.19). It is commercially produced by *Leuconostoc mesenteroides* and *Leuconostoc dextranicus* (lactic acid bacteria). The fermentation medium contains sucrose as a source of carbon, peptone as a source of nitrogen and other essential growth factors. The microbial culture producing an enzyme 'dextran-sucrase' which converts sucrose into dextran and fructose by straight-transglycosylation. The fructose is utilized by the microorganism.

$$\text{n sucrose} \xrightarrow[\text{dextran-sucrase}]{\text{Fermentation}} \text{n(glucose} - H_2O) + \text{n fructose}$$

$$\text{Dextran}$$

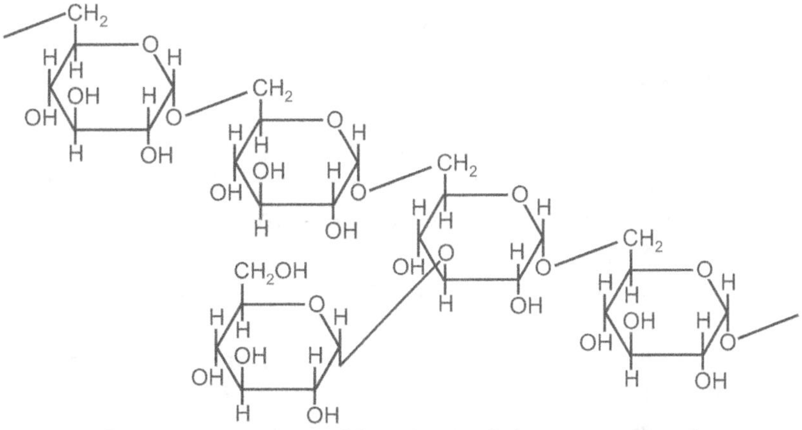

Fig. 5.19: Structure of fragment of dextran molecule

Fermentative production of dextran is similar in many respects to the antibiotic production. Growth of the dextran producing strain is carried out in large fermenters in media containing high percentage of carbohydrates. The average molecular weight of the dextrans produced may be vary with the strain used. Aeration is not required for dextran fermentation because aeration mainly inhibits the process. Many precautions are taken in sterilization of media, adjustment of pH and avoidance of overheating. It is important to prevent the hydrolysis of sucrose to glucose and fructose during sterilization of culture media.

The dextrans produced by the fermentation have molecular weight 2 to 2.5 lakhs. For clinical use, dextran has the molecular weight upto one to 1.1 lakhs. The fermented product is subjected to controlled hydrolysis, followed by fractionation with ethanol or acetone to produce less molecular weight dextran. High molecular weight dextrans may cause renal damage, allergic reactions and interfere with blood matching. They produce colloidal osmotic pressures that are lower than those of small molecules. Acid hydrolysis, thermal degradation and ultrasonic bombardment techniques are used to reduce the molecular sizes of dextran. In acid hydrolysis, dextran is adjusted to a pH 2 and is heated at 90^0C. In thermal degradation, the solution of dextran is heated under pressure at 160^0C in the presence of sodium sulphite, to prevent oxidative degradation and calcium carbonate to neutralise acidity. The bombardment with ultrasonic waves splits the molecules into fragments of the same size in ultrasonic disintegration.

The final dextran molecule is purified by solvent precipitation, adsorption or membrane filtration. The selected fraction again purified to remove reducing sugars (solvent precipitation), fractionation solvents (evaporation under reduced pressure), inorganic solvents (ion exchange), colours (adsorption on to activated charcoal), pyrogens (adsorption on to asbestos or cellulose derivatives) and microorganisms (filtration).

There are different official specifications for Dextran 110 injection (average molecular weight 1,10,000) to confirm that the product is suitable s a plasma substitute. Different chemical techniques are used to detect amount of lead, acetone, reducing sugars, nitrogen, acid and alkali. Biological methods confirm that the preparation is not pyrogenic, sterile and free from proteins.

QUESTIONS

(A) Short answer questions:
1. Draw a flow sheet for production of penicillin.
2. List different species of *Streptomyces* which produce antibiotics.
3. Write the composition of any one media used for production of streptomycin.
4. How will you prepare inoculum for tetracycline production?

(B) Long answer questions:
1. Explain in detail about the down stream process for production of penicillin.
2. Write a note on:
   - (a) Production of streptomycin.
   - (b) Up-stream process of penicillin.
   - (c) Dextran production.
   - (d) Production of vitamin B_{12}.
3. Write in short fermentation process of tetracycline.
4. Explain the production of vitamin B_2 by considering following points:
   - (a) Strains used
   - (b) Inoculum development
   - (c) Fermentation phases
   - (d) Recovery of riboflavin

(C) Multiple choice questions:
1. _____ is an extracellular enzyme produced by most of *Bacillus* species, which hydrolyzes penicillin to penicilloic acid.
   - (a) Lipase (b) Streptokinase (c) Penicillinase (d) Amylase
2. Today, penicillin is produced from _____.
   - (a) *Penicillium notatum*
   - (b) *Penicillium chrysogenum*
   - (c) *Penicillium griseofulvum*
   - (d) All of the above
3. The most suitable pH for production of streptomycin is _____.
   - (a) 5 to 6 (b) 6 to 7 (c) 7 to 8 (d) 8 to 9
4. Dextran is commercially produced by _____.
   - (a) *Streptomyces griseus*
   - (b) *Leuconostoc mesenteroides*
   - (c) *Bacillus subtilis*
   - (d) *Penicillium griseofulvum*
5. Raw material mainly used for commercial production of penicillin.
   - (a) Pepto (b) Corn steep liquor (c) Soya me (d) Glucose

(D) Match the following:

Column 'A'	Column 'B'
(a) Vitamin B_{12}	(i) *Streptomyces aureofaciens*
(b) Streptomycin	(ii) *Propionibacterium shremanii*
(c) Tetracycline	(iii) *Ashbya gossypii*
(d) Vitamin B_2	(iv) *Streptomyces griseus*

(E) Fill in the blanks:
1. Chlorotetracycline is discovered by Duggar which was produced by fermentation of _____.
2. The semisynthetic penicillins are prepared from _____.

■■■

CHAPTER 6

MICROBIAL BIOTRANSFORMATION

CONTENTS

    INTRODUCTION
    ADVANTAGES OF MICROBIALTRANSFORMATION
    METHODS USED IN BIOTRANSFORMATION
    TYPES OF BIOCONVERSION REACTIONS
        Oxidation, Reduction, Hydrolysis,
        Esterification, Isomerization, Amide formation,
        Halogenation, Decarboxylation, Condensation.

INTRODUCTION

Microbial transformation is a biological process in which organic compounds are modified into reversible products. These biotransformation reactions are catalysed by purified enzymes present in microbial cells or pure cultures of microorganisms. Microbial enzymes are highly versatile in nature. Microorganisms are more adoptogenic and they can develop new enzymes for metabolism. Microbial bioconversions are routinely used in the commercial production of steroids, antibiotics, vitamins, prostaglandins, citric acid and many other therapeutic molecules.

Steroids can be produced by chemical synthesis or by microbiological transformations. Steroids are physiologically active compounds which include progesterone, testosterone, cholesterol, ergosterol, corticosterone etc. Steroidal hormones are known to be regulators of metabolism in the animal or human body. Prednisone and prednisolone are effective in the treatment of rheumatoid arthritis and progestogens and oestrogens are used as oral contraceptives. **Mamoli** and **Vercellone** (1937) made the first successful microbial transformation of steroids. **Peterson** and **Murray** (1952) reported the 11-hydroxylation of progesterone using a fungi *Rhizopus arrhizus*. Steroidal transformations are mainly affected by bacteria, actinomycetes and fungi. The structure of a basic steroid is shown in Fig. 6.1 (a). Prostaglandins are naturally occurring hormone-like substances derived biosynthetically from C-20 polyunsaturated fatty acids containing three or four double bonds. They are potent vasoactive substances that play a key role in regulating cellular metabolism. Structurally, prostaglandins are derivatives of prostanoic acid [Fig. 6.1 (b)] and have a cyclopentane ring with two side-chains attached to adjacent carbon atoms. The microbial transformations are commonly reported in different antibiotic classes such as β-lactam, peptide, macrolide, actinomycin, chloramphenicol, novobiocin, griseofulvin, anthracycline, lincomycin etc.

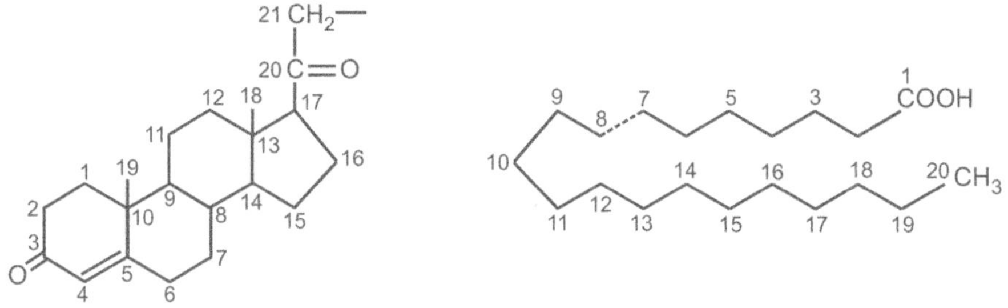

(a) Δ^4 3 – Keto steroid (b) Prostanoic acid

Fig. 6.1: Basic structure of (a) Steroid and (b) Prostaglandins

ADVANTAGES OF MICROBIAL TRANSFORMATIONS

Microbial transformations are brought about by enzymes secreted by selected strains of microorganisms. These reactions are essentially detoxifying mechanisms employed by the microorganisms. Some of the other advantages are listed below:

1. The microbial transformations react specifically. Side reactions do not occur if one enzyme is involved in a biotransformation. The catalytic activity is usually restricted to a single reaction type.
2. Microorganism catalysing bioconversions act a stereospecific catalysts i.e. specific microorganisms must be used to carry out a specific type of transformation.
3. The substrate molecule is usually attacked at the same site, even if several groups of similar reactivity are present (regiospecificity).
4. Microbial bioconversion reactions can be carried out under mild conditions such as neutral pH, room temperature and at normal pressure.
5. Biotransformation reactions can reduce the multistep chemical reaction to a single step.
6. As compared to chemical reactions, microbial transformations require less chemicals, labour, time and money, and release good yield.
7. Microbial transformation can selectively introduce functional groups at certain non-activated positions in a molecule, which can not be attracted by chemical reagents.

METHODS USED IN BIOTRANSFORMATION

Microbial cells serve as a major tool for biotransformation. The main process used for biotransformation is fermentation. Fermentation is carried out in the following phases:

(i) **Phase – I: Growth phase:** In the growth phase, a culture is grown in a nutritionally rich medium. The medium for the growth is simple or of complex type. Aeration and agitation are provided during growth and optimum temperature is maintained. The time of incubation period depends on the type of culture and environmental conditions.

(ii) Phase – II: Transformation phase: Transformation phase begins with the addition of steroids at the end of the growth phase. Steroids may be added simultaneously with the inoculation. Amount of steroid to be added depends on the transforming capacity of the culture, toxicity of substrate or type of product.

An enzyme secreted by the microbial cells acts on the steroid. The desired transformation occurrs under controlled conditions of temperature, pH, agitation, aeration and time.

Steroidal bioconversion is performed by using submerged aeration technique in stainless steel tanks. The media employed are prepared at minimal nutritional levels to allow greater ease of extraction and purification of the transformation product. The selection of medium depends on the type of microorganisms. Glucose or molasses are commonly used as a carbon source for growth of different microorganisms. Microbial transformation requires 24 to 48 hours. After the transformation, microbial growth is separated from the fermentation liquor and extracted with a suitable solvent. Methylene chloride, chloroform, methyl isobutylketone and ethyl acetate solvents are commonly used for extraction of steroids. Products obtained from cells or substrates should be extracted separately. The extracted samples are analysed by using thin layer chromatography, paper chromatography, gas chromatography or high pressure liquid chromatography. The structure of the new product is elucidated by different analytical techniques (IR, NMR, mass, elemental analysis).

TYPES OF BIOCONVERSION REACTIONS

Microorganisms may perform different types of simple or mixed reactions. The bioconversion reactions are classified as follows:

(A) Oxidation:
1. Hydroxylation
2. Dehydrogenation
3. Epoxidation
4. Aromatization

(B) Reduction:
1. Reduction of double bond
2. Reduction of ketones, aldehydes and acids

(C) Hydrolysis   **(D) Esterification**
(E) Isomerization   **(F) Amide formation**
(G) Halogenation   **(H) Decarboxylation**
(I) Condensation

These reactions are described as follows:

(A) Oxidation:

These are the most important reactions of microbial transformations.

1. **Hydroxylation:** Filamentous bacteria and fungi are general used for their versatile hydroxylation at non-activated carbons in a variety of substrates like steroids, prostaglandins, alkaloids and hydrocarbons. Microbial hydroxylation is the involvement of direct replacement of the hydrogen atom on a given carbon. Microbial hydroxylation of steroids at C-11 helps to meet the increased demand for cortisone and hydrocortisone. 11α-hydroxylation, 11β-hydroxylation, 16α-hydroxylation and 21-hydroxylation of steroids are important industrial reactions. Some of the hydroxylation reactions are shown in Fig. 6.2.

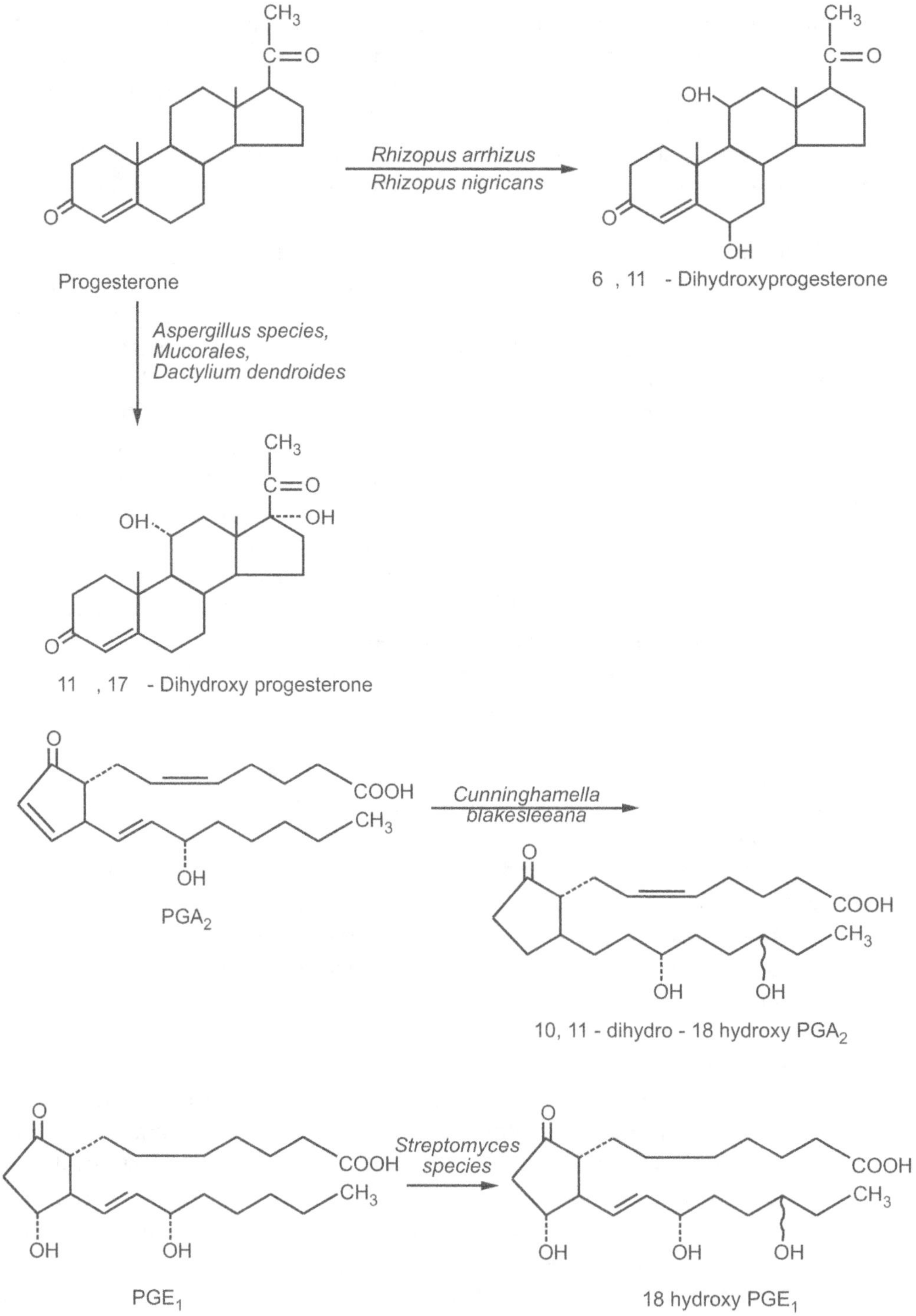

Fig. 6.2: Microbial hydroxylation reactions

2. **Dehydrogenation:** Bacterial and fungal species are capable of dehydrogenation of steroids. Addition of a double bond has been reported for all the four rings of steroid nucleus but majority of microbes attack the ring 'A'. Conversion of cortisone to prednisone and cortisol to prednisolone are shown in Fig. 6.3.

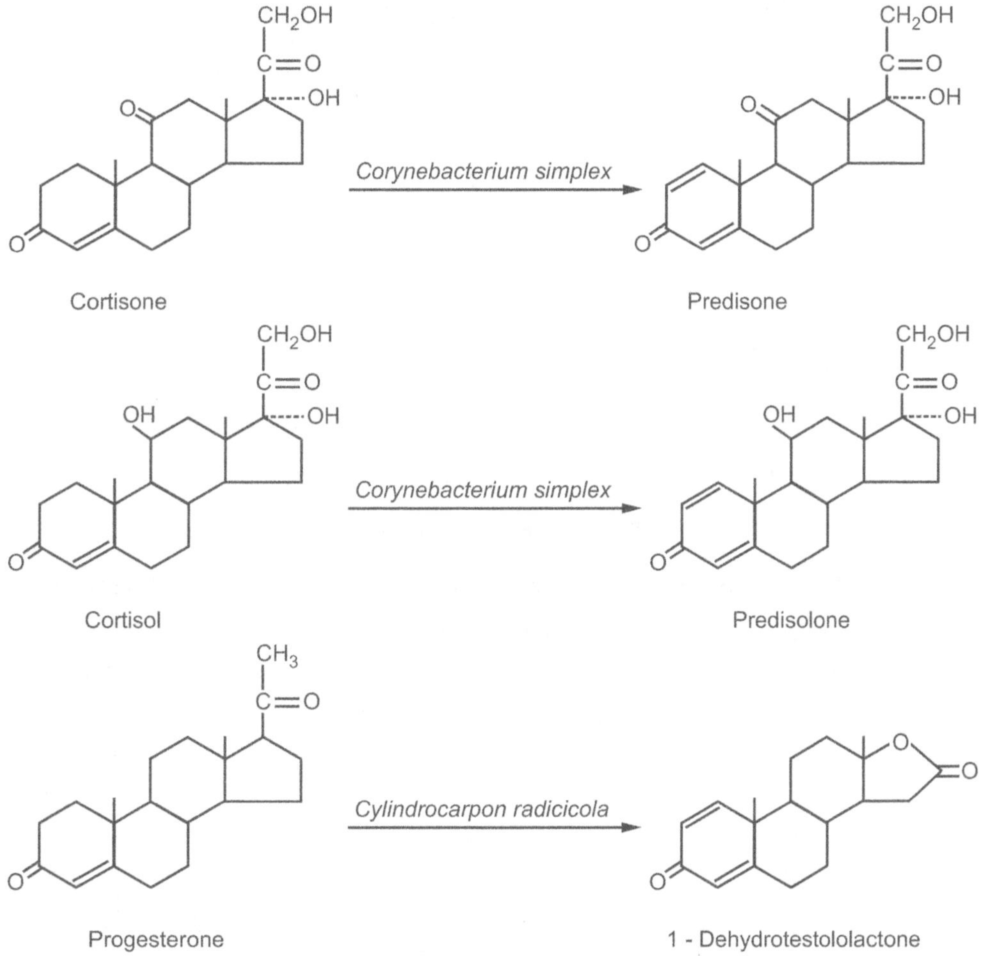

Fig. 6.3: Microbial dehydrogenation reactions

3. **Epoxidation:** Epoxidation is a very rare transformation. The microorganisms which normally hydroxylate saturated steroid will epoxidize the unsaturated analog provided the newly introduced hydroxyl function should be axial in nature. **Bloom** and associates (1956) demonstrated the examples of epoxidation by using *Curvalaria lunata* and *Cunninghamella blakesleena* (Fig. 6.4). These microbial cells normally introduce the 11β–hydroxyl and 14 α–hydroxyl into compound 'S'.

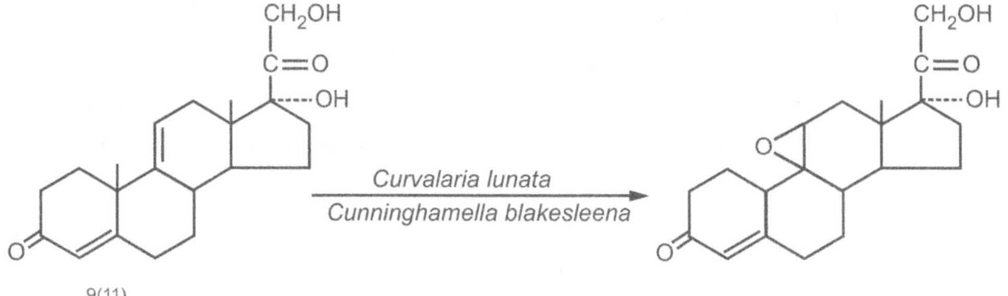

$^{9(11)}$ - Dehydro - compound - 'S'

9, 11 - epoxido - compound - 'S'

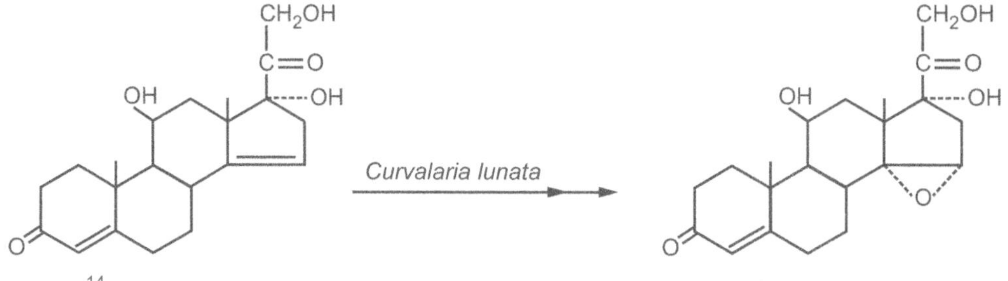

^{14} - Dehydro - compound - 'S'

14, 15 - epoxido - hydrocortisone

Fig. 6.4: Microbial epoxidation reactions

4. **Aromatization:** 19-Hydroxyl cholesterol and 19-hydroxyl-β-sitosterol are converted to estrone with *Nocardia restricta* by aromatisation (Fig. 6.5). C–1–Dehydrogeneration with substrate lacking methyl group at carbon 10 or suitably substituted at carbon 19 results into aromatization.

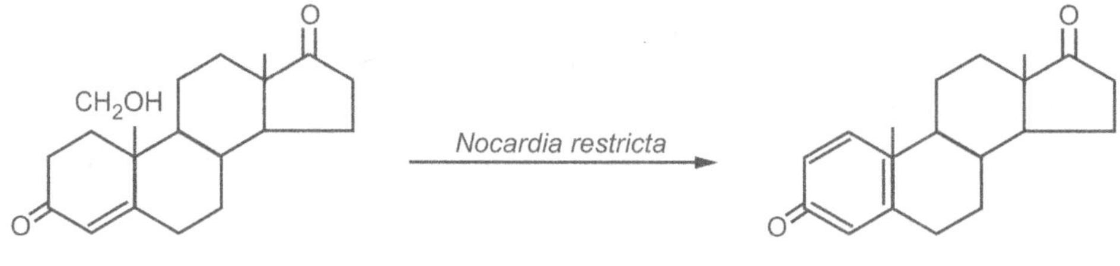

19 - Hydroxy - 4 - androstene 3,17 - dione

Estrone

Fig. 6.5: Formation of estrone by aromatization

(B) **Reduction:**

1. **Reduction of double bond (–C=C–):** The enzymes oxido-reductases catalyse both dehydrogenation and reduction reactions. Ring hydrogenation (reduction) mainly occurs in steroids at Δ^1, Δ^4 and Δ^{16}, Δ^1. The conversion of prednisone to cortisone and prednisolone to cortisol with *Bacillus megatherium* is reported by reduction. The conversion of 4-androstane-

3, 17-dione to androsane-3, 17 dione with *Bacillus putrificus* is reported for Δ^4 hydrogenation. (Fig. 6.6).

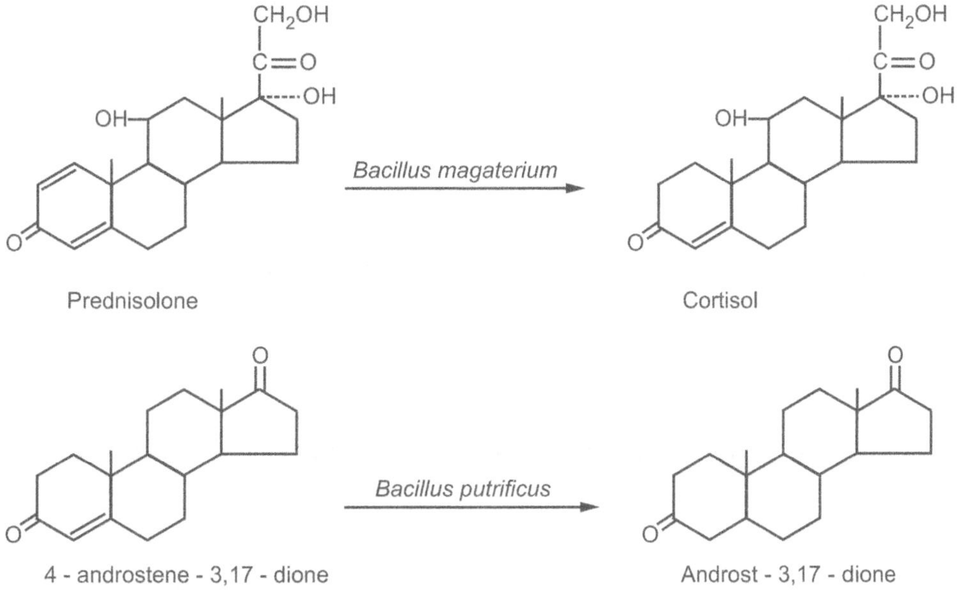

Fig. 6.6: Microbial reduction of steroid (double bond)

Aureobasidium pullulans can perform dehydrogenation of C-15 and C-9 ketone groups alongwith the reduction of the 10, 11 and 13, 14 double bonds in prostaglandins. *Dactylium dendroides* reduces the 10, 11 and 13, 14-double bond and dehydrogenates 15 α-hydroxyl group to 15 ketone moiety. In 15 keto PGF$_{2\alpha}$; the 13(14) double bond is reduced in presence of *Saccharomyces cerevisiae* (Fig. 6.7).

2. Reduction of ketones, aldehydes and acids: Hydroxyl groups at C_6, C_{11} and C_{17}, α-methyl group at C_{16} and Δ^1 unsaturation lead to decrease in the reduction rate in steroids. The presence of electron withdrawing groups at the C-6 in 3 keto-Δ^4 substrate, shift the direction from oxidation to reduction. Reduction of C-20 ketone occurs in presence of *Streptomyces lavendulae* (Fig. 6.8).

Schneider and **Murray** employed yeast to reduce the 9 keto function in prostaglandins. This is an important reaction in the conversion of PGE to PGF. **Miyano** et al performed microbial stereo selective reduction and optical resolution of racemic $\Delta^{8(12)}$– 15 – dehydro PGE$_1$ (Fig. 6.9). Optically active 11-epi-$\Delta^{8(12)}$ – PGE$_1$ is prepared in good yield by *Pseudomonas* species.

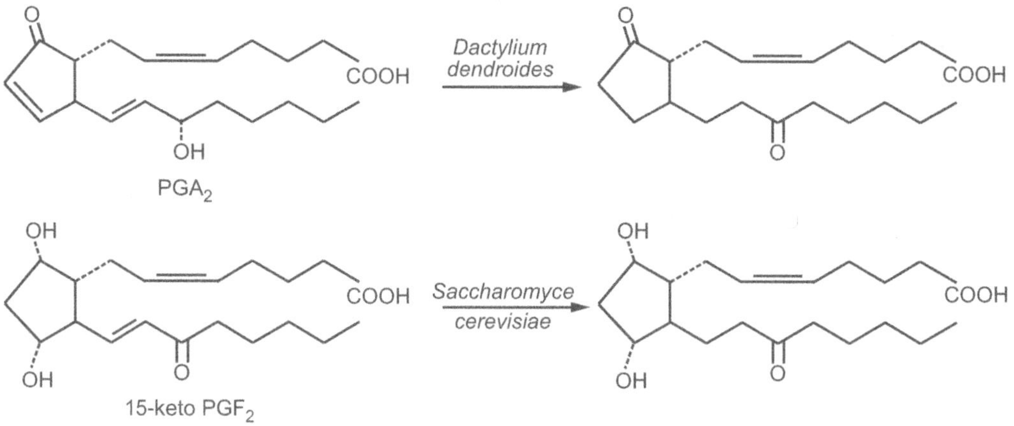

Fig. 6.7: Microbial reduction of prostaglandins (double bond)

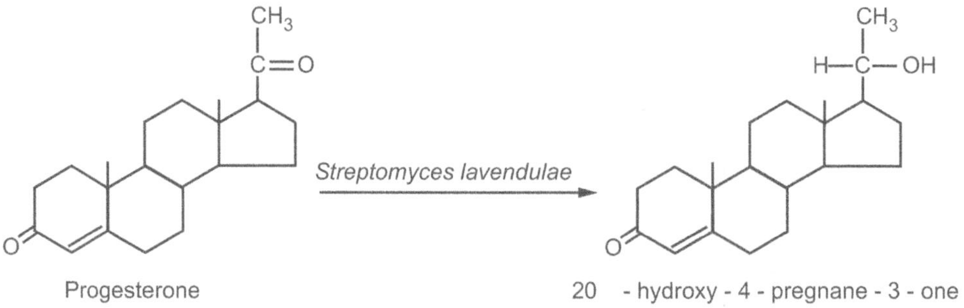

Fig. 6.8: Reduction of C-20 ketones

(C) Hydrolysis:

A large number of esters, lactones, β-lactams, glycosides, epoxides and amides can be hydrolysed by a number of microorganisms. Tartaric acid is prepared from maleic anhydride by hydrolysis of the intermediary cis-epoxy-succinic acid with *Achromobacter tartarogenes*. The 6-aminopenicillanic acid (6-APA) is the intermediate in the preparation of semisynthetic penicillins. Bacterial hydrolysis of benzyl penicillin to 6-aminopenicillanic acid has become an essential step in the manufacturing of semisynthetic derivatives (Fig. 6.10).

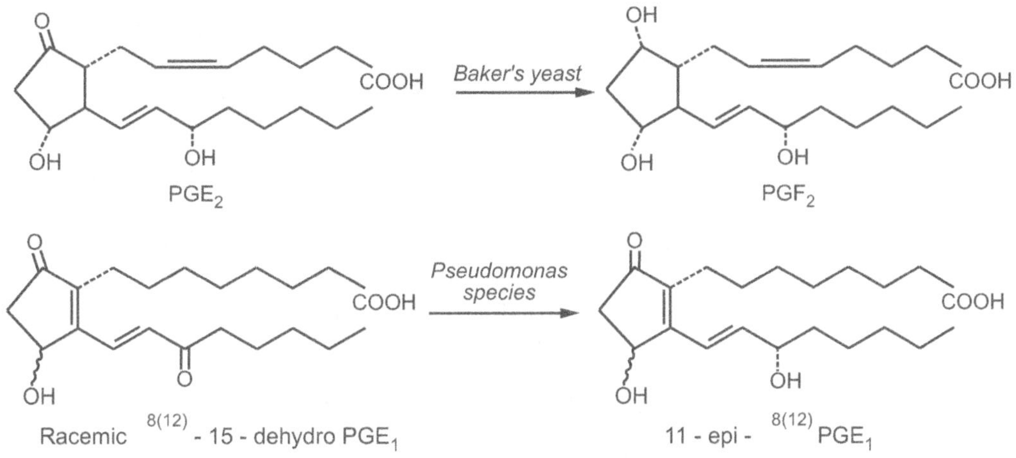

Fig. 6.9: Microbial reduction of ketone in prostaglandins

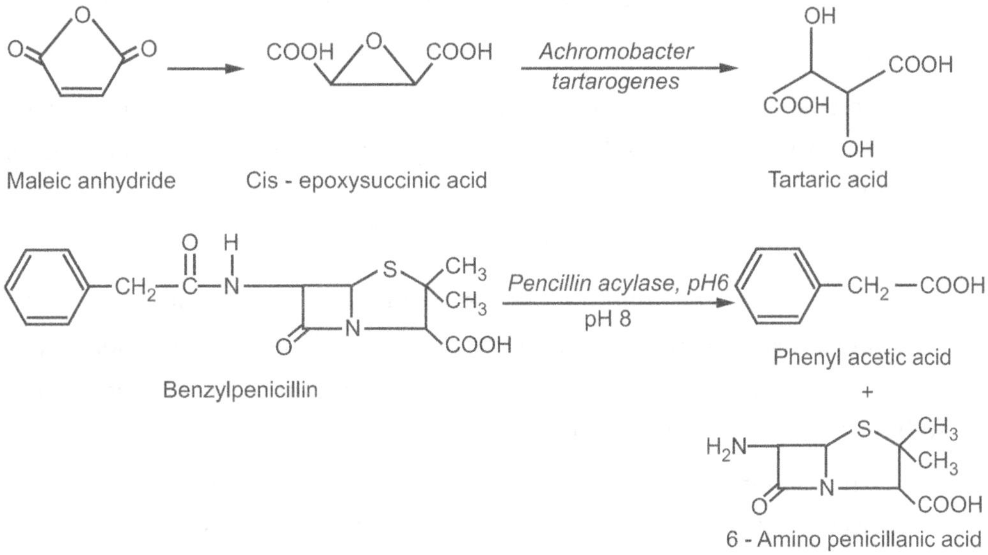

Fig. 6.10: Formation of tartaric acid and 6-aminopenicillanic acid by microbial hydrolysis

The hydrolytic cleavage of prostaglandin esters has been demonstrated by using microbial enzyme systems. *Saccharomyces* species, *Cladosporium resinae, Rhizopus oryzae, Corynespora cassicola* and baker's yeast have been reported for hydrolysis of prostaglandins. *Corynespora cassicola* is used to hydrolyze 15-epi PGA_2 acetate methyl ester. In steroid hydrolysis, 3 and 21-acetates are generally hydrolysed prior to hydroxylation or dehydrogenation. Ester hydrolysis is also frequently accompanied by dehydrogenation (Fig. 6.11).

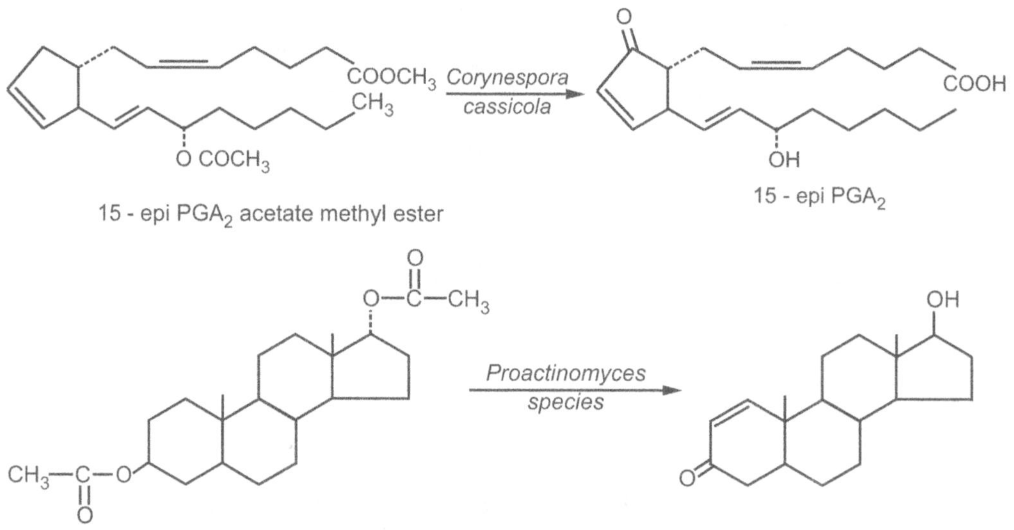

Fig. 6.11: Hydrolysis of prostaglandins and steroids

(D) Esterification:

Microbial transformation by esterification is rarely reported in literature. Different steroids are prepared by esterification using *Sacchromyces fragilis* and *Trichodermaglauca* (Fig. 6.12).

(E) Isomerisation:

Isomerisation is an important process mainly useful for the preparation of high fructose syrup (food sweetener). Microbial isomerisation of prostaglandins is not very important but under basic conditions, PGA (10, 11 double bond) is converted into PGB (8, 12 double bond) without the aid of microorganisms.

Isomerisation of steroids is very common. Deoxycorticosterone is prepared by isomerisation of the double bond from Δ^5 to Δ^4 with *Corynebacterium mediolanum* (Fig. 6.13).

(F) Amide formation:

Amide formation is a relatively rare microbial transformation. **Smith** and his coworkers reported the transformations of steroids with *Streptomyces roseochromogenus* (Fig. 6.14).

(G) Halogenation:

Halogenation reactions are carried out at pH 3. Haloperoxidase enzymes from *Caldariomyces fumago* catalyse the halogenation reactions of steroids (Fig. 6.15).

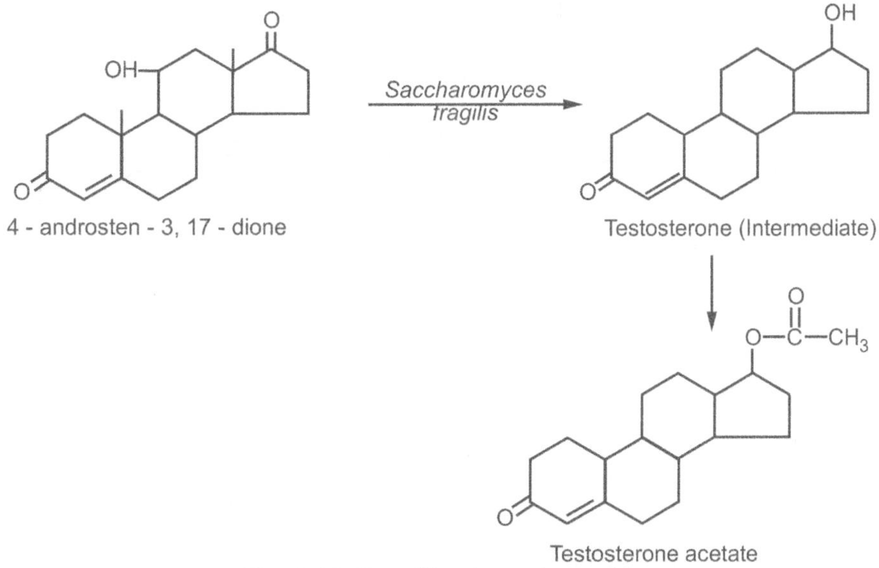

Fig. 6.12: Esterification of steroids

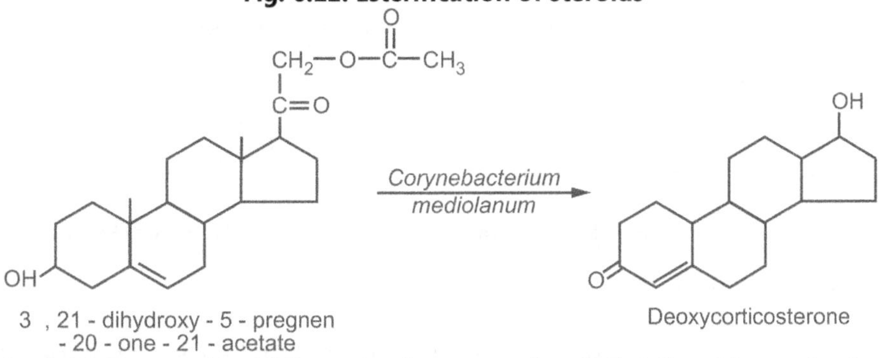

Fig. 6.13: Preparation of deoxycorticosterone by olefinic bond isomerisation

(H) Decarboxylation:

Decarboxylation of aromatic and linear carboxylic acids is very common and of practical importance. L-lysine can be synthesised by stereospecific decarboxylation of meso-α,–α'–diaminopimelic acid (DAP) to L-lysine. The reaction is catalysed by *Bacillus sphaericus* (Fig. 6.16).

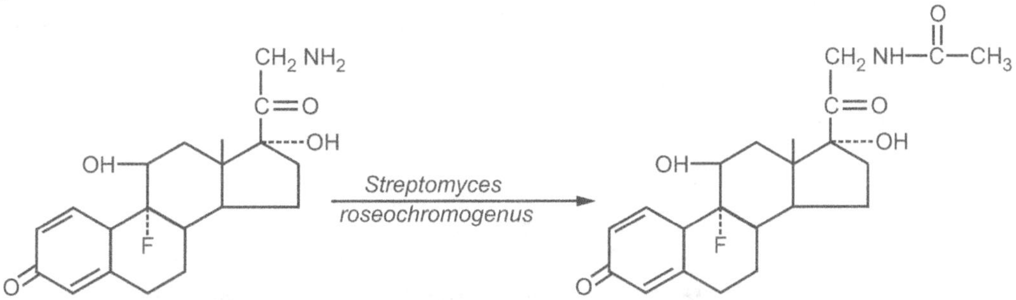

Fig. 6.14: Amide formation with *Streptomyces resoeochromogenus*

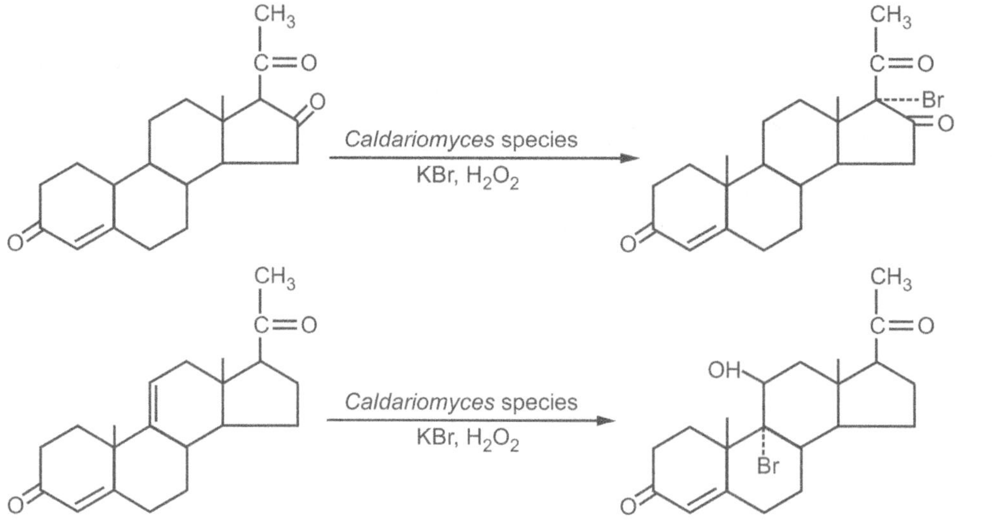

9 (11) - progesterone   9 - bromo - 11 - hydroxy progesterone

Fig. 6.15: Halogenation of steroids

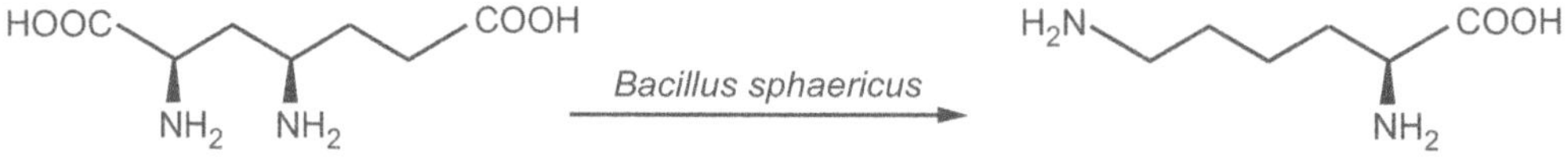

meso - , ' - Diaminopimelic acid   L - Lysine

Fig. 6.16: Formation of L-lysine by decarboxylation

(I) Condensation:

Microbial condensation was utilised in 1934 in the synthesis of natural ephedrine. Acetaldehyde reacts with benzaldehyde in the presence of fermenting yeast and gives (R) – 1 – phenyl – 1 – hydroxy – 2 – propanone. The propanone undergoes reductive condensation with methylamine to yield (1R, 2S) – ephedrine (Fig. 6.17).

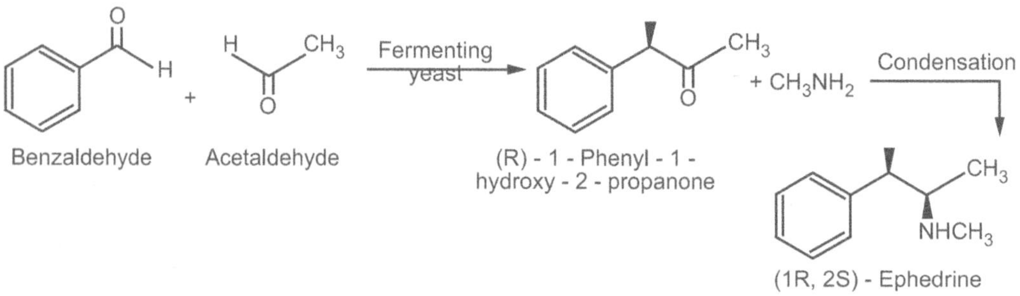

Fig. 6.17: Formation of ephedrine by condensation

QUESTIONS

(A) Short answer questions:

1. What is microbial transformation? Write the advantages of microbial transformations.
2. Write one example of the following types of bioconversions:
   (i) Hydrolysis
   (ii) Esterification
   (iii) Decarboxylation
   (iv) Oxidation

(B) Long answer questions:

1. Explain in detail different biotransformation reactions with special reference to steroids.
2. Write short note on:
   (i) Methods used in biotransformation
   (ii) Microbial transformation by reduction.

(C) Multiple choice questions:

1. Microbial transformations have the following advantages except _____ .
   (a) It can reduce multistep reactions to a single step.
   (b) Reactions can be carried out under mild conditions.
   (c) Reactions are stereospecific and regiospecific.
   (d) It require more chemicals, labour and time.

2. Steroidal transformation mainly occurs at _____ .
   (a) Growth phase   (b) Transformation phase
   (c) Death phase   (d) None of the above

3. Prednisone is produced from cortisone with *Corynebacterium simplex* by dehydrogenation at position _____ .
   (a) Δ^1 (b) Δ^7
   (b) Δ^{13} (d) Δ^{16}

4. Estrone is produced from 19-hydroxy-4-androstene-3, 17-dione with *Nocardia restricta* by aromatization of ring _____ .
   (a) A   (b) B
   (c) C   (d) D

(D) Match the following:

(A)		(B)	
(a)	Microbial epoxidation of steroids	(i)	*Caldariomyces* species
(b)	Halogenation of steroids	(ii)	*Rhizopus* species
(c)	Formation of L-lysine by decarboxylation	(iii)	*Curvalaria lunata*
		(iv)	*Bacillus sphaericus*
(d)	Synthesis of 6β, 11α-dihydroxy progesterone by hydroxylation		

(E) Fill in the blanks:

1. Basic structure of prostaglandin is called _____.

2. 6-Aminopenicillanic acid is produced from benzyl penicillin by using the enzyme _____.

3. Progestrone is transformed to 11 α-hydroxy progesterone by _____.

■■■

CHAPTER 7
INTRODUCTION TO GENETICS

CONTENTS
- INTRODUCTION
- CHEMICAL NATURE OF DNA
- STRUCTURE OF DNA
    - Forms of DNA
- STRUCTURE AND TYPES OF RNA
- PHENOTYPIC AND GENOTYPIC CHANGES
- MUTATION
    - Types of mutation, Mutagenic agents, Spontaneous mutation
- PLASMIDS
- GENETIC MECHANISM OF DRUG RESISTANCE

INTRODUCTION

Genetics is the study of inheritance (heredity) and the variability of the characteristics of an organism. Heredity concerns the exact transmission of genetic information from parents to their progeny. Variability of the inherited characteristics can be accounted for a change either in the genetic makeup of a cell or in the environmental conditions. Genes comprise the genome of cell which may consist of a single DNA molecule or some other small DNA molecules (plasmids). The genotypic variation brought about by changes in genetic information can be due to mutation or loss of plasmids. Each bacterium contains about 1000 genes which are located in its circular chromosome. If the book of information contained is a genome, then paragraph is a loci, the sentences are genes, words are codons and letters are nucleotides.

The 'Central dogma' of molecular biology is that deoxyribonucleic acid (DNA) carries genetic information, which is transcribed onto ribonucleic acid (RNA) and then translated, by ribosomes into particular polypeptide (DNA → RNA → Polypeptide). The essential material of heredity is DNA which is the storehouse of all information for protein synthesis. However, RNA viruses are an important exception in which the genetic material is RNA instead of DNA.

CHEMICAL NATURE OF DNA

Deoxyribonucleic acid (DNA) and Ribonucleic acid (RNA) are the principal genetic materials of living organisms. They are chemically called nucleic acids. The DNA molecule (nucleic acid) is also called polynucleotide. It is a polymer and consists of a long chain of monomers called nucleotides. Each nucleotide consists of three main parts such as cyclic five carbon sugar, purine or pyrimidine base and a phosphate group. The nucleic acids are classified into two types, based on the types of sugars such as ribose nucleic acid (RNA) and deoxyribose nucleic acid (DNA). The sugar present in DNA is a five carbon pentose called 2'-deoxyribose in which the –OH group on carbon 2 of ribose is replaced by hydrogen. (Fig. 7.1)

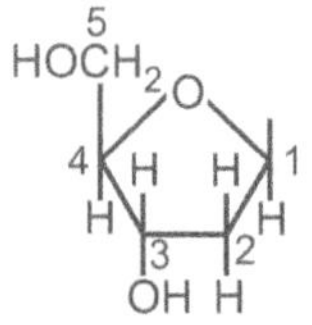

(a) Deoxyribose

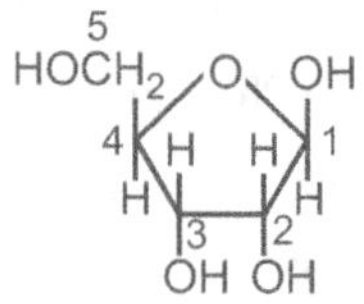

(b) Ribose

Fig. 7.1: Structure of deoxyribose and ribose

Nucleotides contain one of four bases (Fig. 7.2) as adenine (A), guanine (G), thymine (T) or cytosine (C). Adenine and guanine contain two carbon-nitrogen rings (purines) and cytosine and thymine contain a single ring (pyrimidines). Uracil (U) is a third pyrimidine and it is found only in RNA.

Adenine (A)

Guanine (G)

Cytosine (C)

Thymine (T)

Uracil (U)

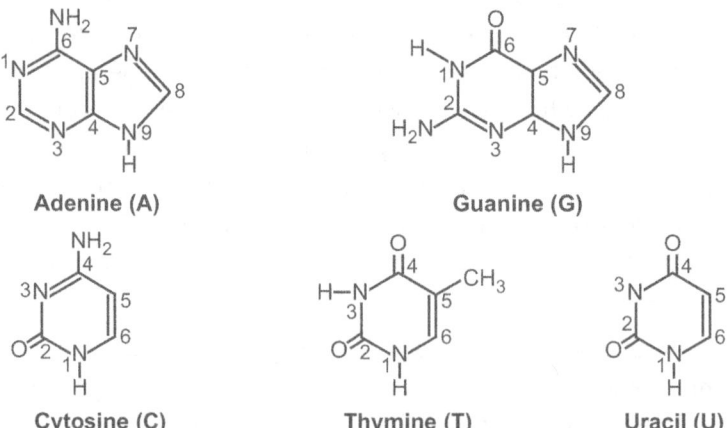

Fig. 7.2: Nitrogenous base of nucleic acids

Nucleotides contain phosphate groups (PO_4) attached to the 5' carbon of the sugar. The nitrogenous bases combined with pentose sugar to form nucleosides and a nucleoside linked with phosphate forms a nucleotide (Fig. 7.3).

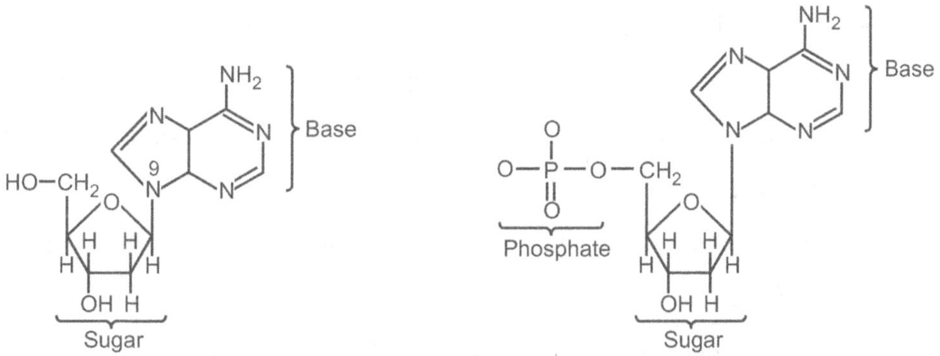

(a) 2'-Deoxyadenosine (Nucleoside) (b) 2' – Deoxyadenosine 5'-phosphate (Nucleotide)
Fig. 7.3: Structure of nucleosides and nucleotides

In DNA, a phosphate group (PO_4^-) is attached to the 3'-carbon of deoxyribose sugar and 5'-carbon of another sugar. Strong negative charges of nucleic acid are due to the presence of phosphate groups. The 5' phosphate of one nucleotide forms a bond with the 3' carbon of the next nucleotide eliminating the –OH group on the 3' carbon during the reaction. The bond is called a 3'-5' phosphodiester bond (Fig. 7.4).

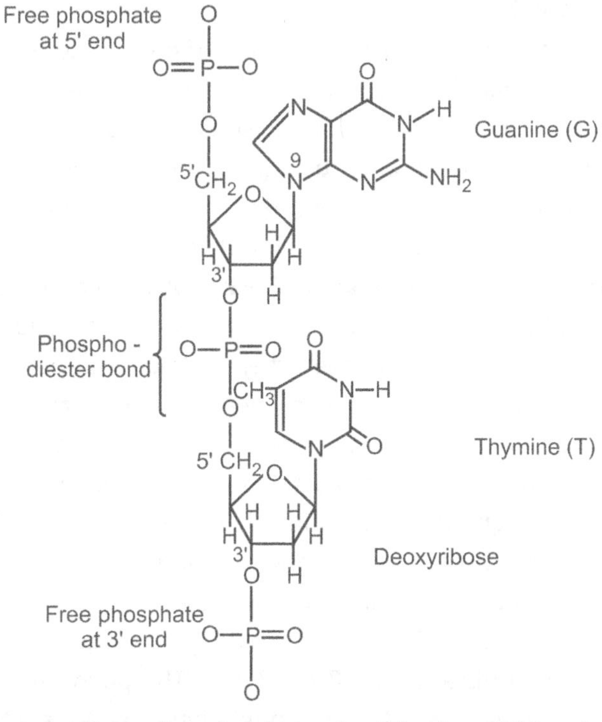

Fig. 7.4: Phosphodiester bonds join nucleotides in a DNA polynucleotide

A chemist **Erwin Chargaff** (1950) established a number of important relationships concerning the contents of individual bases in DNA. Chargaff's equivalence rule has been found to apply almost universally in different organisms. The Chargaff's rules are as follows:

- The total number of purine nucleotides (A + G) is equal to the total number of pyrimidine nucleotides (C + T) i.e. $\frac{(A + G)}{(C + T)} = 1$.
- The amount of adenine (A) is a always equal to the amount of thymine (T) i.e. A = T or $\frac{A}{T} = 1$.
- The amount of guanine (G) is always equal to the amount of cytosine (C) i.e. G = C or $\frac{G}{C} = 1$.
- The numbers (A + T) and (G + C) are the only variables. If (A + T) > (G + C), the DNA is called AT-type and if (G + C) > (A + T), the DNA is called GC – type.

The molar ratio (A + T / G + C) represents a characteristic composition of DNA of each species. In higher plants and animals, A–T composition is higher whereas in the lower plants and animals, bacteria and viruses, it is lower than G–C contents. The base composition has importance in establishing relationship between two species and in taxonomy and phylogeny of species.

STRUCTURE OF DNA

DNA molecule is composed of two chains of nucleotides joined together in the form of a double helix. Each chain has a backbone of alternatively arranged molecules of deoxyribose sugar and phosphates. Each deoxyribose sugar is attached to one of the four nitrogenous bases i.e. purines (adenine, A and guanine, G) and pyrimidines (thymine, T and cytosine, C). The double - stranded nature of the molecule is stabilised by hydrogen bonding between the bases on the opposite strands. Adenine always binds to thymine and guanine to cytosine (Fig. 7.5). **James Watson** and **Francis Crick** (1953) recognised the structure of DNA as a double stranded helix or duplex on the basis of X-ray diffraction data. Adenine of one strand is always paired with thymine of the other by two hydrogen bonds and guanine is paired with cytosine by three hydrogen bonds. There is an equal amount of adenine and thymine in DNA and so also of guanine and cytosine. Ratio of each pair (A+T/G+C) is constant for each species but varies widely from one bacterial species to another.

The DNA is a right handed double helix consisting of two polydeoxyribonucleotide strands twisted around each other on a common axis. The two strands are antiparallel i.e. one strand runs in the 5' to 3' direction while the other in 3' to 5' direction. Only antiparallel polynucleotides form a stable helix. The hydrogen bonds between the two strands are such that they maintain a distance of 20 A° (2 nm). The pitch (turn) of the helix is 34 A° so the spacing between bases is 3.4 A°. The double helix executes a turn every 10 base pairs. The turning of double helix results in the appearance of a deep and wide groove called major groove. The major groove is the site of bonding of specific protein. The distance between two strands forms a minor groove.

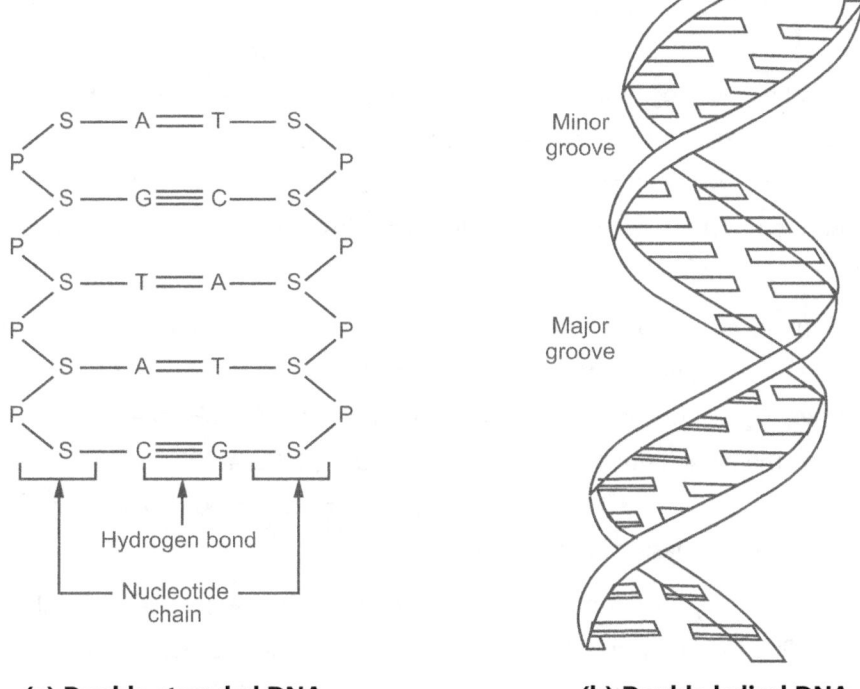

(a) Double stranded DNA (b) Double helical DNA

Fig. 7.5: Structure of DNA

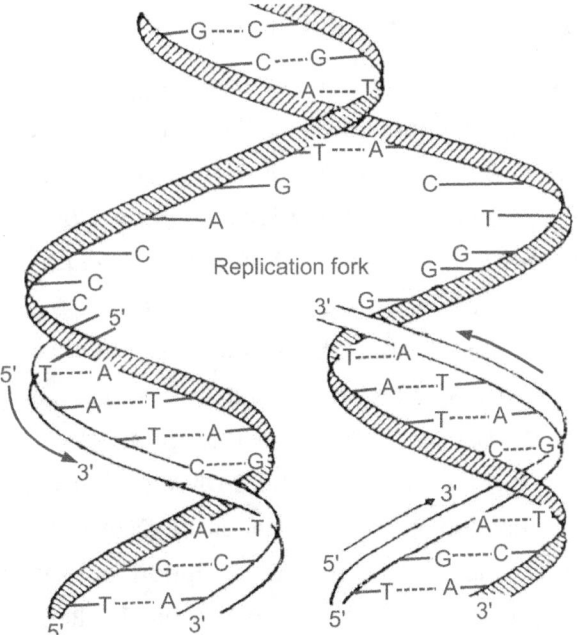

Fig. 7.6: The semiconservative mode of DNA replication

The bases of DNA carry genetic information, whereas the sugar and phosphate groups perform a structural role. The strands are typically complementary to each other thus serve as template during replication to each other. During replication the two chains dissociate and each one serves as a template for the synthesis of new complementary strand. As one strand of each daughter molecule is newly synthesized while other (template) is passed on unchanged form parent DNA molecules. This indicates that the replication of DNA is semiconservative (Fig. 7.6).

Genetic information is stored in DNA as code. The unit of code is known as codon and it consists of a sequence of three bases (code is triplet). Each triplet transcribed on mRNA specifies for a single amino acid but code is 'degenerate'. Hence, more than one codon may exist for the same amino acid. Codons like UAA, UAG and UGA do not code for any amino acid and are known as non-sense codons. They act as punctuation marks, terminating the message for synthesis of a polypeptide.

The bacterial chromosome consists of a double-stranded molecule of DNA and it is about 1000 to 1200 μm in length. The length of DNA is usually expressed in kilobases (kb = 1,000 base pairs). Bacterial DNA is about 4,000 kb and the human genome about 3 million kb long.

Forms of DNA:

The most common form of DNA which has right handed helix called B-form of DNA or B-DNA proposed by **Watson** and **Crick**. The double helical structure of DNA exists in atleast six different forms (A to E and Z). The B-DNA is found in fibres of living cells at a very high 92 percent relative humidity and low ionic strength. However, A-form of DNA is found at 75 percent humidity in the presence of high ionic strength of Na^+, K^+ or Cs^+ ions. C-form of DNA is found at 66 per cent relative humidity in the presence of lithium (Li^+) ions. The B-form of DNA is metabolically stable and undergoes changes to A, C or D forms depending on sequence of nucleotides and concentration of excess salts. The A-form is metastable and quickly turns to the D-form. D-form and E-form rare DNA variants are found only in some DNA molecules which lack guanine. The Z-DNA is a left-handed helix and contains 12 base pairs per turn. The polynucleotide strands of DNA running in antiparallel direction by 'zig-zag' fashion, hence the name Z-DNA. Important features of different forms of DNA double helical structures are summarized in Table 7.1. It is believed that transition between different helical forms of DNA plays a significant role in regulating gene expression.

Table 7.1: Important features of different forms of DNA

Feature	A-DNA	B-DNA	C-DNA	Z-DNA
Helix type	Right-handed	Right-handed	Right-handed	Left-handed
Helical diameter (A°)	23	20	19	18
Base pair per turn	11	10	9.33	12
Rotation per base pair	+ 32.7°	+ 36.0°	+ 38.6°	–30.0°
Vertical rise per base pair (A°)	2.56	3.38	3.32	3.71
Pitch of the helix (A°)	28.15	34	31	45
Conditions	75% relative humidity, Na^+, K^+, Cs^+ ions	92% relative humidity, low ions	66% relative humidity, Li^+ ions	Very light salt concentration

All the organisms contain double stranded DNA except a few viruses which consist of single stranded circular DNA. Single stranded DNA becomes double stranded only at the time of replication. The differences between ss-DNA and ds-DNA are summarized in Table 7.2. Sometimes form triple-stranded DNA due to additional hydrogen bonds between the bases. Thymine can form two Hoogsteen hydrogen bonds to the adenine of A-T pair to form T-A-T. Cytosine can form two hydrogen bonds with guanine of G-C pairs that results of C-G-C. The three negatively charged backbone strands in triple helix enhance electrostatic repulsion. Hence, it is less stable than double helix. Polynucleotides with very high contents of guanine can form four-stranded DNA. The parallel tetrameric structure is called G-quartets and antiparallel structure is referred as G-tetraplexs.

Table 7.2: Difference between ssDNA and dsDNA

ssDNA	dsDNA
• It is circular form.	• It is linear helical form.
• Base pair composition of A, T, G, C is in proportion of 1 : 1.33 : 0.98 : 0.75.	• Base pair composition in dsDNA is equal i.e. A = T and G = C.
• The absorption of uv light increases steadily from 20° to 90°C.	• The dsDNA absorbs uv light (2600A° wavelength) constantly from 0 to 80°C.
• Presence of exposed reactive sites, it does not resist the action of formaline.	• It resists the action of formaline due to closed reactive site.

Prokaryotes and in few viruses, the DNA is organized in the form of closed circle. The two ends of the double helix get covalently sealed to form a closed circle. Sometimes, the covalently closed circles are twisted into super helix or super coils and are associated with basic proteins (Fig. 7.7).

(A) Nucleoids of *E. coli* (B) Closed, circular bacterial DNA (c) Twisted supercoils of dsDNA

Fig. 7.7: The forms of DNA

STRUCTURE AND TYPES OF RNA

Ribonucleic acid (RNA) is structurally similar to deoxyribonucleic acid (DNA), except for two major differences. It has sugar ribose instead of deoxyribose and nitrogenous base uracil in place of thymine in DNA. RNA is the polymer of four nucleotides each one contains D-ribose, phosphoric acid and a nitrogenous base. The bases are two purines (A and G) and two pyrimidines (C and U). RNA is usually a single-stranded polynucleotide. However, this strand may fold at certain places to give a double-stranded structure. There is no specific relation between purine and pyrimidine as well as guanine and cytosine contents due to the single-stranded nature of RNA. Differences between the DNA and RNA molecules are summarized in Table 7.3.

Ribonucleic acid (RNA) present as their genetic material in some plant viruses (e.g. TMV, wound tumour viruses etc.), animal viruses (e.g. influenza viruses, foot and mouth viruses, poliomyelitis viruses etc.) and bacteriphages (e.g. MS_2 etc.). The organisms which have only RNA and it involved in genetic mechanism is called genetic RNA. The genetic RNA of viruses is self-replicating, that is, it can produce by its own replication. This mode of replication is called RNA-dependent RNA synthesis. DNA acts as a genetic material and RNA follows the order of DNA. In such cells the RNA does not have genetic role, is called non-genetic RNA. It is not self-replicating like DNA but it depends on DNA. Therefore, replication of non-genetic RNA is known as DNA-dependent RNA replication. Non-genetic RNA can be divided into three types on the basis of structure and function such as messenger RNA (mRNA), ribosomal RNA (rRNA) and transfer RNA (tRNA).

Table 7.3: Differences between DNA and RNA

Property	DNA	RNA
Origin	It is originated after RNA.	It is more primitive than DNA.
Structure	Double stranded except few viruses (e.g. $\phi \times 174$)	Single stranded except some viruses (e.g. reovirus).
Types	One type	Three types (rRNA, mRNA, tRNA)
Pentose sugar	Deoxyribose	Ribose
Bases	Adenine, guanine, cytosine and thymine	Adenine, guanine, cytosine and uracil
Base pairs	A to T and G to C	A to U and G to C.
Nucleotides	Contains millions of nucleotides (over 4 millions)	Contains few nucleotides (about 12,000)
Present in cell	DNA found in chromosomes. It is also found in mitochondria and chloroplasts.	mRNA is found in nucleolus, tRNA and rRNA.
Functions	It encodes the genetic masses in a form that transcripts.	It translates the transcripts of DNA into proteins.
Reverse transcriptase	It is not required for DNA.	It uses the enzyme during replication.
Examples	Present in almost all living organisms.	Present in some plants, animals and bacterial viruses.

1. Messenger RNA: Francis Jacob and **Jacques Monod** (1961) proposed the name informational or messenger RNA (mRNA) for bearing the transcripts of DNA for protein synthesis on ribosomes. The molecule of mRNA is single-stranded like the rRNA molecule. Its base composition is similar like DNA so that GC contents of mRNA correspond to the GC contents of the genomes total DNA. The total population of mRNA in a cell varies from 5 to 10% of the total cellular RNA. The species of mRNA are short lived and they are broken into ribonucleotides by the enzyme ribonuclease. The sedimentation coefficient of mRNA is 8S and its molecular weight ranges from 5,00,000 to 1,00,000. The mRNA found in prokaryotes shows different properties from that of eukaryotes (Table 7.4).

In prokaryotics, mRNA is complementary to chromosomal DNA and it forms RNA-DNA hybrids after separation of the two DNA strands. Synthesis of mRNA is accomplished with one strand of DNA and that is used as template. The enzyme RNA polymerase joins ribonucleotides and it catalyse the formation of 3'-5'-phosphodiester bonds that form the RNA backbone. The synthesis of mRNA is initiated at 5' end and it grows from 5' end to 3' end. The RNA polymerase attaches to an initiator site of the structural gene, in the promoter and it catalyses mRNA synthesis.

In eukaryotics, the synthesis of mRNA begins with the production of long precursor molecules by RNA polymerase II from the template strand of DNA. This enzyme functions by catalyzing formation of 5' → 3' phosphodiester bonds of the RNA 'backbone' by reading the DNA template in the 3'-5' direction. The developing mRNA is antiparallel and its nucleotides are complementary to those of the DNA template strand. The eukaryotic mRNA is capped at 5'-terminal end by 7-methyl-guanosine triphosphate. This cap helps to prevent the hydrolysis of mRNA by 5'-exonucleases and it also involved in the recognition of mRNA for protein synthesis. The 3'-terminal end of mRNA contains a polymer of adenylate residues (20 to 250 nucleotides) which is known as poly(A) tail and it provide stability to mRNA.

Table 7.4: Difference between prokaryotic and eukaryotic mRNAs

Prokaryotic mRNA	Eukaryotic mRNA
• It do not contain poly (A) at 3' end.	• It contains 200-250 poly (A) residues at 3' end.
• It has short life.	• It has longer life.
• This mRNA is broken down by the ribonuclease into tribonucleotide.	• This is more stable.
• Most of prokaryotes mRNAs are polycistronic.	• Eukaryotes mRNAs are monocistronic.
• Small processing in mRNAs of prokaryotes occurs due to short time between transcription and translation.	• Eukaryotes mRNAs undergo a long processing after being transcribed.
• Its translation starts soon when the mRNAs are being transcribed on DNA template.	• Its translation process begins when transcription process is complete.

2. Ribosomal RNA (rRNA): Ribosomal, stable or insoluble RNA constitutes the largest part (80%) of the total cellular RNA. In prokaryotes rRNA is formed on a part of DNA called ribosomal DNA, while in eukaryotes it is formed in nucleolus containing the nuclear DNA. The rRNAs are found in ribosomes. The ribosomes are of different types such as 80S (eukaryotes) and 70S (prokaryotes). The 80S ribosome consists of 60S and 40S subunits. The 60S ribosomal subunit contains 28S rRNA, 5.8S rRNA and 5S rRNA while 40S subunits contain 18S rRNA.

The 70S ribosomes consist of 50S and 30S subunits. The 50S subunit contains 23S and 5S rRNA while the 30S subunit consists of 16S rRNA.

The rRNA is a single stranded molecule which is twisted at some points to form helical regions. Most of the base pairs are complementary and linked by hydrogen bonds in the helical region (Fig. 7.8). The uncoiled single stranded regions lack the complementary bases. Hence, the ratio of purine: pyrimidine is not equal. The rRNA may play a significant role in the binding of mRNA to ribosomes and protein synthesis.

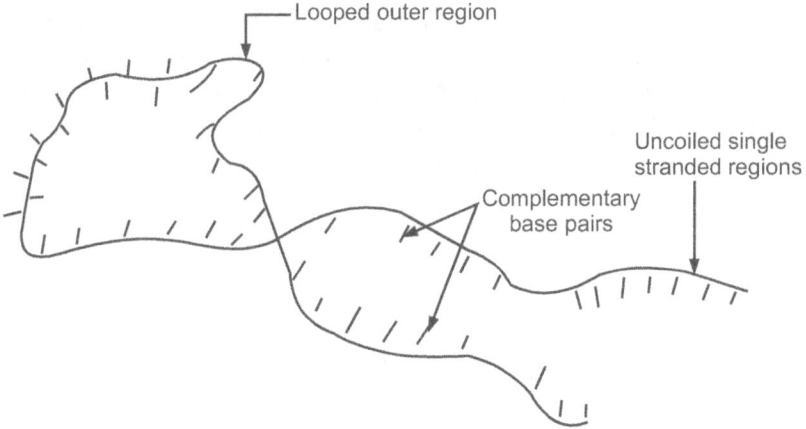

Fig. 7.8: Molecular structure of rRNA

Transfer RNA (tRNA):

Transfer RNA or soluble RNA molecule contains 71 to 80 nucleotides with molecular weight ranging from 25,000 to 30,000 D. It is smaller RNA than mRNA and rRNA and has a sedimentation coefficient of 4S. It accounts for 10 to 20% of the total cytoplasmic RNA. In addition to A, G, C and U bases, some unusual bases are found in tRNA. The unusual bases are 3-methyl cytosine, inosine, dihydrouracil, methyl guanine, dimethyl guanine, ribothymine, pseudouridine, methylinosine etc. These unusual bases are mainly formed by chemical modification by common bases.

Transfer RNA molecule actively engaged in protein synthesis is typically 'clover leaf' like in shape due to intrachain pairing of complementary nucleotides in certain region of the tRNA chain (Fig. 7.9). **Robert Holley** (1968) prepared the clover leaf model for yeast tRNA alanine which includes several known functions of tRNA. A typical structure of tRNA shows following features:

- The single polynucleotide chain of all the tRNA molecule is folded upon itself to form five arms. e.g. acceptor or end terminus arm, dihydrouridine or DHU or D arm, anticodon arm, variable arm and TΨC arm.

- All molecules have guanine residue 'G' at the 5' terminal end and unpaired (single stranded) – CCA sequence at the 3' end. This is called amino acid attachment site or acceptor arm. Adenylic acid (A) acts as amino acid attachment site because amino acids covalently attached to CCA sequence during polypeptide synthesis.

- The acceptor arm consists of 7 base pairs and 4 unpaired bases. The unpaired bases contain a three – CCA bases and a forth variable purine (A or G) at 3' end.

- The dihydrouridine (DHU) or D loop constitutes 8 to 12 unpaired bases. It consists of 15 to 18 nucleotides (3 to 4 base pairs and 8 to 12 unpaired bases) in the loop. It acts as the site for recognition of amino acid activating enzyme amioacyl tRNA synthetase.

- The anticodon stem contains five paired bases and anitcodon loop consists of seven unpaired bases. The middle three nucleotides (from unpaired bases, 3, 4 and 5) act as anticodon which identify three complementary bases of mRNA molecule. This interaction decides about the order of amino acids on polypeptide chain during assemblage in the ribosomes.

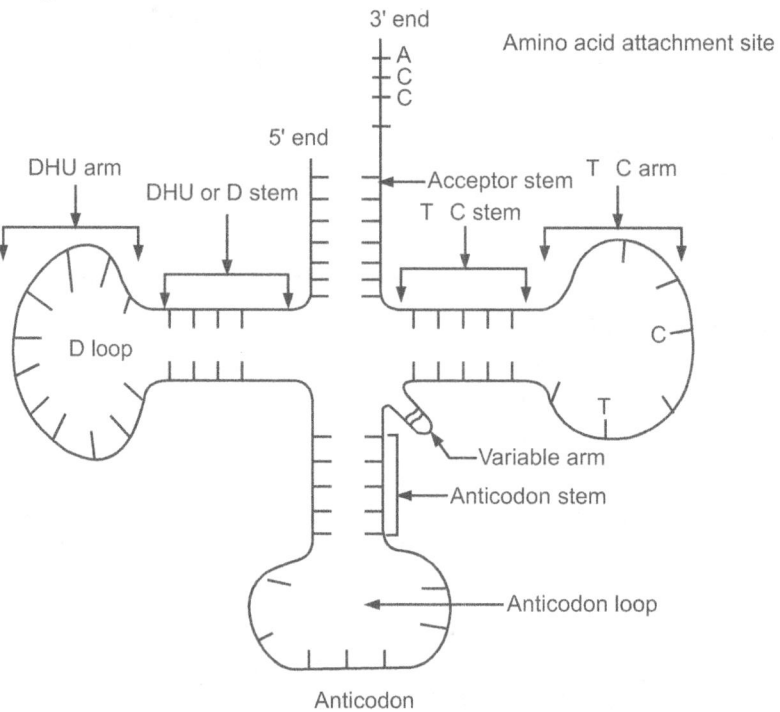

Fig. 7.9: Structure of tRNA

- A variable arm or extra loop may be present in some tRNA which varies in shape, nucleotide content and composition from tRNA to tRNA. It is mainly present in between anticodon arm and TΨC arm.

- TΨC arm consists of a stem of 5 base pairs and a loop of 7 unpaired bases. The TΨC loop consists of a TΨC sequence at 5' → 3' direction. It is involved in the binding of tRNA molecules to the ribosomes.

- The tRNA that initiates protein synthesis is called initiator tRNA. The tRNA specifies methionine as the starting amino acid in eukaryotic protein synthesis and N-methyl methionine in prokaryotes. Hence, the two tRNAs specific to these two amino acids are methionyl tRNA.

- Three dimensional structure (TDS) was proposed by **S.H. Kim** (1973) for yeast phenylalanine tRNA molecule. This TDS takes the shape of letter 'L' with a thickness of 20A°.

PHENOTYPIC AND GENOTYPIC CHANGES

The characteristics expressed by a cell in a given environment are referred as phenotype and the collection of genes encoding these characteristics are called genotype. Phenotype is the physical expression of the genotype in a given environment (Fig. 7.10). Phenotypic changes are temporary to changed conditions of environment. They are readily reversible on restoring original conditions of environment. Bacterial cells from an old culture may exhibit irregular staining and variation in size and shape. If these cells are transferred to a fresh medium, they return to normal morphology. The other examples of environmental influences are synthesis of the enzyme beta galactosidase by *Escherichia coli*, necessary for lactose fermentation. Synthesis of enzyme takes place only when it is grown in a medium containing lactose. Sometimes pigment producing bacteria fail to produce pigment under conditions of laboratory growth, e.g. *Serratia marcescens* produce red pigment at 20 to 25°C whereas pigment is not produced at 37°C.

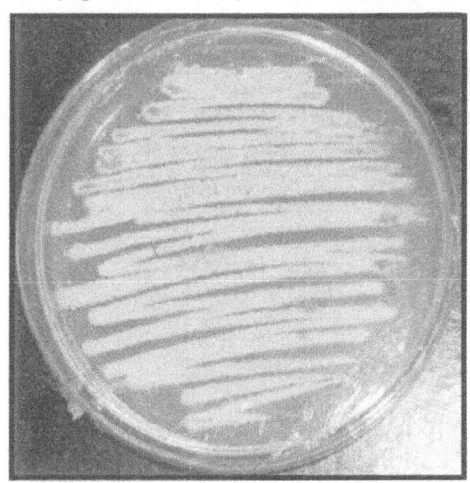
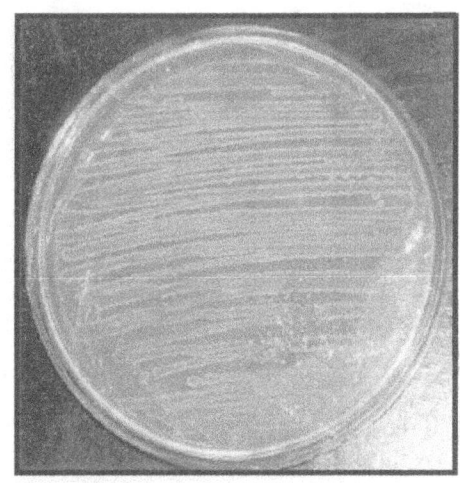

(a) Yeast extract – Meat extract agar   (b) Luria Bertani agar

Fig. 7.10: Characteristics of *Streptomyces* species on two different media

The genotype of a cell is determined by the genetic information contained in its chromosome. Genetypic variations are stable, heritable and are not influenced by the environment. They may occur by mutation or genetic recombination, such as transduction, transformation, conjugation and lysogenic conversion.

MUTATION

Mutation is a random undirected, heritable variation caused by an alteration in the nucleotide sequence at some point of the DNA of the cell. A cell or an organism which shows the effects of mutation is called a mutant. The different form of gene produced by mutation is called alleles. Each gene undergoes mutation with a fixed frequency. Mutation rates of individual genes in bacteria range from 10^{-2} to 10^{-4} per bacterium per division. Alterations in DNA can be caused by chemical or physical means or they can occur spontaneously.

Types of Mutation:

Mutation can be divided conveniently into point mutation, frame shift mutation and multistage mutation.

The substitution of one nucleotide for another in the specific nucleotide sequence of a gene is called point mutation. The substitution of one purine for another purine or one pyrimidine for another pyrimidine is termed a transition type of point mutation. A transversion is the replacement of a purine by a pyrimidine or vice versa. The base-pair substitution may result in one of the three kinds of mutations affecting the translation process. A missense mutation is one in which the triplet code is altered so as to specify an amino acid different from that normally located at a particular position in the protein. Deletion of a nucleotide within a gene may cause premature polypeptides chain termination by generating a non-sense codon and is called non-sense mutation. The altered gene triplet produces a mRNA codon and which specifies the same amino acid because the codon resulting from mutation is a synonym for the original codon and this is called neutral mutation.

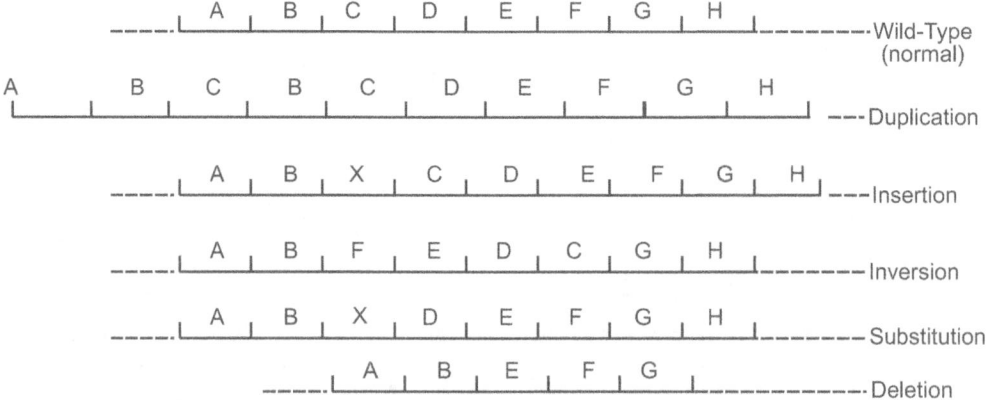

Fig. 7.11: Types of mutations

Frame shift mutations result from an addition or loss of one or more nucleotides in a gene and are termed insertion or deletion (Fig. 7.11) mutations, respectively. This results in a shift of the reading frame. In frame shift mutations, new sequence of amino acids is synthesised from a frameshift reading of the nucleotide sequences of mRNA.

Multisite mutation is called macrolesion. There are extensive chromosomal rearrangements such as inversions, duplications and deletions

Mutations are also classified as induced mutation and spontaneous mutation.

Mutagenic Agents or Mutagens:

Mutagens are chemical or physical agents that increase the rate of mutation and these mutations are called 'induced mutations'. Mutation of an individual gene occurs independently of mutation in other genes. The mutation rate is generally defined as the average number of mutations per cell per division. It is expressed as a negative exponent per cell division. If a mutation occurs once in 1 million divisions, the rate of mutation is 10^{-6}. Generally, the mutation rate for any single gene ranges between 10^{-3} and 10^{-9} per cell division. A variety of mutagens are known to increase the rate of mutation in micro-organisms. These include both physical and chemical agents.

Physical agents: Physical agents commonly used to induce mutations are ultraviolet (UV) light, X-rays, γ-radiations, heat etc. All these agents can cause non-selective mutations. Irradiation of DNA with UV rays generally results in the formation of covalent bonds between thymine molecules on the same strand of DNA yielding thymine-thymine dimers (Fig. 7.12). Most UV mutations are non-sense type of mutations and are the result of a change in one or few bases in the DNA. Many micro-organisms have enzymes that can repair this damage in the dark (dark repair). The light repair system involves a photoactivated enzyme that breaks the bonds between the thymine dimers. This protective mechanism is active only in visible light. X-rays and γ-rays are ionizing radiations and they can cause damage to the DNA but no dimer formation occurs.

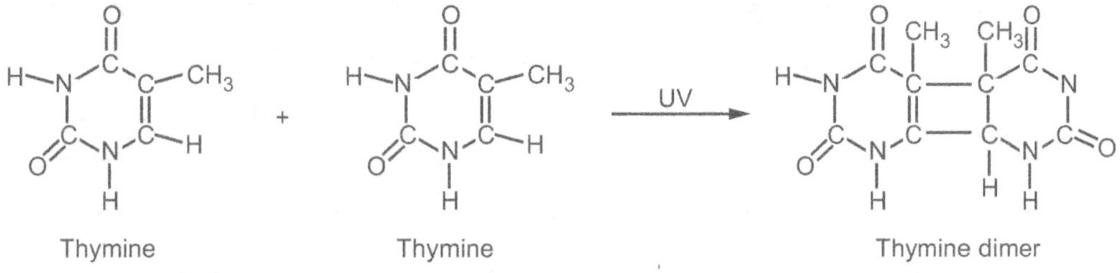

Fig. 7.12: Effect of ultraviolet irradiation on thymine

Chemical agents: Chemical agents used to induce mutations are nitrous acid, hydroxylamine, base analogues (2-amino purine, 5-Bromouracil) alkylating agents such as ethyl ethane sulphonate (EES), ethyl methane sulphonate (EMS), sulfur mustard and nitrosoguanidine. Nitrous acid oxidatively deaminates cytosine to uracil and adenine to hypoxanthine (Fig. 7.13). During subsequent DNA replication, uracil recognises adenine and hypoxanthine pairs with guanine resulting in a AT to GC transition. Base analogues are compounds that are chemically similar to the natural compounds used to synthesize DNA. When base analogous are incorporated into DNA, they do not base pair correctly like the natural bases and cause mispairing and mutations. Alkylating agents are the most potent group of chemical mutagens and they transfer the alkyl group to the carbonyl oxygen of a base. Ethyl methyl sulfonate chemically alters thymine to make it pair with guanine instead of adenine.

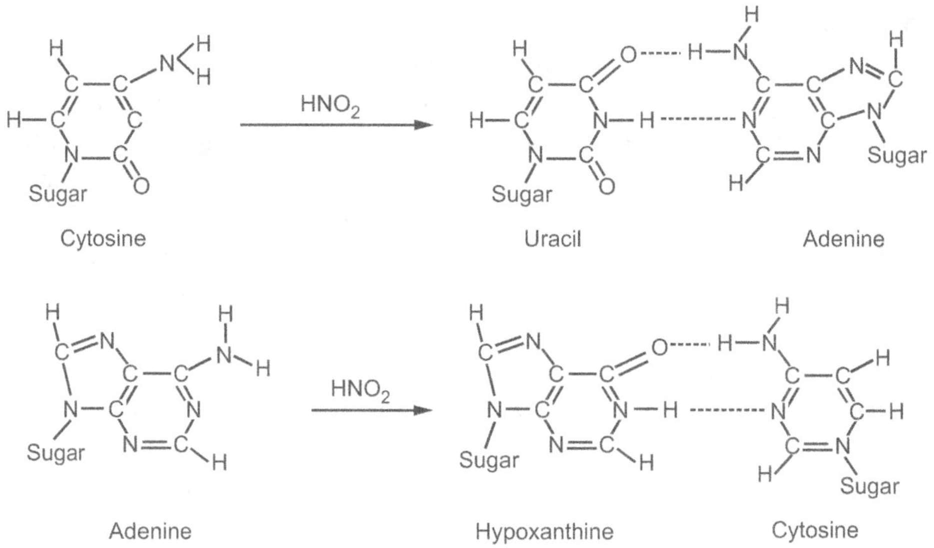

Fig. 7.13: Effect of nitrous acid on cytosine and adenine

Spontaneous Mutation:

Mutations that occur in the absence of all mutagenic agents are called spontaneous mutations. Spontaneous mutation, independent of the environment was first produced by **Salvador Luria** and **Max Delbruck** (1943) by the 'fluctuation test'. They found very wide fluctuations occurring in the numbers of bacteriophage resistant *Escherichia coli* colonies when samples are plated from several separate small volume cultures as compared to samples tested from a single large volume culture (Fig. 7.14).

In fluctuation test, a series of tubes containing 0.5 ml of cells are incubated without phage until a certain population size (10^8 cells/ml) is reached. The cultures are then exposed to phage by pouring the contents of each tube into an agar plate containing phage. The colony counts (phage resistant mutant) from series of similar cultures are then compared with the results of a series of samples taken from one culture (10 ml test tube) started with a similar density of cells/ml and allowed to reach a similar population number (1 ml). The results showed that resistant bacteria arise spontaneously prior to the exposure to phage. A series of similar cultures yielded results different from those obtained with a series of samples from one culture. Luria and Delbruck found that the number of resistant mutants fluctuated from sample to sample indicating that mutants existed in the population prior to exposure to the phage. They concluded that mutations in bacteria occur spontaneously.

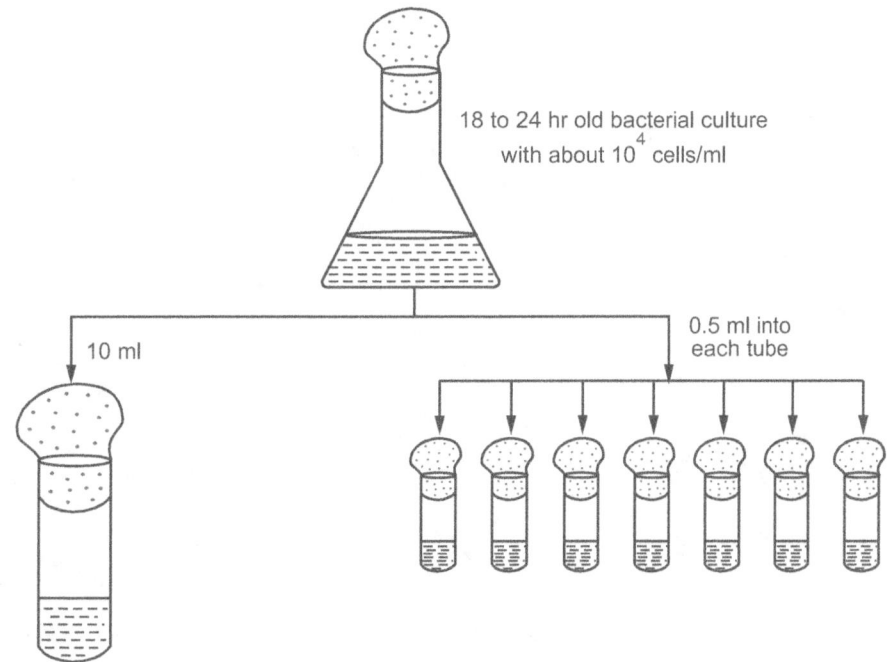

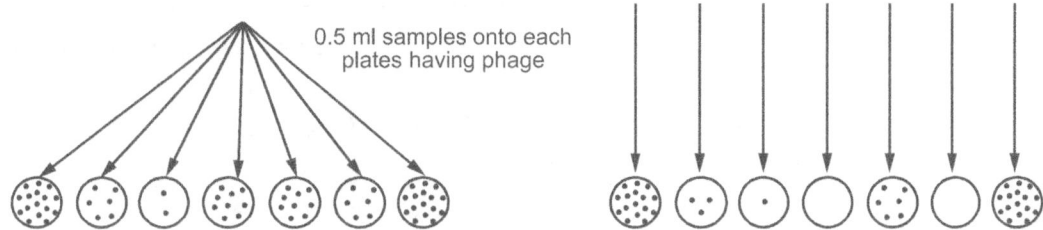

Fig. 7.14: The fluctuation test

These results are further elaborated by **Josua Lederberg** and **Esther Lederberg** by the use of the replica plate technique. The technique consists of first plating a small number of test bacteria on a master plate and incubating it until growth occurred. A sterile velvet pad on a transfer block is then used to inoculate each of the colonies from the master plate onto a plate containing an inhibitor or a selective agent to detect resistant mutants (Fig. 7.15). If resistant mutants are developed on the master plate before exposure to the inhibitor, then such resistant colonies should be located at exactly the same position on each of the replica plates, while if mutation occurred as a consequence of exposure to the inhibitor then the resistant colonies should be at different locations on different replica plates. **Josua** and **Esther Lederberg** found that spontaneous mutations occur in bacteria in the absence of a selective agent. After this conclusion, the replica plate technique has been extensively used as a basic technique for mutant detection.

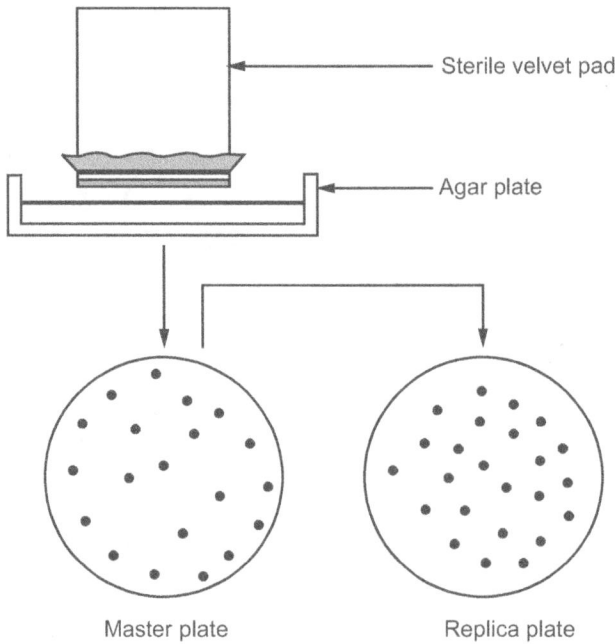

Fig. 7.15: Replica plate technique

PLASMIDS

In addition to chromosomal DNA, most bacteria possess extra-chromosomal genetic materials. These materials are known as plasmid. The general properties of plasmids are as follows:

(i) They are small extrachromosomal piece of genetic material that can replicate autonomously within the host cell.

(ii) They consist of a circular piece of double stranded DNA.

(iii) They can integrate with each other and with the host chromosome which may lead to exchange of genetic material (episome).

(iv) They are not essential for the normal life and cell survival.

(v) They may contain genetic information for controlling their own replication.

(vi) Plasmids may be lost spontaneously or by curing agents.

(vii) They can promote their own transfer by host cell conjugation.

(viii) Plasmids may have some additional properties such as drug or heavy metal resistance, bacteriocin production, toxigenicity etc.

Plasmids vary both in numbers per cell and in size. Each contains 50 to 100 genes. Plasmids can be classified as conjugative or self-transmissible and non-conjugative or nonself transmissible or determinants. The conjugative plasmids are large and self transmissible. They have an apparatus through which they can mediate their own transfer to another cell, e.g. R, F and bacteriocinogen plasmids. Those plasmids which do not possess information for self transfer to another cell are known as non-conjugative plasmids. They can be transferred with the help of transfer factor such as colicin plasmid (Col I) and through the agency of bacteriophages (transduction). A number of properties of bacteria are attributed to extra chromosomal DNA.

Fertility plasmids: The plasmid conferring maleness is known as fertility (F) plasmid. Conjugation in bacteria always proceeds from the male donor cell to the female recipient cell. Microbial cells containing this plasmid are designated F^+ cells and cells without fertility plasmid are designated F^- cells. When F^+ cells conjugate with F^- female cells then all the recipients become F^+ cells. Fertility plasmids code for the genes needed to produce the pili and for the enzymes involved in the transfer of the plasmid.

Composite drug resistant plasmids (Resistance transfer factor – RTF): Many microbial cells possess resistance to multiple drugs and this resistance can be genetically transferred by conjugation. The genes for multiple drug resistance are contained in a DNA plasmid called the r-determinant. This DNA can be mobilised by the resistance transfer factor. The r-determinant plasmid becomes conjugative when it combines with the resistance transfer factor. The two molecules together are called the R-factor. The discovery of RTF was first made in Japan when a strain of *Shiegella dysentriae* was found to be simultaneously resistant to sulphonamides, streptomycin, chloramphenicol and tetracycline. The RTF region of several R-factors has been characterised and found to have molecular weights 60 million daltons while the r-determinants have 10 million daltons. These two segments of the RTF have been found to have different G + C content. These plasmids are genetically labile.

Bacteriocin plasmids: Bacteriocins are protein toxins produced by certain bacteria which inhibit the growth of related bacteria. The formation of a bacteriocin is due to a corresponding plasmid (bacteriocinogen). Ultraviolet rays can induce the bacteriocinogenic strains to form and release the bacteriocins. The bacteriocins produced by strains of *Escherichia coli* are called colicins (B, C, D, E, F, G etc.). Bacteriocins produced by *Serratia marcescens*, *Pasteurella pestis*, *Bacillus megaterium* and *Clostridium perfringens* are marcescins, pesticins, megacins and clostocins respectively.

Degradative plasmids: The degradative plasmids possess genes which control degradation of organic and inorganic compounds. *Pseudomonas* species are capable of metabolizing a large group of organic compounds. The enzymes for octane degradation are contained in a plasmid of *Pseudomonas putida*. The comphor plasmid, octane plasmid or salicylate plasmid control the degradation of camphor, octane or salicylate respectively. These plasmids are transmissible by conjugation within and between *Pseudomonas* strains.

GENETIC MECHANISM OF DRUG RESISTANCE

Three genetic elements are responsible for acquired antibiotic resistance e.g. chromosomes, plasmids and transposons.

Antibiotic resistance is the most common cause of treatment failure in bacterial infectious diseases. Antibiotic resistance is classified as intrinsic resistance and acquired resistance. Intrinsic (innate) resistance suggests that the inherent properties of the bacteria are responsible for preventing antibiotic action. There are many antibiotics active against Gram-positive bacteria (absence of outer membrane) which have no effect on Gram-negative bacteria and vice versa.

Resistance to different antibiotics can arise as a consequence of mutations to chromosomal genes. Mutation can occur due to single base pair changes. Transitions involve the substitution of one purine (A or G) for another and one pyrimidine (C or T) for another. Transversions involve a change from a pyrimidine to a purine and vice versa. Frame shift mutations occur when one or two bases are inserted into the DNA sequence. More extensive changes in the DNA sequence can also occur. Deletions result in the loss of part of the DNA sequence. Insertions add extra base pairs of a gene. Transversions occur when a segment of the DNA is reversed and duplications occur when a segment of the DNA is repeated. A mutation of dihydropteroate synthetase in *Streptococcus pneumoniae* produces an altered enzyme with reduced affinity for sulphonamides. Chromosomal mutations in *Escherichia coli* result in overproduction of dihydrofolate reductase. Hence, higher concentrations of trimethoprim are required to inhibit nucleotide metabolism.

Bacterial chromosome contains all the genes necessary for the growth and replication of cells. Many bacteria also possess additional circular elements of DNA which are capable of replicating and transferring of chromosomes. These extrachromosomal genetic elements are known as plasmids and can code for a number of properties including antibiotic resistance. Plasmids have the ability to transfer within and between bacterial species. This property makes a plasmid acquired resistance much more threatening than chromosomal mutation in terms of the spread of antibiotic resistance. Plasmid transfer normally occurs by conjugation, transduction or transformation. Conjugation requires cell-to-cell contact and involves the transfer of DNA from a donor cell to a recipient cell. Plasmids which can mediate their own transfer are termed conjugative plasmids. Some plasmids which do not posses this property can be transferred if they coexist with a conjugative plasmid (mobilizable plasmids). Gram-positive and Gram-negative bacteria have the ability to conjugate and transfer the plasmids. Transduction is a process whereby DNA is transferred by bacteriophages and plays an important role in the transfer of antibiotic resistance in Gram-positive bacteria e.g. *Staphylococcus aureus, Streptococcus pyogenes*. Certain micro-organisms have the ability to acquire naked DNA from the environment by the process of transformation. *Neisseria gonorrhoeae* have the ability to recognize DNA from their own species and those acquired from the environment.

Plasmids also harbour transposons, which enhances their ability to transfer antibiotic resistance genes. Transposons are mobile genetic elements capable of transferring or transposing independently from one DNA molecule to another. The DNA molecules may be chromosomes or plasmids. Plasmid or transposon-encoded chloramphenicol acetyl-transferases are responsible for resistance by inactivating the antibiotic. Chloramphenicol acetyltransferases convert chloramphenicol to an acetoxy derviative which fails to bind to the ribosomal target.

QUESTIONS

(A) Short answer questions:
1. Define the terms:
   (a) Genetics
   (b) Mutation
   (c) F-plasmid
2. Explain the terms:
   (a) Replica plate
   (b) Messenger RNA
3. Differentiate the following:
   (a) Phenotypic changes and genotypic changes
   (b) Induced mutation and spontaneous mutation
   (c) ssDNA and dsDNA
   (d) DNA and RNA
4. Draw the structure tRNA.

(B) Long answer questions:
1. Explain the structure of 'DNA'.
2. Discuss various types of mutations.
3. Write a note on 'genetics and drug resistance'.
4. What is plasmids? Write the general properties of plasmids.
5. Explain in detail structure and types of RNA.

(C) Multiple choice questions:
1. Which of the following is correct related to RNA _____
   (a) Sugar ribosomes   (b) tRNA is transfer RNA
   (c) Pyrimidine base   (d) All of the above
2. Adenine always binds to _____
   (a) Cytosine   (b) Guanine
   (c) Thymine   (d) None of the above
3. Antibiotic resistance genes chromosome replication is mainly found in _____
   (a) Chromosomal DNA   (b) Plasmid DNA
   (c) Chromosomal and plasmid DNA   (d) None of the above
4. Replacement of purine for purine and pyramidine for pyramidine is known as _____
   (a) Transversion   (b) Translocation
   (c) Transcription   (d) Transition
5. Drug resistance in bacteria is mainly determined by factor _____
   (a) S   (b) R
   (c) B   (d) F
6. cDNA stands for _____
   (a) Complementary DNA   (b) Chromosomal DNA
   (c) Copy DNA   (d) Cohesive DNA

7. DNA is transcribed into RNA in the nucleus and RNA is then translated in the _____
   (a) Cytoplasm
   (b) Nucleus
   (c) ER
   (d) Golgi bodies
8. Which type of cell does not contain double stranded DNA?
   (a) Bacterial cell
   (b) Monoclonal cell
   (c) Adenovirus
   (d) Retrovirus
9. The major DNA form in the cells is _____
   (a) A - DNA
   (b) B - DNA
   (c) C - DNA
   (d) Z - DNA
10. Functional unit of gene is _____
    (a) Cistron
    (b) Exon
    (c) Mutan
    (d) Recan
11. In DNA, cytosine is the complement for _____.
    (a) Guanine
    (b) Thymine
    (c) Uracil
    (d) None of above

(D) Match the following:

A	B
(a) A - DNA	(i) Left handed helix
(b) B - DNA	(ii) Right handed and pitch of helix – 31 A°
(c) C - DNA	(iii) Helical diameter – 20 A°
(d) Z - DNA	(iv) Pitch of the helix – 28.15 A°

(E) Fill in the blanks:
1. _____ is a transposon – encoded enzyme that catalyses transposition.
2. Multiple drug resistance can be passed between bacterial strains by resistance transfer factors which are _____.
3. Structure of DNA of the cell was described by _____.
4. Thymidine dimers are formed in DNA due to the effect of _____.
5. The diameter of the helix of DNA is _____.

CHAPTER 8

DNA REPLICATION, TRANSCRIPTION AND TRANSLATION

CONTENTS
- INTRODUCTION
- DNA REPLICATION
  - Models for DNA replication
  - DNA replication in eukaryotes
- GENE TRANSCRIPTION
  - Transcription in prokaryotes
  - Transcription in eukaryotes
- TRANSLATION (PROTEIN SYNTHESIS)

INTRODUCTION

Deoxyribonucleic acid (DNA) is a macromolecule that carries genetic information from generation to generation. It may be regarded as a reserve bank of genetic information or a memory bank. RNA molecules can perform the cellular functions that are carried out by DNA. Chemically DNA is more stable than RNA. Hence, during the course of evolution, DNA is preferred as a more suitable molecule for long term repository of genetic information. The biological information flows from DNA to RNA and from there to proteins. This is the central dogma of life (Fig. 8.1.).

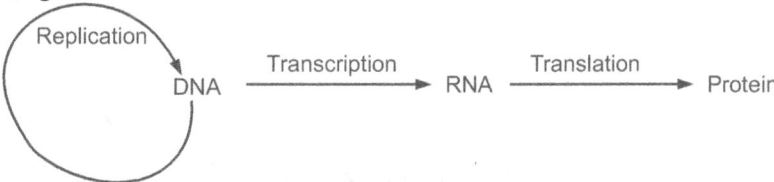

Fig. 8.1: The central dogma of life

DNA REPLICATION

In DNA replication, one parental double-stranded DNA molecule is converted to two identical 'daughter' molecules. It is necessary so that the genetic information present in cells can be passed on to daughter cells following cell division. The DNA is copied by enzymes called DNA polymerases. These act on single-stranded DNA synthesizing a new strand complementary to the original strand. DNA synthesis occurs in the 5' → 3' direction. **Watson** and **Crick** proposed the hypothesis of semiconservative replication (Fig. 8.2). The hydrogen bonds between the base pairs of two strands of double helix are separated from each other. Each purine and pyrimidine base of the stands forms hydrogen bonds with complementary free nucleotides to be involved in polymerization in the cell. The free nucleotides from phosphodiester bonds with deoxyribose residue resulting in formation of a new polynucleotide molecule. This type of duplication in which one polynucleotide chain acts as a template to direct the synthesis of a new chain complementary to itself is termed as 'semiconservative replication'. It forms two daughter helix, each containing one old template strand and one new complementary strand.

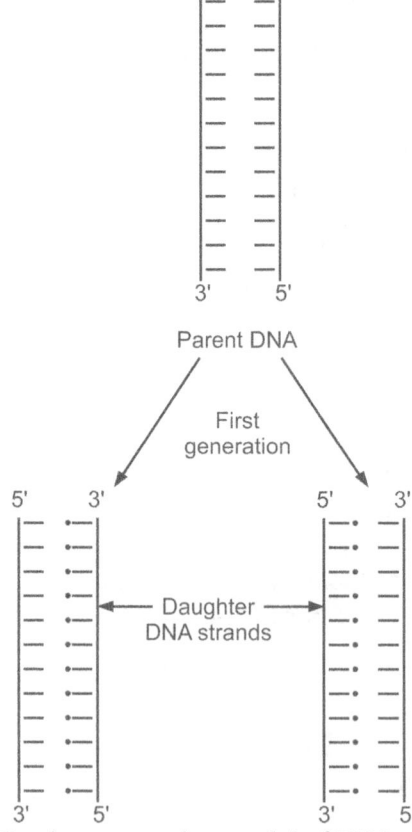

Fig. 8.2: Semi-conservative model of DNA replication

Meselson-Stahl Experiment: Matthew Meselson and **Franklin Stahl** (1957) provided the experimental support for **Watson's** and **Crick's** model for DNA replication which is called Meselson-Stahl experiment. They grow *E. coli* cells for many generations in a medium containing heavy isotopic nitrogen (^{15}N) and this cells contains ^{15}N – labelled DNA. The DNA isolated from these cells had a density about 1% greater than that of normal (^{14}N) DNA [Fig. 8.3 (a)]. The mixture of heavy (^{15}N) and light (^{14}N) DNA can be separated by centrifugation to equilibrium in a cesium chloride (CsCl) density gradient.

The cells grown in the ^{15}N medium were transferred to a fresh medium containing less dense isotopic nitrogen (^{14}N) and was allowed to multiply several times. In the first generation, DNA was extracted which was found to be hybrid of $^{15}N - {}^{14}N$ [Fig. 8.3 (b)]. This strand was lighter than ^{15}N and heavier than ^{14}N. The DNA bands were formed at a specific position in the density gradient. The cells were again allowed to double in number in the ^{14}N medium. The isolated DNA product of the second generation exhibited two bands [Fig. 8.3 (c)] in the density gradient (light DNA and hybrid DNA). This was the semi-conservative nature of DNA.

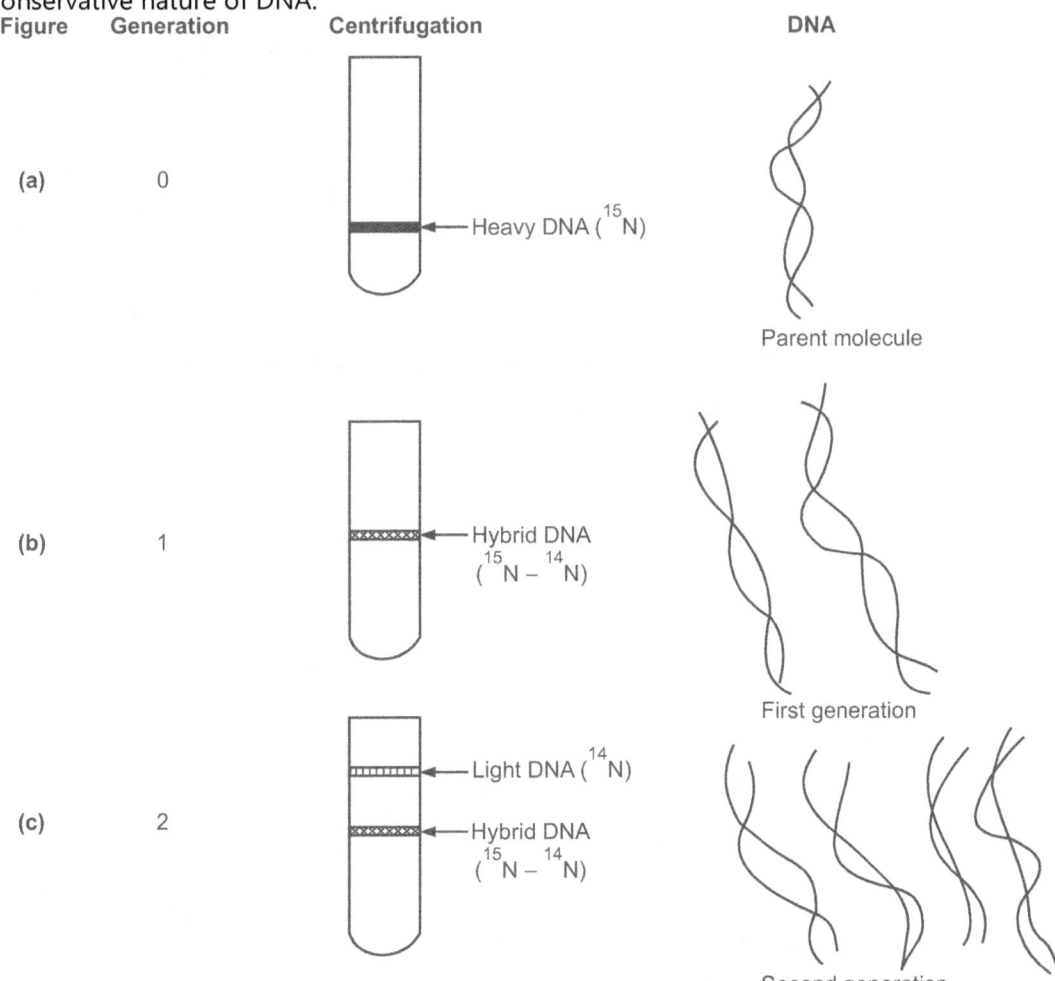

Fig. 8.3: Meselson – Stahl experiment

Models for DNA replication:

The pattern of DNA replication in prokaryotes differs from that of eukaryotes due to the nature of prokaryotic DNA. Different techniques are used for replication of circular DNA molecules which occur in bacteria and for the linear chromosomal DNA molecules present in eukaryotes. The general methods for DNA replication is discussed as follows:

Theta (θ) mode: The simplest and most common form of replication for bacteria (circular DNA) involves a single origin of replication from which two replication forks progress in opposite directions. This mode is called 'theta' because intermediate structures resemble the Greek letter θ (Fig. 8.4). In this process, a circular parental chromosome is replicated to two circular daughter chromosomes. One strand of the parental DNA molecule is conserved and a complementary strand is newly synthesized.

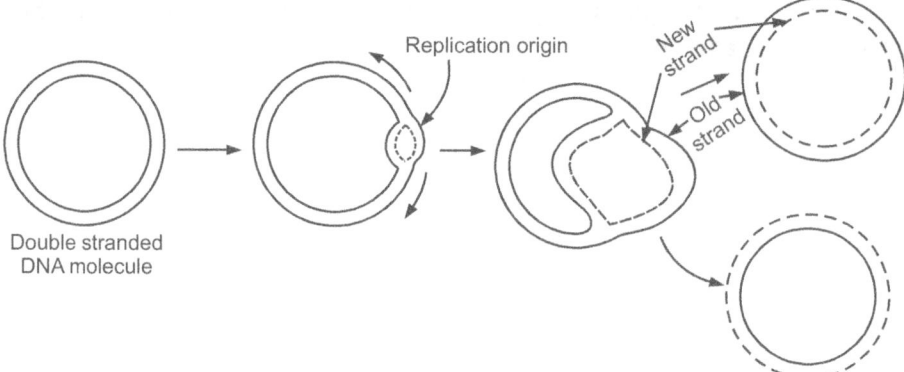

Fig. 8.4: Replication of bacterial DNA by the theta mode

Sigma (σ) on Rolling Circle Mode:

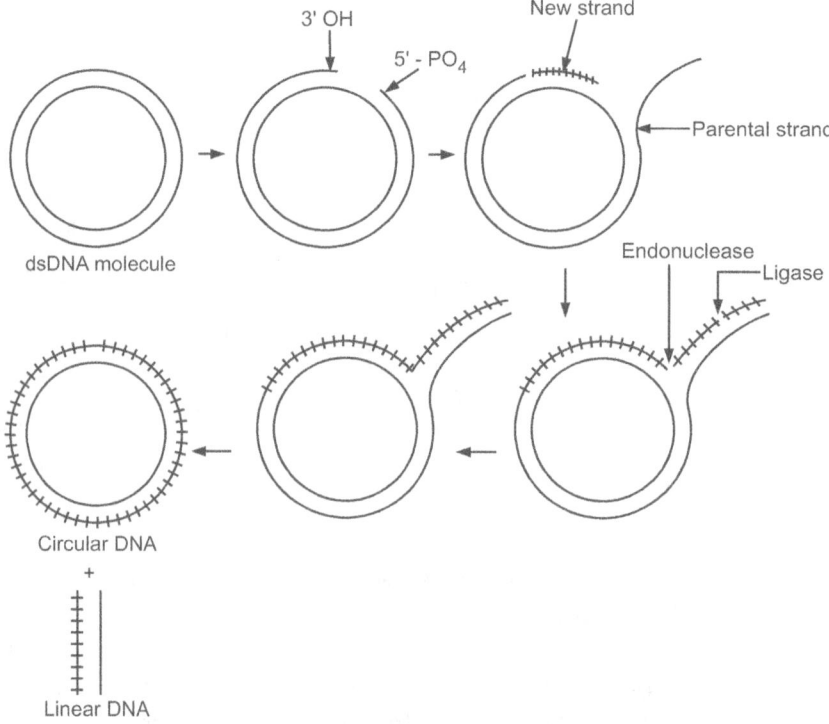

Fig. 8.5: Sigma mode of DNA replication

The double stranded circular DNA molecule is nicked at a specific point exposing 3'-hydroxyl and 5-phosphate terminal groups. The complementary circular strand serves as a template for the synthesis of a new strand. It is covalently linked to the 3'-OH end of the nicked parental strand. As this strand grows at the 3'-OH end, the 5'-PO_4 end of the same strand is displaced to form a 'tail' on the circle (Fig. 8.5). The short fragments are joined together by polynucleotide ligase. The circular parental molecule is converted to two daughter molecules (one circular and one linear). This mode is called sigma because intermediate structures have the Greek letter sigma (σ). This type of DNA replication is carried out by some bacteriophages (λ and $\phi \times 174$), bacteria (in sexual conjugation) and by certain eukaryotes during oogenesis.

Linear Mode and replication Fork: All eukaryotic organisms and some viruses have linear DNA molecules. Replication of linear DNA molecules is initiated at specific sites by the formation of replication bubbles (Fig. 8.6). Prokaryotes and small viral linear DNA molecules may have only one point of initiation per molecule. Large DNA molecules of eukaryotes may have hundreds of initiation points per molecule. Replication may occur in either a unidirectional or bidirectional (Fig. 8.7) manner from each origin. However, the well accepted model for replication of eukaryotic DNA is the bidirectional model.

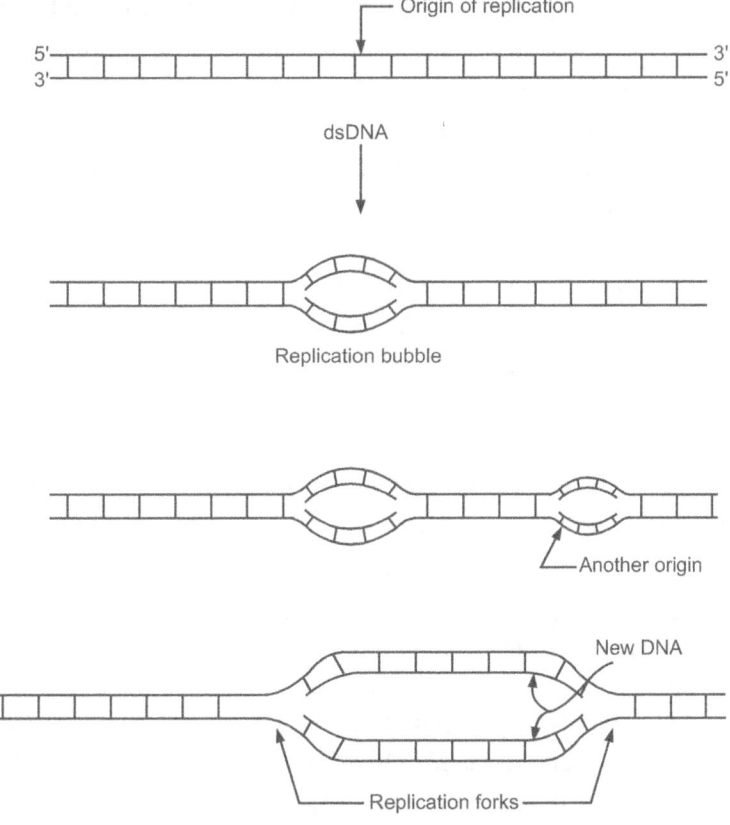

Fig. 8.6: Replication origin and replication forks

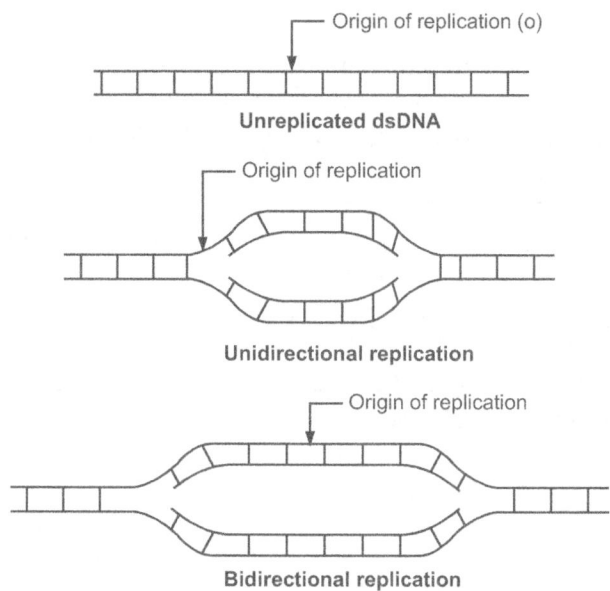

Fig. 8.7: Unidirectional and bidirectional replications

During DNA replication, the double helix DNA is progressively unwound producing segments of single-stranded DNA which can be copied by DNA polymerases. Unwinding of the double helix begins at a distinct position called the replication origin. Replication origins usually contain sequences rich in weak A-T base pairs. The region where the helix unwinds and new DNA is synthesized is called the replication fork. As the replication fork moves along the parental DNA, the two new DNA strands must grow in different directions. A new strand of DNA is always synthesized in the 5'-3' direction.

Reiji Okazaki and colleagues (1960) found that one of the new DNA strands is synthesized in short pieces called 'okazaki fragments' (Fig. 8.8). This work ultimately led to the conclusion that one strand is synthesized continuously and the other discontinuously. The continuous strand (leading strand) is synthesized continuously as the DNA polymerase moves toward the replication fork. The discontinuous (lagging) strand is synthesized in pieces of about 1000 nucleotides as the DNA polymerase moves away from the replication fork.

DNA helicase enzymes bind to both the DNA strands at the replication fork. This enzyme move along the DNA helix and separate the strands. Single stranded DNA binding (SSB) proteins bind to only single-stranded DNA. It separates two strands and provide the template for new DNA synthesis. A short piece of RNA (RNA primer) is needed to start synthesis on the lagging strand. DNA polymerase removes the RNA primer and the enzyme DNA ligase joins the newly made DNA fragments.

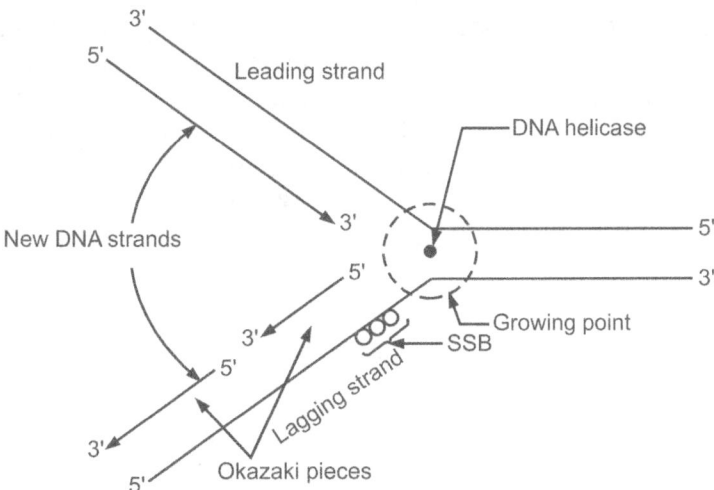

Fig. 8.8: Replication of leading and lagging strand

DNA Replication in eukaryotes:

Replication of DNA in eukaryotes closely resembles that of prokaryotes. The DNA molecules in eukaryotic cells are larger than those in bacteria and are organized into complex nucleoprotein structures. Multiple origins of replication is a characteristic feature of eukaryotic cell. Three different DNA polymerases (I, II, III) are known in prokaryotes. DNA polymerase I (Kornberg enzyme) and DNA polymerase II are meant for DNA repair. DNA polymerase III (poll II) enzyme plays an essential role in DNA replication. Like bacteria, eukaryotes have several types of DNA polymerases and Greek letters are used to number of these enzymes.

- **DNA Polymerase α (alpha):** This relatively high molecular weight enzyme is also called cytoplasmic polymerase. It is found both in nucleus and cytoplasm. It is responsible for the synthesis of RNA primer for both the leading and lagging strands of DNA.

- **DNA polymerase β (beta):** This enzyme is also called nuclear or small polymerase and it is involved in the repair of DNA.

- **DNA polymerase γ (gamma):** This enzyme is called mitochondrial polymerase and is encoded in the nucleus. It is involved in the replication of mitochondrial DNA.

- **DNA polymerase δ (delta):** This enzyme is associated with and stimulated by a protein called proliferating cell nuclear antigen (PCNA). This enzyme has $3' \rightarrow 5'$ proofreading exonuclease activity and appears to carry out both leading and lagging strand synthesis in a complex comparable to the dimeric bacterial DNA polymerase III.

- **DNA polymerase ε (epsilon):** This enzyme is PCNA independent and occurs in mammalian HeLa cells and budding yeast. It plays major role in DNA synthesis on the lagging strand and proof-reading function.

Many DNA viruses encode their own DNA polymerases and some of these have become targets for pharmaceuticals. The DNA polymerase of the herpes simplex virus is inhibited by acyclovir, a compound developed by **Gertrude Elion**. The difference in the DNA replication between bacteria and human cells, attributed to the enzymes, are successfully used in antibacterial therapy to target bacterial replication.

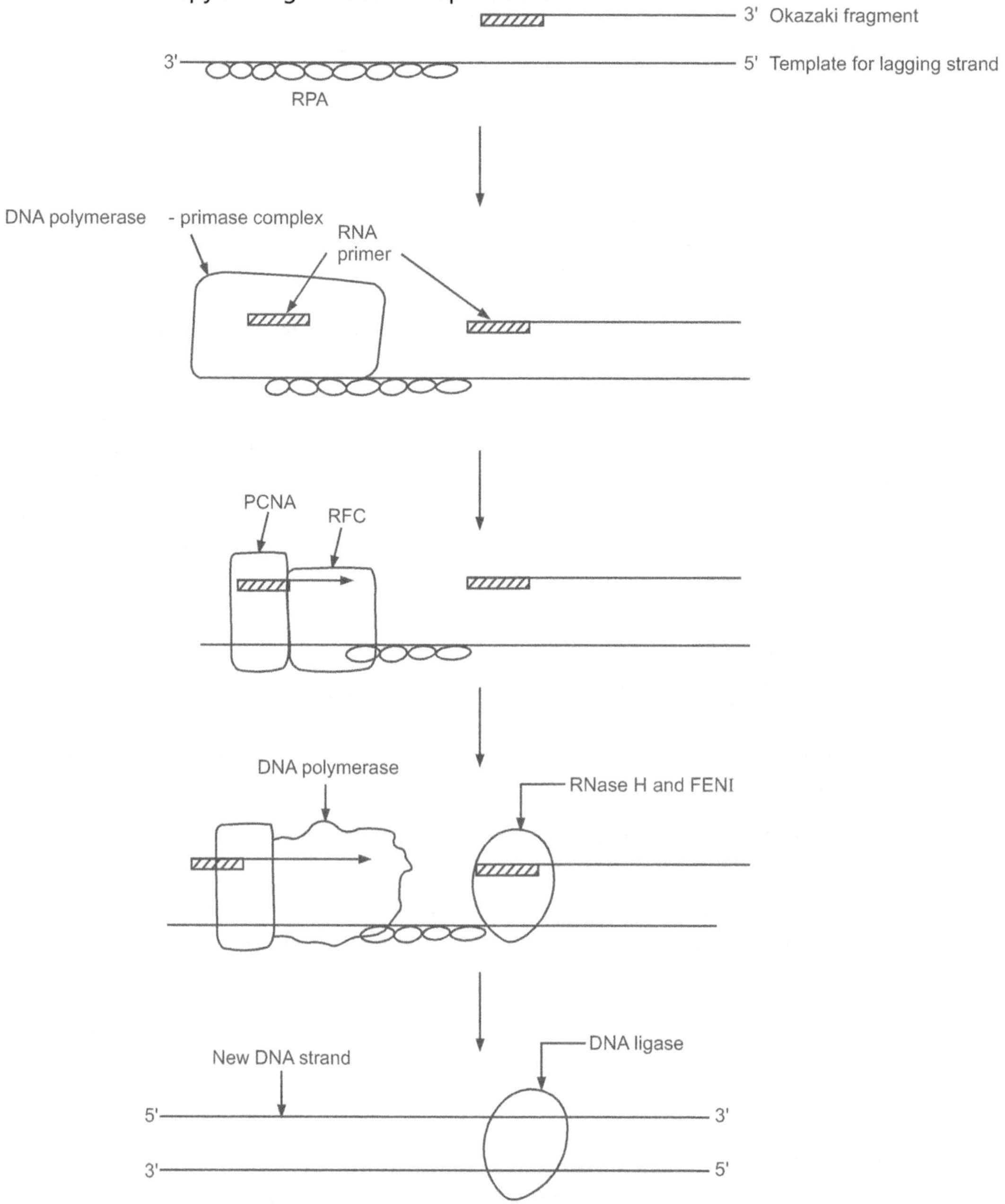

Fig. 8.9: DNA replication on the lagging strand in eukaryotes

DNA replication in prokaryotes and eukaryotes is attained in discrete units, called replicons. The number of replicons may vary in a genome from one in bacteria (*Escherichia coli*) and 500 in yeast to several thousands in plants and animals. A typical mammalian cell has 50 – 1,00,000 replicons, each of which replicates 40-200 Kb of DNA.

The replication on the leading (continuous) stand of DNA is simple and it involves DNA polymerase δ and proliferating cell nuclear antigen (PCNA). The replication on the lagging (discontinuous) strand in eukaryotes is more complex. The parental strands of DNA are separated by the enzyme helicase. A single-stranded DNA binding protein (replication protein A, RPA) binds to the exposed single-stranded template and it has opened by the replication fork. The enzyme primase forms a complex with DNA polymerase α which initiates the synthesis of *Okazaki* fragments. The primase activity of pol α-primase complex is capable of producing 10-bp RNA-primer. The enzyme activity is then switched from primase to DNA polymerase α which elongates the primer by the addition of 20 to 30 deoxyribonucleotides. Replication factor C (RFC) binds to elongated primer and it servers as a clamp loader. It also catalyses the assembly of proliferating cell nuclear antigen (PCNA) molecules. The DNA polymerase δ binds to the sliding clamp and elongates the Okazaki fragment to a final length of about 150 to 200 bp. (Fig. 8.9). RNase H and flap endonuclease I (FENI) are involved to remove the RNA primer. The new *okazaki* fragment is elongated and finally sealed in DNA ligase.

GENE TRANSCRIPTION

Transcription is the first stage of gene expression and it involves the synthesis of RNA from a DNA template by RNA polymerase. Gene expression is accomplished by the transfer of genetic information from DNA to RNA molecules and then from RNA to protein molecules. RNA molecules are synthesized by using the base sequence of one strand of DNA as a template in a polymerization reaction that is catalysed by enzymes called DNA-dependent RNA polymerases or simple RNA polymerases. The two complementary DNA strands have different roles in transcription. The strand that serves as template for RNA synthesis is called the template strand. The DNA strand complementary to the template

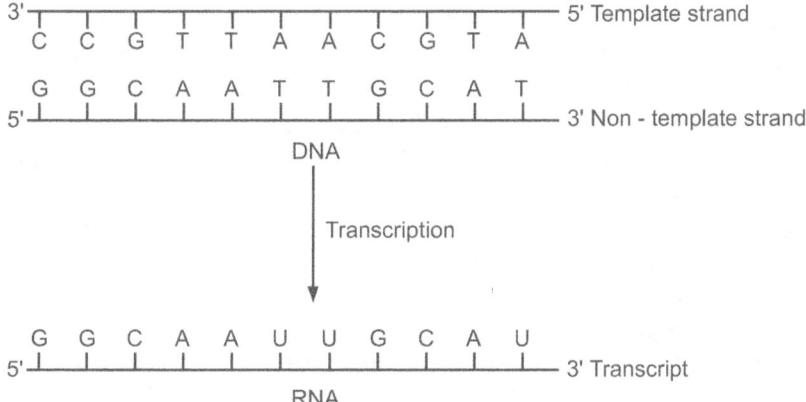

Fig. 8.10: Synthesis RNA from DNA (Transcription)

(non-template or coding strand) is identical in base sequence to the RNA transcribed from the gene, with 'U' in the RNA in place of 'T' in the DNA. RNA is produced using the template strand and the RNA molecule synthesized is a copy of the non-template strand (Fig. 8.10). The RNA molecule synthesized is called a transcript and may subsequently undergo translation to produce a protein. RNA synthesis involves the polymerization of ribonucleotide triphosphates and it occurs in the opposite direction to the template strand.

The entire molecule of DNA is not expressed in transcription. RNAs are synthesized only for some selected regions of DNA. During replication, the entire chromosome is usually copied but transcription is more selective. There exist certain differences in the transcription between prokaryotes and eukaryotes.

Transcription in prokaryotes:

Transcription involves three different stages in prokaryotes such as initiation, elongation and termination. RNA is synthesized by a single RNA polymerase enzyme which contains multiple polypeptide subunits. RNA polymerase of *Escherichia coli* is a complex holoenzyme with five polypeptide subunits (2α, 1β, $1\beta'$, 1σ factor). The sigma (σ) factor may dissociate from the other subunits to form core enzyme (2α, 1β, $1\beta'$).

Initiation: The enzyme RNA polymerase plays a major role in recognition and binding of initiation site. The specific region on the DNA where the enzyme binds is known as promoter region. Promoter region contains specific DNA sequences that acts as points of attachment for the RNA polymerase. In *Escherichia coli,* two sequence elements recognized by the RNA polymerase known as the – 10 sequence and –35 sequence. The – 10 sequence is called Pribnow's box (TATA box), whereas – 35 region is called the recognition site. The Pribnow's box is found as a part of all prokaryotic promoters. It consists of 6 nucleotide basis (TATAAT), located on the left side about 10 bases away from the starting point of transcription (Fig. 8.11). The double helix DNA partially dissociates at Pribnow's box (– 10 box), which is rich in weak A-T bonds to give an open promoter complex. This open complex then allows tight binding of the RNA polymerase with subsequent initiation of RNA synthesis.

Elongation: RNA is synthesized from 5' end to 3' end and (5' $\rightarrow$ 3') antiparallel to the DNA template. Chain elongation occurs by core enzyme that move along the DNA template. The region of template that has been transcribed regains its double helical form behind the bubble and the next region of DNA which is to be transcribed unwinds. The unwound area contains the newly synthesized RNA base-paired with the template DNA strand and extends over 12 to 17 bases. The newly formed RNA transcript consists of a triphosphate group at 5' and free – OH group at 3' end.

Termination: The process of transcription stops by termination signals. There are two types of mechanisms that brings about termination such as rho-independent termination and rho-dependent termination.

The rho-independent termination is brought about by the formation of hairpins of newly synthesized RNA. This occurs due to the presence of palindromes. It synthesises an RNA transcript that becomes folded to form a stem and loop structure of about 20 bases. This step-loop structure causes RNA polymerase to pause a disrupt the RNA-DNA hybrid at 5' end.

Rho-dependent termination requires the Rho protein (factor) encode by rho-gene. It binds to the growing RNA of weakly to DNA, and in the bound state it acts as ATPase and terminates transcription. The termination of transcription involves the release of the transcript and the core enzyme which may then reassociate with the sigma subunit and it starts another round of transcription.

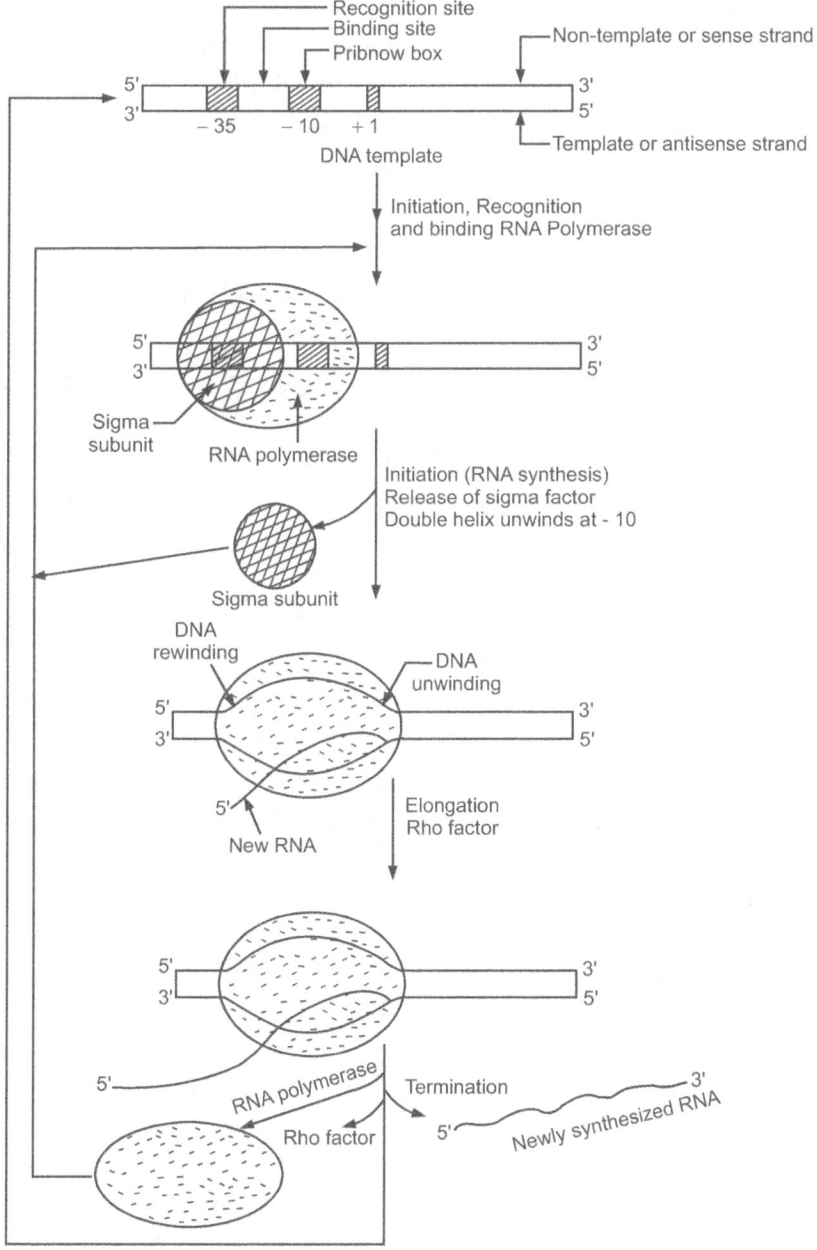

Fig. 8.11: Synthesis of RNA from DNA template (transcription)

Transcription in Eukaryotes:

Transcription is more complicated process in eukaryotes compare to prokaryotes. In eukaryotes, three different RNA polymerases transcribe the genes for the four types of RNAs.

RNA Polymerase I: It is located in the nucleolus. RNA polymerase I enzyme transcribes genes encoding three of the four ribosomal RNAs (18S, 28S and 5.8S). It is responsible for the synthesis of precursors for the large ribosomal RNAs.

RNA Polymerase II: It is found in the nucleoplasm of the nucleus. The main function of this enzyme is synthesis of messenger RNAs (mRNAs) and some small nuclear RNAs (snRNAs). RNA polymerase II can recognize thousands of promoters that vary greatly in sequence.

RNA Polymerase III: It is located in the nucleoplasm. It synthesizes the transfer RNAs (tRNAs), 5S rRNAs and some other small specialised RNAs.

RNA polymerase II is central to eukaryotic gene expression and a huge enzyme with 12 subunits. The process of transcription by Pol II can be classified in the form of phases such as assembly, initiation, elongation and termination.

The core promoter is needed for the transcription machinery to start RNA synthesis at the correct site. The core promoter elements are Inr (initiator) and TATA box (Goldberg – Hogness box). Initiator spans the transcription initiation start site (+1) while the TATA element located at −30 position. Promoters contain various combinations of core promoter elements and promoter proximal elements. Enhancers are also required for the maximal transcription of a gene. It contains a variety of short sequence elements. Activators mainly bind to these elements and with other protein complexes.

RNA polymerase II and general transcription factors (GTFs) are mainly responsible for initiation of transcription. All three eukaryotic RNA polymerases require GTFs in order to initiate transcription. RNA polymerase is attached to the TATA box with the help of a series of transcription factors specific to RNA polymerase II (TFIIA, TFIIB etc). These bind to the DNA around the TATA box and form a platform for binding RNA polymerase II. Transcription factors can bind in a specific order as TFIID binds first followed by TFIIA and TFIIB. The RNA polymerase II then binds followed by TFIIF, E, H and J to produce a functional complex capable of initiating transcription (Fig. 8.12). TFIIH has DNA helicase activity that promotes the unwinding of DNA near the RNA start site and it creates a open complex. TFIIE and TFIIH are released during synthesis of initial 60 to 70 nucleotides of RNA. RNA polymerase II enters in the elongation phase of transcription. Elongation is accompanied by the release of many transcription factors and is enhanced by elongation factors. Transcription is terminated when the RNA transcript is completed. PolII is dephosphorylated and recycled.

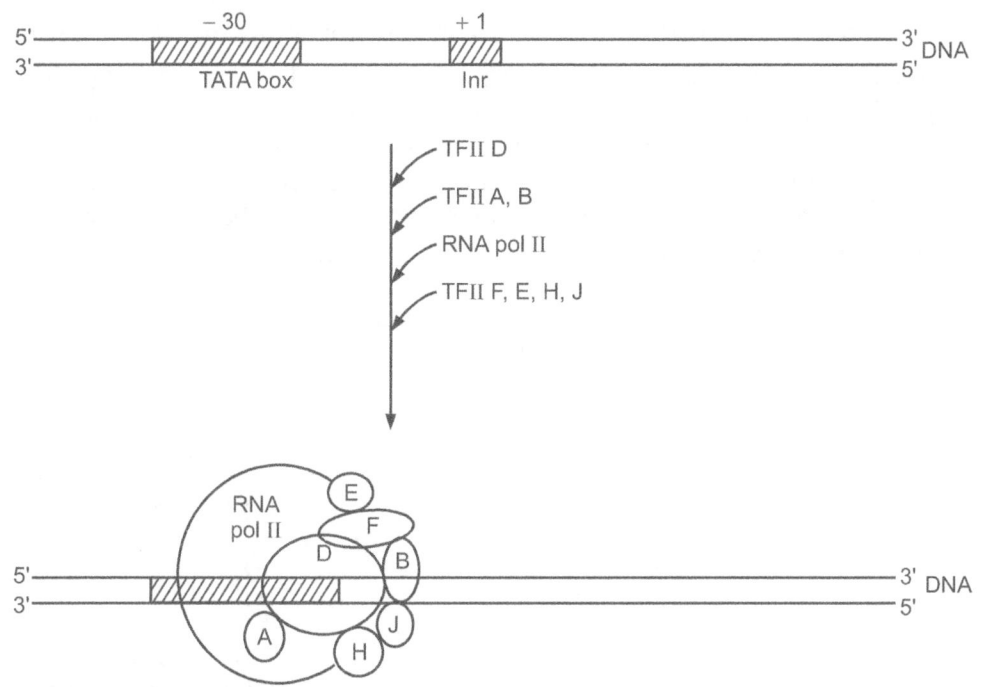

Fig. 8.12: Binding of RNA polymerase II and transcription factors

TRANSLATION (PROTEIN SYNTHESIS)

The biosynthesis of a protein or a polypeptide in a living cell is called as translation. The genetic information stored in DNA is passed to RNA (transcription) and it expressed in the language of proteins (translation). Translation occurs by similar mechanisms of prokaryotes and eukaryotes and it is described in five stages.

1. Activation of amino acids (Aminoacyl tRNA synthetases).
2. Initiation (Binding of a ribosome to mRNA).
3. Elongation (Repeated addition of amino acids).
4. Termination and release (Release of new polypeptide chain).
5. Folding and post-translational processing (polypeptide must fold into three-dimensional conformation and it may undergo enzymatic processing).

Translation requires the use of energy by the cell which is provided by the hydrolysis of GTP and ATP. Guanosine-triphosphate (GTP) is used for ribosome movement and in binding of accessory factors. Adenosine triphosphate (ATP) is used to change tRNAs and in removing secondary structure from mRNA. Protein synthesis requires many components such as amino acids, ribosomes, mRNA, tRNA, protein factors and energy sources (ATP and GTP).

Activation of Amino Acids:

Cytoplasm contains 20 different amino acids and they are activated by a specific activating enzyme known as the aminoacyl synthetase and ATP before the attachment with its specific tRNA. The correct amino acid is attached to the tRNA by a type of enzyme called an aminoacyl-tRNA synthetase (aminoacylation / charging). The process of transfer of activated amino acids to tRNA is called charging of tRNA. The tRNAs are specific to their specific amino acid (e.g. tRNA^{ala} – for alanine). First, the amino acid and ATP bind to the specific aminoacyl – tRNA synthetase enzyme. Enzyme then catalyses a reaction in which the ATP loses two phosphates and is coupled to the amino acid as AMP to form aminoacyl – AMP (Fig. 8.13). The tRNA molecule binds to the enzyme, which transfers the amino acid from the aminoacyl – AMP to the tRNA to form aminoacyl-tRNA. The aminoacyl-tRNA molecule produced is then released from the enzyme.

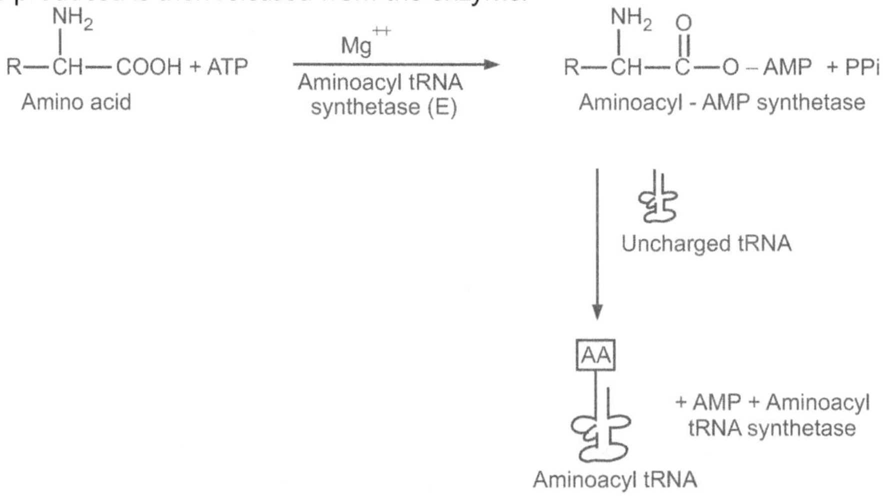

$$\text{R-CH(NH}_2\text{)-COOH + ATP} \xrightarrow[\text{synthetase (E)}]{\text{Mg}^{++} \text{ Aminoacyl tRNA}} \text{R-CH(NH}_2\text{)-C(=O)-O-AMP + PPi}$$

Amino acid → Aminoacyl - AMP synthetase

↓ Uncharged tRNA

↓ + AMP + Aminoacyl tRNA synthetase

Aminoacyl tRNA

Fig. 8.13: Formation of charged tRNA (aminoacyl tRNA)

Initiation:

The first step in translation involves the binding of the small ribosomal subunit to the mRNA and use of specific initiating tRNA molecule. In prokaryotes, tRNA molecule is acylated with the modified amino acid (N-formyl methionine). Both tRNA^{fMet} and tRNA^{Met} recognize the codon AUG but only tRNA^{fMet} is used for initiation. The tRNA^{fMet} molecule is first acylated with methionine and an enzyme adds a formyl group to the amino group of the methionine. In eukaryotes, the initiating tRNA molecule is charged with methionine but formylation does not occur.

The initiation of polypeptide synthesis in prokaryotes requires 30S and 50S ribosomal subunit, mRNA, tRNA^{fMet}, initiation factors (IF-1, IF-2 and IF-3), GTP and magnesium ions. Eucaryotic cells have at least nine initiation factors (eIF2, eIF2B, eIF3, eIF4A, eIF4B, eIF4E, eIF4G, eIF5, eIF6). The initiation factors bind to 30S ribosomal subunit in the presence of GTP to form 30S-IF complex. The 30S-IF complex binds to the region of the mRNA with The AUG initiation codon. Each mRNA at its untranslational region consists of a ribosome binding site for every polypeptide in the form of polycistronic message. This ribosome binding site (5'-AGGAGGA-3') is known as **Shine-Dalgarno** sequence which is important in the binding of mRNA to the 30S-IF complex.

The ribosome has three important binding sites such as aminoacyl-tRNA binding site (A), peptide binding site (P) and exit site (E). The A site receives all the incoming charged tRNA, whereas the P site possesses the previous tRNA with the new polypeptides. The tRNA^{fMet}

directly binds with 'P' site. The E site is the site from which the 'uncharged' tRNAs leave during elongation. Factor IF-1 binds at the A site and prevents tRNA binding at this site during initiation.

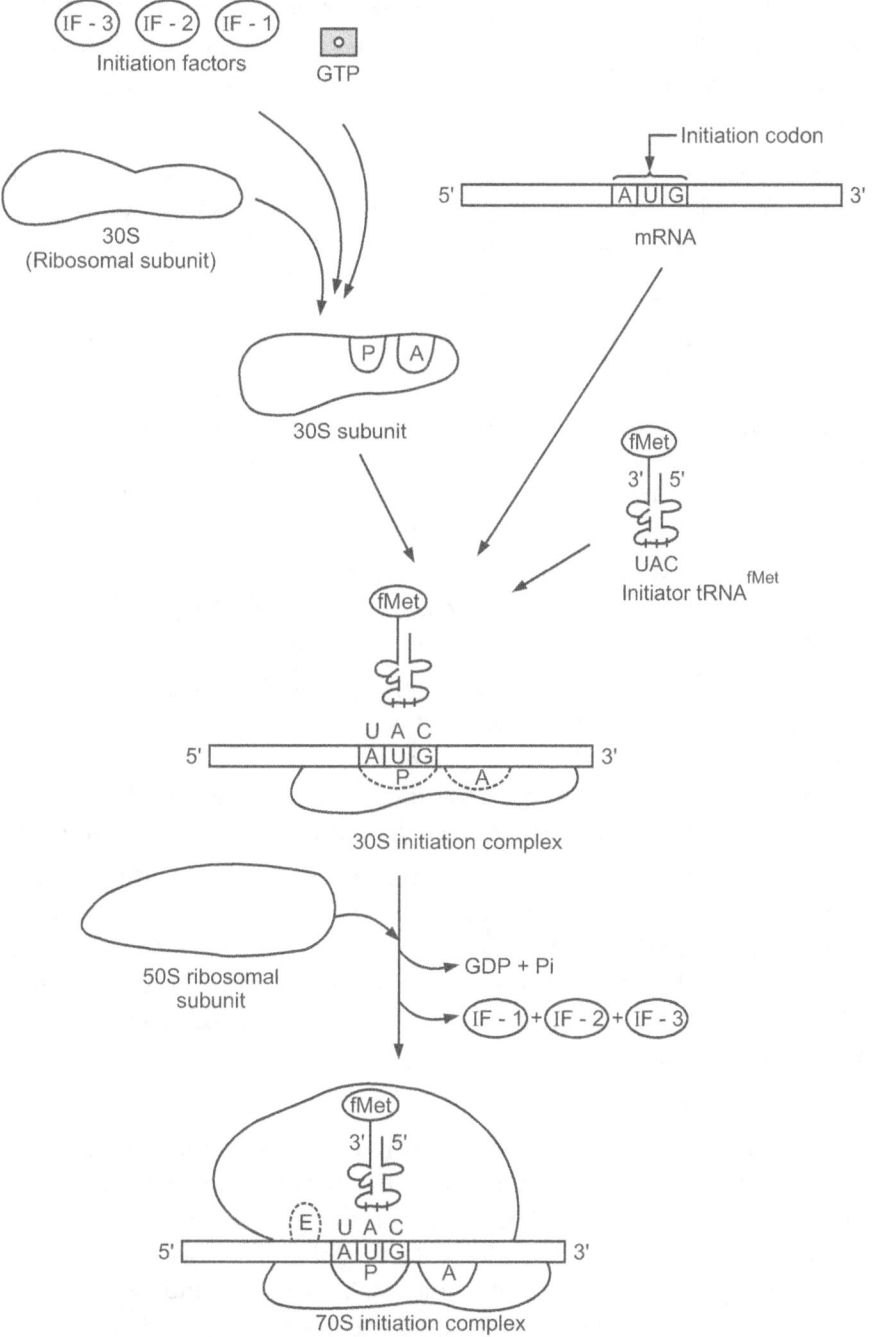

Fig. 8.14: Formation of initiation complex in prokaryotes

The IF-2 which has combined with GTP, permits the initiator tRNA (tRNA^{fMet}) to bind to the 30S ribosomal subunit (Fig. 8.14). A 30S ribosome unit is bound with 50S unit to produce 70S initiation complex. Similarly, in eukaryotes the 40S initiation complex is attached to 60S ribosomal subunit and forms the complete 80S initiation complex. The GTP bond to IF2 is hydrolyzed to GDP and Pi, which are released from the complex. All three initiation factors also depart from the ribosome. The initiation complex is now ready for elongation.

Elongation:

Elongation requires the initiation complex, aminoacyl-tRNAs, GTP and elongation factors. The addition of amino acids to the growing polypeptide chain as per codon on mRNA is called elongation of chain. Elongation of chain occur in three phases.

1. Binding of aminoacyl-tRNA.
2. Peptide bond formation.
3. Translocation.

1. Binding of aminoacyl-tRNA: The ribosome (70S) possess the tRNA^{fMet} in the P-site, whereas the A site is free to receive the next aminoacyl-tRNA according to the codons on mRNA. Aminoacyl-tRNA bind to the protein elongation factor EF-Tu and a molecule of GTP. GTP hydrolysis releases EF-Tu-GDP and EF-Tu is recycled. Second elongation factor (EF-Ts) binds to EF-Tu and displaces the GDP (Fig. 8.15). GTP binds to the EF-Tu-EF-Ts complex to produce EF-Tu-GTP complex by releasing EF-Ts. Aminoacyl-tRNA binds to the EF-Tu-GTP and that complex can bind to the A site in the ribosome.

2. Peptide bond formation: A peptide bond is formed between the two amino acids bounded to their tRNAs to the A and P sites on the ribosome. First, the bond between the amino acid and the tRNA in the P site is breaked and form free fMet and its tRNA. The peptide bond is formed between the free fMet and the Ser attached to the tRNA in the A site (Fig. 8.15). The enzyme peptidyl transferase catalyses the formation of peptide bond.

3. Translocation: The ribosome moves to the next codon of the mRNA (towards 3'-end) after the formation of peptide bond. This process is called translocation. Translocation requires the activity of another protein elongation factor, EF-G (In eukaryotes, eEF-2). An EF-G-GTP complex binds to the ribosome and GTP is hydrolyzed to supplies energy to move mRNA. Translocation of ribosome occurs alongwith displacement of the uncharged tRNA away from the 'P' site.

Termination and Release:

The polypeptide chain is continuously elongated until a termination codon on mRNA reaches to ribosome. The termination of translation is signaled by one of three stop codons such as UAA, UAG and UGA. The ribosome recognize a stop codon with the help of proteins called termination factors or release factors (RF). In prokaryotes, there are three release factors (RF-1, RF-2, RF-3). RF-1 recognizes UAA and UAG and RF-2 recognizes UAA and UGA. The RF-3 activates the RF-1 and RF-2, hence, it is called 'stimulatory(s) factor'. In eukaryotes, there is only one RF protein (eRF-1) which is active with codons UAA, UAG and UGA.

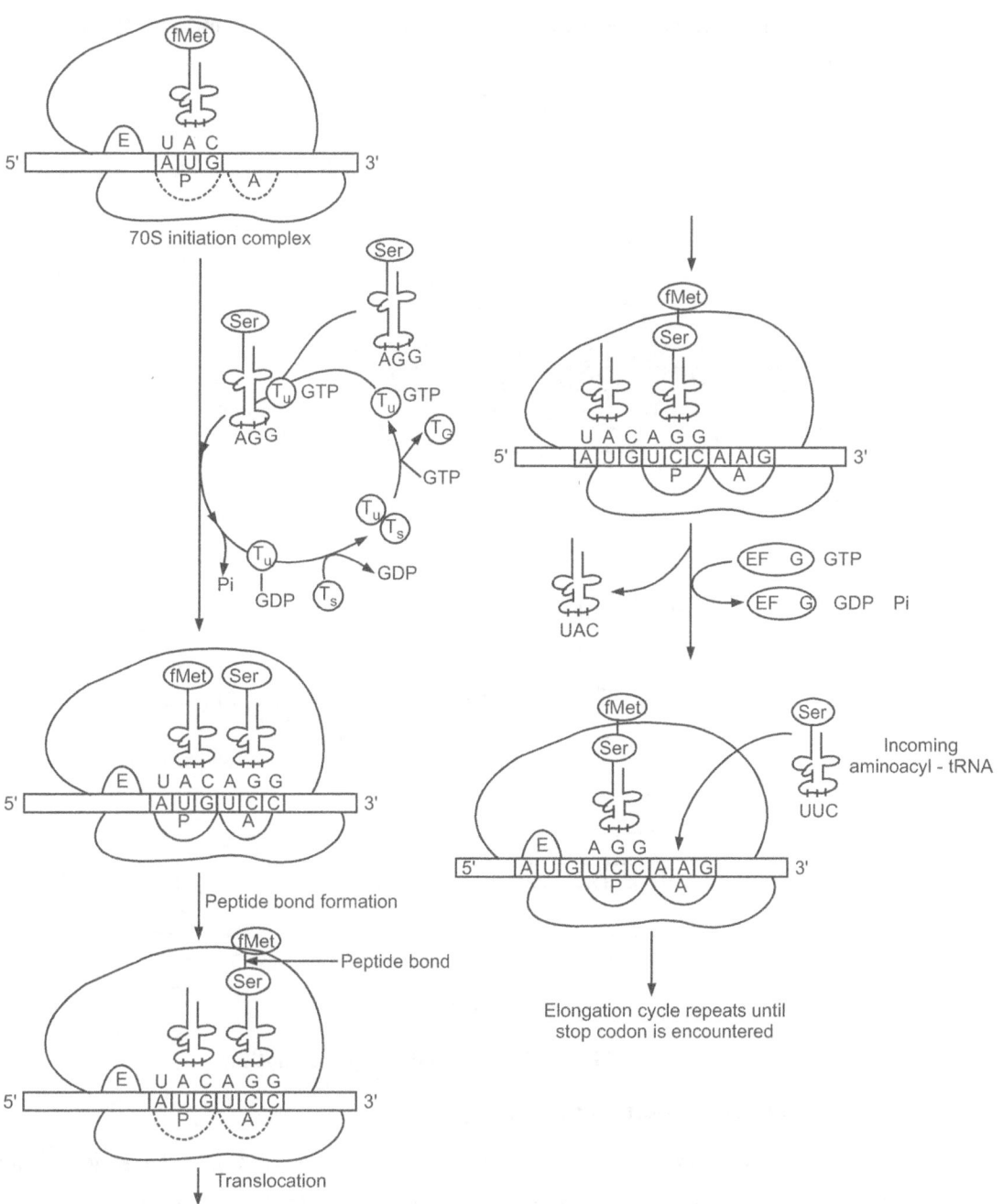

Fig. 8.15: Elongation stages of translation

The specific termination events triggered by the release factors are release of the polypeptide from the tRNA in the P-site of the ribosome, release of the tRNA from the ribosome and the dissociation of the two ribosomal subunits and the RF from the mRNA (Fig. 8.16).

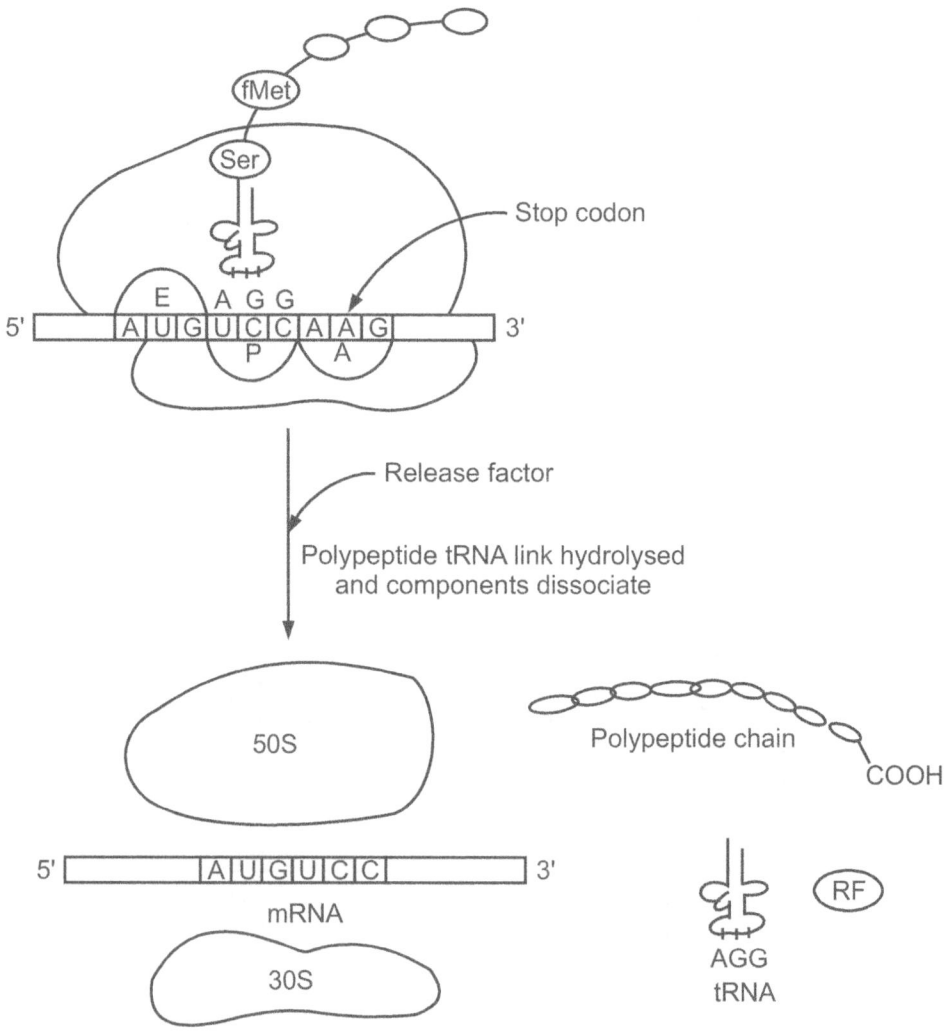

Fig. 8.16: Termination of translation

Folding and post-translation processing:

After release, some of the processing events occur in the polypeptide chain. These modifications include protein folding, trimming by proteolytic degradation, intein splicing and covalent changes which are collectively known as post-translational modifications. Many different chemical modifications of the side chains of amino acids or the amino and carboxyl termini of proteins are found. Modifications may involve addition of small groups such as methylation, phosphorylation, acetylation and hydroxylation. Some modifications may occur by the addition of larger molecular structures such as lipid and oligosaccharides.

QUESTIONS

(A) Short answer questions:
1. Draw the diagram of elongation stages of translation.
2. What is DNA replication?
3. Explain the following:
   (a) DNA polymerase β
   (b) Okazaki pieces
   (c) Initiator tRNA^{fMet}
   (d) Stop codon

(B) Long answer questions:
1. Explain in detail models of DNA replication.
2. Discuss the DNA replication process in eukaryotes.
3. How gene transcription in prokaryotes is different from eukaryotes.
4. Write a note on:
   (a) Meselson-Stahl experiment
   (b) Protein synthesis.

(C) Multiple choice questions:
1. Meselson-Stahl experiment _____ is used as density gradient.
   (a) CsCl
   (b) CaCl
   (c) NaCl
   (d) KCl
2. In RNA synthesis, termination is caused by _____ factor.
   (a) Delta
   (b) Polymerase
   (c) Penta
   (d) Rho
3. In DNA replication, two strands are separated by enzyme called _____.
   (a) Helicases
   (b) RNA polymerases
   (c) DNA ligase
   (d) Endonuclease
4. Synthesis of RNA from DNA template is known as _____
   (a) Replication
   (b) Transcription
   (c) Transformation
   (d) Translation

5. Replication of eukaryotic DNA is initiated by many sites by the formation of _____
   - (a) Bubbles
   - (b) Circles
   - (c) Strands
   - (d) Splits

(D) Match the following:

A	B
(a) Synthesis of RNA from DNA	(i) Nucleases
(b) DNA degradation	(ii) Ribonucleases
(c) RNA degradation	(iii) DNA polymerases
(d) DNA synthesis	(iv) DNA-dependent RNA polymerase

(E) Fill in the blanks:

1. Amino acids are activated for protein synthesis through a reaction catalyzed by _____ synthetase.
2. The synthesis of DNA using DNA as a template is called _____.

CHAPTER 9
GENETIC RECOMBINATION (GENE TRANSFER)

CONTENTS

    INTRODUCTION
    CONJUGATION
    TRANSDUCTION
        Generalised transduction
        Specialised transduction
    TRANSFORMATION
    PROTOPLAST FUSION
    PLASMID (Ti AND Ri) MEDIATED GENE TRANSFER

INTRODUCTION

Genetic recombination is the formation of a new genotype by exchange of genetic material between two different chromosomes which have similar genes at corresponding sites (homologous chromosomes).

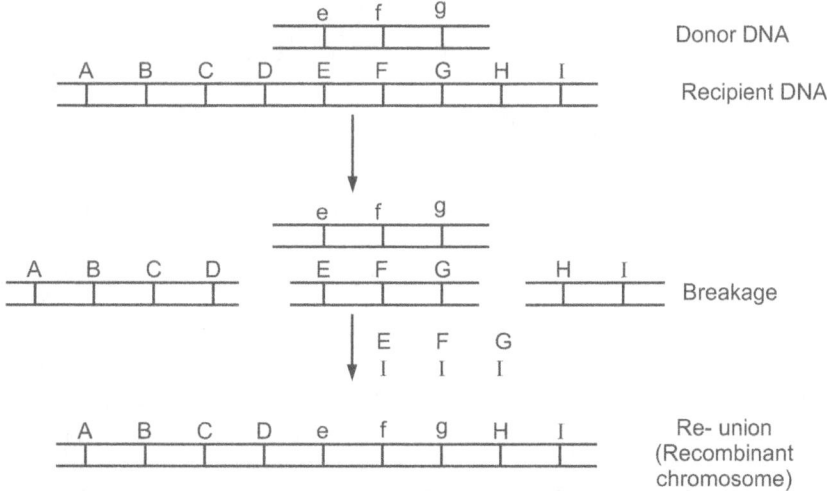

Fig. 9.1: Breakage and re-union model of bacterial recombination

In bacterial recombination, usually only a portion of the chromosome from the donor cell (male) is transferred to the recipient cell (female). The recipient cell thus forms a merozygote and recombination can take place. The general recombination mechanism is shown in Fig. 9.1. Bacterial recombination may occur by direct or indirect gene transfer method or sexual or asexual process. Genetic recombination can occur by different types of gene transfer techniques i.e. conjugation, transduction, transformation, protoplast fusion etc.

CONJUGATION

Bacterial conjugation was first reported by **Joshua Lederberg** and **Edward Tatum** (1946) who proved the process of transfer of genetic material by cell to cell contact. **Lederberg** and **Tatum** produced two auxotrophic strains (58-161 and W677) of *Escherichia coli* K12 by mutation. The strain 58-16 was found unable to synthesize, amino acid methionine and vitamin biotin and hence, genotype of this strain is represented as: thr^+ len^+ $meth^-$ bio^-. The strain W677 cannot produce amino acids like threonine and leucine.

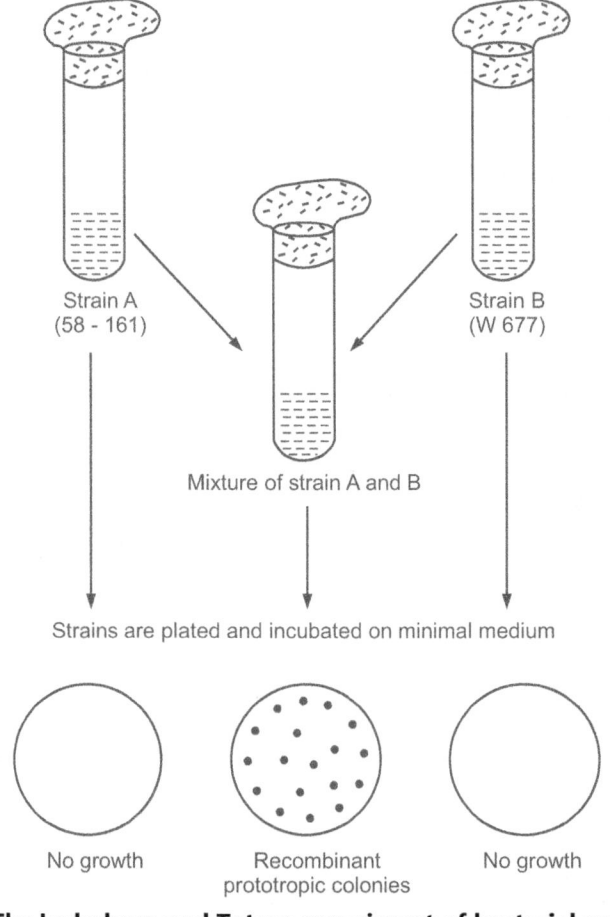

Fig. 9.2: The Lederberg and Tatum experiment of bacterial conjugation

The genotype of this strain (W677) is $meth^+$ bio^+ $thr-$ len^-. These mutant strains cannot grow on the minimal medium. These mutant strains are called the auxotrophic and the wild strain is called as prototroph (Fig. 9.2). Mixing of two auxotrophs and plating on minimal medium (absence of growth factors) produce the prototroph (i.e. thr^+ len^+ $meth^+$ bio^+). These prototroph cells have the capacity to synthesize all four growth factors. This experiment indicates that recombination was brought by direct cell contact or process of conjugation.

The evidence for cell-to-cell contact was provided by **Bernard Davis** (1950) by using U-shaped tube (Fig. 9.3). Two separate pieces of curved glass tubes were prepared and fused at the base to form a U-shape with a sintered glass filter which permitted the passage of the nutrient medium. The filter did not allow bacteria to pass from both the ends of U tube. Nutrient medium was inoculated with different auxotrophic strain of *Escherichia coli*. The culture medium was made to pass through the filter from one arm to the other by altering pressure. The strains from both the arms of U-tube were plated on minimal medium and incubated for growth. The bacterial colonies or prototrophs did not appear on medium which indicates the contact between the two auxotrophs cells was essential for the formation of recombinant prototrophs.

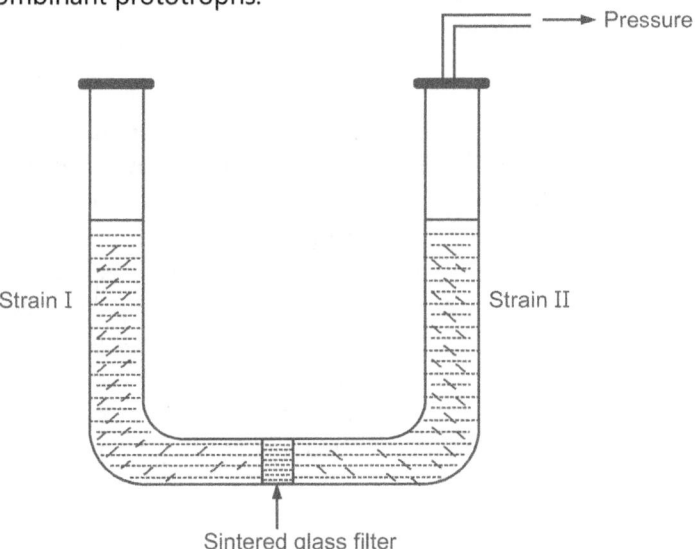

Fig. 9.3: Bernard Davis U-tube experiment

Conjugation is a natural process found in certain bacterial species involves the active passage of genetic material from one cell to another cell by means of the sex pili. Male cells contain in a small circular piece of DNA (plasmid), which is in the cytoplasm called the sex factor of F-factor (fertility factor). These donor cells are referred as F^+ cells and recipient cells are referred as F^- cells (absence of fertility factor). However, in $F^+ \times F^-$ crosses, the male replicates its sex factor and one copy is transferred to the female recipient. The F^- cells is converted to an F^+ cell and it itself acts as donor cell (Fig. 9.4). Therefore, as long as the cell grow, the conjugation process can continue in an infectious way with repeated transfer for the sex factor. The presence of F-factor in a bacterial cell determines its autonomous replication and sex pili formation. The F-factor remains in two stages as plasmid and as episome. The F-plasmid replicates independently but sometimes it is integrated with the normal chromosome of the bacterium. Therefore, it is referred as episome. The bacterial conjugation process is commonly observed in *Escherichia, Shigella, Pseudomonas* and *Vibrio* species.

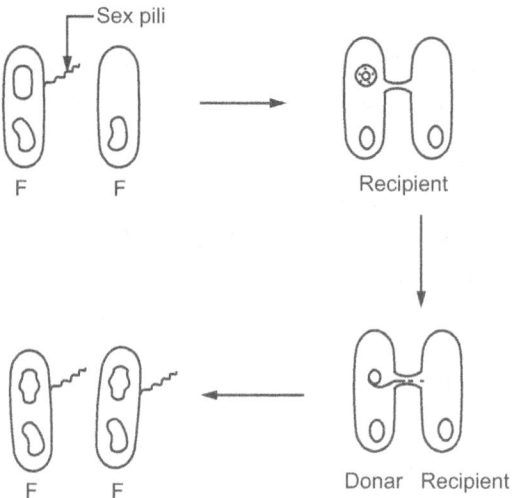

Fig. 9.4: Process of conjugation

The chromosomes of F^+ cell integrates with F-plasmid then these cells are called high frequency recombination (Hfr) cells. High frequency recombination cells arise from F^+ cells in which F-factor becomes integrated into the bacterial chromosme (Fig. 9.5). They differ from F^+ cells in that the F-factor of the Hfr is rarely transferred during recombination. Thus, in Hfr × F^- cross, the frequency of recombination is high and the transfer of F-factor is low and in $F^+ \times F^-$ cross, the frequency of recombination is low and the transfer of F-factor is high. When F-factor is excised from the chromosome of an Hfr strain with some chromosomal genes then these cells are called F' cells. The plasmid in an F' cells is self-replicating. The excision of an F' plasmid from an Hfr strain occurs about once for every 10 cells divisions.

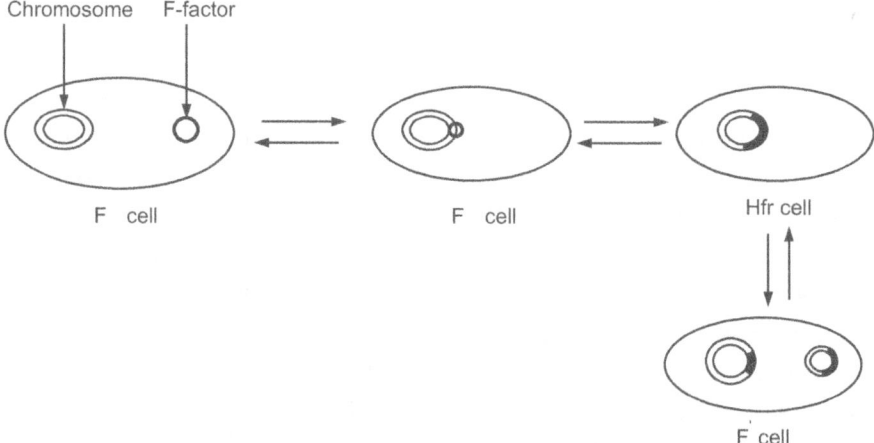

Fig. 9.5: Formation of high frequency recombination (Hfr) and F' cell

TRANSDUCTION

The transfer of genetic material from one cell to another by a bacteriophage is called transduction. Bacterial genes may be transferred from strain to strain using bacteriophages as vectors. This genetic transfer technique was discovered by **Norman Zinder** and **Joshua Lederberg** (1952) while searching for sexual conjugation in *Salmonella* species. They mixed auxotrophic mutants together and isolated prototrophic recombinant colonies from selective nutritional media by using **Davis** U-tube experiment (Refer Fig. 9.3). Auxotrophic strains were added in each arm of U-tube and separated by a microporous sintered glass filter. The prototrophs were found in one arm of the tube that indicated some phenomenon other than conjugation was involved. It was subsequently observed that the active component was a bacteriophage which was carried by one of the strains in the prophage condition. Some bacterial cells have the ability to carry phage DNA within their own DNA and such cells are called as lysogenic bacteria. In such bacteria, the prophage, under certain conditions multiplies and destroys the host cell with the release of a number of phage particles. These phages can infect other bacteria and carry the bacterial DNA to the recipient cells. Such phages are called as 'transducing phages'. These are two fundamentally different transduction processes such as generalized (unrestricted) transduction and specialized (restricted) transduction.

Generalised or unrestricted transduction

Transduction mediated by virulent phages is called generalized transduction because it transfers any portion of the bacterial chromosome from one cell to another. Virulent phages infect bacteria by adhering to the surface of the host cell and inject the DNA into it. The phage DNA directs the cell to make phage components as DNA and protein. These phage components assemble into mature phage particles that are released from the cell after cell lysis. These particles may subsequently infect other susceptible cells, completing the lytic cycle (Fig. 9.6).

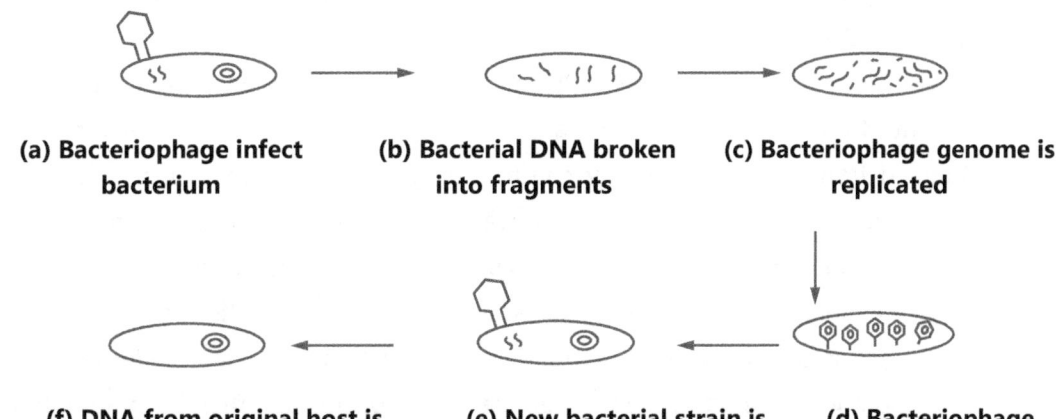

(a) Bacteriophage infect bacterium

(b) Bacterial DNA broken into fragments

(c) Bacteriophage genome is replicated

(f) DNA from original host is inserted into genome of its new host

(e) New bacterial strain is infected by bacteriophage

(d) Bacteriophage particles are formed

Fig. 9.6: Process of generalised transduction (lytic cycle)

Specialised or restricted transduction:

Some temperate phages can transfer only a few restricted genes of the bacterial chromosome to the receipient bacterial cell. This transfer of bacterial genes adjacent to prophage only to the recipient chromosome is called specialized transduction.

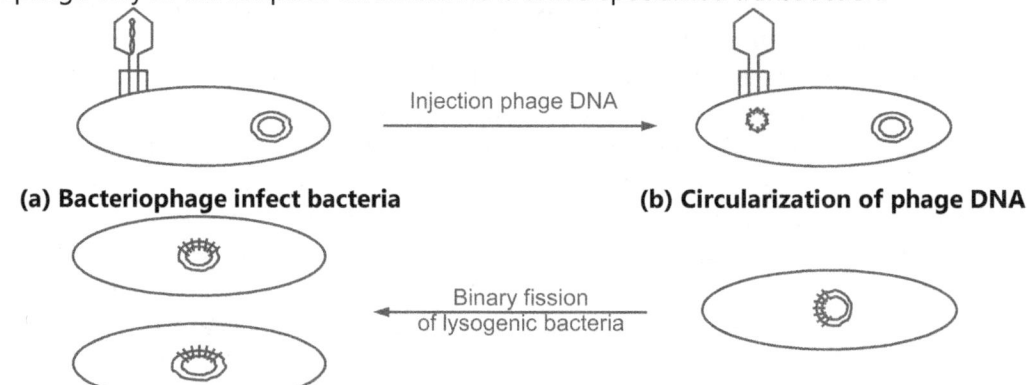

(a) Bacteriophage infect bacteria   (b) Circularization of phage DNA

(d) New bacteria with prophage   (c) Integration of phage DNA with host chromosome

Fig. 9.7: Process of specialized transduction (lysogeny)

Morse and **Lederberg** (1956) found that in the lambda (λ) phage the transducing activity was restricted to the galactose locus. Temperate phages have two types of life cycles such as lytic cycle and lysogenic cycle. When a phage genome is introduced in the bacterial cell, it becomes integrated with bacterial chromosome as prophage. The prophage behaves like a segment of the host chromosome and replicates synchronously in bacterial cell. This is called lysogeny (Fig. 9.7). Under certain conditions (e.g. UV light or chemicals), the prophages enter the lytic cycle and kill the hosts.

TRANSFORMATION

Transformation is the process whereby cell free or naked DNA containing a limited amount of genetic information is transferred from one bacterial cell to another. The DNA is obtained from the donor cell by natural cell lysis or by chemical extraction. Donor DNA passes into recipient through the cell wall and cell membrane of the recipient cell. DNA having molecular weight from 3,00,000 to 8 million daltons is most suitable for transformation. Once DNA enters into a cell, it integrates into chromosome of recipient cell. One strand is degraded by deoxyribonucleases while other strand undergoes base pairing with a homologous part of the recipient cell chromosome and then becomes integrated into the recipient DNA (Fig. 9.8).

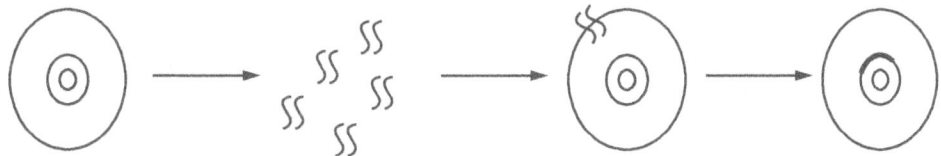

(a) Donor cell   (b) Donor DNA fragments   (c) Binding of donor DNA fragments to recipient cell   (d) Integration of single strand of donor DNA (Transformed cell)

Fig. 9.8: Bacterial transformation

Bacterial transformation was first discovered by **F. Griffith** (1928) during his investigations of pneumococcal infections in mice. He had found that in *Streptococcus pneumonia*, virulence to mice was related to the presence of a capsular material and the absence of capsule made the bacteria avirulent. The wild type strain is surrounded by a polysaccharide capsule and forms a colony with a smooth (s) surface. This strain is pathogenic (virulent) and causes severe infection of pneumonia. A mutant strain does not have the capsule and it forms a colony with a rough (R) surface. The mutant (R) strain is non-pathogenic (avirulent). Griffith's experiments involved the infection of mice with heat killed and living preparations from two strains of *Streptococcus pneumoniae*. Injection of avirulent mutant 'R' bacteria or heat killed virulent 'S' bacteria did not cause any harm to mice. Injection of a mixture of the two bacterial types [R and S (heat-killed)] killed some mice and live, virulent 'S' bacteria recovered from these animals (Fig. 9.9). The strain 'R' type acquired the ability to produce capsules and become virulent. This induction in change of 'R' strain was called transformation. **Griffith** thought that the transferring agent was a protein.

Avery, **Macleod** and **McCarty** (1944) showed that the substance responsible for transformation was DNA. Their studies with purified DNA from the smooth (S) cells and its ability to transform rough cells in a test tube explained the observations made by **Griffith**. From this experiment, it was concluded that the heat killed capsulated cells carried the information for the synthesis of the capsule which was transferred to the live non-capsulated cells. Transformation has now been demonstrated in *Streptococcus, Bacillus, Escherichia, Neisseria, Hemophilus, Salmonella, Rhizobium, Xanthomonas, Staphylococcus* and *Streptomyces*. It is now possible to introduce intact plasmids by artificial transformation into bacteria, yeast, plants and animals. The development of artificial transformation is important for recombinant DNA technology.

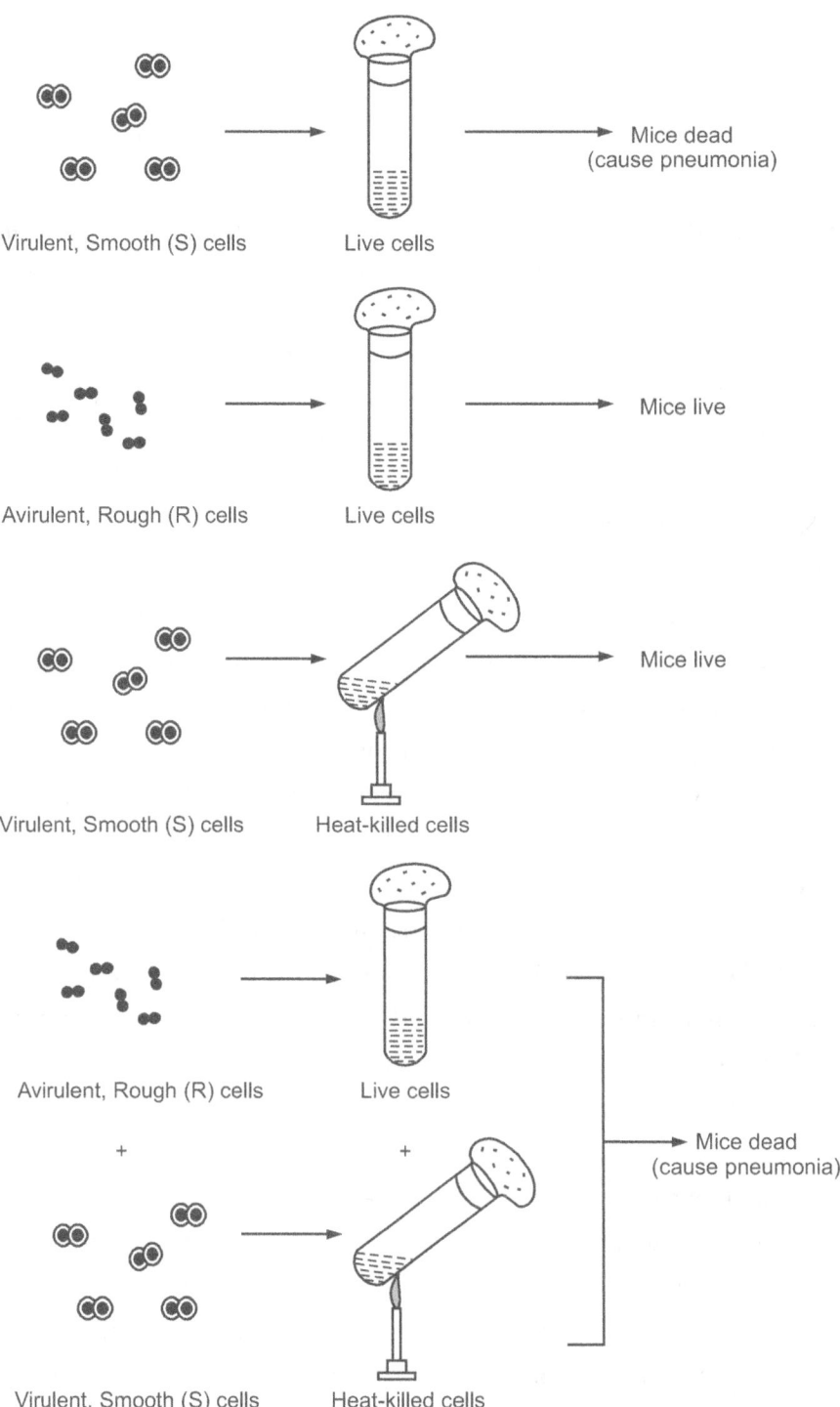

Fig. 9.9: Griffith's transformation experiment with *Streptococcus pneumonia*

PROTOPLAST FUSION

Protoplast fusion can take place by the joining the cell membrane and generation of cytoplasmic bridges. In this technique, two genetically distinct strains are mixed with the use of lyzozyme and then fused in the presence of polyethylene glycol. The fused protoplast cells are grown into vegetative cells. Recombinant *Bacillus megaterium* is obtained by this method of protoplast fusion. Fusion can be obtained between members of different kingdoms as well as unrelated cells. This process is common among the bacteria which do not possess a defined cell wall structure. Gene transfer by protoplast fusion is also called as genetic transfusion. (For details, please refer Chapter 17).

PLASMID (Ti AND Ri) MEDIATED GENE TRANSFER

Many plants have received attention for DNA cloning and expression of foreign DNA in plant cells. Major work is done on soil-borne bacteria such as *Agrobacterium tumefaciens* causing crown gall disease and *Agrobacteirum rhizogenes* causing hairy root disease on the stems of numerous plants. *Agrobacterium* plasmids (Ti and Ri) have been used for introduction of genes of desirable traits into plants. Explants are commonly used for gene transfer. These explants are co-cultured with *Agrobacterium* containing vector with modified foreign gene. The transformed colonies are selected and used for regeneration of whole plant. These plants are tested for the transfer of gene with the help of screenable markers (reporter genes). The reporter genes are also transferred along with desired genes.

Agrobacterium tumefaciens contains plasmid which induces tumour in plants (For detail, please refer Chapter 18), these plasmid is called as Ti-plasmid (180 to 250 Kb). Ti-plasmid contains T-DNA region of about 23 to 25 Kb which is transferred into plant cells. *Agrobacterium tumefaciens* mainly present in soil and cause infection to dicotyledonous plants. Bacterial species secrete lipopolysaccharide which help in attachment with polygalacturonic acid fractions of plant cell wall. Phenolic compound (acetosyringone) is secreted from the wounded cells walls of plants which induces the vir genes of Ti-plasmids. Vir genes encode an enzyme which nick the double stranded T-DNA on the same strand at two points. It produces single stranded DNA molecules and are carried into plant cells. A desired DNA fragment can be cloned in the region of Ti plasmid which will introduce the DNA fragment into plant genome. *Agrobacterium rhizogenes* causes formation of adventitious roots and this rhizogenicity has been correlated with the presence of a large plasmid (Ri-plasmid). Plasmid of this species also contains a T-DNA which causes the development of hairy roots. Ri-plasmid of *Agrobacterium rhizogenes* is useful for production of secondary root systems for ability to resist anoxia from flooding of the soil and better anchorage of plants.

QUESTIONS

(A) Short answer questions:
1. Define the terms:
   (a) Conjugation
   (b) Specialised transduction
2. Explain in short Griffith's experiment for bacterial transformation.

(B) Long answer questions:
1. What is bacterial recombination? Explain the different techniques used for gene transfer?
2. Write a note on:
   (a) Protoplast fusion
   (b) Davis U-tube experiment.

(C) Multiple choice questions:
1. The process in which temperate virus can transfer specific bacterial genes that are located near the viral integration site is called _____
   (a) Generalised transduction
   (b) Specialised transduction
   (c) Conjugation
   (d) Transformation
2. Drug resistance in tuberculosis is due to _____
   (a) Transformation
   (b) Transduction
   (c) Conjugation
   (d) Mutation
3. The transfer of foreign gene into another cell is done by the following method _____
   (a) Transduction
   (b) Microinjection
   (c) Transformation
   (d) All of the above
4. The highest rate of conjugation and recombination is associated with the _____
   (a) F-plasmid
   (b) R-plasmid
   (c) C-Plasmid
   (d) M-plasmid

(D) Match the following:

A	B
(a) Somatic cell hybridization	(i) Transformation
(b) Griffith experiment	(ii) Transduction
(c) Lytic cycle	(iii) Conjugation
(d) Hfr and F cell	(iv) Protoplast fusion

(E) Fill in the blanks:
1. The process of transfer of genetic information from one cell to another by cell to cell contact is called _____.
2. The process is which a bacterial virus integrates into the host genome is called _____.
3. The vehicle used to carry a gene for cloning is called _____.
4. The viral DNA does not replicate but is integrated into the host genome and is known as _____.

■■■

CHAPTER 10

RECOMBINANT DNA TECHNOLOGY
(GENE CLONING)

CONTENTS
- INTRODUCTION
- ENZYMES ACTING ON DNA
  - Restriction enzymes, S1 nuclease, alkaline phosphatase
  - DNA polymerase, reverse transcriptase, DNA ligase
- INSERTION OF TARGET DNA INTO VECTOR
- CLONING VECTORS
  - Plasmid vectors (pBR 322 plasmid), bacteriophase vectors,
  - Cosmid vectors, shuttle vector, yeast vector, expression vector
- TRANSFORMATION AND GROWTH OF CELLS
- SELECTION OF RECOMBINANT CLONES

INTRODUCTION

The deliberate modification in genetic material of an organism by changing the nucleic acid directly is called gene manipulation or genetic engineering or gene cloning and is accomplished by several methods which are collectively known as rDNA (recombinant DNA) technology. DNA cloning is an important technique that allows specific DNA sequences to be separated from other sequences and copied so that they can be obtained in large amounts permitting detailed analysis. DNA cloning is used to isolate new genes allowing them to be investigated and characterized. In 1997, world's first mammalian clone (Dolly) was developed from a non-reproductive cell of an adult animal through cloning by nuclear transplantation.

The various strategies outlined for gene cloning along with the basic steps are discussed as follows:

- Isolation of target DNA or DNA fragment.
- Insertion of target DNA into suitable vector.
- Cloning vectors.
- Isolation and identification of recombinant genes.

The DNA fragments to be cloned are called foreign DNA or passenger DNA or DNA insert. The desired DNA inserts can be obtained from genomic library, cDNA libraries, chemical synthesis and amplification through PCR (polymerase chain reaction). All these processes are possible only due to enzymes such as restriction endonucleases, S1 nuclease, alkaline phosphatase, DNA polymerase, ligase, reverse transcriptase etc.

ENZYME'S ACTING ON DNA

Genetic engineering is based on different types of enzymes. Some enzymes used in gene cloning are given in Table 10.1.

Table 10.1: Enzymes used in DNA cloning

Enzyme	Function
Restriction enzyme	Cuts both strands of dsDNA within a symmetrical recognition site resulting in blunt or sticky ends.
Alkaline phosphatase	Removes terminal phosphates (PO_4) from either the 5' or 3' end (or both).
Reverse transcriptase	Synthesize of DNA copy of an RNA molecule.
S1 Nuclease	Cleaves a strand opposite to a nick on the complementary strand.
DNA polymerase I	Fills gaps in duplexes by stepwise addition of nucleotides to 3' ends.
Exo nuclease III	It cleaves from the end of linear DNA and digest dsDNA from 3' end.
Terminal transferase	Adds homopolymer tails to the 3'–OH ends of a DNA strand.
Polynucleotide kinase	Adds a phosphate to the 5'–OH end of dsDNA or ssDNA or RNA.
Bacteriophage λ exonuclease	Removes nucleotide from the 5' end of a duplex to expose single-stranded 3' ends.
Taq polymerase	DNA polymerase isolated from *Thermus aquaticus* which operates at 72°C (in PCR) and stable above 90°C.
DNA ligase	It joins two DNA molecules or fragments.

Restriction enzymes:

The ability to join DNA molecules together for cloning is dependent on the type of enzymes occur in bacteria. These restriction enzymes are called restriction endonucleases or molecular scissors. Restriction endonucleases recognize specific sequences in the incoming DNA and cleave the DNA into fragments.

The existence of these enzymes was first postulated by **Werner Arber** in the early 1960s while studying bacterial viruses. He found that when virus DNA entered in the bacteria, it was cut into small pieces. **Arber** also proposed that the restriction enzymes act at specific sites on the viral DNA. **Hamilton Smith** and his colleagues (1970) isolated the first restriction enzyme (*Hind* III) from *Haemophilus influenzae*. This enzyme recognizes a particular target sequence in a duplex DNA molecule and breaks the polynucleotide chain.

The restricton enzymes name is designated by a three letter abbreviation for the host organism (e.g. *Escherichia coli* – *Eco*). A strain or type identified is written as subscript (e.g. *Eschierichia* coli strain K – *Eco* K). Roman numerals are used to indicate the different restriction – modification systems in a strain, when more than one enzyme is obtained from the same organism (e.g. *Haemophilus influenzae*, serotype d, enzyme III – *Hind* III). Some commonly used restriction enzymes are given in Table 10.2. Arrows indicate in the table are the recognition sites.

There are three distinct types of restriction endonucleases: Type I, Type II and Type III. These enzymes are differentiated by their mode of action. Type I restriction endonucleases cleave DNA at random sites that can be more than 1000 base pairs (bp) from the recognition sequences. This type of enzymes are most complex and not useful in gene cloning as their cleavage sites are non-specific e.g. *Eco* K, *Eco* B, etc. Type (II) restriction endonucleases enzymes cut within the recognition sequence and are used for gene cloning studies giving rise to discrete DNA fragments of defined length and sequence. The first type (II) enzyme to be isolated was *Hind* III by **Hamilton Smith** in 1970. They are most stable enzymes that require Mg^{++} as cofactor. The recognition sequences are usually 4 to 6 bp long and palindromic. Type (II) restriction endonucleases are used for restriction mapping and gene cloning. Type (III) restriction endonucleases are intermediate between the type (I) and type (II) enzymes. They cleave to DNA about 25 bp from the recognition sequence e.g. *Eco* P1, *Eco* P15 etc. Type (I) and type (III) restriction enzymes are not used in gene cloning.

Type (II) enzymes are the most important and they cut DNA molecules at specific sequences usually 4 to 8 bases. The sequences recognized are palindromes. In a palindrome, the base sequence in the second half of a DNA strand is the mirror image of the sequence in its first half (Fig. 10.1 a). In a palindrome with rotational symmetry, the base sequence in the first half of one strand of the DNA double helix is the mirror image of the second half of its complementary strand [Fig. 10.1 (b)]. Some restriction enzymes make staggered cuts on the two DNA strands, leaving two to four nucleotides of one strand unpaired at each resulting end. These unpaired strands are called as cohesive ends or sticky ends [Fig. 10.2 (a)].

Table 10.2: Source and cleavage sites of restriction enzyme

Restriction endonuclease	Source	Cleavage sites
Hind III	*Haemophilus influenzae* – d	↓ 5' – AAGCTT – 3' 3' – TTCGAA – 5' ↑
Eco RI	*Escherichia coli* RY 13	↓ 5' – GAATTC – 3' 3' – CTTAAG – 5' ↑
Hpa I	*Haemophilus parainfluenzae*	↓ 5' – GTTAAC – 3' 3' – CAATTG – 5' ↑
Kpn I	*Klebsiella pneumoniae*	↓ 5' – GGTACC – 3' 3' – CCATGG – 5' ↑
Bam HI	*Bacillus amyloliquefaciens* H	↓ 5' – GGATCC – 3' 3' – CCTAGG – 5' ↑
Bgl II	*Bacillus globiggi*	↓ 5' – AGATCT – 3' 3' – TCTAGA – 5' ↑
Sal I	*Streptomyces albus* G	↓ 5' – GTCGAC – 3' 3' – CAGCTG – 5' ↑
Sau 3AI	*Staphylococcus aureus* 3AI	↓ 5' – GATC – 3' 3' – CTAG – 5' ↑
Pst I	*Providencia stuartii*	↓ 5' – CTGCAG – 3' 3' – GACGTC – 5' ↑
Nla III	*Neisseria lactamica*	↓ 5' – CATG – 3' 3' – GTAC – 5' ↑
Taq I	*Thermus aquaticus* YTI	↓ 5' – TCGA – 3' 3' – AGCT – 5' ↑

Certain type (II) restriction enzymes cleave both strands of DNA at the same base pairs but in the centre of recognition sequence. These DNA fragments are called flush ends or blunt ends [Fig. 10.2 (b)].

```
5' – GAA ↑ AAG – 3'              5' – GAA  |  TTC – 3'
3' – CTT  |  TTC – 5'             3' – CTT  ↓  AAG – 5'
```

(a) Sequence in a DNA double helix (b) Palindrome with rotational symmetry

Fig. 10.1: A palindrome sequence (the arrow represents the axis of symmetry)

```
         ↓
5' – GAATTC – 3'     Eco RI        5' – G          + AATTC – 3'
3' – CTTAAG – 5'     ⇌              3' – CTTAA              G – 5'
         ↑           Ligation                      Sticky ends
```

(a) Cohesive or sticky ends

```
         ↓
5' – GGCC – 3'       Cleavage      5' – GG    +    CC – 3'
3' – CCGG – 5'       ⇌              3' – CC         GG – 5'
         ↑           Ligation                      Blunt ends
```

(b) Flush or blunt ends

Fig. 10.2: Cohesive and flush ends of DNA fragments

S1 Nuclease:

S1 nuclease degrades the single stranded DNA or single strand protrusion of double stranded DNA with cohesive ends. By the action of S1 nuclease, cohesive ends are converted into blunt ends [Fig. 10.3 (a)]. *Bal* 31 nuclease is very specific single stranded endodeoxyribonuclease. It degrades both 3' and 5' strands of DNA molecule and shortens the fragments. These fragments possess flush ends at both the termini. [Fig. 10.3 (b)].

```
5' – AG – 3'          S1 nuclease        5' – AG – 3'
3' –TCTTAA – 5'       ⟶                  3' – TC – 5'
```

(a) Formation of blunt ends by action of S1 nuclease

```
5' – GGAATT – 3'      Bal 31 exonuclease     5' – GGAA – 3'
3' –CCTTAA – 5'       ⟶                      3' – CCTT – 5'
```

(b) Effect of *Bal* 31 exonuclease on DNA molecule

Fig. 10.3: Action of nuclease

Alkaline phosphatase:

Sometimes cohesive ends of plasmids, instead of joining with foreign DNA join the cohesive end of the same DNA molecules. This problem is overcomed by using alkaline phosphatase. Broken plasmids are treated with alkaline phosphatase to digests the terminal 5' phosphonyl group. The fragments of the foreign DNA to be cloned are not treated with this enzyme, hence, the 5' end of foreign DNA fragment can join to 3' end of the plasmid.

The recombinant DNA has a nick with 3' and 5' hydroxyl ends. Ligase can joint both the ends of hybrid DNA if the 5' end is phosphorylated. Ligase and alkaline phosphatase enzymes are used to prevent recircularization of the vector and increase the frequency of production of recombinant DNA.

$$5' - GG_{OH} - 3' \quad \xrightarrow{\text{Alkaline phosphatase}} \quad 5' - GG - 3'$$
$$3' - CCAATTA_P - 5' \quad \quad \quad \quad \quad \quad 3' - CCAATTA_{OH} - 5'$$

DNA polymerase:

The DNA polymerase was investigated by **A. Kornberg** and coworkers (1956) is *Escherichia coli*. Polymerase enzymes are classified as DNA polymerase I, II and III (DNA pol I, II and III). DNA polymerase enzymes polymerizes the DNA synthesis on DNA template and also catalyses a 5' → 3' and 3' → 5' exonucleolytic degradation of DNA. This enzyme is called replicase when it replicates the DNA molecules and is inherited by daughter cells. It requires the four deoxyribonucleotide triphosphates (dATP, dGTP, dTTP and dCTP), DNA template, primer and Mg^{++} for the catalysis of polymerization. DNA polymerase I has a single polypeptide chain of about 1000 amino acid residues (mol. wt. – 109,000). The addition of mononucleotide to the free – OH end of a DNA chain is catalysed by DNA pol I. It also catalyses 3' → 5' and 5' → 3' exonucleases activity. DNA polymerase II (DNA pol II) catalyses 3' → 5' exonuclease activity (mol.wt. – 120,000). DNA polymerase III (mol. wt. – 140,000) is more active as compare to DNA pol I and DNA pol II.

Reverse transcriptase:

Reverse transcriptase is used to synthesize complementary DNA (cDNA) or copy DNA by using mRNA as a template and construction of cDNA clone bank. Retroviruses (which have RNA as genetic material) contain RNA dependent DNA polymerase (called reverse transcriptase) which produces single stranded DNA.

DNA ligase:

DNA ligases seal the cut ends of two DNA molecules. **Mertz** and **Davis** (1972) demonstrated that cohesive termini of cleaved DNA molecules could be covalently sealed with *Escherichia coli* DNA ligase and it produce recombinant DNA molecules.

There are two types of DNA ligases: *E. coli* DNA ligase and T_4 DNA ligase. DNA ligase catalyses the formation of phosphodiestir bonds between 3'–OH and 5'–PO_4 group of a nick and turns into an intact DNA. The T_4 DNA ligase enzyme requires ATP as co-factor while the *E. coli* DNA ligase enzyme requires nicotinamide adenine dinucleotide (NAD^+) as a co-factor for joining reaction of the nick. The cofactor splits and forms an enzyme – adenosine monophosphate (AMP) complex. The complex binds to the nick which must expose a 5'–PO_4 and 3'–OH group and makes a covalent bond in the phosphodiester chain. T_4 DNA ligase enzyme has the ability to join the blunt ends of DNA fragments while *E. coli* DNA ligase joins the cohesive ends produced by restriction enzymes. The role of DNA ligase in DNA cloning is shown in Fig. 10.4.

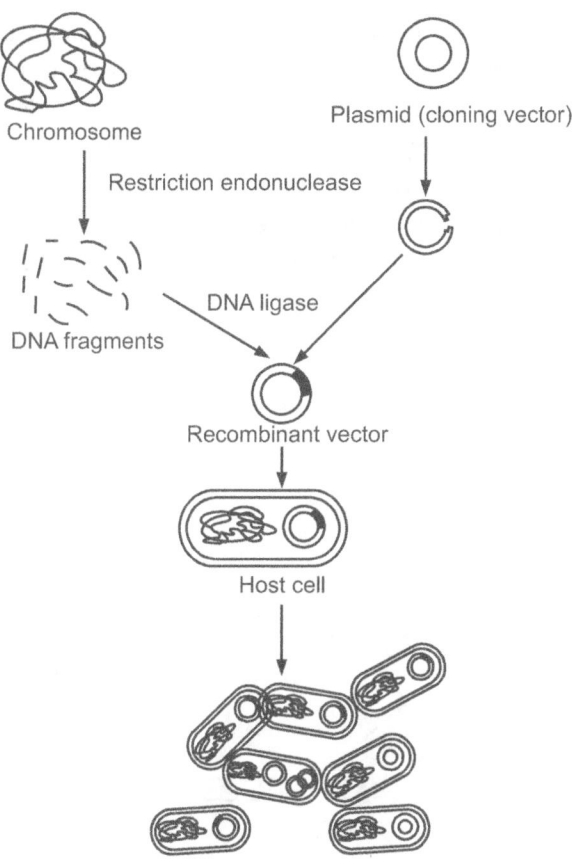

Fig. 10.4: DNA cloning and role of DNA ligase

INSERTION OF TARGET DNA INTO VECTOR

Insertion of DNA fragment into a vector can be performed when both the target gene and vector are cut with the same restriction enzyme to produce identical cohesive ends. The 3' ends of DNA strands always carry a free hydroxyl group, while their 5' ends contain phosphate group. The ends of DNA strands produced by restriction enzymes have to be modified for gene cloning. The 5' phosphate group of vector DNA is removed by alkaline phosphatase treatment to prevent vector circularization during DNA insert integration. Cohesive ends are converted to blunt ends by removing protruding nucleotides using S1 nuclease, which degrades single stranded protruding DNA.

Type II restriction enzymes mainly form fragments having sticky or blunt ends and such DNA fragments are not easily ligated with cloning vectors. The new DNA sequences are created by inserting synthetic DNA fragments called linkers (Fig. 10.5). Inserted DNA fragments with multiple recognition sequences for restriction endonucleases are called polylinkers. Linkers are short, chemically synthesized, double-stranded oligonucleotides.

Linkers are ligated to the blunt ends of DNA to be cloned by using T_4 DNA ligase. These DNA are cut to generate fragments with sticky ends by using specific restriction enzymes. Adaptors are also short, chemically synthesized DNA double strands which can be used to link the ends of two DNA molecules which have different sequences at their ends (Fig. 10.5). Adaptor is used in the 5'-hydroxyl form to prevent self-polymerization. The foreign DNA plus ligated adaptors is phosphorylated at the 5'-termini and ligated into the vector previously cut with *Bam* HI. Adaptors are used to develop sticky ends.

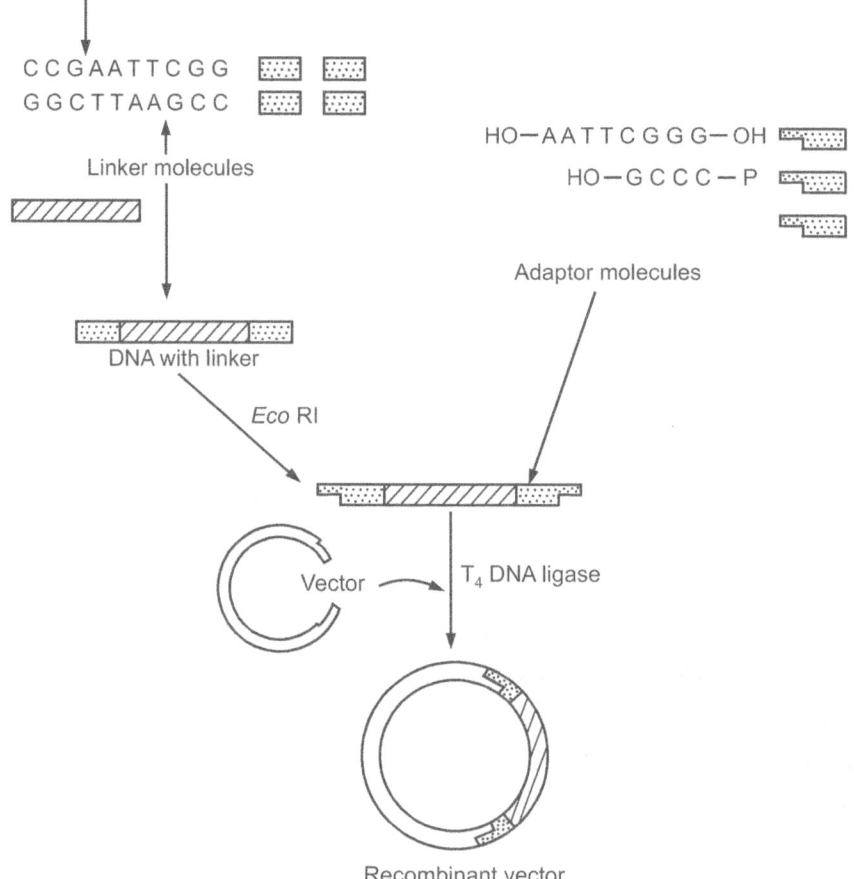

Fig. 10.5: Role of linker and adapter molecules in gene cloning

The homopolymer sequences are added to the foreign DNA fragments to be cloned and vector used by terminal transferase enzyme. The terminal transferase reaction is used to add tail to blunt ended DNA with protruding 3-hydroxyl terminus. Vectors and inserts are treated separately so that poly dA tails build on the 3' termini of one and poly dT tails on the other (Fig. 10.6). The homopolymer tails form a stable, hybrid recombinant DNA in the absence of ligation.

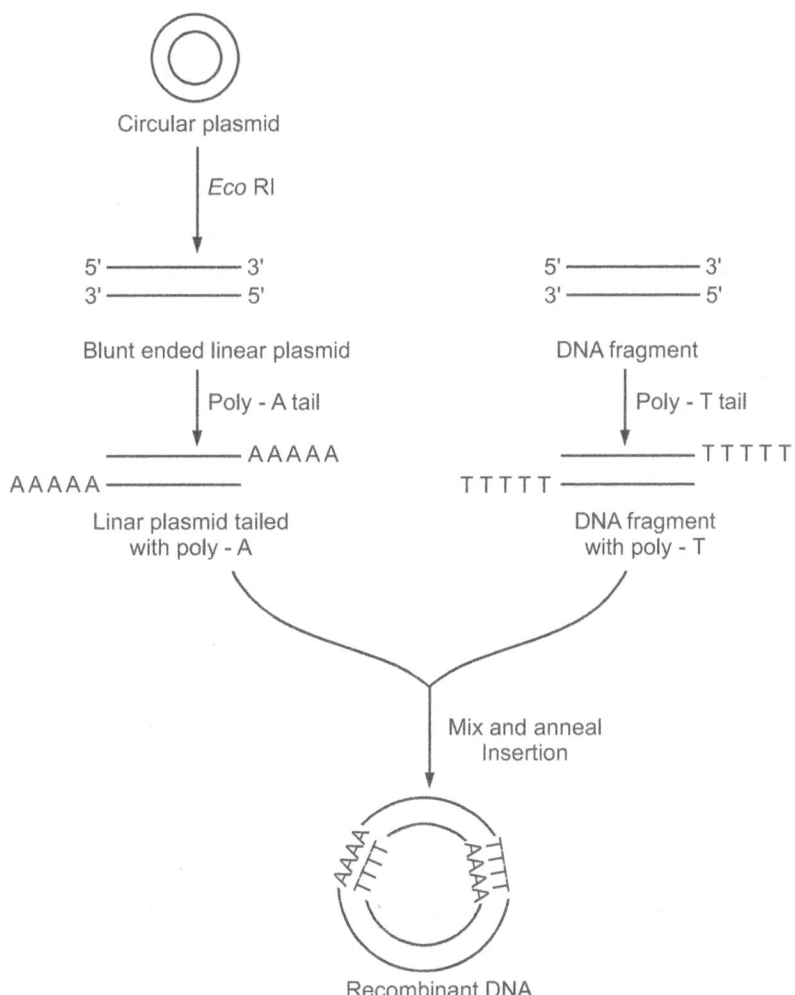

Fig. 10.6: Use of homopolymer tails in recombination

CLONING VECTORS

The vectors are the DNA molecules that carry of foreign DNA segment and replicate inside the host cell. Cloning vectors are also called vehicle DNA because they act as carrier of genes. All vectors used for propagation of DNA inserts in a suitable hosts are called cloning vectors. Any extra-chromosomal small genome is used as a vector e.g. plasmid, bacteriophage, cosmid, bacterial artificial chromosome, phagemid, yeast, shuttle, expression etc. These vectors must possess the following characteristics.

- It must be replicate (ori gene) autonomously in host cell.
- It must be easy to isolate, purify and introduce into the host cells.
- The vector should contain suitable marker genes (tetR, kanR, ampR) that allow easy selection of transformed cells.

- It must have the ability of intergrate either itself or the DNA insert.
- The vector must contain specific control systems like promoters, terminators, operators, etc.

Plasmid vectors:

Plasmids are the extrachromosomal, self replicating, double stranded and circular DNA molecules present in the bacterial cell. Naturally, occurring bacterial plasmids size range is 5000 to 400,0000 bp. Plasmids are widely used as cloning vehicles. The number of plasmids in a bacterial cell can be increased to about 1000 per cell. This process of increasing the number of plasmids is called amplification.

Plasmids are introduced into bacterial cells by a process called transformation. The plasmid is digested with a restriction enzyme and converted into a linear molecule with sticky ends. The foreign DNA is also digested with the restriction enzyme to produce the same sticky ends. Plasmid and foreign DNA are mixed to form circular recombinant plasmids. These recombinant plasmids are introduced into host cells (*Escherichia coli*) by the process of transformation. In this process, a naked DNA from donor strain is transported into cell cytoplasm of the host cell. Plasmid DNA and host cells (*E. coli*) are mixed and incubated at 0°C in a $CaCl_2$ solution. These cells are given heat shock treatment by shifting the temperature to 38 to 42°C. Some cells are treated by the process of electroporation. In this method, host cells are incubated with the plasmid DNA and subjected to a high-voltage. The transformed bacteria are spread on surface of agar plates. Individual colonies are cultured in conical flask containing liquid medium and large amounts of plasmids are produced. Some of the important plasmid cloning vectors are given in the Table 10.3. The small size of the plasmids (about 3 kbp) enhances the transformation efficiency and easy to purify from bacterial cultures. The plasmid contains two genes (tet^R, amp^R) that shows the resistance to antibiotics such as tetracycline and ampicillin. Hence, it is easy to isolate the antibiotic resistant colonies on surface of agar plates. The pBR 322 is one of earliest, popular and most widely used plasmid of 4362 bp.

Table 10.3: Plasmid cloning vectors

Vectors	Selective markers	Cloning sites
pBR 322	amp^R, tet^R	EcoRI, BalI, BamHI, SalI, SphI, PvrI
pBR 325	amp^R, tet^R, cm^R	EcoRI, PstI, HindIII, BamHI, SalI
pMB 9	tet^R	EcoRI, SmaI, HindIII, BamHI
pACYC 184	tet^R, cm^R	EcoRI, BamHI, HindIII
pRK 2501	tet^R, kan^R	EcoRI, BglI, HindIII
pBD 6	kan^R, str^R	BamHI
pBC 16-1	tet^R	EcoRI, HindIII

pBR 322 plasmid: The pBR 322 is the first artificial vector developed by **Boliver** and **Rodriguez** (1977) from *Escherichia coli* plasmid ColEl. In the name pBR, p stands for plasmid, B is for **Boliver** and R is for **Rodriguez**, the scientists who developed cloning vector pBR 322. Some plasmid names are derived from the places they were developed.

The pUC name is obtained from University of California. Plasmid pBR 322 consists of genes for origin of replication for resistance to amplicillin (amp^R) and tetracycline (tet^R) unique recognition for 20 restriction enzymes. Structural features of pBR 322 plasmid are shown in Fig. 10.7. Out of 20 sites, six of these sites (*Bam*HI, *Sph*I, *Sal*II, *Xma*III, *Nru*I and *Eco*RIV) are present within the gene coding for tetracycline resistance, two sites (*Hind*III and *Cla*I) are located within the promoter of the tetracycline resistance gene and three sites (*Pst*I, *Pvu*I and *Sca*I) within the gene that provide resistance to ampicillin. Insertion of the DNA fragment into the plasmid using restriction enzyme *Pst*I or *Pvu*I, places the DNA insert within ampicillin resistance gene (amp^R). Cells containing such as pBR 322 recombinant plasmid may grow in presence of tetracycline but not in presence of ampicillin. In *Bam*HI or *Sal*I restriction enzymes are used then the DNA insert in placed within the tetracycline resistance gene. Bacterial cells containing such type of recombinant plasmid may grow on ampicillin but not on tetracycline. This characteristics allows on easy selection of a single bacterial cell having recombinant pBR 322 from other types of cells. **Messings** and collegues (1983) developed the pUC vector as a derivative of pBR 322. Vector (pUC) is smaller and it contains all the essential parts of pBR 322.

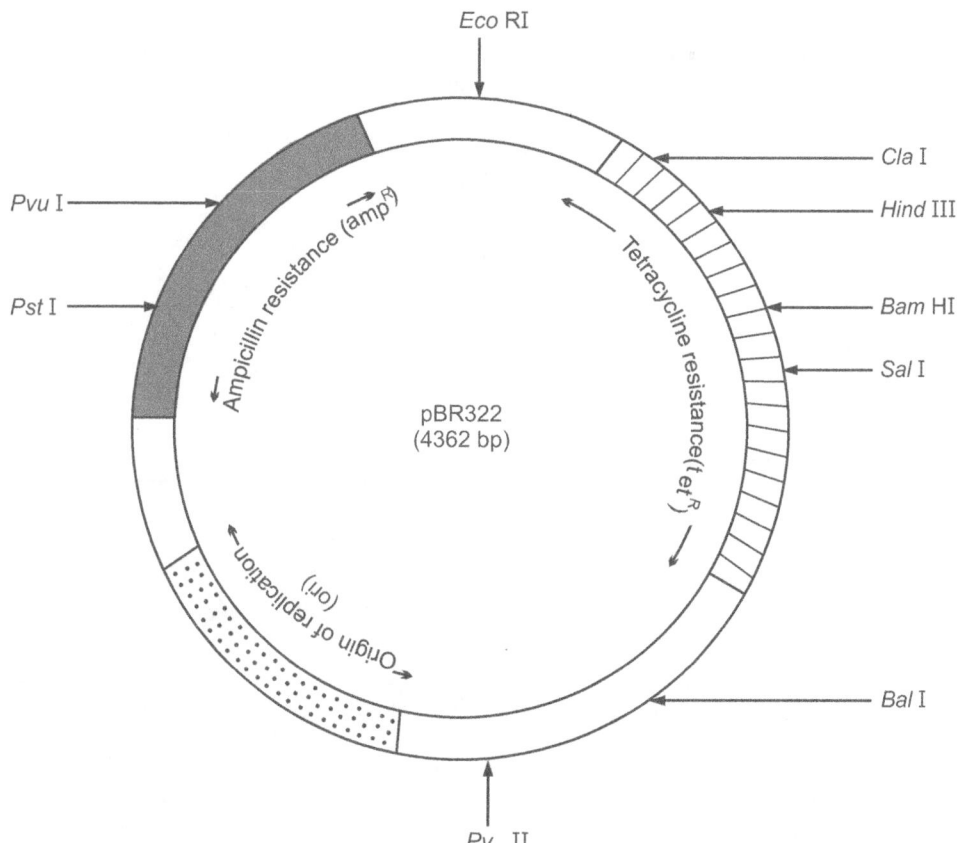

Fig. 10.7: Structural features of pBR 322 vector

Bacteriophage vectors:

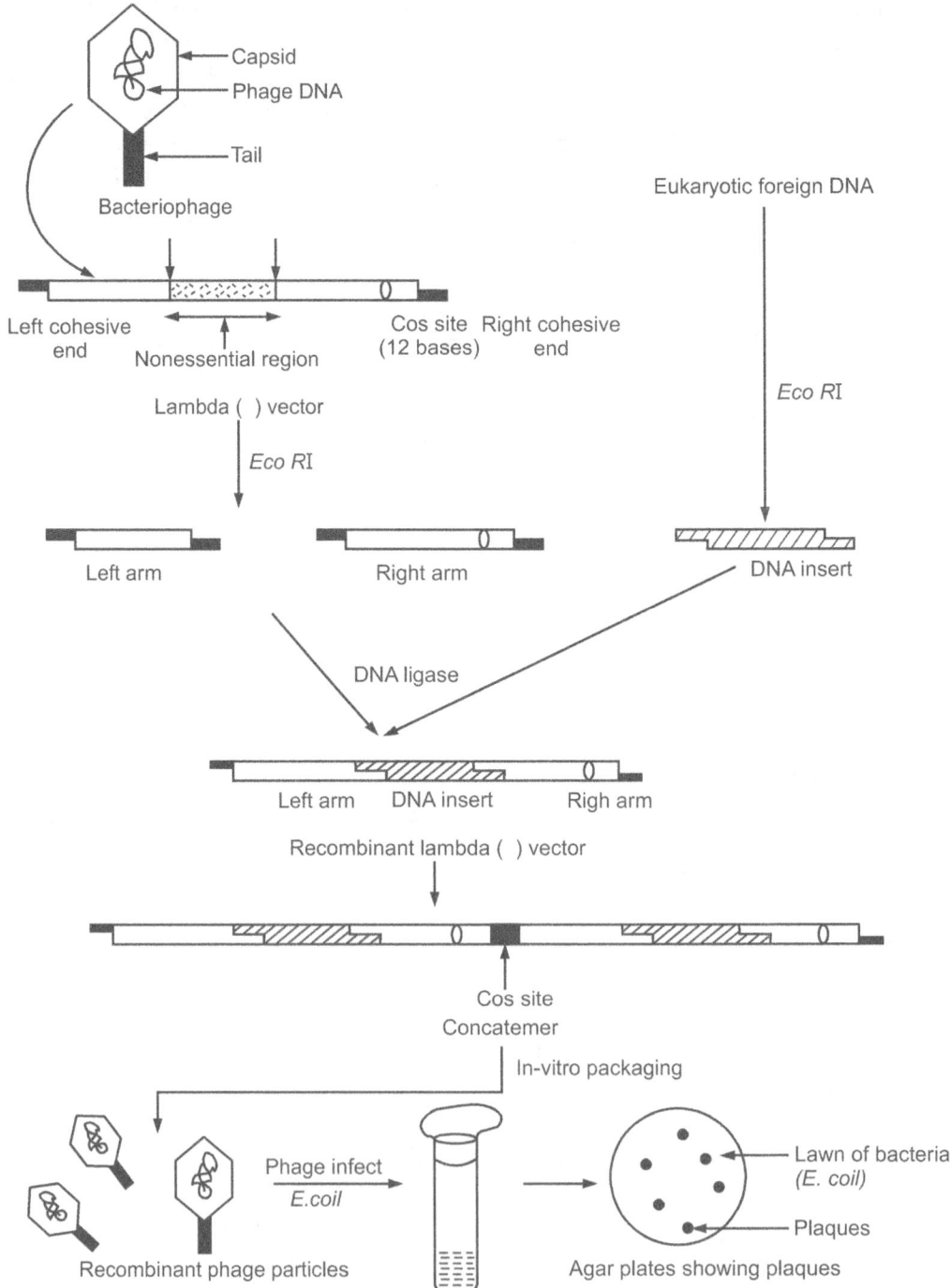

Fig. 10.8: Cloning target DNA with bacteriophage lambda (λ) vector

Bacteriophages (phages) are the viruses that infect bacterial cells by injecting their genetic material (DNA or RNA). Most of bacteriophages lyse the bacterial cells by the infection (lytic cycle). Some phage chromosome integreates into the bacterial chromosome and multiplies as lysogenic cycle. The prophage may dissociate from the bacterial chromosome and follow the lytic cycle. Most commonly used *Escherichia coli* phages are λ (lambda), M13 and Fd phages. Phage vectors are most efficient than plasmids (15 kb) for cloning of large fragments of over 25 kb. These vectors are easy to screen in large number of phage plaques than bacterial colonies.

Bacteriophage lamba (λ) DNA has been widely used as cloning vectors. The phage λ is contained within the head attached to a tail. DNA exists as a linear double stranded molecule (48.5 kbp) in the phage head but in host cells, the cohesive ends anneal to form a circular molecule necessary for replication. The sealed cohesive ends are called cos sites (sites of cleavage). It amplifies by rolling mechanism into several genomes joined end to end forming a concatemer (Fig. 10.8) which is the precursor for packaging of λ genome into phage heads. The recombinant phage DNA is inserted (in vitro) into phage capsids by a process called packaging. It involves mixing the recombinant DNA with a packaging extract containing phage capsid proteins and processing enzymes. *E. coli* cells are infected by recombinant phage particles and then these cells are spread on agar plate. It produces a continuous sheet of bacteria called a lawn which contains small clear areas. These correspond to areas of lysis produced by infection with bacteriophage and are called plaques (Fig. 10.8). The plaques are isolated and used to generate large amounts of recombinant DNA by infection of fresh cultures of *Escherichia coli*.

Cosmid vectors:

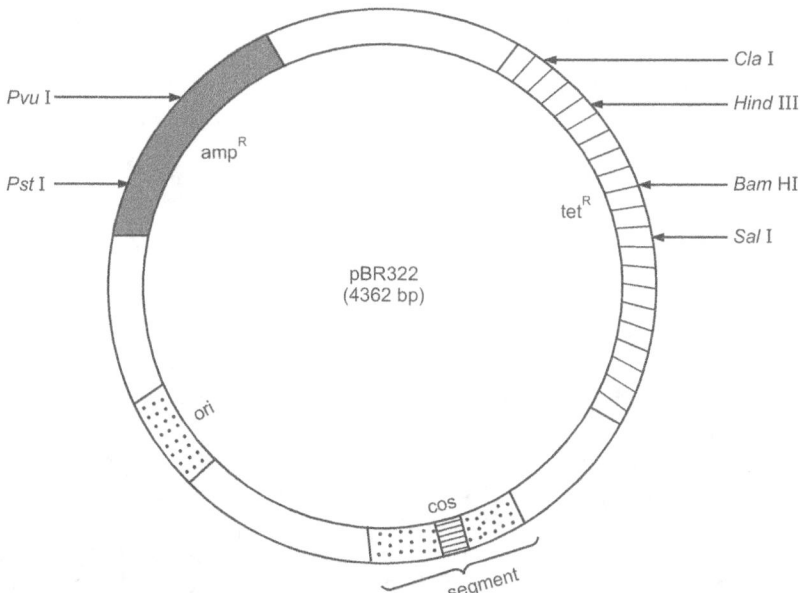

Fig. 10.9: Cosmid vector containing pBR 322 modules and a λ segment

Cosmids (cos site + plasmid) are the hybrid vectors derived from plasmids which contain *cos* site of phage lambda. Cosmids has unique restricton sites, replication origin and selectable markers from the plasmid (Fig. 10.9). It is prepared using recombinant DNA techniques. The cos sequences occur at one end of lambda DNA molecule and it is responsible for its insertion into the phage capsid. The presence of cos sites on cosmids allows them to be packaged into phage capsids. The recombinant cosmid is packaged into lambda capsids and used to infect *E. coli*. Cosmids are small 7 kb or less and lambda capsid can accommodate upto 52 kb. Hence, cosmids can accommodate upto 45 bp long DNA inserts.

Shuttle vector:

Specific recombinant plasmids incorporate multiple replication origins and other elements that allow them to be used in more than one species (*E. coli* or yeast). Plasmids which are propagated in cells of two or more different species are called shuttle vectors. Such vectors (Fig. 10.10) possess two origin for replication (ori^E, ori^{Euk}). The ori^E functions in *Escherichia coli* and ori^{Euk} functions in eukaryotic cells like yeast. The important gene are *ori* (origin for replication in *E. coli*), amp^R (ampicillin resistance), ars (autonomously replicating sequence), cen (centromere of yeast) and *leu*-2 (complements of a defective gene encoding for leucin).

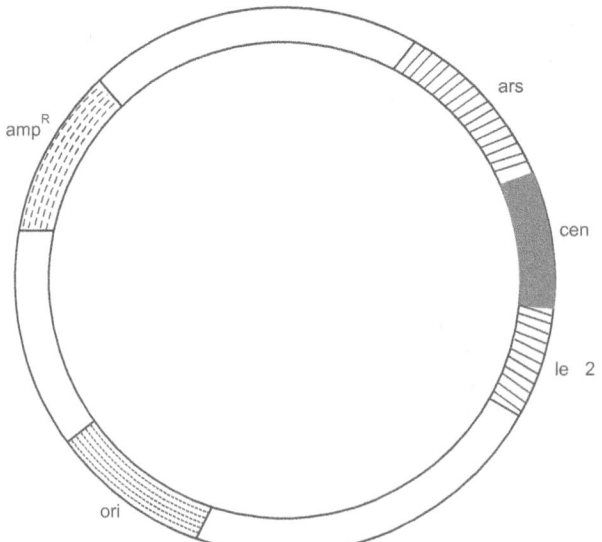

Fig. 10.10: A typical shuttle vector constructed for yeast and *Escherichia coli*

Yeast vectors:

Yeast is a unicellular eukaryotic microorganism. It reproduces sexually as well as asexually by budding. Yeast cells contain their own plasmid (6318 bp long) known as 2 μm plasmid. It is present in many strains in 50 to 100 copies/cell and used as a vector for foreign genes. Yeast plasmid contains an origin of DNA replication (ori), cis-action region (REP 3) and two genes (REP1 and REP2). This plasmid (about 50%) of the 2 μm plasmid is essential for its replication and maintenance in high copy number. The half part of the plasmid is combined with a portion of pBR 322 to form a shuttle vector (Fig. 10.11).

The pBR 322 plasmid segment contains the origin of replication (ori) for *E. coli*, amp^R selectable marker gene and HIS 3 yeast gene. This plasmid vector contains several restriction sites for insertion of DNA segments.

David and colleagues (1987) developed yeast artificial chromosome (YAC) by using new techniques where DNA segment of several thousand base pairs (1 Mb) can be cloned. Yeast artificial chromosome contains all the essential features of a chromosome required for its propagation in a yeast cell. A typical linear YAC contains origin of replication, a centromere, selectable marker gene and telomeres to stabilize the ends of the chromosome (Fig. 10.12). For cloning, yeast artificial chromosome is digested with restriction enzyme such as a *Bam*III and *Eco*RI. Recombinant YAC are produced by inserting a large fragment of genomic DNA. Digestion with restriction enzymes generates two separate DNA arm (Fig. 10.13).

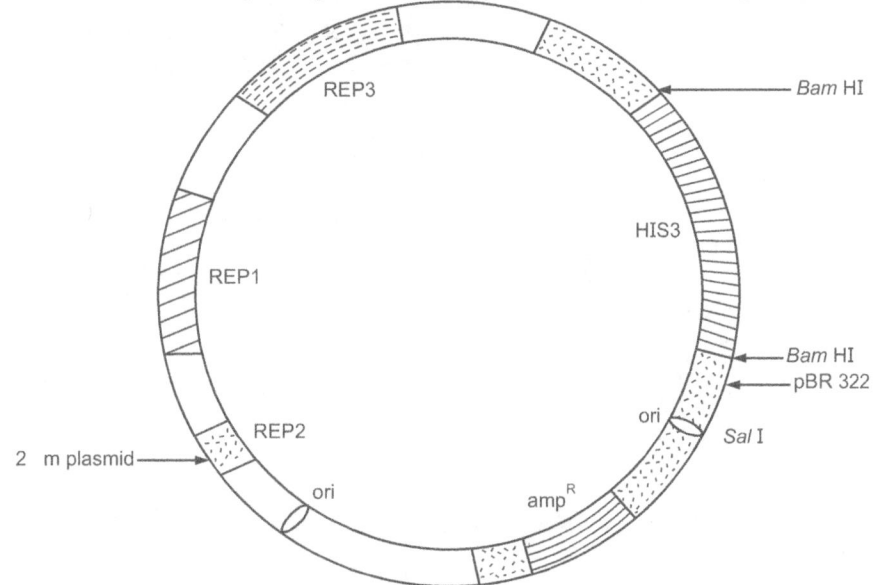

Fig. 10.11: Yeast plasmid (shuttle) vector for *Escherichia coli* and yeast

Each separate arm contains telomeric end and one selectable marker. A large segment of DNA (upto 2×10^6 bp) is ligated to the two arms to create a yeast artificial chromosome (YAC). The YAC is transferred in yeast cells prepared by removal of the cell wall (spheroplasts). The transformants that contain YAC can be identified by change in colour of colonies (red colour – transformed colonies, white colonies – non-transformed colonies).

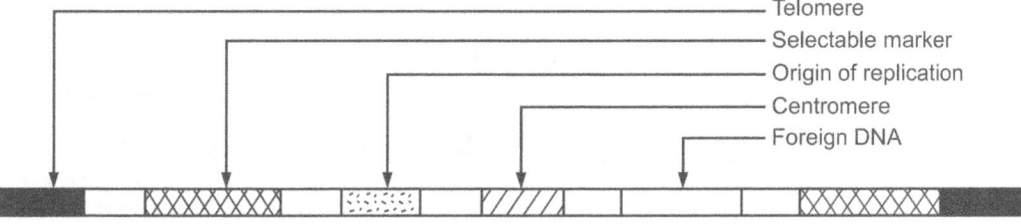

Fig. 10.12: Linear yeast artificial chromosome (YAC)

Yeast artificial chromosomes have been widely used to construct maps of parts of the human genome. It is mainly used for cloning of very large (upto 100 kb) DNA segments for mapping of complex eukaryotic chromosomes. Bacterial artificial chromosomes (BAC) and P1 artificial chromosomes (PAC) vectors are used similar to yeast artificial chromosomes.

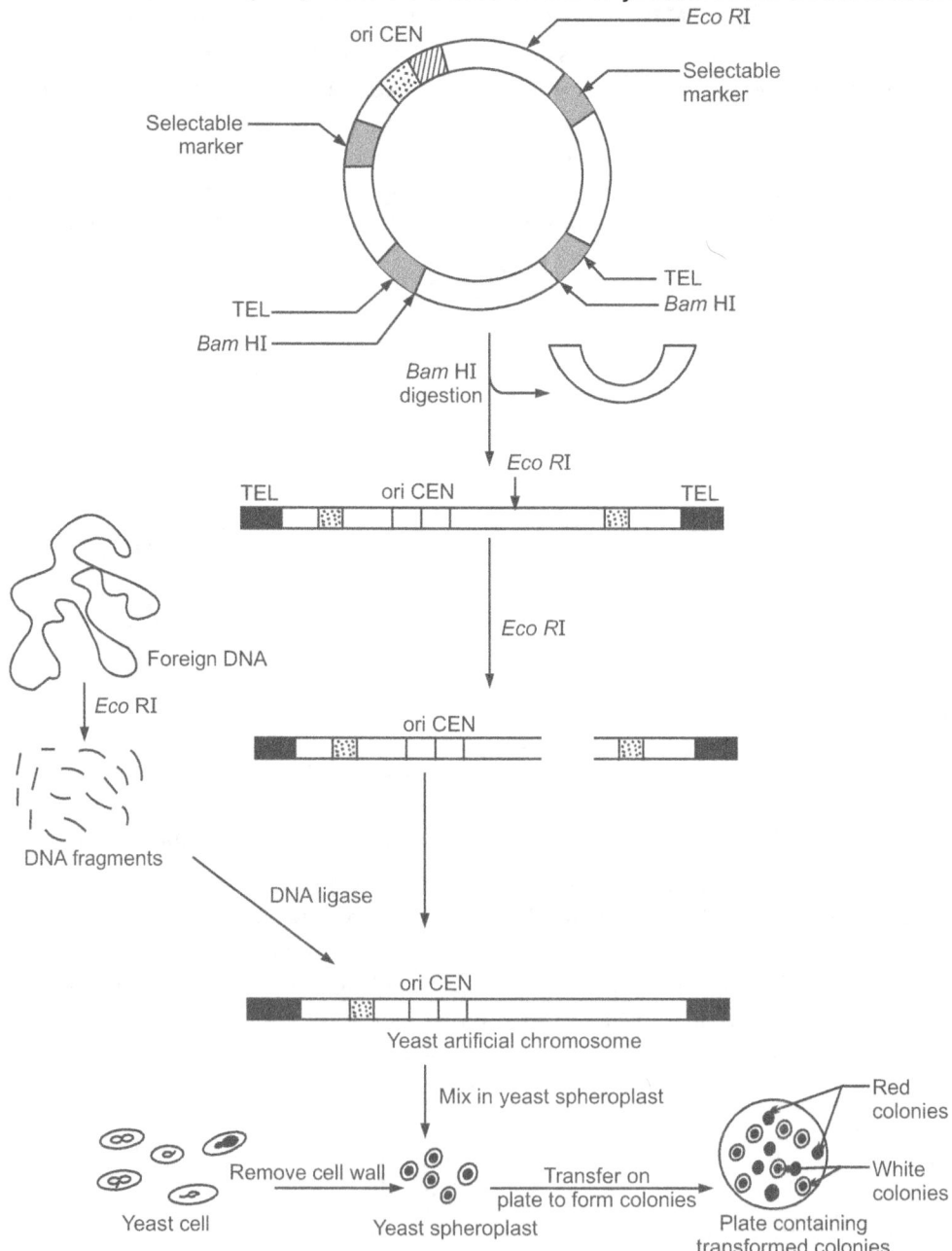

Fig. 10.13: Role of YAC in gene cloning

Expression vector:

Recombinant DNA technology is used to produce high amount of proteins by addition of desired gene into the blast cell. Expresion of cloned genes is carried out by inserting a 'promoter sequence' and a 'terminator sequence'. The cloning vectors which contain the signals for protein synthesis are called expression vectors (Fig. 10.14). Plasmids have been extensively modified to incorporate control elements designed for high level expression of inserted target gene. These control elements contain ribosomes, promoters, polylinkers and terminator sequence. The gene to be expressed is inserted into one of the restriction sites in the polylinker. The promoter allows efficient transcription of the inserted gene. The transcription termination sequence mainly improves the amount of stability of the mRNA produced. The ribosome binding site provides sequence signals needed for efficient translation of the mRNA derived from the gene. In addition, origin of replication and a marker gene (resistant to antibiotic) is incorporated in expression vectors. Lambda PL, lac Z, trip and lac promoters are commonly used to construct expression vectors. The trc and tac promoters are also used which are hybrid promoters derived from lac and trp promoters.

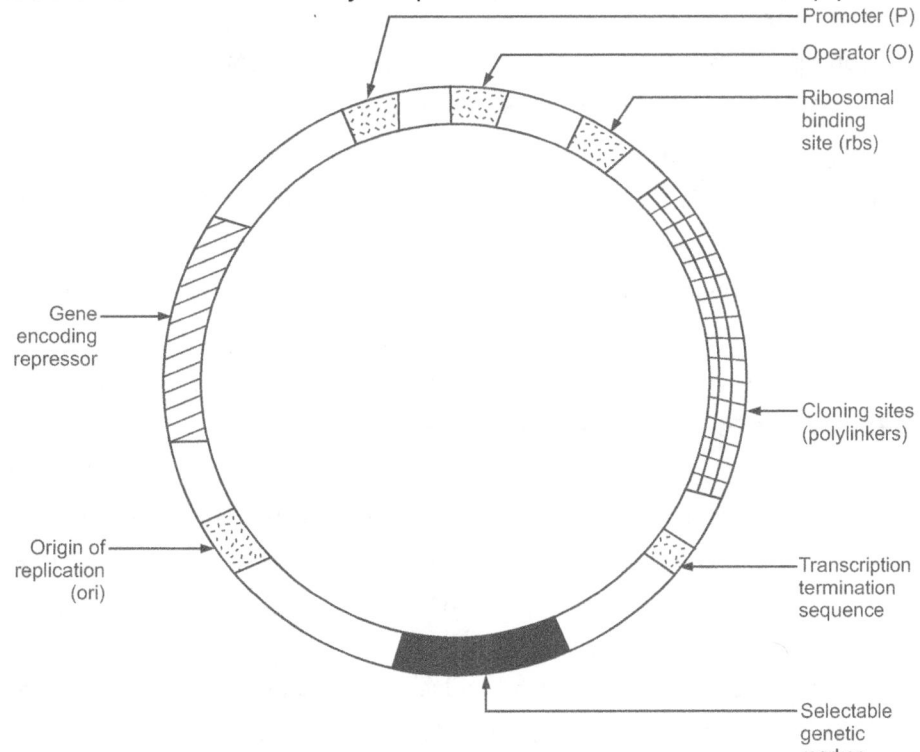

Fig. 10.14: Ideal *E. coli* expression vector

TRANSFORMATION AND GROWTH OF CELLS

Mandell and **Higa** (1979) developed the procedure of transformation of rDNA in bacterial cells. Recombinant DNA is allowed to enter into a suitable host cell for expression of foreign DNA. The recombinant vector is mainly introduced into *Escherichia coli* to select the recombinant from the unchanged vector and to obtain many copies of the DNA insert or recombinant vector. The specific method is selected for transformation and it depends on types of vectors and host cells. The main methods used for gene transfer (rDNA) into host cells are transformation and transfection.

Transformation:

The recombinant plasmids are introduced into host cells (*Escherichia coli*) by the process called transformation. Plasmid DNA and host cells are mixed and pretreated with $CaCl_2$ at low temperature to enter plasmid DNA (rDNA) into bacterial cell. The transformed bacterial cells are spread on surface of agar plates for growth (For detail, please refer section-plasmid vectors).

Transfection:

Lambda (λ) phage is used to transfer the foreign DNA into *Escherichia coli* cell by the process called transfection (a hybrid of transformation and infection). The vectors containing λ phage cos sequences are in-vitro packaged into empty λ phage heads and forms complete λ particles. These phage particles are used to infect *Escherichia coli* cells. The vectors are also used to transform *E. coli* cells directly as naked DNA ($CaCl_2$ method). Infection by phage particles containing DNA insert is more efficient than direct transformation (For detail, please refer section – bacteriophage vectors). Other than *E. coli*, *Bacillus subtilis*, yeasts and mammalian cells are commonly used as cloning hosts.

SELECTION OF RECOMBINANT CLONES

The main objective of cloning experiments is to isolate the cells that contain recombinant vector from non-transformed cells. Recombinant cells express the characters while the non-recombinants do not express the characters or traits. Different methods are used for screening or selection of recombinants.

Direct selection:

Many times, cloned DNA itself codes for resistance to the antibiotic ampicillin (amp^R) and the recombinants can be allowed to grow on minimal medium containing ampicillin. Such recombinants can grow on medium and form colonies that contain amp^R gene on its plasmid vector.

Hybrid arrested translation (HART):

In this method, the portion of mixture (mRNAs) is used for in vitro translation and it serves as the control. The remaining portion of the mRNA mixture is subdivided and mixed with denatured recombinant DNA molecule. The mixture is incubated under suitable conditions favouring annealing. The DNA insert present in a given clone is hybridize with the complementary mRNA. The mRNA mixture is used for in vitro translation and the resulting mixture of polypeptides is subjected to electrophoresis. The protein bands obtained in each sample are compared with those obtained from the control mRNA. The DNA insert causing the absence of desired protein are identified and isolated.

Hybrid selection:

In hybrid selection method, recombinant vectors are purified, denatured and fixed separately to a solid support (nitrocellulose filter discs). The DNA attached to each disc hybridizes with its complementary mRNA. The mRNA bound to each disc is isolated separately and used for in vitro translation. The resulting polypeptides are identified by electrophoresis. The identification of specific polypeptide may be facilitated by using antibodies specific to it. The antibodies may be used for western blotting (Refer – blotting techniques) or RNA blotting methods.

Colony hybridization or nucleic acid hybridization:

This method is used to identify those bacterial colonies in a Petri plate which contain specific DNA sequence (Fig. 10.15). The bacterial colonies are replica-placed or phage plaques are directly lifted on nitrocellulose filters. The filter disc is removed and put on blotting paper soaked with 0.5 N NaOH solution. The alkali diffuses into filters, lyses bacterial cells and denatures their DNA. The disc is neutralized by tris (hydoxy methyl) amino methane HCl buffer by maintaining high concentrations of the salt. The cDNA is fixed properly by baking at 80°C. The disc is incubated with a solution containing radioactive chemical labelled probe (p^{32}) at suitable conditions. The probe hybridizes any bound DNA that contains sequences complementary to probe. The unhybridized probe is removed by washing. Colonies that develop positive X-ray image are compared with water plate and these colonies are picked up for further studies.

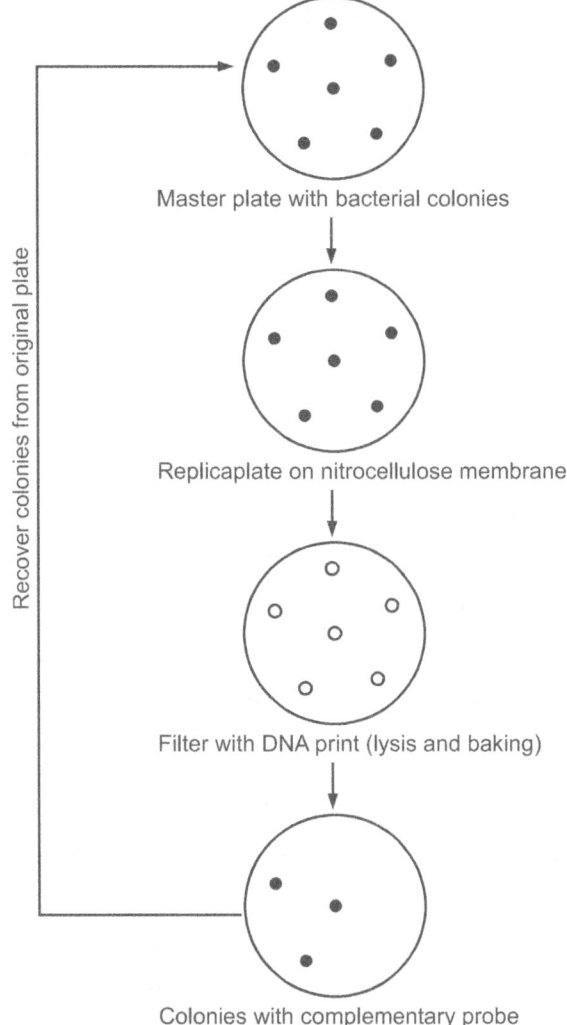

Fig. 10.15: Colony hybridization

QUESTIONS

(A) Short answer questions:
1. Define vector. Write the features of a good vector.
2. Write the role of following in gene cloning
    (a) Linkers
    (b) *Eco* RI
    (c) DNA ligase
    (d) Radioactive probe (p^{32})
3. List different enzymes used for gene cloning.
4. What is concatemer? Write its applications of gene cloning.

(B) Long answer questions:

1. Explain various types of vectors for *E. coli*.
2. Describe in detail the various methods for the integration of DNA inserts into the vector.
3. Write a note on:
   (a) Colony hybridization
   (b) Cosmid vectors
   (c) Yeast vectors
   (d) Transformation and growth of rDNA.
4. Explain the role of restriction enzymes in gene cloning.
5. Write in short about different techniques used for selection of recombinant clones.

(C) Multiple choice questions:

1. _____ enzyme is isolated from *Thermus aquaticus*.
   (a) Taq polymerase   (b) Taq ligase
   (c) Taq kinase   (d) Taq nuclease

2. The pBR 322 is the first artificial vector developed from _____.
   (a) *B. subtilis*   (b) *Saccharomyces cerevisiae*
   (c) *Escherichia coli*   (d) Hepatitis B virus

3. Which one of the following is a restriction endonuclease?
   (a) *Taq* pol   (b) *Bam* HI
   (c) *Eac* HII   (d) *Sta* PII

4. Sequence specific enzymes that cleave DNA to give sticky ends are _____.
   (a) Restriction endonucleases (b) DNA ligases
   (c) Beta-lactamases   (d) DNA methylases

(D) Match the following:

A	B
(a) DNA ligase	(i) Synthesize a DNA copy of an RNA molecule
(b) Alkaline phosphatase	(ii) Adds a phosphate to the 5' – OH ends
(c) Polynucleotide kinase	(iii) Removes terminal PO_4
(d) Reverse transcriptase	(iv) Joins two DNA molecules

(E) Fill in the blanks:
1. *Hind* III restriction endonuclease is prepared from _____.
2. Plasmids which are propagated in cells of two or more different species are called _____ vectors.

CHAPTER 11

TECHNIQUES OF GENETIC ENGINEERING

CONTENTS

    INTRODUCTION
    ISOLATION OF DNA
        Shotgun method, DNA from mRNA
    GENE LIBRARY
        Genomic library, cDNA library
    SITE-DIRECTED MUTAGENESIS
    RESTRICTION FRAGMENT LENGTH POLYMORPHISM (RFLP)
    DNA FINGERPRINTING
    GENE SYNTHESIS AND GENE MACHINE
    GENE (DNA) SEQUENCING
    HUMAN GENE THERAPY

INTRODUCTION

The most important application of molecular genetics in biotechnology is genetic engineering or recombinant (rDNA) technology. Genetic engineering is the process of producing an organism that contains a gene or genes not naturally present in that organism. This technique (Fig. 11.1) has tremendous potential of developing microorganisms that are able to produce many useful products which are difficult or impossible to produce by other methods. This is a useful tool for the production of vaccines and antigens. Recombinant DNA technology has also been used for the production of proteins of therapeutic interest such as human insulin, interferons, human growth hormone, tissue plasminogen activator, tumour necrosis factor, interleukin-2, fibroblast growth factor, erythropoietin and other biologicals.

The basic technique of recombinant DNA technology is simple. Plasmid DNA from *Escherichia coli* and chromosomal DNA from another organism are cleaved with a restriction enzyme, mixed and ligated with DNA ligase. The recombinant DNA molecule is then

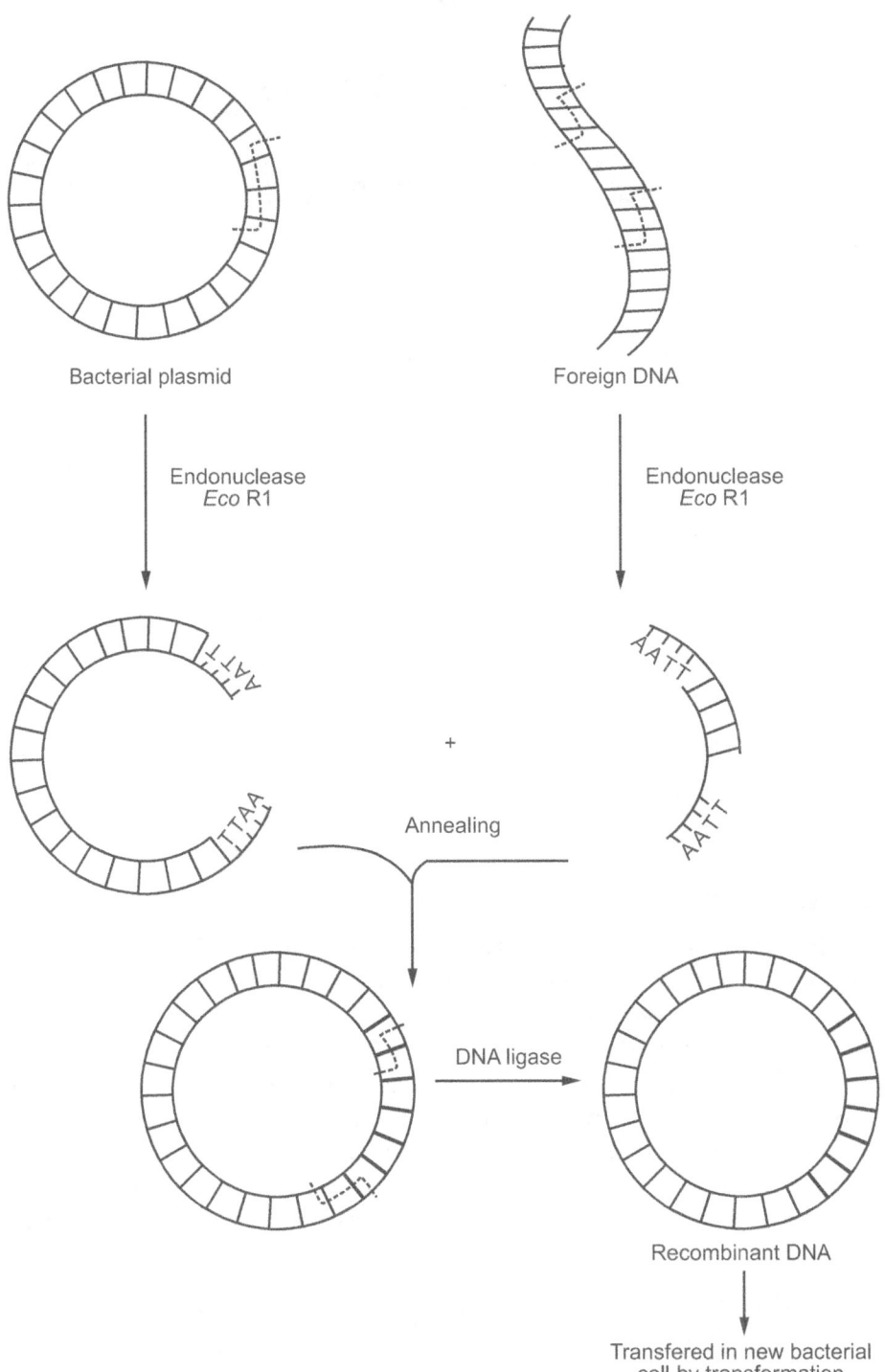

Fig. 11.1: Preparation of recombinant DNA by genetic engineering

introduced into *Escherichia coli* where foreign chromosomal DNA can replicate. It is linked to a plasmid which has an origin of replication and the genes in the donor segment are said to be cloned and the DNA molecule that carries it is known as vector.

Insertion of the gene into the DNA carrier molecule is done with restriction endonucleases. These enzymes are present in bacteria and naturally function to protect against invading DNA molecules. Restriction endonucleases *Eco* RI, *Hind* III, *Bgl* H, *Pst* I and *Sma* I are obtained from *Escherichia coli, Haemophilus influenzae, Bacillus globigii, Providencia stuarti* and *Serratia marcescens* respectively. These enzymes cut DNA molecules at specific base sequences that occur in palindromic order. Type I restriction endonucleases recognises a specific sequence but makes cuts only within the recognition sites. Type II restriction endonucleases are used in genetic engineering. These enzymes make two single strand breaks, one break in each strand. These breaks may be at the centre of symmetry (flush or blunt ends) or at same relative location in each strand generating complementary or cohesive or sticky ends that can overlap for two to four bases. Fragments of DNA cut can be rejoined by a sealing or ligating enzyme known as DNA ligase. The most commonly used ligase commercially available is that encoded by phase T_4.

ISOLATION OF DNA

The DNA of microorganisms contains thousands of genes. Isolation of required gene from the entire DNA is the major tool of genetic studies. Shotgun and mRNA (hybridization and reverse transcriptase) methods are commonly used for isolation of DNA.

Shotgun method:

DNA is isolated from the organism like bacteria, virus, plant or animal. Restriction enzymes such as *Eco*RI is used to break the DNA into many fragments. This DNA is called as 'foreign DNA'.

Plasmid DNA is isolated from host cells (*E. coli*) by dissolving outer membrane of cells by detergents. The plasmids are separated from chromosomal DNA in an ultracentrifuge. Plasmid rings (pDNA) are converted into linear form by using restriction enzyme. Foreign DNA fragments are mixed with linear plasmid DNA. Random association between the two types of DNA takes place by hydrogen bonding at the cohesive ends. The foreign DNA becomes inserted into plasmid DNA to form a larger ring or a longer linear form and covalent joining occurs by DNA ligase. The new DNA is called 'recombinant DNA' (Fig. 11.2).

The 'recombinant DNA' or chimera plasmids are placed in a solution containing calcium chloride and *Escherichia coli* bacteria. Recombinant plasmids enter into the bacterial cell through the membrane by heating at 42°C to 44°C for 2 to 5 minutes. These bacterial cells

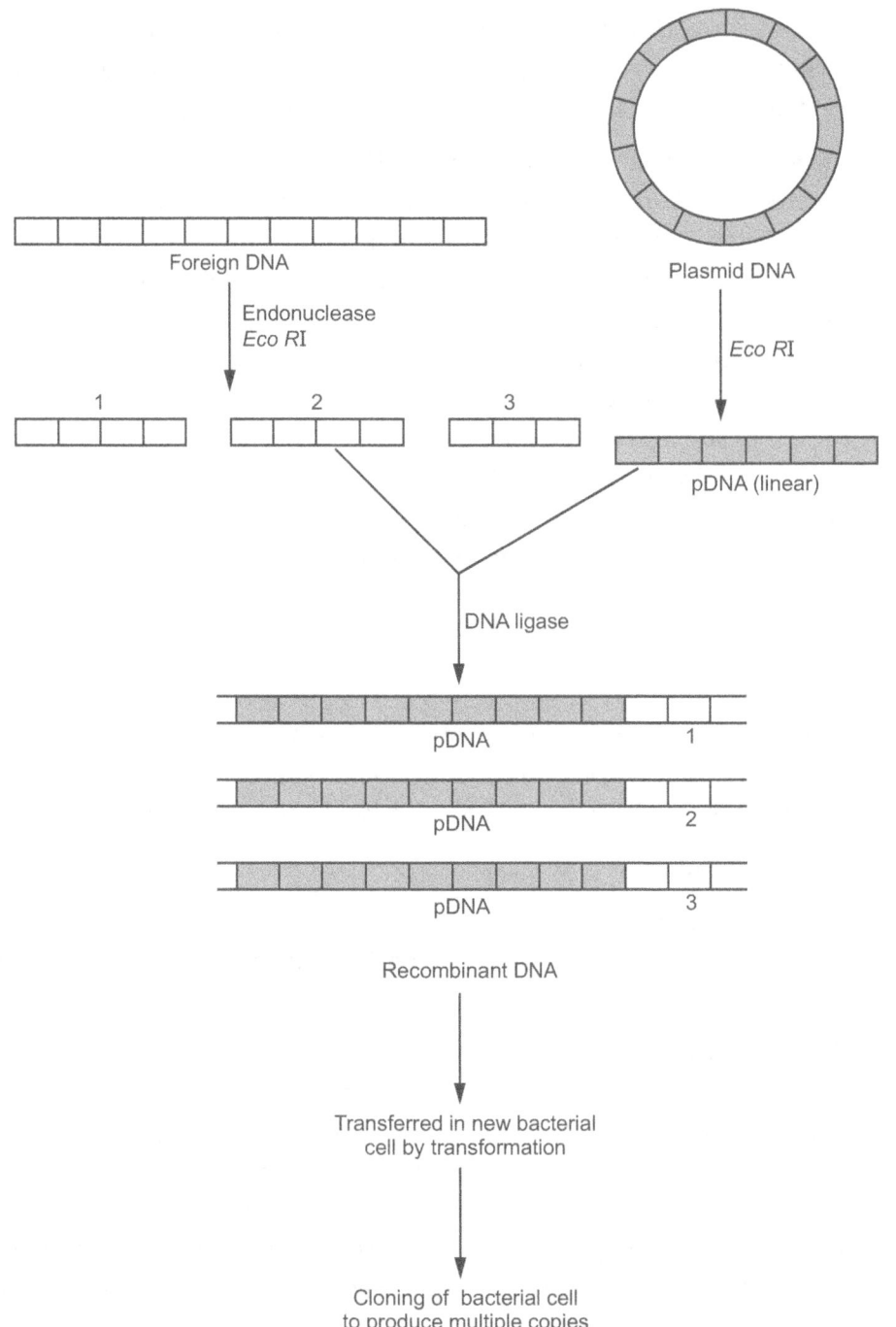

Fig. 11.2: Shotgun method for isolation of genes

are spread on a nutrient medium and they grow in the form of colonies. Each colony contains individuals with specific segments of foreign DNA in their plasmids.

DNA from mRNA:

DNA is obtained from mRNA by the:

(i) Hybridization method and

(ii) Reverse transcriptase method.

(i) Hybridization method:

In this method, double-stranded DNA (dsDNA) is isolated from organism and treated with heat or alkali. This dsDNA is converted into the single-stranded form (ssDNA) by denaturation. The ssDNA strands are mixed with mRNA transcribed by the gene. The mRNA pairs with the complementary region of DNA to form a DNA-RNA hybrid (Fig. 11.3). The DNA-RNA complex is isolated and DNA is separated from RNA. The ssDNA is converted to dsDNA by the action of polymerase enzyme. Hybridization method is useful for isolating genes which exist in multiple copies.

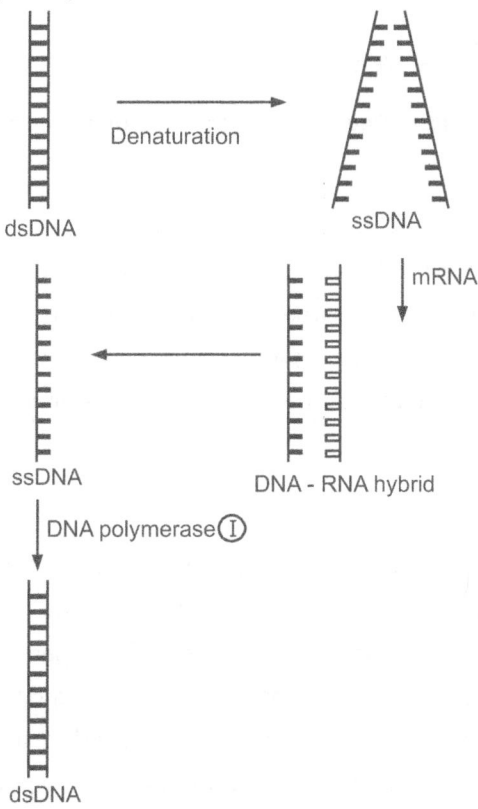

Fig. 11.3: Hybridization method (Isolation of DNA from mRNA)

(ii) Reverse transcriptase method:

Purified mRNA of the required gene is used as a template to transcribe ssDNA by the action of reverse transcriptase. The ssDNA (complementary DNA) is converted to dsDNA by using the enzyme DNA polymerase (I) of *E. coli*

The enzyme (S_1 nuclease) breaks the covalent linkage between the two DNA strands. Poly (dT) or poly (dA) tails are added to dsDNA by the action of the enzyme terminal transferase in the presence of TTP or ATP respectively. Double stranded DNA is spliced to vector DNA and cloned to produce multiple copies (Fig. 11.4).

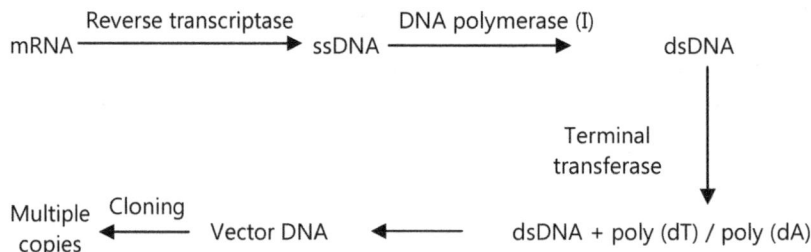

Fig. 11.4: Reverse transcriptase method for isolation of gene

GENE LIBRARY

A DNA (gene) library is the collection of different DNA sequences from an organism where each sequence has been cloned into a vector for ease of purification and analysis. The combination of restriction enzymes and various cloning vector allows the entire genome of an organism to be packed into a vector. A collection of these different recombinant clones is called a library. Depending on the source of DNA, library can be classified as (i) genomic library and (ii) cDNA library.

Genomic library:

A genomic library is a collection of plasmid clones or phage lysates containing recombinant DNA molecules. A genomic library is prepared from the total DNA of a cell or tissue. The complete genome of a particular organism is cleaved into thousands of fragments of appropriate size by mechanical shearing or by partial digestion of the DNA by restriction endonucleases. The fragments produced in partial digests with enzymes having four base (tetrameric) recognition sites are more appropriate size for cloning as compare to six base (hexameric) sites. The enzymes *Hae* III (GG/CC), *Alu* I (AG/CT) or *Sau* 3A (/GATC)

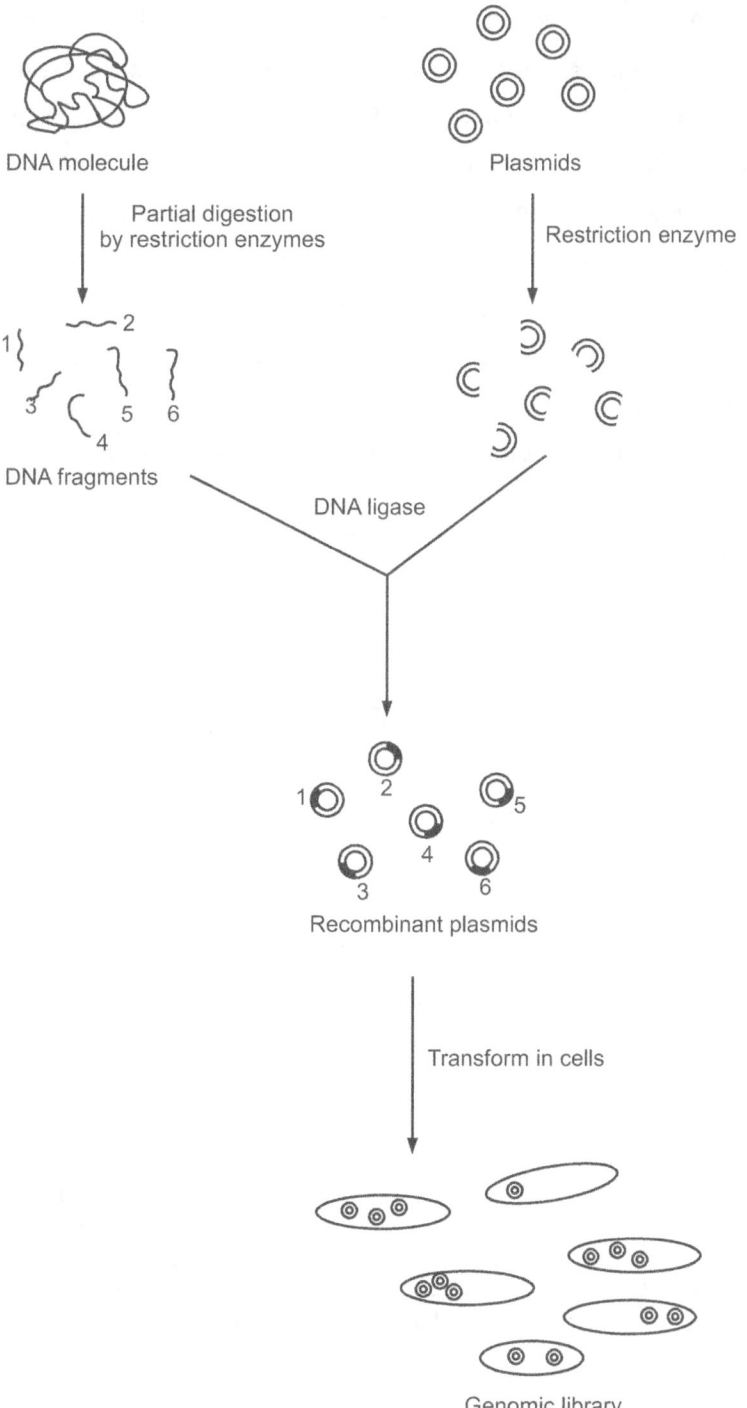

Fig. 11.5: Preparation of genomic library

have been used for constructing genomic libraries. DNA fragments of proper size are selected for cloning by removing large and small fragments by centrifugation or agarose gel electrophoresis. The cloning vector (BAC, YAC, lambda (λ) or cosmids) is cleaved with the same restriction endonuclease and ligated to the genomic DNA fragments (Fig. 11.5). Each vector consists of different fragments of DNA. The ligated DNA mixture is used to transform bacterial or yeast cells to produce a library of cell types. All transformed cells grow into a colony or clone. Colonies containing desired DNA fragments are identified by DNA or colony hybridization. A set of overlapping clones represent a catalog for a long continuous segment of a genome (contig). A well characterized library may contain thousands of long contigs. The known sequences within the library can provide landmarks for genomic sequencing projects.

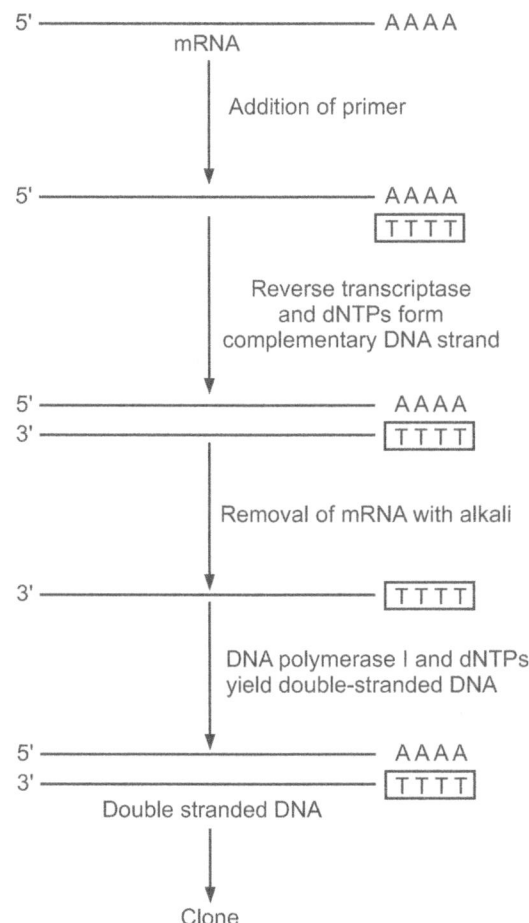

Fig. 11.6: Preparation of cDNA library from mRNA

cDNA library:

The cDNA library can be prepared by using mRNA. The mRNAs are highly processed, intro free representatives of DNA. The mRNAs are unstable. Hence, they are not directly cloned. The double stranded cDNA is prepared by following steps:

(i) First-strand DNA synthesis on the mRNA template.
(ii) Removal of the RNA template and
(iii) Second-strand DNA synthesis using the first DNA strand as a template (Fig. 11.6).

The resulting double-stranded DNA fragments are inserted into a suitable vector and cloned, creating a population of clones called cDNA library.

SITE-DIRECTED MUTAGENESIS

Site-directed mutagenesis is a 'in-vitro' technique, which allow the introduction of mutations at specific site on a genome. It involves the change of cloned target DNA either by deletion, substitution or insertion of the same into the host cell for the production of a functional protein. It is possible to remove a DNA segment and replace it with a synthetic one (Fig. 11.7). The simplest method of site directed mutagenesis is the single-primer method. This method involves priming in vitro DNA synthesis with a chemically synthesized oligonucleotide (7 to 20 nucleotides long) that carries a base mismatch with the complementary sequence. A single stranded clone of the wild type gene is produced by using an M13 phage based vector. A synthetic oligonuclotide with a desired sequence change at one position is hybridized to a single stranded copy of the gene. The hybridization is performed under the conditions of low stringency i.e. temperature (low) and cation (high) concentration. The hybridized clone as a primer in the presence of DNA polymerase, synthesizes second DNA strand. The slightly mismatched duplex recombinant plasmid is used to transform bacteria. The duplex DNA replicates in bacterial cell and produce either wild type or mutant plasmids (Fig. 11.8). The clones can be screened by DNA (nucleic acid) hybridization with ^{32}p-labelled oligonucleotide as probe. Site directed mutagenesis is commonly used to produce novel proteins and enzymes e.g. βlactamase, subtilisin etc.

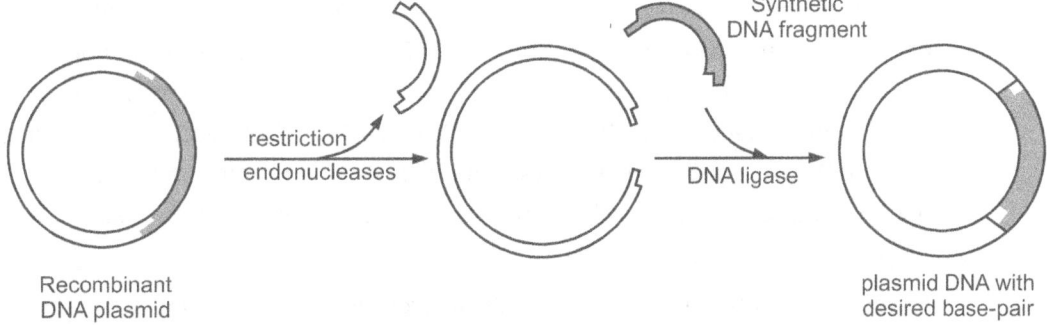

Fig. 11.7: Site-directed mutagenesis by replacing DNA-fragment

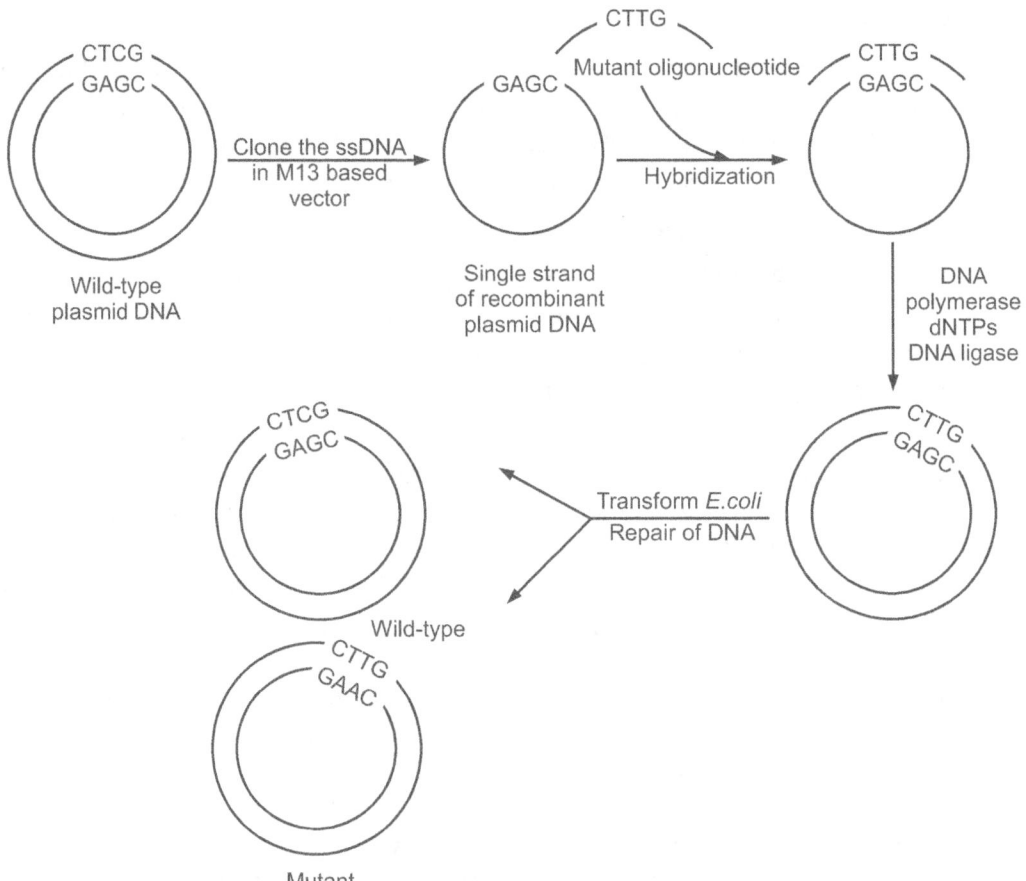

Fig. 11.8: Oligonucleotide site-directed mutagenesis

RESTRICTION FRAGMENT LENGTH POLYMORPHISM (RFLP)

Most restriction enzymes cleave DNA molecules in a site specific manner. The genomic DNA from an individual organism is digested with single or more restriction enzymes and this result in fragmentation with variation in length. These fragments are known as restriction fragment length polymorphisms (RFLPs). The size of the restriction fragments can be determined by agarose gel electrophoresis (Fig. 11.9). Single nucleotide polymorphisms (SNPs) can be detected by the sensitive PCR method. Variation obtained in one DNA fragment with that specific enzyme used for digestion is called one RFLP. The detection of restriction fragment length polymorphisms (RFLPs) relies on a specialized hybridization procedure called Southern blotting.

Extract and purify genomic DNA from different individuals having some differences and isolate separately. Digest DNA samples by restriction endonuclease and subject to gel electrophoresis of each individual on the same gel slab. DNA fragments are transferred from gel to nitrocellulose filters by using Southern blotting. The filters with small fragments, homologous to the probe can be detected by autoradiography after hybridization. The hybridized fragments of genomic DNA is called RFLP. Amplified fragment length polymorphism (AFLP) is the combination of restriction fragment length polymorphism (RFLP) and random amplified polymorphic DNA (RAPD) which is very sensitive in detecting polymorphism throughout the genome. RFLP and SNP maps are useful in the human genome sequencing project. It gives information about various single gene and multigenic diseases. RFLPs can be used to establish linkage groups by the process of chromosome walking. Restriction fragment length polymorphisms (RFLPs) are also used to prepare chromosome maps in rice, tomato, maize, mice, humans etc.

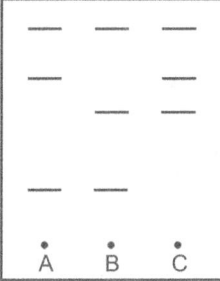

Fig. 11.9: RFLPs of three individuals (A, B and C) after hybridization

DNA FINGERPRINTING

DNA fingerprinting or DNA typing or DNA profiling method is important in forensic biochemical laboratories. It is mainly used to provide evidence in paternity and criminal cases. DNA fingerprints of the mother, child and alleged father are compared for paternity determination. Paternal bonds in child's DNA fingerprint must match with the alleged father for positive paternity identification. In forensic application, the DNA fingerprint obtained from cells at a crime scene is compared with a DNA fingerprint from cells provided by the suspect. It is possible to identify burnt dead body be DNA profiling.

Alec Jeffreys (1984) developed this technique of DNA fingerprinting in University of Leicester, England. Variable number of tandem repeats (VNTRs) is the key of DNA profiling because on the basis of number of repeats present in VNTRs, the length of segment is measured. The length of fragments of DNA containing the repeated sequences is also known as RFLP.

In the method of DNA profiling, DNA is isolated from blood, semen or any other DNA containing cells. Isolated DNA is cut into small fragments with restriction endonucleases and subjected to Southern blotting. The DNA bands appearing on membrane are hybridized with ^{32}P-DNA probe and passed through X-ray (Fig. 11.10). Specific DNA sequences appearing on two X-ray films are identified and confirmed.

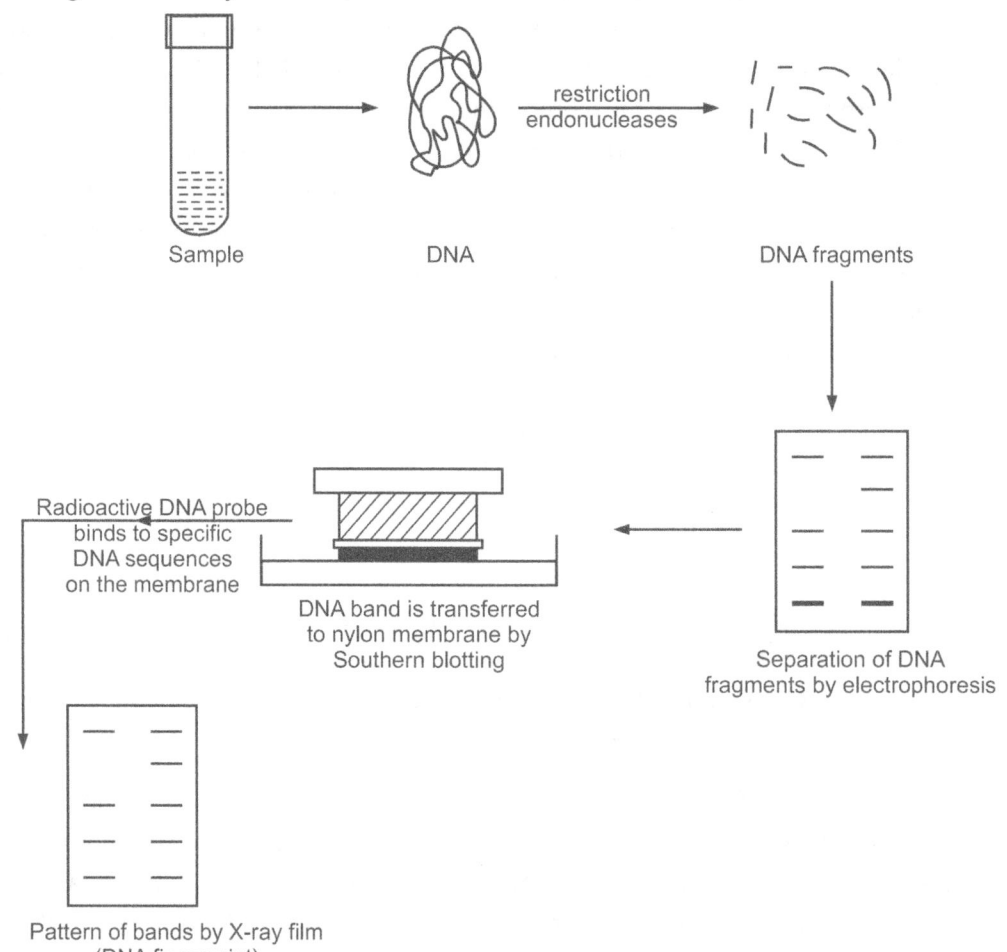

Fig. 11.10: DNA fingerprinting process

GENE SYNTHESIS AND GENE MACHINE

Har Govind Khorana and **K. L. Agarwal** (1970) synthesized the structure of gene for an alanine tRNA from yeast. Chemical synthesis of DNA has found wide applications in genetic engineering as total gene synthesis, primers for DNA and RNA sequencing, site directed mutagenesis, structure determination etc. The genes can be artificially synthesized by following methods.

Synthesis of a gene for yeast alanine tRNA:

R. W. Holley and his coworkers (1965) found detailed structure of yeast alanine tRNA containing 77 nucleotides. **Khorana** and his co-workers had a experience of synthesizing DNA of known base sequences. They found that it was difficult to assemble 77 base pairs of nucleotides in ordered form. They synthesized the short deoxynucleotide sequence which was joined by hydrogen bonding to form a long complementary strand. Double stranded pieces were prepared by using polynucleotide ligase.

Fifteen oligonucleotides ranging from pentanucleotide (five bases) to an icosanucleotide (twenty bases) are prepared. The chemical synthesis is performed by condensation between the –OH group at 3' position of one deoxynucleotide and the PO_4 group- at 5' position of the second deoxynucleotide. All other functional groups, not taking part in condensation, is protected using specific protective groups. Fifteen single stranded oligonucleotides are used to prepare three large double stranded DNA fragments. These three fragments contained, segment A-consisted of the first 20 nucleotides in which nucleotides 17-20 being single stranded, segment B-having nucleotide residues from 17 to 50 in which single stranded region being 17 to 20 and 46 to 50 and fragment C-consisting of nucleotide residues 46 to 77 with single stranded region 46 to 50 (Fig. 11.11). The above three segments (A, B and C) are joined by using the enzyme polynucleotide ligase to produce the complete gene for alanine tRNA.

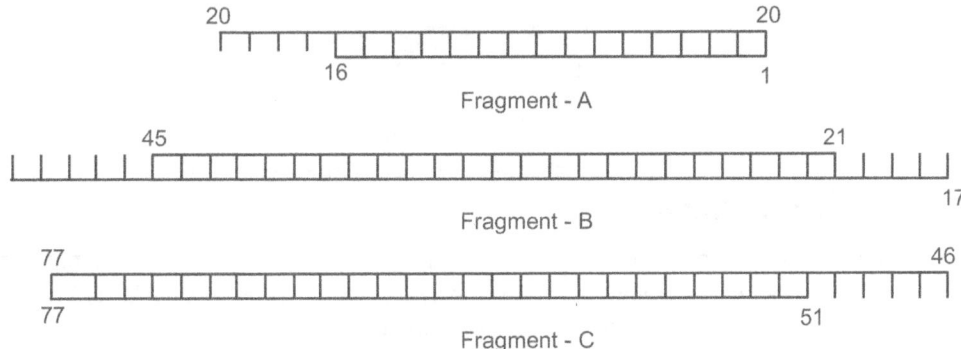

Fig. 11.11: The duplex DNA fragments (A, B and C)

Gene synthesis from mRNA:

RNA directed DNA polymerase enzyme is used for synthesis of DNA from RNA template. Hence, this technique is also called as enzymatic synthesis of gene (For detail-refer Gene library or Isolation of DNA).

The gene can be synthesized rapidly and in high amount with the help of fully automated commercial instrument called gene synthesis machine or automated polynucleotide synthesizer. The synthesis of gene is based on development of silica-based supports, which are insoluble and provide support for solid phase synthesis of DNA chains and development of stable deoxyribonucleoside phosphoramidites as synthons which are stable to oxidation and hydrolysis. These techniques can be used to prepare DNA molecules more than 100 nucleotides long within a short period. Different types of gene machines are used for synthesis of DNA, under the control of a microprocessor. Separate reservoirs (nucleotides A, T, C and G) are connected with a tube to synthesizer coloumn (Fig. 11.12) packed with small silica beads. These beads provide support on which DNA molecules are assembled. The desired sequence is entered on a keyboard. The microprocessor automatically opens the valves of the containers of nucleotides, reagents and solvents required for each step and it is controlled by microcomputer control system.

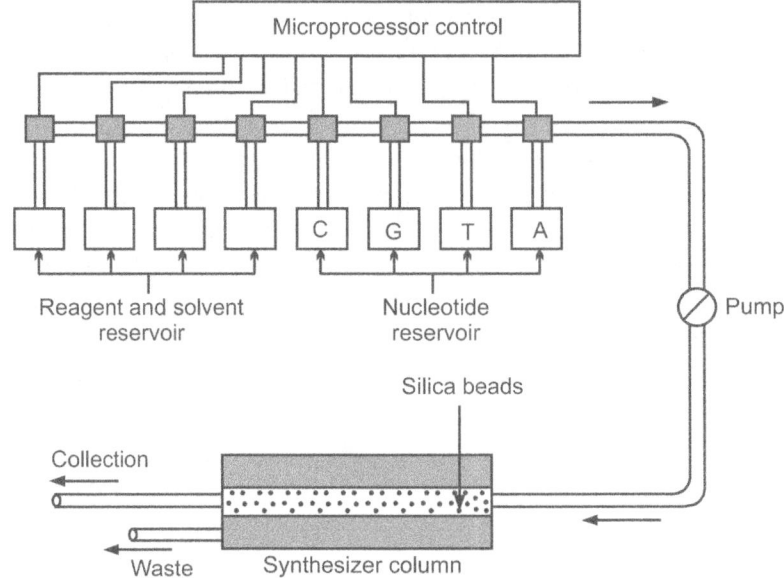

Fig. 11.12: Working of gene machine

GENE (DNA) SEQUENCING

Gene sequencing is a fundamental requirement for modern gene manipulation. The first DNA sequence was studied of the cohesive ends of phage λ DNA (12 bases long). The method used was derived from RNA sequencing and it was not applicable to large scale DNA sequencing. The new method (plus and minus sequencing) was used to sequence the 5386 bp phage. This method was superseded (1977) by chemical degradation method developed by **Maxam and Gilbert** and dideoxy chain termination method of **Sanger**. The methods used for DNA sequencing are classified as **Maxam** and **Gilbert's** chemical degradation method, **Sanger's** dideoxynucleotide chain termination method and automated DNA sequencing.

Maxam and Gilbert's chemical degradation method:

In the chemical degradation method, the DNA molecule is radiolabelled with ^{32}P at either its 5' end by using polynucleotide kinase or its 3' end by terminal transferase. One end of radiolabelled double stranded DNA is removed by using endonuclease. The DNA is then partially modified with chemical reagents specific for the different bases and cleaved at the modified nucleotides. This generates a set of molecules differing in length but with the same isotopically labelled terminus. These fragments of different length represent unique pairs of 5' and 3' cleavage products in the random collection. All these fragments are separated by gel electrophoresis and fragments containing labelled terminus are observed in autoradiogram (Fig. 11.13).

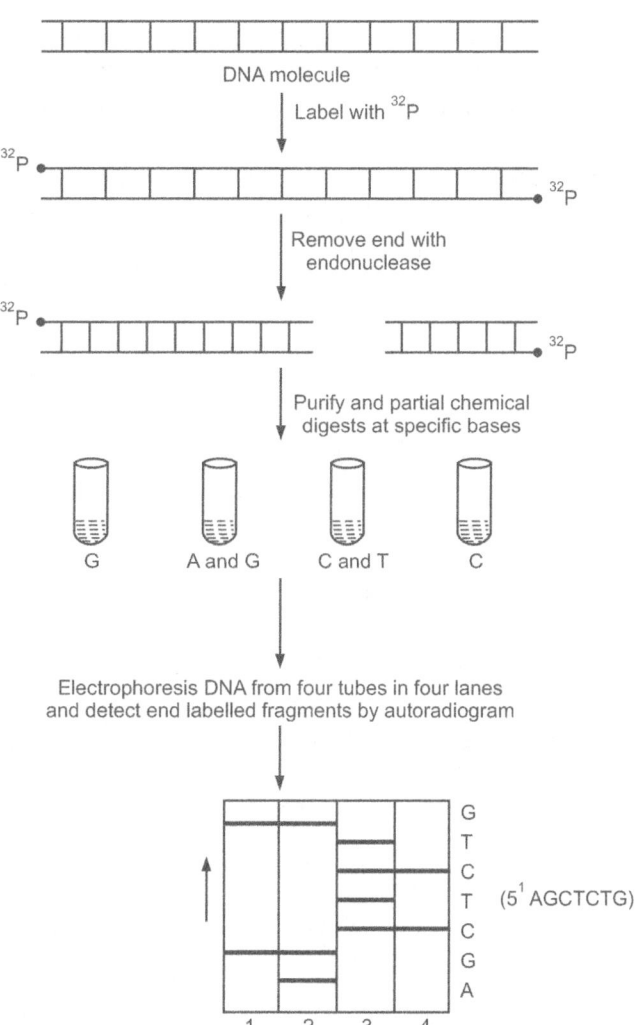

Fig. 11.13: Maxam and Gilbert's method for DNA sequencing

Sanger's dideoxynucleotide chain termination method :

The **Sanger's** chain termination method is more superior than **Maxam** and **Gilbert's** chemical method because chain method is more efficient and simple to perform. **Sanger** first developed the method for DNA sequencing, in which utilized DNA polymerase to extend DNA chain length. This method is called plus minus method. **Sanger** formulated a technique to identify the DNA sequence by providing a ssDNA solution of nucleotides of perticular type. This method is time consuming and not possible for whole genome sequencing.

Sanger developed a more powerful method utilizing single stranded DNA as the template for DNA synthesis. This method is called dideoxynucleotide chain termination method. Dideoxynucleotides are used as triphosphates (ddNTP) and can be incorporated in a growing chain but they terminate synthesis. They differ from dNTPs as they lack a –OH group on the 3' carbon of the ribose sugar. Hence, they prevent formation of a phosphodiester bond with the next nucleotide to be added and prevent further elongation. Different DNA polymerases like *E. coli* DNA polymerase (I) (Klenow fragment), genetically modified DNA polymerase from the phase T7 (sequence) and *Taq* DNA polymerase have been used for the sequencing reaction. All DNA polymerases require short regions of double stranded DNA to initiate DNA synthesis on a single stranded template. This is provide by the addition of a short single-stranded DNA molecule known as primer.

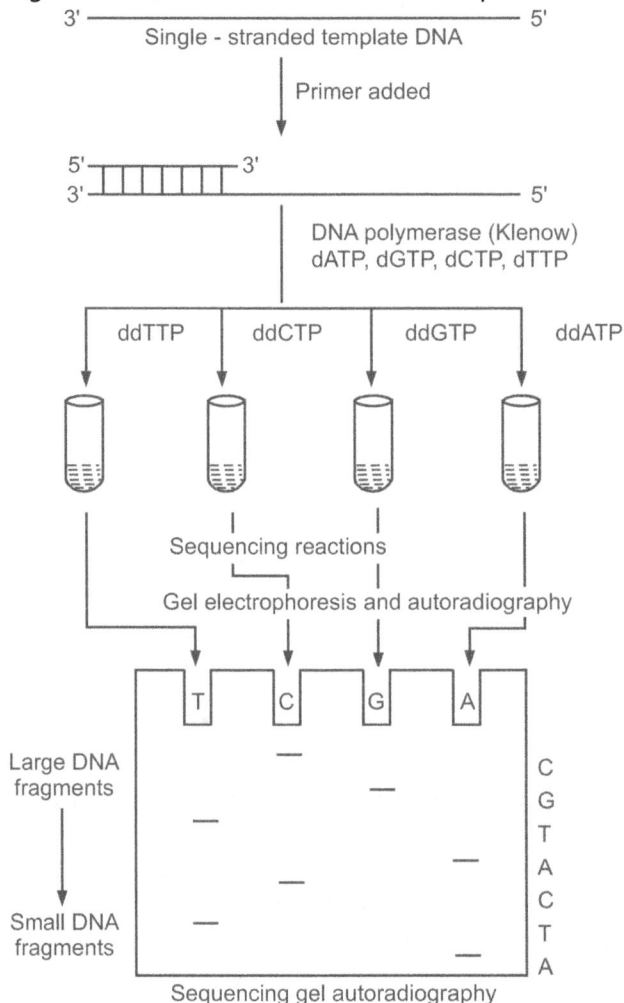

Fig. 11.14: DNA sequencing by dideoxy chain termination method

For the sequence of DNA molecule, four separate enzyme reaction are performed in separate reaction tubes (Fig. 11.14). Each tube containing template DNA (cloned in M13 phage) in single-stranded form, DNA polymerase, primer, each of the four deoxynucleotide triphosphates, dNTPs (dATP, dGTP, dCTP and dTTP) and modified nucleotide, dideoxynucleotide triphosphate, ddNTPs (ddATP, ddGTP, ddCTP and ddTTP). The concentration of ddNTPs should be maintained to about 1% of the concentration of dNTPs. The ratio of dNTP to ddNTP in the reaction mixture is carefully adjusted so that a dideoxy moiety is incorporated only occasionally in place of its deoxy homologues. All four reactions produce a population of partially synthesized DNA fragments of different lengths, all sharing a common 5' end, all are radioactivelly labelled and all of which are terminated by a dideoxynucleotide. The synthesized DNA molecules are separated according to size by electrophoresis on polyacrylamide gels. The gel is used for autoradiography so that the position of different bands in each lane can be visualized. DNA sequence is obtained by reading the bands on autoradiogram of four lanes.

Automated DNA sequencing:

Automated DNA sequencing technique includes semi-automated systems in which electrophoresis of DNA and analysis of sequencing reactions is carried out by instruments controlled by computers (Fig. 11.15). In this method, the four ddNTPs are labelled by the covalent attachment of a different coloured dye. All labelled ddNTPs are added in single capillary tube. The DNA fragments of different colours are separated by their respective size in a single electrophoretic gel. All DNA fragments are illuminated with a laser beam that excites the dye label to emit fluorescence. The instrument identifies the dye from the wavelength of the emitted fluorescence. The sequence of the colours emitted from specific peaks is detected for DNA sequences. This information is directly supplied to a computer system which determines the sequence. Automated DNA sequencing leads good quality sequence data with less error as compared to manual sequencing. Each sequencing reaction requires one tube and one lane on the gel compared with four per sample required for manual sequencing. Speed and scope of DNA sequencing is changed because of new modified DNA sequencer. DNA sequencing is one of important technique of molecular genetics and is widely used for identification of newly isolated bioactive microbial species.

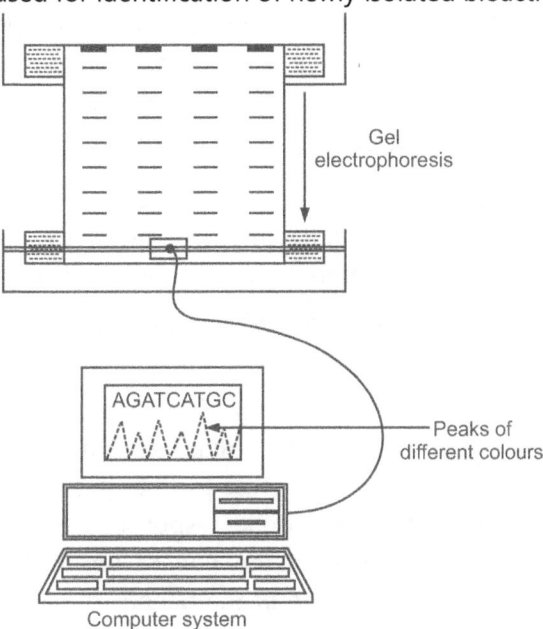

Fig. 11.15: Automated DNA sequencing

HUMAN GENE THERAPY

Gene therapy is the method used to treat disease by modifying the genetic information in the cells of the patient. Gene therapies are aimed to treat or eliminate the cause of disease by gene transfer. The first clinical study was initiated in USA in 1990. The desired gene must usually be packed into a vector system capable of delivering it safely inside the intended recipient cells. A variety of vectors can be used to affect gene transfer (Table 11.1).

Table 11.1: Vector systems used to deliver genes into mammalian cells

Types	Example
Viral based vector systems	Adenoviruses, Retroviruses, Herpes virus, Polio virus, Vaccinia virus, Adeno associated virus
Non-viral based vector systems	Electroporation, particle acceleration, nucleic acid containing liposomes, molecular conjugates, direct injection of naked DNA, $CaPO_4$ precipitation.

There are two strategies for gene transfer, (i) In-vivo approach, in which involves introduction of genes directly into the target organs of an individual (patient therapy) and (ii) ex-vivo approach, in which cells are isolated for gene transfer in vitro followed by transplantation of genetically modified cells back into the patients.

Gene delivery has become quite easy with the availability of many viral, non-viral and physical delivery systems. Retroviruses effectively enter various cell types and integrate their genome into the host cell genome in stable form. Hence, retroviruses are potential vectors for gene therapy. Adenovirus can transfer genes to both proliferating and quiescent cells and it efficiently transfers gene by in vivo method. Various approaches have been tried for effective transfer of genes to appropriate site. These approaches are classified as follows.

(a) **Gene modification** – replacement therapy, corrective gene therapy.

(b) **Gene transfer** – physical methods as gene gun, microinjection, naked DNA, electoporation etc. chemical methods as oligonucleotides, cationic liposomes etc and biological methods as mammalian artificial chromosomes, viral vectors etc.

(c) **Gene transfer in specific cells lines** – somatic gene therapy, germline gene therapy.

More than 4000 genetic diseases have been characterized and studied. These diseases are caused by lack of production of a single gene product or due to the production of a mutated gene product. The slow progress to treat genetic diseases is likely due to number of factors. Identification of actual gene responsible for disease, proper gene-delivering vectors, complexicity of disease, limited patient population etc are major problems for development of gene therapy. Some of the genetic diseases under clinical trial are listed in Table 11.2.

Table 11.2: Gene therapies in clinical studies

Disease	Vector	Gene transfer	Therapeutic agent/gene	Target cell/ tissue
Cytic fibrosis	Adeno virus	In vivo	CFTR	Nasal epithelium
Limb ischaemia	Naked DNA	In vivo	VEGF	Muscle cells
Haemophilia	Retrovirus	In vivo	Factor VIII / IX	Hepatocytes, muscles
Alzheimer's disease	Retrovirus	Ex vivo	NGF	Tumour cells
Parkinson's disease	Retrovirus	Ex vivo	TH	Fibroblast
AIDS	Retrovirus	Ex vivo	HIV antigen	T cells
Cancer	Cationic lipid	In vivo	HLA B7	Tumour cells
Cancer	Retrovirus	Ex vivo	Interleukins	Tumour cells
Cancer	Adenovirus	In vivo	P 53	Tumour cells

Most of the clinical trials involving gene therapy have been directed to tumour cells. Introduction of TNF gene into tumour in-filtrating lymphocytes, insertion of a copy of a tumour suppresser gene into cancer cells and killing of tumour cells by transfection with the thymidine kinase gene of the herpes simplex virus are the major techniques used for gene therapy in cancer.

QUESTIONS

(A) Short answer questions:

1. Explain the following:
    (a) Primer
    (b) PFGE
    (c) cDNA library
    (d) Automated DNA sequencing
2. Write the role of site directed mutagenesis in strain improvement.
3. Explain the applications of DNA fingerprinting.
4. Explain in short synthesis of gene for yeast alanine tRNA.

(B) Long answer questions:

1. What is RFLP? Explain.
2. Explain different methods used for gene sequencing.

3. Write a short note on:
   (a) Gene therapy
   (c) Gene machine
4. Describe in short different methods used for isolation of DNA.
5. Explain the different electrophoresis techniques used for separation of DNA, RNA and protein molecules.
6. Explain the applications of polymerase-chain reaction.

(C) Multiple choice questions:
1. An enzyme that cleaves DNA at a specific site is called _____ .
   (a) Restrictive ribonuclease
   (b) Restrictive endonuclease
   (c) Trypsin
   (d) All of the above

2. The most widely used carrier for gene therapy is _____ .
   (a) *Escherichia coli*
   (b) *Staphylococcus aureus*
   (c) Adenovirus
   (d) Vaccinia virus

3. Site-directed mutagenesis can be achieved by the following technique _____.
   (a) PCR
   (b) RT-PCR
   (c) LCR
   (d) RAS

(D) Fill in the blanks:
1. A _____ is a collection of plasmid clones or phage lysates containing recombinant DNA molecules.
2. The powerful method utilizing single stranded DNA as the template for DNA synthesis is developed by **Sanger** called _____ chain termination method.

■■■

CHAPTER 12

BLOTTING TECHNIQUES AND GEL ELECTROPHORESIS

CONTENTS
    INTRODUCTION
    BLOTTING TECHNIQUES
        Southern blotting,
        Northern blotting,
        Western blotting,
        Dot and slot blotting
    DNA PROBES
    GEL ELECTROPHORESIS
    POLYMERASE CHAIN REACTION (PCR)

INTRODUCTION

Blotting techniques are applied in the isolation and quantification of specific nucleic acid sequences and in the study of the organization, intracellular localization, expression and regulation. These techniques describe the immobilization of sample nucleic acids on a nylon or nitrocellulose membranes. The blotted nucleic acids are then used as 'targets' in subsequent hybridization experiments. DNA, RNA and proteins are easily separated by blotting method. The main blotting procedures are:

- Southern blotting
- Northern blotting
- Western blotting or protein blotting
- Dot and slot blotting.

Agarose gel electrophoresis, pulsed field gel electrophoresis (PFGE), polyacrylamide gel electrophoresis (PAGE), sodium dodecyl sulphate polyacrylamide gel electrophoresis (SDS – PAGE) and two-dimensional electrophoresis techniques are used for separation of DNA, RNA and protein molecules.

The development of polymerase chain reaction (PCR) or gene amplification method in 1983 was a major breakthrough in molecular biology. This technique was developed by **Kary Mullis** at Cetus Corporation (biotech company) in Emery Ville, California. The details of PCR techniques are described by **Erlich** (1989) in his edited book 'PCR Technology'. It is an in-vitro method for producing large amounts of specific DNA fragment of defined length and sequence from a small amount of complex template. PCR is now considered as a basic tool for the molecular biologist.

BLOTTING TECHNIQUES

Blotting techniques are widely used analytical tools for the specific identification of desired DNA or RNA fragments. Blotting refers to the process of immobilization of sample nucleic acids or solid support. The blotted nucleic acids are then used as targets in the hybridization experiments for their specific detection.

Southern blotting:

The original method of blotting was developed by E. M. Southern (1975) to identify the locations of genes and other DNA sequences on restriction fragments separated by gel electrophoresis. In Southern blotting technique, a sample of DNA containing fragments of different sizes are subjected to electrophoresis using either polyacrylamide or agarose gel.

DNA molecule is cut into small fragments by restriction enzyme and passed through agarose gel by electrophoresis method. It results into separation of DNA molecules based on their size. The DNA is then denatured into single strands by exposing the gel to alkaline solution. Gel is added on the top of the buffer saturated filter paper. It is covered with nitrocellulose filter overlayed with dry filter paper (Fig. 12.1). The buffer moves from the bottom of filter paper by the capillary action and DNA is trapped in the nitrocellulose membrane. This process is known as blotting. The nitrocellulose membrane is removed from the blotting stack and DNA is permanently immobilized on the membrane by baking at $80^{\circ}C$ or ultraviolet induced cross-linking.

Single-stranded DNA has a high affinity for nitrocellular filter membrane. Hence, the membrane is treated with a solution containing 0.2% each of Ficoll, polyvinylpyrrolidone and bovine serum albumin. This treatment prevents non-specific binding of the radioactive probe. The membrane is placed in a solution of labelled RNA, single-stranded DNA or oligodeoxynucleotide (probe). These labelled nucleic acid is used to detect and locate the complementary sequence, it is called probe. The probe containing the sequence of interest is hybridized or annealed with the immbolized DNA on the membrane. After the hybridization reaction, the membrane is washed to remove the unbound probes. The washed membrane is exposed to X-ray film that detects the presence of the radioactivity in the bound probe. The film is developed to reveal bands indicating positions in the gel of the DNA fragments that are complementary to the radioactive probe.

The Southern blotting technique is very sensitive method and it is used to map the restriction sites around a single copy gene sequence in any genome. It is also used in preparation of restriction fragment length polymorphism (RFLP) maps, DNA finger printing, identification of the transferred genes etc. Nitrocellulose paper being very fragile is now replaced by nylon membrane.

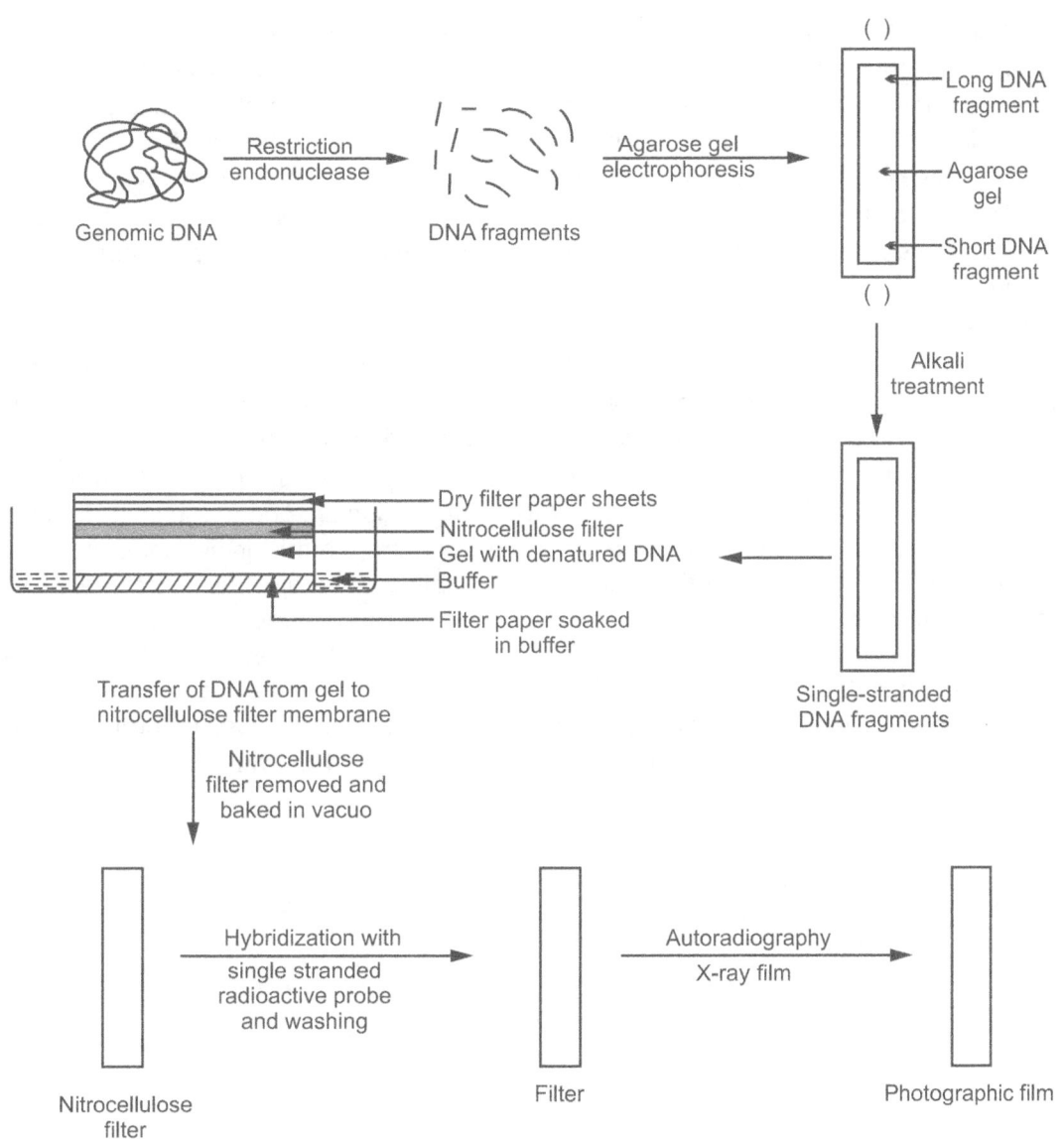

Fig. 12.1: Procedure of Southern blotting technique

Northern blotting:

Alwine et al (1979) devised a technique in which RNA bands are blot transferred from the gel onto chemically reactive paper. An aminobenzyloxymethyl cellulose paper prepared from Whatman paper 540 after a series of simple reactions. It is diazotised and rendered into the reactive paper. It becomes available for hybridization with radio-labelled DNA probes. The hybridized bands are found out by autoradiography. **Alwine's** method extends that of Southern method and hence, it has given the jargon term 'Northern blotting'.

Thomas (1980) found that mRNA bands can also be blotted directly on nitrocellulose paper under appropriate condition and it can be hybridized with a labeled DNA or RNA probe. Hybrids are treated with S-1 nuclease with RNAase which digests the single stranded RNA/DNA probe. Structure of mRNA is revealed to the extent to which mRNA protects the nucleic acid probe. In this technique, preparation of reactive paper is not required.

Northern blotting are mainly useful in studies of gene expression. It is also used to determine whether a particular gene is transcribed in all tissues of an microorganism or only certain tissues.

Western blotting:

Towbin et al (1979) developed the western blotting or protein blotting or electroblotting technique to findout the newly encoded protein by a transformed cell. Polyacrylamide gel electrophoresis is used for the separation and characterization of proteins.

Proteins are extracted from transformed cells and separated by using sodium dodecyl sulphate polyacrylamide gel electrophoresis (SDS – PAGE). Sodium dodecyl sulphate acts as a denaturant for proteins during electrophoresis. After electrophoresis, individual proteins are detected by using specific antibodies and polypeptides can also be transferred to a nitrocellulose membrane. The transfer of proteins from gels to nitrocellulose membranes is called western blotting. It is performed by using an electric current, hence, it is called electroblotting method (Fig. 12.2). Electric field is applied to cause the migration of proteins from the gel to nitrocellulose filter paper. Nitrocellulose membrane is used for probing with a specific labelled antibody. The antibody is labelled with ^{125}I and the signal is detected again with autoradiography.

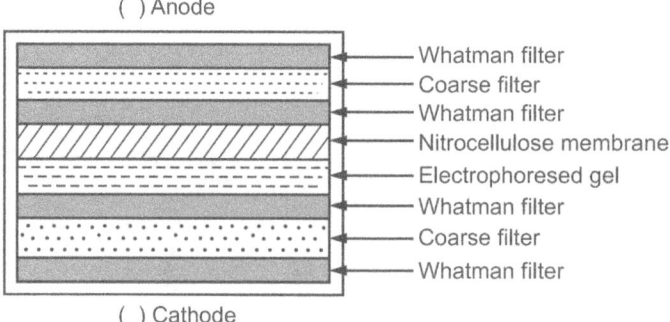

Fig. 12.2: Electo blotting or western blotting apparatus

Dot and slot blotting:

Dot and slot blotting is used to detect the presence of a given sequence of DNA/RNA in the non-fractionated DNA. The procedure is made simple by excluding purification steps, electrophoresis and blotting of gel. The sample of DNA or RNA from different individuals or tissues are transferred onto a nitrocellulose filter in form of dots or slots. Hence, this method is called as dot and slot blotting. The DNA is first denatured and then the filer is baked at 80°C to fix the DNA. The nitrocellulose filter is treated with the appropriate radioactive single stranded DNA probe. The membrane is then hybridized with radioactively labelled probe

(DNA or RNA) and dots are detected by autoradiography (Fig. 12.3). The intensity of dot will indicate the relative concentration of a sequence related to the probe in the DNA sample.

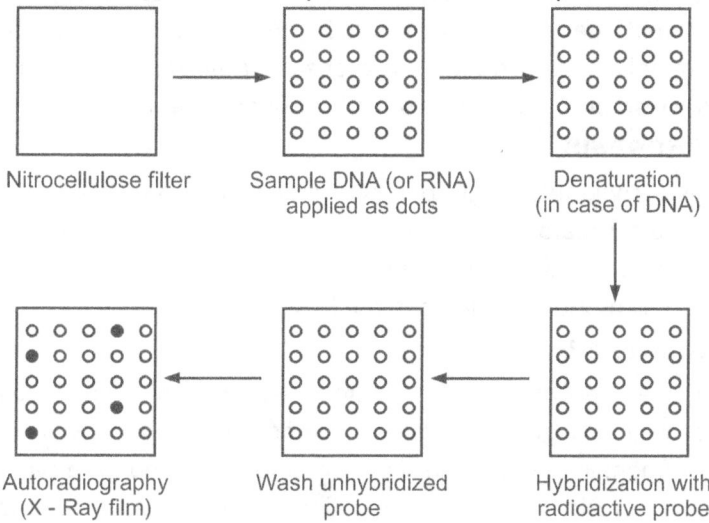

Fig. 12.3: Dot blot method

DNA PROBES

DNA probes are radiolabelled pieces of single-stranded DNA that will bind to DNA that is complementary to the probe using hybridizing technique. These probes contain unique nucleotide sequences which can be used for the detection of homologous DNA by hybridisation. DNA probes are commonly used in the diagnosis of infectious diseases based on unique sequences of DNA or RNA. Every microorganism contains a unique nucleotide sequences that distinguishes it from every other species. A genetic composition of cells is in essence, a fingerprint that can be used for its identification. This technique is based on hybridization of test DNA with a DNA probe. A DNA probe is a sequence of DNA which is tagged with an easily detectable marker like radioactive isotope or an enzyme. If the test DNA is present in the sample it will conjugate with itself the DNA probe. These probes can be designated that are totally specific for any given genus or species of micro-organism.

The method of developing a nucleic acid probe (DNA or RNA) is to cut or isolate sequences from the nucleic acid of the cell using a set of enzymes (restriction endonucleases). These DNA fragments obtained by enzymes digestion and separation on gel can be transferred from the gel by blotting to nitrocellulose paper or nylon membranes that bind the DNA. The DNA bound to the membrane is converted to the single-stranded form and treated with radioactive single-stranded DNA probes. These will hybridise with homologous DNA to form radioactive double-stranded segments. DNA hybridization can be detected on X-ray film. This sensitive technique (DNA hybridization) was devised by **E. M. Southern** and hence, it is called as Southern blotting. This technique has wide applications in DNA analysis. The RNA mixture is separated by gel electrophoresis, blotted and identified using labelled DNA or RNA probes. This technique for the analysis of RNA is called northern blotting. A similar technique used for the identification of proteins (antigens) is called immunoblotting (western blotting). Protein antigen mixture is separated by sodium dodecyl sulfate - polyacrylamide gel electrophoresis (SDS-PAGE), blotted onto nitrocellulose strips and identified by radiolabelled antibodies as probes. The western blot test is commonly used as the confirmatory test for the diagnosis of HIV antibody in sera.

GEL ELECTROPHORESIS

Electrophoresis technique is applied for separation of DNA, RNA and proteins. These charged molecules are separated depending on their net charges, size and shapes. DNA molecules have negative charges and hence they migrate to anode. The small size DNA molecules move faster through the gel than the larger molecules.

Agarose gel electrophoresis:

Agarose is a linear polymer of D-galactose and 3, 6-anhydro-L-galactose which is extracted from seaweeds algae. The gel is composed of agarose. It is convenient for separating of DNA fragments ranging in size from a few hundred base pairs to about 20 kb. Agarose gel electrophoresis is used for separation of large sized macromolecules because these gels are porous and have large pore size. Nucleic acids are loaded into slots (called wells) of the agarose gel and allowed to migrate from cathode to anode by using electric field (Fig. 12.4). The pores in the gel act to sieve the molecules. The migration of the DNA molecules through the pores of the matrix must play an important role in molecular weight separations (Fig. 12.5). All the molecules of a particular size move at approximately the same rate through the gel, forming a band. The bands of DNA in the gel are stained with the intercalating dye ethidium bromide and detected by visible fluorescence (Fig. 12.6) when the gel is illuminated with UV light.

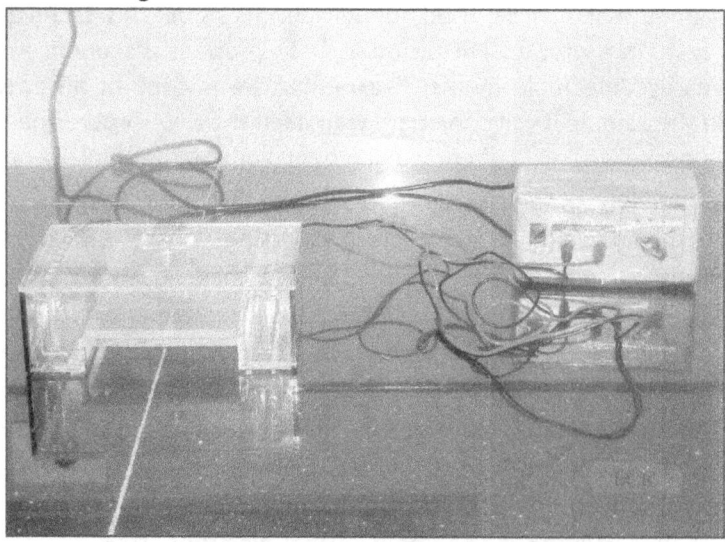

Fig. 12.4: Gel electrophoresis assembly

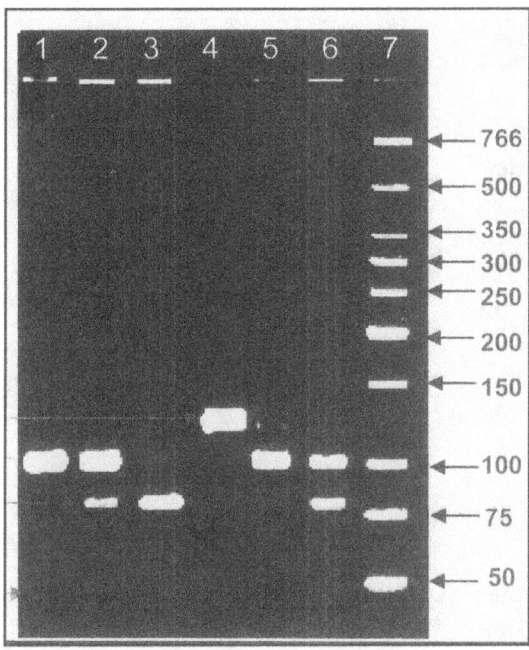

Fig. 12.5: DNA molecules are separated by gel electrophoresis as per molecular weight

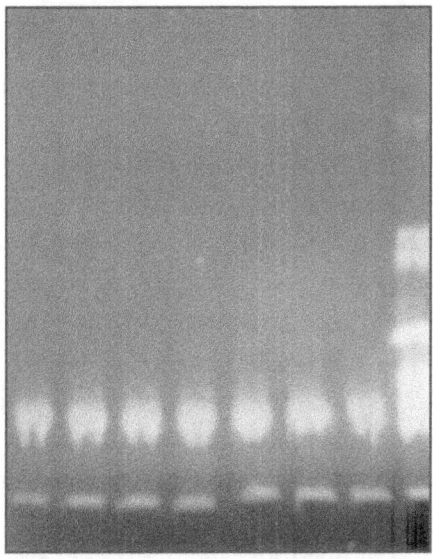

Fig. 12.6: DNA isolated by gel electrophoresis are visible by fluorescence

Pulsed field gel electrophoresis (PFGE):

In pulsed field gel electrophoresis, molecules of size 10 Mb can be separated in agarose gels. **Schwartz** and **Cantor** (1984) developed this technique for separation of long DNA molecules. This is achieved by causing the DNA to periodically alter its direction of migration by regular changes in the orientation of the electric field with respect to the gel. The larger molecules require more time to reorient than the smaller molecules (Fig. 12.7). Direction, intensity and duration of the electric field are set independent for each of the different fields.

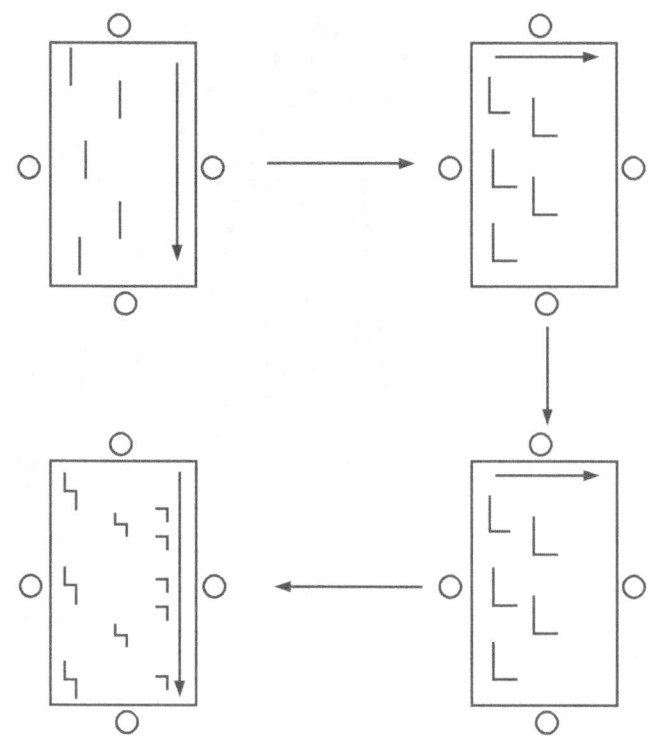

Fig. 12.7: Pulsed field gel electrophoresis (PFGE)

Polyacrylamide gel electrophoresis (PAGE):

The most widely used method for determining the purity of a protein is polyacrylamide gel electrophoresis (PAGE). Polyacrylamide has a smaller pore size than agarose and hence, it is preferred for smaller DNA fragments of 10 to 1000 nucelotides in length. Polyacrylamide gel is inert and stable at different conditions of pH, temperature and ionic strength with very high resolution. Pore size of gel can be changed by varying the concentration of acrylamide and biacrylamide monomers.

Some proteins are treated with an ionic detergent (sodium dodecyl sulfate, SDS) before the polyacrylamide gel electrophoresis because such proteins are not separated due to similar charge mass ratio. This electrophoresis is called as sodium dodecyl sulfate polyacrylamide gel electrophoresis (SDS – PAGE). Sodium dodecyl sulfate (SDS) denatures and binds to proteins at a ratio of one molecule of SDS per two peptide bonds. It is used in conjunction with 2-mercaptoethanol or dithiothreitol to reduce and break disulfide bonds to separate polypeptides. The smaller polypeptides move faster than the larger polypeptides towards anode (Fig. 12.8). The separated polypeptides in the acrylamide gel are visualized by staining with coomassie blue dye. (Fig. 12.9)

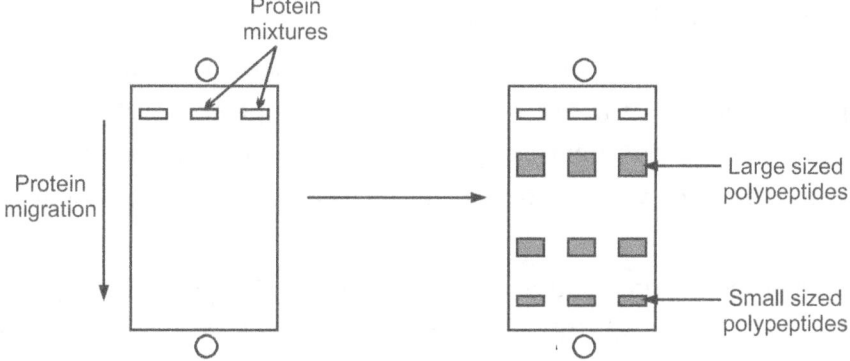

Fig. 12.8: Separation of proteins by SDS-PAGE

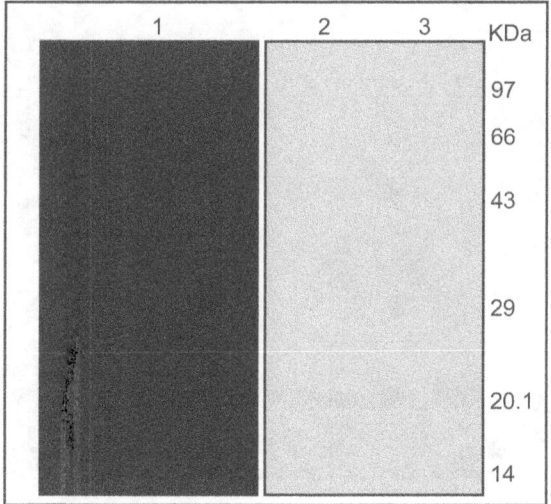

Fig. 12.9: SDS-PAGE staining with coomassie blue dye

Two-dimensional electrophoresis:

A mixture of protein is separated by two-dimensional electrophoresis. The first dimension uses the iso-electric focusing and the second dimension is SDS-PAGE. Isoelectric focusing is used on conjunction with SDS-PAGE. Proteins have electric charges which depends on the conditions of medium (pH) and type of molecules. These molecules have net negative charge and net positive charge or iso-electric point (no charge) at different pH of buffer. Ampholytes (ionic buffers) and an applied electric field are used to generate a pH gradient within a polyacrylamide matrix. Proteins migrate through the region of the matrix where the pH matches their isoelectric point and the pH at which a molecule's net charge is zero. Two dimensional electrophoresis is commonly used for separating the components of complex mixtures of proteins.

POLYMERASE CHAIN REACTION (PCR)

PCR is an in-vitro method for producing large amounts of specific DNA fragment of defined length and sequence from a small amount of complex template. In this technique, microgram quantities of DNA from picogram produce amounts of starting material. Target DNA, primers, polymerase and nucleotides are combined in a test tube for multiplication of genetic material.

DNA is amplified by polymerase chain reaction (Fig. 12.10) in an enzymatic reaction which undergoes multiple incubations at three different temperatures. Each PCR contains four important components.

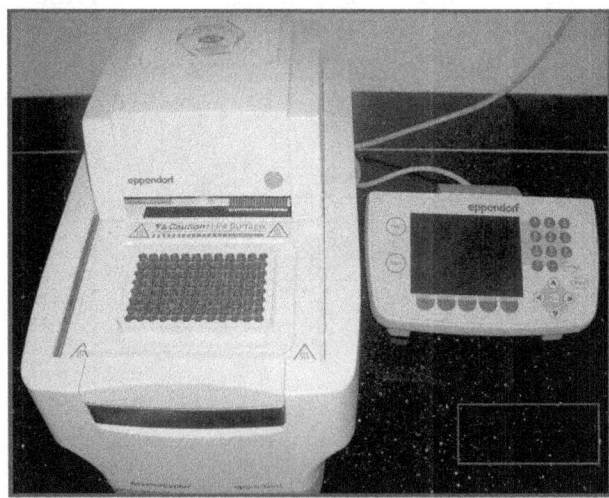

Fig. 12.10: Polymerase chain reaction (PCR) machine (thermal cycler)

DNA Template: Any source that contains one or more target DNA molecules to be amplified can be taken as template. RNA can also be used for PCR by first making a DNA copy using the enzyme reverse transcriptase.

Primers: Each PCR requires a pair of oligonucleotide primers. These are short single-stranded DNA molecules obtained by chemical synthesis. These primers are designed to anneal on opposite strands of target sequence so that they will be extended towards each other by addition of nucleotides.

DNA polymerase: The most commonly used enzyme in PCR is *Taq* DNA polymerase isolated from a thermostable bacterium called *Thermus aquaticus*. It survives at 95°C for 1 to 2 minutes and has a half life for more than 2 hours at same temperature. The DNA polymerase binds to a single-stranded DNA and synthesizes a new strand complementary to the origin strand. The role of this enzyme in PCR is to copy DNA molecules.

Deoxynucleotide triphosphates: PCR requires four deoxynucleotide triphosphates, dNTPs (dATP, dGTP, dTTP, dCTP) which are used by the DNA polymerase as building blocks to synthesize new DNA.

Polymerase chain reaction (PCR) involves three stages which are as follows (Fig. 12.11):
1. Melting of DNA (95°C) to convert double stranded DNA to a single stranded DNA (denaturation).
2. Promoting the primers (at 50 - 65°C) to attach themselves to either end of the target strip (annealing of primers).
3. Extension of the primers by DNA polymerase to form new double-stranded DNA across the segment by sequential addition of deoxynucleotides (primer extension). When the temperature is again raised the new strands separate and the process begins again. Temperature profile of typical PCR cycle is shown in Fig. 12.12.

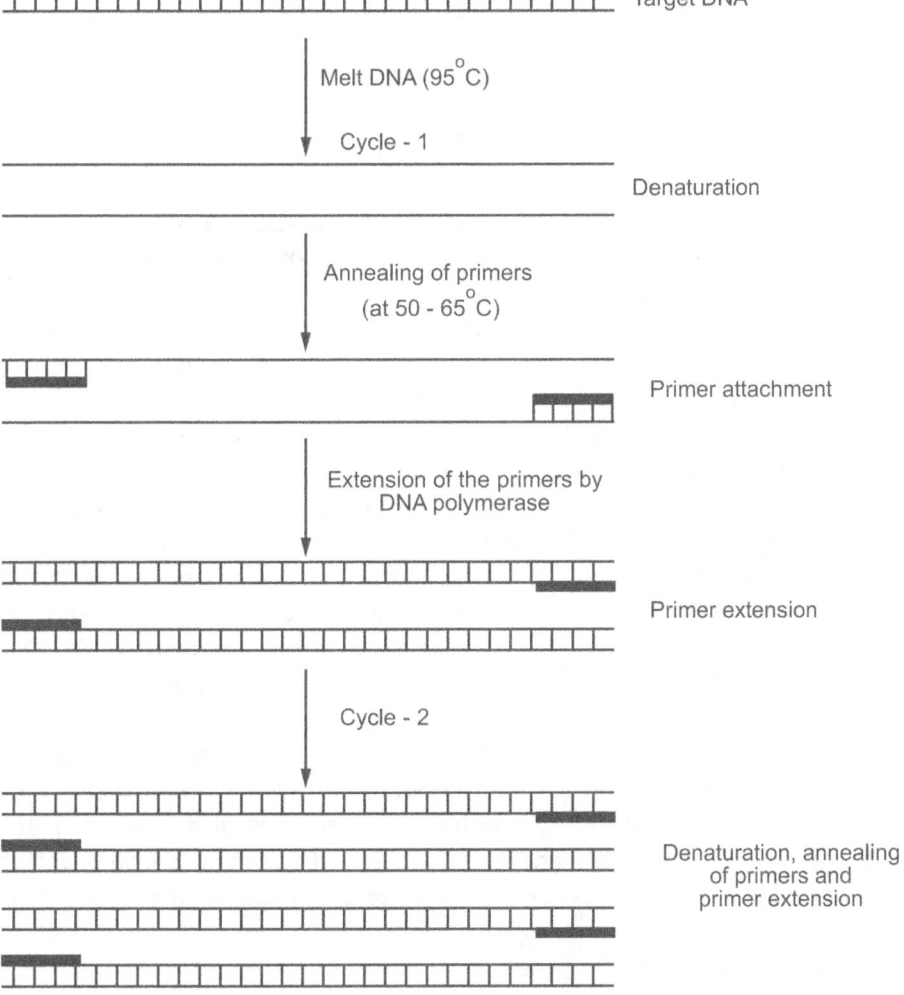

Fig. 12.11: Polymerase chain reaction (PCR)

The oligonucleotide primers are designed to hybridise the region of DNA flanking a desired target gene sequence. The primers are then extended across the target sequence using DNA polymerase derived from *Thermus aquaticus* (Taq) in the presence of free deoxynucleotide triphosphate. These three steps constitute one cycle of the reaction. These steps are repeated by manipulating the temperature, by using the PCR machine. A cycle takes about 3 to 5 minutes and after 30 cycles (about 3 hours), a single copy of DNA can be multiplied into 1,000,000 copies.

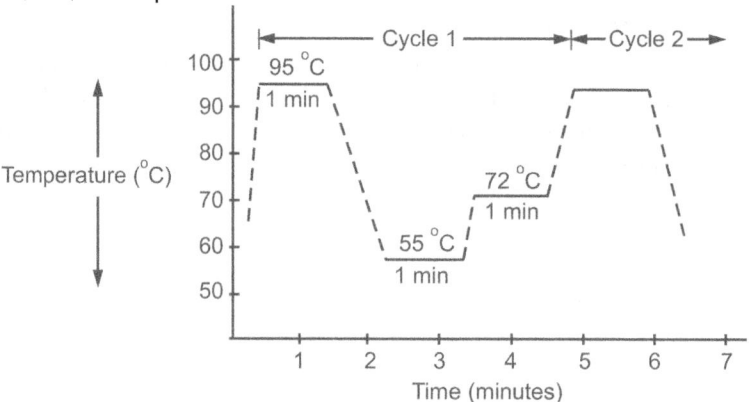

Fig. 12.12: Temperature profile of a typical PCR cycle

RNA polymerase chain reaction is a modification of PCR technique which allows amplification beginning from an RNA template.

Recent research in the field of polymerase chain reaction has led to the development of the techniques contributing to the effectiveness of the method. PCR is a highly versatile technique. Important variations of PCR are as follows:

Inverse PCR: PCR can be used to the amplification of those DNA sequences which are away from the primer and not of those which are flanked by the primer. The sequences to be amplified may be cloned in a vector and border sequence of the vector may be used as a primer in such a way that the polymerization proceeds in reverse direction.

Anchored PCR: In this method only one primer is used. One strand is copied first and then poly G tail is attached at the end of the newly synthesized strand. This allows the use of complementary homopolymer, poly-C, to be used as primer for copying the DNA single strands generated by PCR. It gives rise to the complete DNA duplex that can be amplified normally.

RT-PCR: Reverse transcription-mediated PCR includes a single application combining the process of cDNA synthesis (by reverse transcription) and PCR amplification. It can also be applied to double stranded cDNA also which is synthesized from mRNA using the enzyme reverse transcriptase. Thermostable enzyme rT_{th} uses RNA templates from cDNA synthesis and thus allows single enzyme RT-PCR viral reverse transcriptase from avian murine virus (AMV RTase).

Asymmetric PCR: It is used to generate single-strand copies of a DNA sequence which can be directly used for DNA sequencing. The two primers (100 : 1 ratio) are such adjusted in the reaction mixture that one of them is exhausted about 10 or more cycles. After these cycles, only a single strand of DNA segment is copied and these copies are the ideal starting materials for DNA sequencing. This variation is known as asymmetric PCR.

AP-PCR: Arbitrary primed PCR (AP-PCR) is a type of random amplified polymorphic DNA (RAPD) where single primers of 10 to 50 bases are used to amplify genomic DNA in PCR. **Welsh** and **McCleland** (1990) developed the arbitrary primed – PCR and carried out finger printing of genomes with arbitrary primers.

Polymerase chain reaction is useful in diverse areas of molecular biology, medicines and biotechnology.

Diagnosis of pathogens: PCR is commonly used for diagnosis of infections caused by viruses (e.g. HIV–1, HIV–2, Herpes simplex virus, Hepatitis B virus etc.), bacteria (*Mycobacterium tuberculosis, Helicobacter pylori, Mycoplasma pneumoniae* etc), fungi (*Candida albicans*) and protozoa (*Toxoplasma gondii, Trypanosoma cruzi* etc).

Diagnosis of plant pathogens: Various plant pathogens are detected by using PCR such as viruses (plum pox virus, cauliflower mosaic virus), fungi (*Verticillium* spp., *Laccaria* spp., *Phytophthora* spp. etc), mycoplasms bacteria (*Agrobacterium tumifaciens, Rhizobium leguminosarum, Xanthomonas* compestris etc) and nematodes (*Meloidogyne incoginta*) etc.

Inherited diseases: Inherited disorders are caused by gene mutations passed on from parents to their children e.g. hemophilia, cystic fibrosis etc. PCR is used to amplify gene sequences which can then be screened for disease causing mutations.

Research: PCR is used extensively as a research tool for identification of new species. Many bioactive microbial species are isolated from various extreme environment such as soil, water, air, sediments etc. DNA fingerprinting of new microorganisms is carried out to confirm their identity by comparing with the DNA sequences of known microorganisms.

Cancer research: Polymerase chain reaction has been widely used in studies for the role of genes in cancer. Tumour-supressor genes and mutations in oncogenes have been identified in DNA from tumors using PCR-based strategies.

Biotechnology: PCR has played major role in the production of recombinant proteins. Insulin and growth hormones are recombinant proteins, widely used as drugs and recombinant vaccines are developed for hepatitis B virus. It is an important tool in the biotechnology industries of research institutes.

Forensic science: PCR is most applicable in forensic science where it is being used in search of criminals through DNA fingerprinting technology. PCR allows amplification of DNA from individual hairs, stains of blood or seminal fluid having partially degraded DNA. Analysis of variable sequences is also used in tissue typing to match organ donors with recipients.

DNA polymorphism: PCR is used to study DNA polymorphism in the genome using known sequences as primers. PCR can be used to study RFLPs (restriction fragment length polymorphisms) as well as RAPDs (random amplified polymorphic DNA).

Gene therapy: PCR proves to be immense help in monitoring a gene in gene therapy experiments. This PCR technology provides shortcuts for many cloning and sequencing applications.

QUESTIONS

(A) Short answer questions:
1. Explain the following:
   (a) Primer
   (b) PFGE
   (c) Northern blotting

(B) Long answer questions:
1. What are DNA probes? Explain.
2. Write a short note on:
   (a) PCR
   (b) Western blotting
3. Explain in detail principle and applications of Southern blotting.
4. Explain the different electrophoresis techniques used for separation of DNA, RNA and protein molecules.
5. Explain the applications of polymerase-chain reaction.

(C) Multiple choice questions:
1. Polymerase chain reaction is useful in the diagnosis of _____ .
   (a) HIV
   (b) Fever
   (b) Diabetes
   (d) None of the above
2. The polymerase chain reaction is _____ .
   (a) A method of gene amplification
   (b) A type of DNA repair
   (c) Require for ligation of DNA ends
   (d) Essential for chromosome replication
3. RT - PCR stands for _____.
   (a) Random temperature PCR
   (b) Random template PCR
   (c) Reverse transcriptase PCR
   (d) Real time PCR

(D) Match the following:

A	B
(a) Southern blotting	(i) Studies of gene expression
(b) Northern blotting	(ii) Identify the locations of genes
(c) Western blotting	(iii) Detect the sequence of DNA/RNA in the non-fractionated DNA
(d) Dot and slot blotting	(iv) Characterization of proteins.

(E) Fill in the blanks:
1. The most widely used method for determining the purity of a protein is _____ gel electrophoresis.
2. The bands of DNA in the gel are stained with _____ dye and detected by visible fluorescence when the gel is illuminated with UV light.
3. _____ blot method is useful to detect the presence and location of gene segment in restriction digest of genomic DNA.

■■■

CHAPTER 13
HEALTHCARE BIOTECHNOLOGY

CONTENTS
- INTRODUCTION
- HUMAN INSULIN
- INTERFERONS
- HUMAN GROWTH HORMONE: SOMATOTROPIN
- SOMATOSTATIN
- PURIFICATION AND ANALYSIS OF BIOTECH PRODUCTS

INTRODUCTION

The development of recombinant technology has created an enormous potential for the pharmaceutical industries. Cloned genes are utilized commercially in medicals, agriculture, and pharmaceuticals for the production of valuable products. Genes are responsible for the expression of the proteins and these proteins and peptides are easily prepared by using recombinant technology. The recombinant proteins provide a high level of sensitivity and specificity as compared to natural proteins which are isolated from plants, animals and microorganisms. The biological activity of expressed protein is dependent on the choice of host, type of host cell, characters of host cell substrate, recombinant culture etc. Preparation of recombinant proteins by transgenic animals is most important system for production of pharmaceutical useful proteins. Erythropoietin (EPO), human insulin, somatotropin, somatostatin, interferon's, tissue plasminogen activator, interleukins, hepatitis B vaccine, granulocyte colony stimulating factor (G – CSF) etc, are the important biologicals (Table 13.1) prepare by recombinant DNA technology.

Table 13.1: Important recombinant proteins and their applications

Proteins/Peptides	Applications
Human insulin	Diabetes mellitus
Interferons	Hepatitis, cancers, hairy cell leukemia, genital warts
Tissue plasminogen activator	Coronary thrombolysis (anticoagulant)
Erythropoietin	Anemia associated with renal failure

Contd.

Hepatitis B vaccine	Vaccination
Granulocyte colony stimulating factor (G – CSF)	Bone marrow transplantation
Human growth hormone	Pituitary dwarfism
DNase	Cystic fibrosis
Tumour necrosis factor	Cancer treatment
Interleukins – 1, 2, 3	Immune disorder and tumours

HUMAN INSULIN

Human insulin is one of the smallest protein secreted by Islet of Langerhans (β-cells) of pancreas which catabolizes glucose in blood. It is used for the patients suffering from diabetes mellietus who is not capable to metabolize sugars. Insulin was first derived using recombinant technology from *Escherichia coli* in 1982 for human use.

Insulin is composed of two polypeptide chains (A and B) linked via disulfide bonds. Polypeptide chain A contains 21 amino acids and chain B contains 30 amino acids. Insulin chains (A and B) are derived from preproinsulin which is synthesized in β-cells of Islets of Langerhans containing 109 amino acids. When preproinsulin passes through the cell membrane of the synthesizing cells, then delinked first 23 amino acids and forms proinsulin containing 86 amino acids (Fig. 13.1). Finally, proinsulin is converted to insulin by the action of proteolytic enzymes such as endopeptidase and thiol-activated carboxypeptidase.

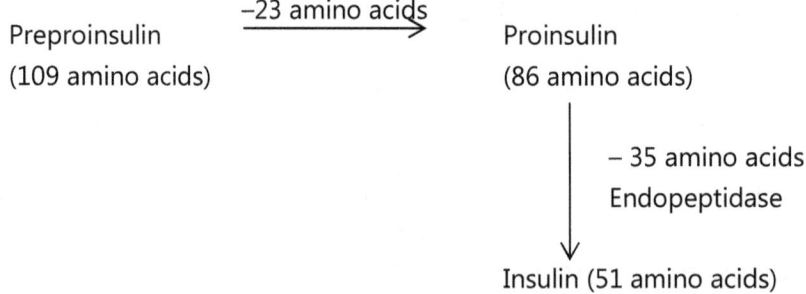

Fig. 13.1: Conversion of preproinsulin to insulin

Insulin is easily prepared by recombinant DNA technology from synthetic gene or from mRNA separated from rat pancreas. **Itakura et al** (1977) chemically synthesized DNA sequence for A and B chains of insulin. The synthetic A and B genes are separately inserted into two pBR 322 plasmids by the side of β-galactosidase gene. The recombinant plasmids are separately transferred into *Escherichia coli* cells (Fig. 13.2). The bacterial cells are grown in large fermenter by using proper nutrients and optimized physical conditions. The product contains large chimeric protein consisting of the A chain or B chain attached to naturally occurring *Escherichia coli* protein. These two chains (A and B) are obtained by detaching from β-galactosidase through cyanogen bromide (CNBr). The chain A and chain B are joined (in vitro) to form insulin by sulphonating the two peptides with sodium disulphonate and sodium sulphite.

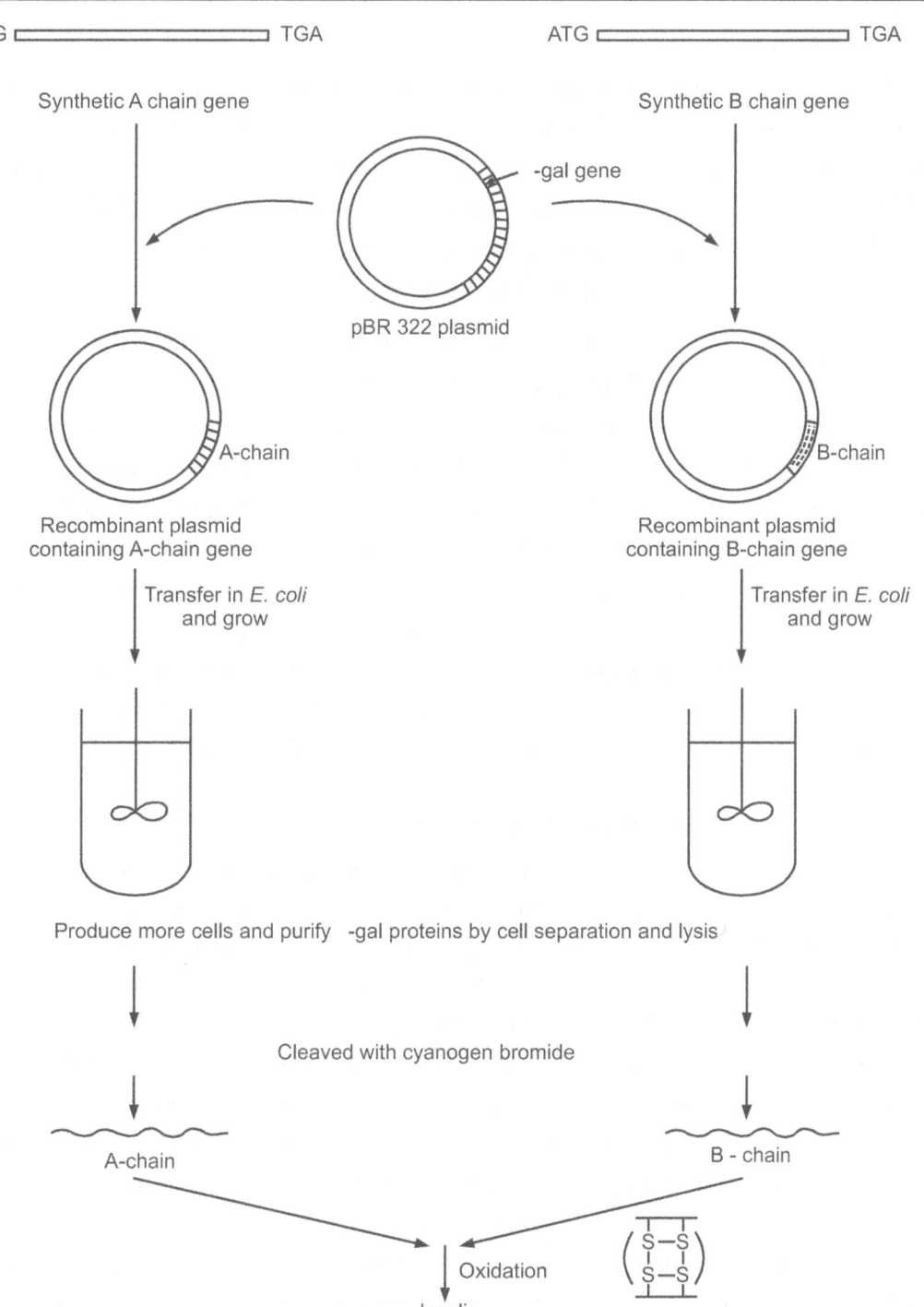

Fig. 13.2: Production of insulin by recombinant DNA technology

INTERFERONS

Alec Issacs and **Jean Lindermann** (1957), two British scientists discovered a glycoprotein naturally produced by cells called interferon. Interferons are the set of small proteins which are secreted by cell in response to viral infections. Human interferons are about 145 amino acid long and its molecular weight is between 20,000 to 30,000 daltons. They are classified into three types based on their physicochemical and antigenic properties.

(i) Alpha interferon (IFN- α) or leukocyte interferon

(ii) Beta interferon (IFN - β) or fibroblast interferon.

(iii) Gamma interferon (IFN - γ) or immune interferon.

Interferons mainly inhibit viral replication (antiviral agent) and also protect the cell from other intracellular parasites. It activates natural killer cells and macrophages, stimulates B cells and increases cell resistance to many microbial infections. They have a significant role in treatment of hepatitis B, cancer and other viral diseases.

Human interferon gene are inserted in *Escherichia coli* for production of interferon by recombinant DNA technology. The DNA sequence coding for human leukocyte interferon is attached to the yeast alcohol dehydrogenase gene in a plasmid. The recombinant plasmid is introduced into yeast cells of *Saccharomyces cerevisiae*. In yeast cell, plasmid grows easily to replicate into glycoproteins. Plasmids are also successfully replicate in *Escherichia coli* but production is slow as compared to yeast cells.

HUMAN GROWTH HORMONE: SOMATOTROPIN

Somatotropin, the human growth hormone (hGH), is secreted by the anterior lobe of pituitary glands which consists of 191 amino acid residues. Its molecular weitht is 22,000 daltons. Secretion of somatotropin is regulated by somatostatin and growth hormone releasing hormone produced by hypothalamus. Human growth hormone deficiency in children is responsible for dwarfism i.e. shorter adult height.

Humatrope (somatotropin recombinant) is easily produced by recombinant DNA technology. Complementary oligonucleotides are ligated to form one synthetic stand of small DNA fragment. It contains the coding sequence for the first 24 amino acids of mature human growth hormone. Second segment of gene is produced by extracting mRNA from human pituitary gland. This gene is converted into cDNA by treatment with reverse transcriptase and restriction endonucleases. The synthetic DNA and cDNA molecules are ligated to yield a new fragment which contains the complete coding sequence of hormone growth hormone DNA. This gene is ligated into a restriction site just down stream of the lac promoter/operater region cloned on a plasmid (Fig. 13.3).

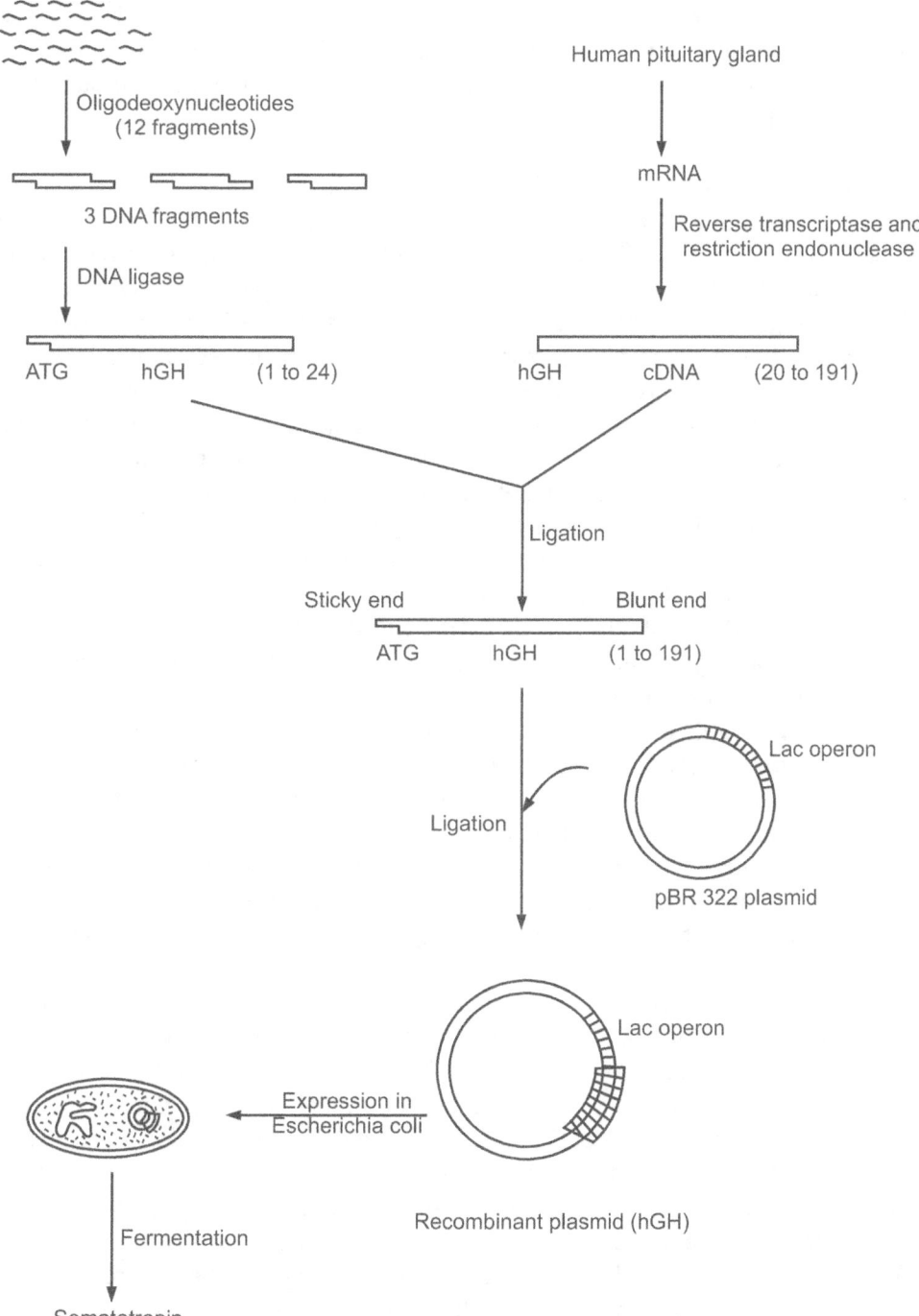

Fig. 13.3: Production of somatotropin by recombinant DNA technology

The recombinant plasmids are inserted in *Escherichia coli* and grown by fermentation. Somatotropin is isolated from intact cell and it possess additional methionine residue at the amino terminus. The human growth hormone is purified by different methods to remove methionine from the met-hGH molecules.

SOMATOSTATIN

Somatostatin is synthesized in the hypothalamus to control release of several other hormones from pituitary glands. It mainly inhibits the secretion of insulin, glucagon and growth hormones. It is the first 14 residue polypeptide hormone prepared in bacterial cell.

Somatostatin gene (double stranded synthetic gene) is synthesized chemically by the annealing the eight single stranded DNA fragments. The synthesized oligonucleotide gene contained 52 base pairs. Out of 52 base pairs, 42 code for somatostatin and other provides two sticky ends for the insertion into plasmid. Expression vector is prepared from plasmid pBR 322 in which contains control region and β-galactosidase gene. The synthetic (somatostatin) gene is inserted into the plasmid near C-terminus of β-galactosidase (Fig. 13.4). Recombinant plasmid pBR322 is then introduced in *Escherichia coli* for expression. The cells synthesis fused protein consisting of NH_2-termined segment of a β-galactosidase fragment joined by methionine to somatostatin. The fused protein is purified and treated with cyanogen bromide (CNBr) to form somatostatin.

PURIFICATION AND ANALYSIS BIOTECH PRODUCTS

The recovery and purification of biotech products is based on protein separation techniques, contaminants and purity requirements of the product. Purification protocol and analysis method is designed by considering the presence of probable protein and other contaminants into the products. Stability profile of the product, ionic strength, surface properties, optimum temperature, pH range, freeze-thaw stability, molecular weight, electrophoretic mobility etc are essential in purification and storage of protein products. Various chromatographical techniques are used for purification of biotechnologically products such as affinity chromatography, ion exchange chromatography, size exclusion chromatography, charge transfer chromatography, hydrophobic interaction chromatography etc.

Affinity chromatography method is used for separation of proteins based on their selective affinity towards different adsorbents, cofactors, substrates, antibody, chelated metal ion and on molecular recognition interaction such as antigen-antibody, enzyme-cofactor, hormones-receptor affinity. The main drawbacks in affinity chromatography are cost, time required in obtaining suitable ligand and harsh conditions required for elution which can damage the protein. Ion-exchange chromatography is one of the important and high-resolution purification technique for proteins. Anion and cation exchangers are used in this technique. Protein separation is dependent on ionic strength, which is equal to half of the sum of the concentrations of all ions present, each multiplied by the square of ion change. Hydrophobic interaction chromatography (HIC) method is used for separation of proteins based on differences in their hydrophobicity under mild adsorption and elution conditions that generally prevent denaturation of proteins. All proteins after their purification can be quantified and proteins which are enzymes are assayed by catalytic effect.

Quality control of biotech products includes raw material testing, process control, documentation and aseptic processing. They are tested for sterility, safety in experimental animals and product potency. Proteins are relatively unstable. They are degraded by oxidation, denaturation, aggregation, proteolysis etc. Hence, these products may be lyophized to avoid degradation. Carbohydrates, inorganic salts, bulking agents, amino acids, polyhydric alcohols, surfactants are commonly added into dosage form as a stabilizing agents.

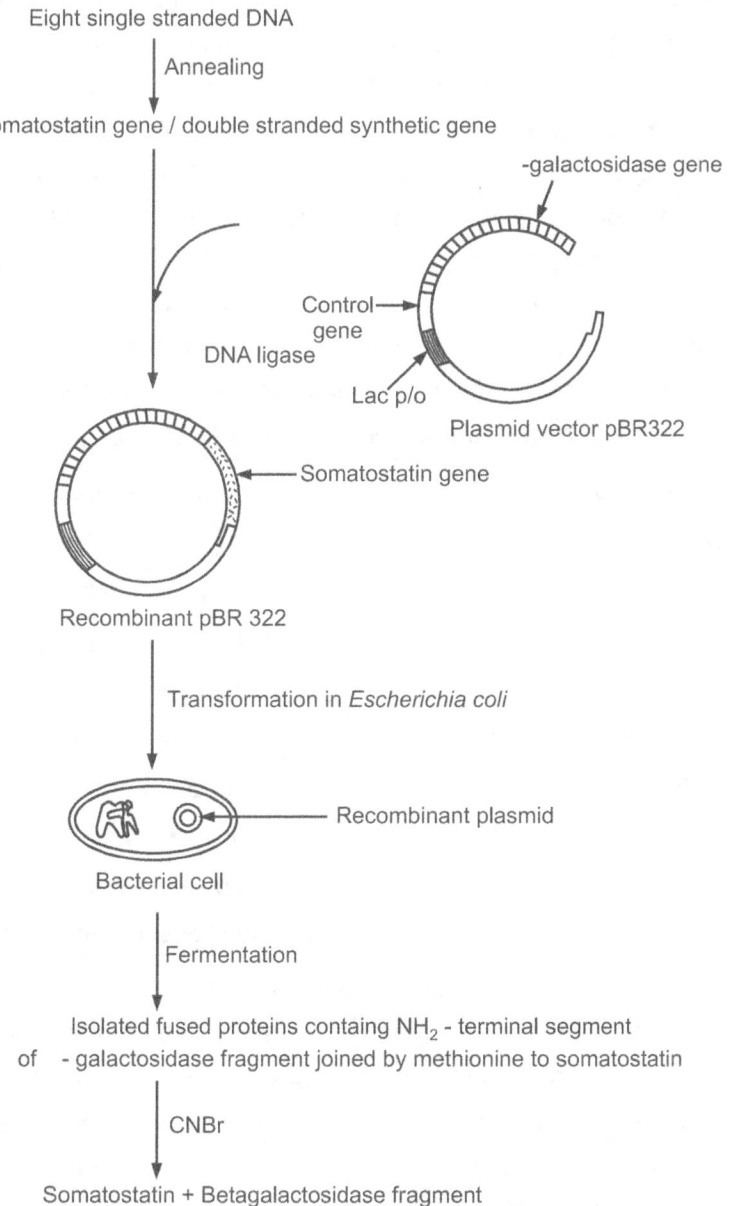

Fig. 13.4: Production of somatostatin by rDNA technology

Analysis of biotech products are performed by using chemical methods, chromatographic techniques, biotechnological methods, microbiological and immunological bioassays. These products also require reference standards in their analysis for the comparison. Protein contents are determined by using Lowry assay, Bradford method, fluorescent method, bicinchonic acid (BCA) assay, UV-spectrophotometry and Kjeldhal nitrogen determination method. Amino acid analysis techniques are used for determination of amino acid composition of proteins and peptides. Amino-terminal and carboxy-terminal protein sequencing are useful methods of protein quantitation and it gives information about primary structure of proteins. Peptide mapping is highly specific identity method. N-terminal and C-terminal peptides are separated, identified and confirmed genetic stability. Protein purity and homogeneity are commonly determined by the process of electrophoresis. The methods of electrophoresis are sodium dodecyl sulfate-polyacrylamide gel electrophoresis (SDS-PAGE), High performance capillary electrophoresis (HPCE) and IEF. Chromatographic techniques such as HPIEC, HPSEC, RP-HPLC, and HIC are used in quantitation of proteins to determine purity of such products (Table 13.2).

Table 13.2: Determination of impurities in biotech products

Impurities or contaminants	Method for detection
Aggregated protein	SDS-PAGE
Amino acid substitutions	Peptide mapping, MS
DNA	DNA hybridization, spectroscopy
Endotoxin	Bacterial endotoxin test, pyrogen test
Host cell and media proteins	SDS-PAGE, Immunoassays
Monoclonal antibodies	SDS-PAGE, Immunoassays
Microorganisms	Microbial limit test
Protein mutants	HPLC, Peptide mapping
Viruses	Cytopathic effect, Hemadsorption

Chromatographical separation of protein is more difficult because of multiple modes of interaction of proteins with chromatographical support. Raman spectroscopy and circular dichroism are employed in the characterization of proteins and polypeptides.

Radioimmuno assays (RIAs) and enzyme-linked immuno-sorbent assays (ELISA) are employed in identification and quantitation of proteins. These assays are based on specific high affinity antigen-antibody interactions and visualized by radio-labelled or enzyme-linked antigens or antibodies. Sandwich ELISA (DAS-ELISA) and double antigen coating ELISA (DAC-ELISA) are also used for protein characterization and impurity profiling. The assays that mimic the biological effect of product (biomimmetic assays) are employed to measure the activity of the product. Animal model assays, cell culture based assays and physicochemical or in vitro assays are three major types of biomimmetic assays.

QUESTIONS

(A) Short answer questions:

1. What are interferons? Write the role of yeast cells in preparation of interferons by recombinant technology.

2. Write different techniques used for purification of biotech products.

(B) Long answer questions:

1. What is healthcare biotechnology? How will you prepare human insulin by rDNA technology?

2. Write a note on

    (a) Production of somatostatin.

    (b) Analysis of biotech products

3. Explain the production and use of human growth hormone somatotropin.

(C) Multiple choice questions:

1. Insulin is made up of .... amino acids.

    (a) 119 (b) 51

    (c) 86 (d) 35

2. Fibroblast interferon is also called ....

    (a) Immune interferon (b) Leukocyte interferon

    (c) Alpha interferon (d) Beta interferon

(D) Match the following:

A		B	
(a)	Erythropoietin	(i)	Pituitary dwarfism
(b)	Human growth hormone	(ii)	Cystic fibrosis
(c)	DNase	(iii)	Cancer treatment
(d)	Tumour necrosis factor	(iv)	Anemia in renal failure

(E) Fill in the blanks:

1. Human insulin is used for treatment to patients caused _____.

2. _____ the human growth hormone (hGH), is secreted by the anterior lobe of pituitary glands which consists of 191 amino acid residues.

■■■

CHAPTER 14

BLOOD AND BLOOD PRODUCTS

CONTENTS
- INTRODUCTION
- WHOLE BLOOD AND BLOOD COMPONENTS
- COLLECTION AND STORAGE OF BLOOD AND BLOOD PRODUCTS
- ANTIBODIES AND ISOAGGLUTININS
    - Blood Groups
    - Coagulation of Blood
    - Anticoagulants
- BLOOD PRODUCTS
    - Concentrated Human Red Blood Corpuscles
    - Dried Human Plasma
    - Human Plasma Protein Fraction
    - Dried Human Serum
    - Human Fibrinogen
    - Human Thrombin
    - Human Fibrin Foam
    - Human Normal Immunoglobulin
    - Human Albumin
    - Control of Blood Products
- PLASMA SUBSTITUTES
    - Polyvinylpyrrolidone
    - Gelatin
    - Hydroxyethyl Starch
    - Perfluorochemicals
    - Stroma Fee Haemoglobin
    - Dextran

INTRODUCTION

Blood is composed of a clear, straw - coloured, watery fluid called plasma in which several different types of blood cell are suspended. It is an important regulator and a mirror of proper functioning of body cells. It circulates the throughout the body by the circulatory system.

Blood transports oxygen from lungs to the tissues and carbon dioxide from the tissues to the lungs for excretion. It also used to transports nutrients from the alimentary tract to the tissues and cell wastes to the excretory organs (kidney). Blood also plays important role in transport of hormones to target tissues, protective substances to area of infection and clotting factors to part of ruptured blood vessels. Blood makes up about 7-8% of body weight consisting 5.6 litres in a 65 to 70 kg weight in adult. The temperature of blood is about 38°C and pH is 7.4. Blood volume and the concentration of its many constituents are kept within narrow limits by homeostatic mechanisms.

Hospital blood blanks and blood centres provide a wide range of services to patient by prescription of doctor. It includes whole blood, platelets, granulocytes, single donar plasma, frozen plasma etc. The use of blood and its components is accompanied by some risk of accidental transmission of infectious agents e.g. Hepatitis, AIDS, herpes simplex, syphilis, malaria, infectious mononucleosis etc. The risk of microbial contamination is different depending on selection of donors and preparation techniques. The accidental pathogenic infection is prevented by careful screening of blood donors and finished products.

WHOLE BLOOD AND BLOOD COMPONENTS

Whole blood is blood that has been aseptically withdrawn from humans who are certified by a physical as being free of transmissible disease and mixed with a suitable anticoagulant. Whole human blood is the final mixture of blood and anticoagulant solution contains not less than 9.7% w/v of haemoglobin. Whole blood is a mixture of a plasma and blood cells (Fig. 14.1).

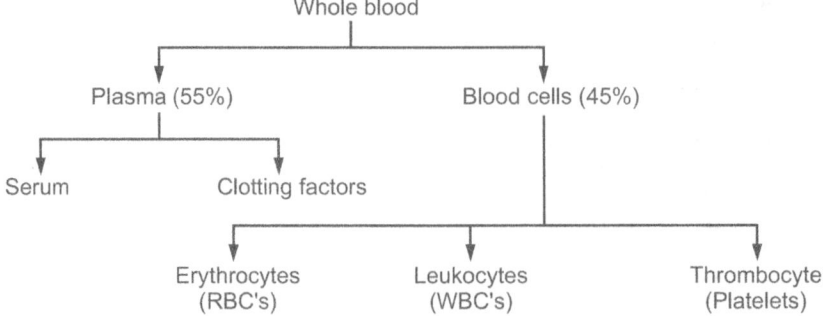

Fig. 14.1: Components of blood

The blood plasma is made up of water (92%), plasma proteins, inorganic salts, nutrients, waste materials, hormones and gases. Albumins are the most abundant plasma proteins. The main function of albumin is to maintain normal plasma osmotic pressure and it act as carrier molecules for free fatty acids, some drugs and hormones. Fibrinogen is responsible for coagulation of blood. Immunoglobulins are complex are complex proteins produced by lymphocytes that play an important part in immunity which interact with antigen to form antigen-antibody complex. Electrolytes are used for muscle contraction (calcium ions), transmission of nerve impulses (calcium and sodium ions) and maintenance of acid-base balance (phosphate ions). Nutrients such as glucose, amino acids, fatty acids, glycerol, vitamins and mineral salts are absorbed from the alimentary tract and are used by body cells for energy, heat repair and for synthesis of other blood components. Gases such as oxygen, carbon dioxide and nitrogen are transported round the body dissolved in plasma. Urea, creatinine and uric acid are the waste products of protein metabolism. They are formed in the liver and carried in blood to kidneys for excretion.

Blood cells contains erythrocytes, leukocytes and thrombocytes (Fig. 14.2). Blood cells are synthesized mainly in red bone marrow. The active cellular bone marrow is called red bone marrow where as the inactive marrow is called yellow marrow. The blood cells are derived from stem cell called Hemopoietic/Pluoripotent stem cell. The process of blood cell formation is called haemopoiesis.

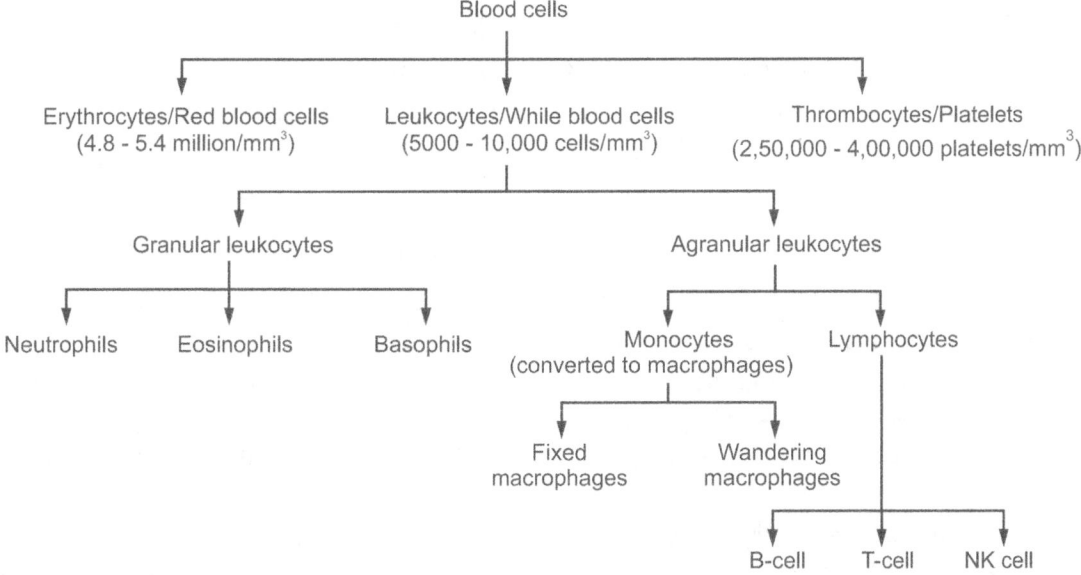

Fig. 14.2: Types of blood cell

Erythrocytes: Red blood cells are biconcave disc like shape without nucleus and their diameter is 7-8 mm. The main function of erythrocytes is in gas transport (O_2 and CO_2). The biconcavity shape of cell, increases their surface area for gas exchange and it contains large pigmented protein (haemoglobin) responsible for gas transport. The Red Blood Cells (Male : 4.5 - 6.5 × 10^{12}/l or 4.5 - 6.5 million/mm^3, Female : 3.8 - 5.8 × 10^{12}/l or

3.8 - 5.8 million/mm³) and haemoglobin content (male : 13-18 g/100 ml, Female : 11.5 - 16.5 g/100 ml) are routine and useful assessments made in clinical practice.

Leukocytes: White blood cells are nucleated, non-hemoglobin containing largest blood cells. These cells play important function in defence and immunity and blood count is about 5,000 to 10,000 cells/mm³. The cells contains nuclei and some have granules in their cytoplasm. Leukocytes are divided into granulocytes (polymorphonuclear leukocytes) and a granulocytes (Table 14.1).

(i) Granulocytes: There cells have different shaped nuclei (polymorphonuclear leukocytes) and granules (granulocytes) in the cytoplasm. The cells are divided into three types depending upon the staining characteristics of the granules. Eosinophils are stained by red acidic dye eosin and hence they are called acidophils or eosinophils. Basophils take up alkaline methylene blue (basophils) and neutrophils take both dyes (purple color).

Table 14.1: Normal count and characteristics of Leukocytes

Leukocytes	Number × $10^9/l$	Percentage of total	Nucleus shape	Cell diameter (μm)
Granulocytes				
Neutrophils	2.5 to 7.5	60 to 70	One to four lobed	10 to 12
Eosinophils	0.05 to 0.45	2 to 4	Usually two lobes	10 to 12
Basophils	0.015 to 0.1	0.5 to 1	Irregular and usually bilobed	8 to 10
Agranulocytes				
Monocytes	0.2 to 0.8	3 to 8	Oval or Kidney shaped	12 to 20
Lymphocytes	1.6 to 3.6	20 to 25	Generally round	6 to 13

Neutrophiles are small, fast and highly mobile and squeeze through the capillary walls in the affected area of diapedesis. They are transferred to area of infection by chemical substances (chemotaxins) which are released by damaged cells. These cells engulf and kill bacteria by phagocytosis. Eosinophils also plays minor role as phagocytosis but their specialized role in parasitic infections.

Eosinophils are less active as phagocytes compare to neutrophils but their specialized role appears in elimination of parasites. Eosinophils releases certain toxic chemicals from granules when they attaches to parasites. Eosinophils accumulate at the site of allergic reactions and mast cells release eosinophils chemotatic factor which attracts these cells at the site of infection.

Basophils and mast cells releases histamine (inflammatory agent), heparin (anticoagulant), bradykinin, serotonin and other lysosomal enzymes. It amplify the overall inflammatory response.

(ii) Agranulocytes: Agranulocytes make up 25 to 40% of the total leukocyte count. They have a large nucleus and granules (small size) cannot be seen under light microscope. Hence, they are called as agranular leukocytes. Agranulocytes are two types as manocytes and lymphocytes.

Manocytes are the largest while blood cells and they are actively motile and phagocytic. Some cells circulate in the blood while others migrate into the tissues where they develop into macrophages. Macrophages are actively phogocytic and it plays diverse range of protective functions. They synthesize and release of cytokines and interleukin-1 and play important role in inflammation and immunity.

Lympocytes are divided into B-cells, T-cells and natural killer cells. They circular in the blood and present in large numbers in lymphatic tissue such as lymph nodes and the spleen. The lymphocyte is the basic cell responsible for both cellular and humoral immunity. B-lymphocytes respond to antigens by differentiating into antibody producing plasma cells while T-lymphocytes are responsible for cell mediated immunity.

Thrombocytes: Thrombocytes or platelets are disc shaped, non-nucleated discs, 2 to 4 μm in diameter, derived from the cytoplasm of megakaryocytes in red bone marrow. The normal blood platelet count is 200-350 × $10^9/l$ and life is around 5 to 9 days. Many platelet come together and form platelet plug at the damaged site. This helps repairing of mild vascular damage and blood clotting (hemostasis). Platelets release certain chemical mediators which promote vascular spasm and blood clotting.

COLLECTION AND STORAGE OF BLOOD AND BLOOD PRODUCTS

The blood is collected aseptically from the median cubital vein, in front of the elbow. Blood serves as a transport medium for carrying all its different components to and from the different organs of the body. Blood is collected in sterile plastic bags or medial research council blood bottles containing an anticoagulant solution. During collection the bottle is gently shaken to mix blood and anticoagulant solution. This collected blood is known as 'whole blood' transfusion. One unit of donated blood may be divided into components as red cell concentrates, fresh frozen plasma, platelet concentrates etc.

Transfusion medicine is a specialized branch of hematology that is concerned with the study of blood groups, along with the work of a blood bank to provide a transfusion service for blood and other blood products. Blood bank involves testing of blood from both donors and recipients to ensure that every individual recipient is given blood that is compatible and safe.

Blood is withdrawn, not more than 420 ml at once, transfer to plastic containers, sealed and cooled to 4 to 6°C. Refrigerators are commonly used for storage of blood components. The temperature in all areas of refrigerator must be maintained at between 2-6°C. The interior of refrigerator must be clean, insulated and well organization of storage areas which are properly labeled and designated for cross matched blood, labelled blood and outdated blood. All blood storage refrigerators must contain recording thermometers and audible alarms. Temperature records are maintained for atleast 5 years as a part of blood blank records. A freezer that can achieve a storage temperature of – 20°C or lower is required for storing fresh frozen plasma and cryoprecipitate.

The whole blood or its components may be procured by the primary health centre or any hospital from the Government blood banks, Indian red cross society blood banks or regional blood transfusion centres.

ANTIBODIES AND ISOAGGLUTININS

Human plasma contains antibodies of various types, which are almost entirely concentrated in Fractions II and III. Some of there occur naturally, others arise as a result of infection or are stimulated by artificial immunization.

Blood groups:

Human being can be divided into various categories on the basis of blood groups. Individuals have different types of antigen on the surfaces of their red blood cells. These antigens are mainly lipoproteins or glycoproteins. The antigenic characters of RBCs are inherited and the antigen detection of all blood groups is based on the principle of hemagglutination. There are many different collections of red cells surface antigens, but the most important are the ABO and the Rhesus systems.

The ABO System: The first sign of the haemolytic antigen-antibody reaction in agglutination. Hence, red-cell antigens are called agglutinogens and plasma antibodies involved in reaction is called agglutinins. About 55% of the population has either A-type antigens (blood group A), B - type antigens (blood group B) or both (blood group AB) on their cell surface. The remaining 45% have neither A nor B type antigens (blood group O). The corresponding antibodies are called anti-A and anti-B. Blood group A individuals can not make anti-A but make anti-B. Blood group B individuals make only anti-A. Blood group O make both but Blood group AB can not make any antibodies (Table 14.2).

Table 14.2: Blood groups and their interactions

Blood group	Antigenon RBCs (agglu-tinogen)	Plasma antibody (agglutinin)	Donate to	Receive from
A	B	Anti-B	A or AB	A or O
B	B	Anti-A	B or AB	B or O
AB	A and B	None	AB	A, B, AB, O (Universal recipient)
O	O	Anti-A and Anti-B	A, B, AB, O (Universal donor)	O

Rhesus Blood Group System (Rh factor): Landsteiner and Wiener (1940), first observed this antigenic factor on RBCs of rhesus monkey. About 85% of people have this antigen (Rhesus positive, Rh^+) and remaining 15% people not contain Rhesus antigen (Rhesus negative, Rh^-). Rhesus positive individuals do not make anti-Rhesus antibodies but Rhesus negative individuals are capable of making anti-Rhesus antibodies. In haemolytic disease of the newborn, the mother's immune system makes antibodies to the baby's red blood cells, causing destruction of fetal erythrocytes. The antigen system involved is usually the Rhesus (Rh) antigen.

Coagulation of blood

The clotting of blood is very important process and it depends on the existence of a complex system of reactions involving plasma proteins, platelets, tissue factors and calcium ion. The process of prevention of blood loss (by formation of solid gel) is called hemostasis. Different mechanisms involved in hemostasis are vasoconstriction, platelet plug formation, blood clotting and fibrinolysis.

Immediately after a blood vessel is ruptured, the trauma stimulus to contract the wall of vessel. Platelets come into contact with a damaged blood vessel and adhere to the damaged wall. They release serotonin (5-hydroxytryptamine) and thromboxane which constricts the vessel. The adherent platelets clump to each other and release other substances, including adenosine diphosphate (ADP) which attract more platelets to the site. This makes the platelets swell and become sticky to adhere more cells. This process is known as platelet aggregation which helps creating a platelet plug inside the vessel.

Blood clotting (coagulation) is a complex process of plasma to injury. The factors involved in blood clotting are given in Table 14.3 as per order of discovery. These clotting factors activate each other in a specific order to form prothrombin activator. Prothrombin activates the enzyme thrombin, which converts inactive fibrinogen to insoluble threads of fibrin. (Fig. 14.3).

Table 14.3: Blood clotting factors

Factor	Synonyms
I	Fibrinogen
II	Prothrombin
III	Tissue factor (thromboplastin)
IV	Calcium (Ca^{++})
V	Labile factor, proaccelerin, AC-globulin
VII	Stable factor, proconvertin
VIII	Antihaemophilic factor A, antihaemophilic globulin (AHG)
IX	Antihaemophilic factor B, Christmas factor
X	Stuart Prower factor
XI	Antihaemophilic factor 'C', Plasma thromboplastin antecedent (PTA)
XII	Hageman factor, Antihemophilic factor 'D'
XIII	Fibrin stabilizing factor

[**Note:** Factor VI does not exist]

The final common pathway can be initiated by extrinsic and intrinsic pathways. The extrinsic pathway is activated rapidly following tissue damage and releasing a complex of chemicals called thromboplastin or tissue factor, which initiates coagulation. The intrinsic pathway is slower and is triggered when blood comes into contact with damaged blood vessel lining.

The breakdown of clot or fibrinolysis is the process of removing the clot and healing the damaged blood vessel. Plasminogen (inactive substance) is present in the clot and is converted to the enzyme plasmin. Plasmin initiates the breakdown of fibrin to soluble products and removed by phagocytosis.

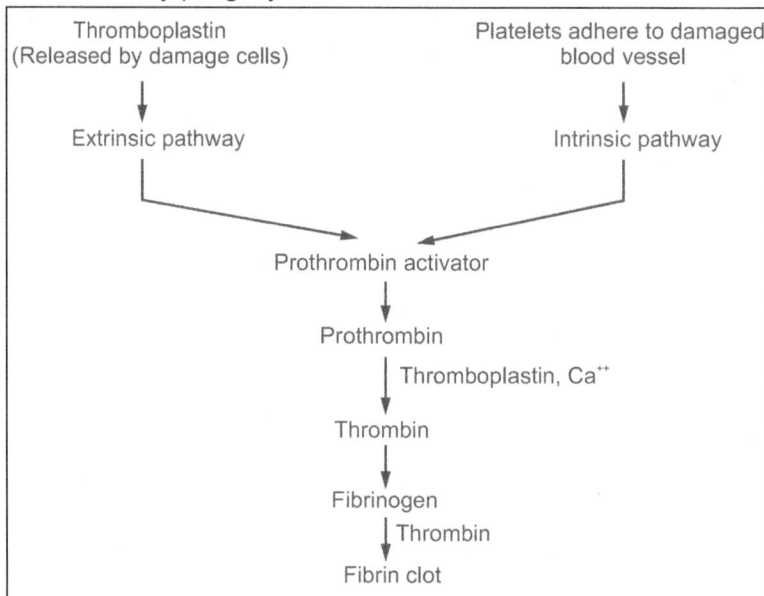

Fig. 14.3: Process of blood clotting

Anticoagulants:

Anticoagulants are substances or drugs which delay coagulation of blood. Anticoagulant are citrates, heparin and disodium edentate. Citrates (Acid-citrate-dextrose, ACD) is most often used as blood anticoagulant and has the composition containing sodium acid citrate (2 to 2.5 g), dextrose (3 g) and water for injection to make 120 ml. The citrate prevents clotting by binding the calcium ions as unionized calcium citrate. Calcium is essential to several steps in the clotting process. Hence, it is removed from blood to prevent clotting.

Heparin is a naturally occurring anticoagulant made by the mast cells. Heparin and heparin substitutes are combine with antithrombin III, then this complex interact with certain activated clotting factors such as factors IX, X, XI and XIII to prevent the conversion of prothrombin to thrombin. This complex interacts with thrombin in high concentrations to inhibit conversion of fibrinogen to fibrin. It also inhibits the aggregation of patelets.

Disodium edetate is a chelating agent and it has a strong affinity for divalent metals. It firmly bind to calcium and print clotting.

BLOOD PRODUCTS

Blood centres and blood banks provide a wide way of services which reach the patient on prescription usually through a hospital blood bank or transfusion service. The major blood products includes whole blood, conc. human, R.B.C., dried human plasma, platelets, human thrombin etc. (Fig. 14.4). These are called as blood and blood products. They are distinguished by the fact that they are prepared locally in blood center and are dispensed in the form of individual units identified by donor.

Concentrated Human Red Blood Corpuscles

Concentrated Red Blood Cells (RBCs) are units of whole blood with most of the plasma removed. It is prepared by centrifugation or undisturbed sedimentation for the separation of plasma and anticoagulant solution. The quantity of fluid removed is not less than 40% of the total volume of whole human blood. A certain amount of plasma is left to ensure optimal cell preservation and maintain viscosity for administration. All surfaces that come in contact with the red cells and plasma must be sterile and free from pyrogen. The containers containing concentrated human red blood cells are stored at a temperature between 2° and 8°C. It may be stored for a period not longer than that for which the whole human blood from which it is prepared. However, if the seal is broken during processing, the product must be used within 24 hours.

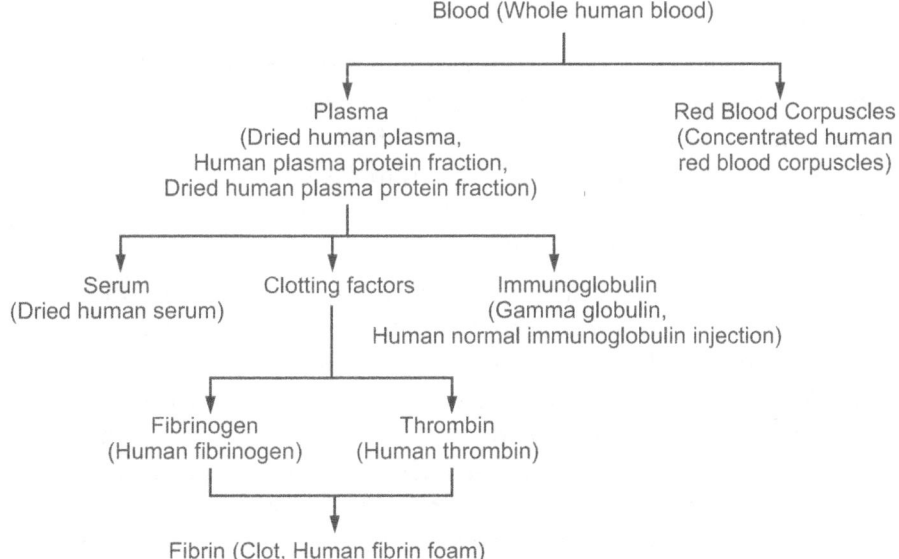

Fig. 14.4: Blood products

The haemoglobin concentration of the final preparation is not less than 15.5% w/v.

The final container must be labeled with the reference number of the whole human blood from which the preparation is made, the ABO and Rh groups of the whole human blood, the date of collection of the whole human blood from which the preparation is made, the date after which the preparation is not suitable for transfusion and the storage conditions. This product is used principally in the treatment of anaemia. Red blood cell fractions are also administered to patients with sickle cell anaemia and new born babies suffering from haemolytic disease.

Dried Human Plasma

Dried plasma has several advantages compare with whole blood. It can be given to patients of any blood group and well stored plasma can be used for five years. Dried plasma can be stored at room temperature (below 20°C) if protected from light.

The plasma of same donors contains haemagglutinating antibodies of the ABO system which on transfusion into patients of certain blood groups may cause intravascular agglutination and haemolysis. This risk can be avoided by neutralization of the haemogglutinins with the soluble blood group substances present in the plasma of other donors of appropriate blood groups. The most satisfactory ratio for mixing is A (9 parts) : 0 (9 parts) : B or AB (2 Parts).

Viral jaundice (infective hepatitis and homologous serum jaundice) is one of the most serious ill effects of transfusion of plasma. Control of infection is partly effected by refusing to accept donors with a history of jaundice but not all cases are recognized. Attempts have been made to kill the infective viruses by treatment with ultraviolet irradiation or β-propiolactone or in combination of both. But treated plasma shows electrophoretic and other abnormalities.

Dried plasma is usually prepared from time-expired citrated blood. The supernatant fluid is separated by centrifugation or undisturbed sedimentation. Batches of not more than ten bottles are pooled, choosing the correct ratio of blood groups of neutralize powerful agglutinins. The pools are kept of 4 to 6°C while samples are tested for sterility. Pools which have passed the test for sterility are then redistributed in transfusion bottles in quantities suitable for freeze drying or sublimation drying.

In pre-freezing, the plasma bottles are sealed with bacteriologically efficient fabric pads covered by ring-type closures and then centrifuged at − 18°C. The content freezes in a shell round the walls of the bottle in a similar manner to formation of the roll tube used in microbiology. This process provides large area for sublimation and the maximum area for heat transfer (Fig. 14.5). In primary drying, then plasma bottles containing frozen material are mounted horizontally in the drying chamber and a high vacuum is applied. The ice sublimes on to a condensing coil (− 50°C) and a small heater provides the latent heat required for evaporation. The primary drying process leaves products with about 2% moisture and this is removed in the secondary drying process. Secondary drying is preformed is another chamber by vacuum desiccation over phosphorus pentoxide. The final product is left with about 0.5% of moisture. Each fabric seal is replaced by on MRC type closure perforated by a plugged hypodermic needle. The bottles are returned to the secondary drying chamber, re-evacuated and then the vacuum is broken with dry sterile nitrogen. Finally, the needles are removed and the closure is protected with a sterile cap.

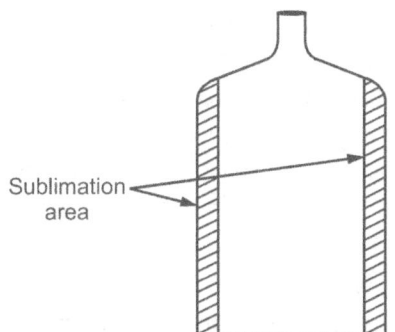

Fig. 14.5: Container showing large surface area of sublimation

The dried plasma is a cream-coloured powder, free from streaks of red or pink indicative of red cells or haemoglobin. It is reconstituted with water for injection equivalent to the original volume of plasma at room temperature. It must dissolve completely within ten minutes. The protein content is not less than 45 gm/lit. Dried plasma is stored in dry conditions, below 20°C and protected from moisture, light and oxygen. The containers must be labelled in addition to general requirements containing the names and percentages of anticoagulant and other contents, the quantity of water for injections required for reconstitution and the protein content. It must be used immediately (before 3 hr.) after reconstitution. Reconstituted plasma is a alternative to whole blood in conditions where there is no loss of red cells. In emergencies, to restore blood volume when whole blood is not available or while awaiting the results of compatibility tests. It also used in acute fibrinogen deficiency. Reconstituted plasma is used in patients suffering from severe burns, scalds or crush injury.

Fresh frozen plasma is prepared by centrifugation from whole human blood within a few hours of its collection from the donor. It is stored in frozen state (below – 30°C). Frozen plasma is used after by immersion in a water both at a temperature not exceeding 37°C for 45 min. It is used as a source of factor VIII for treating minor hemorrhage is mildly affected haemophiliacs.

Human plasma protein fraction

Human plasma protein fraction is a sterile aqueous solution by proteins of plasma or serum containing albumin and globulins. It is an isotonic solution containing 4.0 to 5.0% w/v of total protein and prepared by fractionating pooled citrated plasma. The plasma or serum is obtained from healthy human donors and free from detectable agents of infection transmissible by transfusion of blood or blood derivatives. Mainly, hepatitis B surface antigen and HIV antibodies are carried out by suitable sensitive methods.

The fractionation procedures is used make use of following facts:
(i) Proteins are precipitated from solutions without denaturation by the addition of organic solvents such as diethyl ether or ethanol.
(ii) The different proteins are minimally soluble at different pH values.
(iii) Solubility in presence of organic solvents is differentially affected by variations in the salt concentration.

In a series of precipitation steps in which these factors are carefully controlled, various components are separated by centrifugation from a single pool of plasma. The final sedimented paste of proteins containing the desired component in concentrated form is dissolved in a suitable solvent, the composition of which is carefully controlled with respect to pH, ionic strength and temperature. The final product contain not less than 85% of the total protein is albumin. The solutions obtained are freeze-dried to remove residual organic solvent and gives stable product.

The product is dissolved in water and sufficient quantities of a suitable stabilizer, such as sodium caprylate or acetyl tryptophan is added to allow the preparation to be heated for several hours without denaturation of proteins. Sodium chloride is added to make the preparation isotonic but no antibiotic or antimicrobial preservative is added at any stage during preparation. The solution is sterilized by filtration and distributed aseptically into sterile containers. The solution in its final container is heated at $60 \pm 0.5°C$ for ten hours to destroy the viruses of infective hepatitis and homologous serum jaundice. The containers are then incubated at 30 to 32°C for not less than 14 days or at 20 to 25°C for not less than 4 weeks and examined visually for evidence of microbial contamination. It must be stored between 2 and 25°C and protected from light.

Dried human plasma protein function is prepared by freeze drying human plasma protein fraction. Both are used for the same purposes as dried plasma.

Dried Human Serum

Dried human serum is prepared in the same way as dried plasma except that the blood is collected into dry bottles and allowed to clot. The supernatant serum is pooled, bottled and freeze-dried. Its storage and use are the same as for dried plasma except that it can not be used as a source of fibrinogen.

Human Fibrinogen

Fibrinogen is a soluble plasma protein with a molecular weight of 3,40,000. The fibrinogen molecules are elongated and in clotting process, they interact irreversibly to form a three-dimensional network of a semi-solid polymer (fibrin). The polymerization of fibrinogen is brought about by the action of an enzyme, thrombin, which is obtained from the activation of prothrombin.

After separation from plasma by fractionation, the precipitate is collected by centrifugation and dissolved in a citrate-saline solution. The citrate binds calcium ions and prevents spontaneous clotting of the product. The solution is freeze-dried to obtain dried human fribrinogen, yielding a white powder or friable solid. The dried powder is mixed with the stated volume of water for injection to reconstitute for use. The contents are mixed gently so as to avoid frothing. The cloudy solution obtained after 20 to 30 min. contains 10-15 gm./lit. of fibrinogen. The fibrinogen content is determined by adding thrombin to a known volume of solution and measuring the protein content of the separated and washed clot.

Dried human fibrinogen is stored in dry conditions, protected from light and temperature below 25°C. The solution is used immediately after preparation (before 3 hours). It is used for the treatment of fibrinogen deficiency. It is also used in conjunction with thrombin to repair severed nerves and to aid the adhesion of grafts.

Human Thrombin

Human thrombin is the enzyme that converts fibrinogen to fibrin. The prothrombin obtained from the fractionation of plasma is washed with distilled water and dissolved in citrate saline. Prothrombin is converted to thrombin by adjustment to pH7 and adding thromboplastin in the presence of calcium ions. The solution is clarified, sterilized by filtration and freeze-dried. It is reconstituted with saline solution when required.

Dried human thrombin is stored in dry conditions, protected from light and temperature below 20°C. Thrombin is mixed with fibrinogen to produce fibrin clot and it is used in surgery to suture severed nerves and to assist adhesion of skin grafts. The clot also acts as haemostat.

Human Fibrin Foam

Human fibrin foam is prepared by adding thrombin into the solution of fibrinogen and mix immediately to form foam. The semi-solid foam of fibrin is poured into trays, freeze-dried and sterilized by dry heat at 130°C for three hours. It is issued in suitable size and shape pieces in sealed sterile containers. The fibrin foam is stored below 20°C temperature and protected from light.

Fibrin foam is used as absorbable surgical haemostatic agent. It is usually impregnated with human thrombin and applied locally.

Human Normal Immunoglobulin

Human normal immunoglobulin is a sterile solution or freeze-dried preparation containing immunoglobulins, mainly immunoglobulin G (I_gG), together with smaller amount of other plasma proteins. Human immunoglobulin is the name given to that fraction (IgG Immunoglobulin), separated from human plasma. This fraction was previously known as γ-globulin or immune serum globulin. When the fraction is prepared from random pools of human plasma it is called human normal immunoglobulin.

Human normal immunoglobulin is obtained from source materials such as blood, plasma, serum or placentae frozen immediately after collection from healthy donors. This preparation is a solution of IgG immunoglobulin separated from random pools of plasma. Each pool is derived from not less than 1500 individual donations of blood. The paste obtained by solvent precipitation is freeze-dried and then dissolved in a suitable solvent, usually sodium chloride (0.9% w/v) solution or glycine (2.25 w/v) solution. Tiomersal (0.01%) or other bactericide in suitable concentration is added and pH is adjusted to 6.8 ± 0.4. The solution is sterilized by filtration and distributed into previously sterilized containers and sealed. The liquid preparation is clear pale yellow or light brown in colour. A trace of flocculent protein may precipitate during storage. The freeze-dried preparation is a white to slightly yellow powder or solid, friable mass.

It is stored at temperature between 2-8°C with protection from light. Its use is based on the fact that adults have been exposed to a variety of virus infections. Plasma collected from large number of different donors contains useful levels of a number of important antiviral antibodies. Normal immunoglobulin is effective in preventing measles, rubella, chickenpox, infective hepatitis and bacterial infections.

Human Albumin

Human albumin is sterile, non-pyrogenic preparation of serum albumin obtained by fractionating blood, plasma, serum or placentas from healthy human donors. It is tested individually for the absence of hepatitis B surface antigen, HCV antibodies and HIV antibodies and complies with other tests and requirements prescribed by the appropriate national control authority.

Human albumin is prepared from pooled source materials by precipitation with organic solvents under controlled conditions of pH, ionic strength and temperature. Residual organic solvent is removed by freeze drying or other suitable treatment. The product is dissolved in sufficient water to obtain a suitable concentration. The preparation is free from antimicrobial agent but may contain sodium acetyltryptophanate with or without solution caprylate as a stabilizing agent. The solution is sterilized by filtration and transfer aseptically into final containers. The solution is heated at 60°C for 10 hours so as to prevent the transmission of infections agent. It is then normally incubated at 30 to 32°C for a further 14 days and subsequently examined for any signs of microbial growth. Human albumin is stored at a temperature between 2 to 25°C and protected from light.

Human serum albumin (HSA) is the single most abundant protein in blood. Its normal concentration is approximately 42 g/lit., representing 60% of total plasma protein. HSA is responsible for over 80% of the colloidal osmotic pressure of human body, hence, it retain sufficient fluid within blood vessels. Human serum albumin preparations are given to patients suffering from kidney, liver diseases and as plasma volume expander in patients suffering from shock due to heavy loss of blood. Hyperoncotic albumin solutions may be used to cause transient diuresis in edematous patients or in those undergoing renal dialysis.

Control of Blood Products

All the blood products can save life but many products are dangerous become heavily contaminated with microorganisms. Rigorous application of good manufacturing practice (GMP) with regard to the manufacture of blood products is required to minimize the risk of pathogen transmission. Most GMP or related guidelines contain sections that address issues particularly relevant to the production of blood products. The risk of contamination of blood during processing is minimized by using closed systems and strict aseptic technique. The official standards and labeling are designed to reduce the hazards and prepare quality blood products.

Identification: All blood products contain proteins, hence, standard methods are used in protein identification. Precipitation tests with specific antisera are used to show that only human serum proteins are present in dried serum, dried plasma, the plasma protein fractions, fibrinogen, thrombin and immunoglobulin. Different types of gamma globulin are identified by their sedimentation rate in an ultra-centrifuge. Fibrinogen and thrombin are identified by their clotting behaviour. Normal immunoglobulin is identified by a suitable immunoelectrophoresis technique. Whole blood is identified by determination of the blood group under the ABO and Rh system.

Assay: Whole blood and concentrated human red blood corpuscles assay is performed by determining haemoglobin content by photometric haemoglobinometry. Protein content of many blood products are detected by chemical method except thrombin and fibrin foam. For assay of thrombin, a clotting dose being the amount of thrombin required to clot 1 ml of fibrinogen (0.1%) is saline buffered at 7.2 in 15 seconds. Determination of K and Na ions in plasma protein fraction ensure the electrolyte balance of the recipient.

Solubility: All solid preparations are soluble in an appropriate volume of the usual solvent in a specified time. Solubility parameter helps in detection of deteriorated protein constituents. Normal immunoglobulin solubility is determined by adding the volume of the liquid stated on the label and allow it to stand at 20°C for 15 minutes, it dissolves completely.

Sterility and pyrogens: All blood products must comply with the official tests for sterility and some preparation that are exposed to special risk of contamination with pyrogen due to lengthy processing must also pass the pyrogen test. Pyrogen test for normal immunoglobulin is performed by injecting per kg of the rabbit's mass a volume equivalent to 0.5 g of immunoglobulin but not more than 10 ml per kg of body mass.

Blood products are routinely tested for sterility, identity, pyrogenicity, solubility, stability, assay, abnormal toxicity, loss on drying, protein and moisture contents etc. The quality of the plasma protein fractions is also controlled by electrophoretic, immunoelectrophoretic, ultracentrifugal and chromatographic analysis; assay of specific activities such as coagulation factor or antibody activity; and tests of heat stability. All blood products are properly labelled with all official specifications, storage conditions, contents, expiry date, dose etc.

PLASMA SUBSTITUTES

The limited supplies of blood, risk of transmitting serum hepatitis and the cost involved in storing, cross matching, processing and dispensing blood and blood products stimulates to find substitutes of non-human origin that could be used to restore the blood volume. The majority of blood substitutes are used as plasma expanders. These blood substitutes are used to maintain blood pressure by providing vascular fluid volume after haemorrhage, burns or shock. Standard electrolyte solutions or physiological saline have been shown to be effective but relatively inefficient plasma volume expanders. The electrolyte solutions (crystalloid fluids) are diffuse out of the vascular system or distribute over the entire extra cellular fluid space. Hence, large volume of crystalloid fluids are required to result in effective plasma volume expansion. Colloidal fluids contain larger molecules that diffuse slowly across the semipermeable capillary membranes. These fluids such as dextran, gelatin, starch derivates are used as effective plasma expanders. The major drawbacks of colloidal therapy are high cost and the risk of prompting a hypersensitivity reactions. The ideal properties of plasma substitutes are as follows:

- Low cost, ease of preparation and ready availability.
- Isotonic, equal to blood plasma.
- Same colloidal osmotic pressure as whole blood.
- Viscosity similar to plasma.
- Freedom from toxicity, antigenicity, pyrogenicity and confusing effects on important tests.
- High stability in liquid form at normal and sterilizing temperatures and storage.
- Low rate of excretion or destruction by the body and complete elimination from the body.
- A high molecular weight such that the molecules do not easily diffuse through the capillary walls.

Polyvinylpyrrolidone

Polyvinylpyrrolidone, a synthetic colloid was introduced by Germany in the Second World War for the treatment of shock. It was marketed in this county in the 1950s but it was not used further because of suspected carcinogenicity.

Gelatin

Gelatin is produced by partial acid or partial alkaline hydrolysis of animal collagen. It has a wide variety of therapeutic and pharmaceutical uses. Gelatin solution (4%) or succinylated gelatin is also used as a plasma expander. Rapid infusion of the gelatin solution has been known to initiate hypersensitivity reactions. Gelatin is excreted quickly and mostly via the urine.

Hydroxyethyl starch

Starch is the energy storage polysaccharide of plants and is analogous functionally and structurally to glycogen, the energy storage polysaccharide molecule of animals. Starch is composed of two types of glucose polymers such as amylose (linear molecule) and amylopectin (branched molecule). Amylopectin is well tolerated when infused intravascularly into animals but is rapidly hydrolyse by amylase. Amylopectin molecule is modified and make it more stable within the plasma by substituting hydroxyethyl groups to crate hydroxyethyl starch (HES).

HES solutions contain a heterogeneous solution of HES molecules with an average molecular weight of 69,000, similar to albumin. Hydroxyethyl starch appears to be an extremely well-tolerated plasma expander. Allergic reactions to HES are distinctly uncommon. The incidence of allergic reactions to HES was 0.085% compared with 0.011% for albumin infusion. The important adverse effect of HES infusion appears to be some impairment of coagulation after moderate (20 ml/kg) doses.

Hydroxyethyl starch has been well studied for its efficacy as a plasma volume expander. HES solution (6%) in saline increases plasma volume from 71% to 230% of the volume infused. The colloid osmotic pressure is increased significantly following HES infusion. HES infusion as good hemodynamic effect. In comparative studies of fluid therapy patients, in fusing HES solutions (6%) has increased central venous pressure, cardiac output and ventricular strike work, with efficacy equivalent to that of 5% albumin infusion. HES and dextran both effectively raise colloid osmotic pressure and plasma volume, through the plasma volume increase may be greater and more sustained following infusion of higher molecular weight dextrans.

Perfluorochemicals

Perfluorochemicals (PFCs) are 8 to 10 carbon fluorinated hydrocarbons and used as an oxygen carrying blood substitute. Fluosol (Fluosol - DA 20%) is a fluorocarbon emulsion of perfluorodecalin and perfluorotripropylamine. This emulsion is prepared by using poloxamer 188 (Pluronic F-68) or egg yolk phospholipid as a emulsifying agent and hydroxyethyl starch is added to increase oncotic pressure. Fluosol emulsion can absorb, transport and release both oxygen and carbon dioxide. It is used as an effective oxygen carrier during coronary angioplasty. Fluorocarbon emulsions (20%) can be administered regardless of blood type. It is free from blood borne pathogens and is stable for years at room temperature.

Perfluorochemical emulsions are eliminated unchanged through the airways. The particle size of the fluosol emulsion is small (0.1 μ), which contributes to elimination through the alveolar membrane. There is some uptake of PFC emulsions by the reticuloendothelial cells. The plasma half-life of fluosol is about 17 hours after infusion of 20 ml/kg.

Stroma-free Hemoglobin

Hemoglobin is principal protein found in erythrocytes. Human hemoglobin is a tetramer of molecular mass 64 kDa consisting of two α-chains (141 amino acids) and two β-chains (146 amino acids). Each of the four polypeptide chains has heme as prosthetic group and it is responsible for oxygen binding of hemoglobin.

Human hemoglobin solutions has number of advantages, including the potential to develop a stable, oxygen-binding, colloid volume expander with no antigenicity. Renal toxicity is the main problem with hemoglobin solutions which has led to the development of stroma-free hemoglobin solutions. There are highly purified hemoglobin solutions, free from erythrocytic membrane fragments, which are responsible for renal toxicity.

Stroma-free hemoglobin solutions are prepared from the hemolysis of washed, outdated, banked, human packed erythrocytes. Pure crystalline hemoglobin is produced by sequentially crystallization and washing of hemolysate. This protein is stored in dry form or it may be reconstituted into a solution. These preparations are relatively stable and shelf-life is greatly prolonged if stored in frozen state.

Stroma-free hemoglobin has high ability to bind oxygen. The oxygen half-saturation pressure (P-50) of stroma-free hemoglobin solutions varies from 12 to 16 torr compared with a value of 26 to 27 torr for fresh blood. This increased oxygen affinity is due to the loss of tetrameric hemoglobin, the lack of 2, 3-diphosphoglycerate (2, 3-DPG) and a higher pH compared with the intracellular erythrocyte pH. The increased affinity for oxygen by stroma-free hemoglobin solutions could lead to inadequate release of oxygen to the tissues. The major problem with stroma-face hemoglobin is their rapid clearance from the vascular space due to renal excretion and reticuloendothelial cell uptake.

Hemoglobin is conjugated to additional high molecular weight substances (dextran, polyethylene glycol) to prolong vascular retention, reduce antigenicity and potent plasma volume expansion properties. Polymerized hemoglobins are prepared by cross-linking with gluteraldehyde to prolong product half-life by preventing disassociation into dimmers or manomers. Hemoglobin has been successfully produced by recombinant DNA technology is *Escherichia coli* and *Saccharomyces cerevisiae*. Human hemoglobin α and β genes have been expressed in a wide variety of prokaryotic and eukaryotic systems, including transgenic plants and animals.

Dextran

Dextrans are polysaccharides (Refer Fig. 5.19) produced by the conversion of sucrose into long glucose polymers (Fig. 14.6) by the bacterial enzyme dextransucrase isolated from *Leuconostoc mesenteroides*.

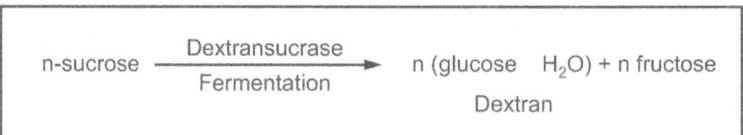

Fig. 14.6: Production of dextran

Dextrans of various molecular masses usually 1, 40, 60, 70 or 110 kDa are often used as plasma expanders. Two dextran solutions are now most widely used, a 6% solution with an average molecular weight of 70,000 (dextran 70) and a 10% solution with an average weigh to 40,000 (dextran 40)).

Fermentation production of dextran is similar in many respects to the antibiotic production. Growth of the dextran producting strain is carried out in large fermenters in media containing high percentage of carbohydrates. The dextran produced by the fermentation have molecular weight 2 to 2.5 lakhs. For clinical use, dextran have the molecular weight upto one to 1.1 lakhs. Less molecular weight dextrans are produced by the process of acid hydrolysis, thermal degradation, ultrasonic disintegration and seeding the fermenter with low molecular weight dextran (Refer Chapter 5, Page 5.18). The final dextran molecule is purified by solvent precipitation, adsorption or membrane filtration.

Higher molecular weight dextrans (mainly dextran 70, 75 and 110) are used to promote short-term expansion of plasma volume thus preventing shock due to blood loss. A solution of these dextrans (6% w/v) exerts an osmotic pressure similar to that of plasma proteins. The initial dose of 500 to 1000 ml is administered by intravenous infusion but not more than 20 ml/kg of body weight. In addition to plasma volume expansion, dextran solutions are also used as antithrombotic effects, probably mediated by inhibition of platelet aggregation and to improve blood flow. The low molecular weight dextrans mainly responsible for improvement of microcirculatory flow by decreasing the viscosity of blood and inhibiting erythrocytic aggregation. The low molecular weight dextran (40 kDa) shows similar therapeutic effects to the high molecular weight dextrans, although it must be used at higher concentrations (10% w/v) in order to achieve the same osmotic pressure.

The rate of renal excretion of dextran depends on molecular size and it mainly excreted unchanged in the urine. Large molecules not excreted in the urine slowly diffuse into the interstitium where uptake into the retriculoendothelial cells. Dextran molecules has severe side effects such as renal failure, coagulation disorders, congestive heart failure, hypervolemia, hypersensitivity, severe dehydration and allergic reactions. The dextrans may interfere with cross-matching of blood if unsuitable dilutions of erythrocytes and serum are used.

QUESTIONS

(A) Short answer questions:
1. What is blood? Write the importance of blood donation.
2. Write in short process of blood clotting.
3. Enlist different plasma substitutes. Write the ideal properties of plasma substitutes.
4. Explain in short quality control of blood products.

(B) Long answer questions:
1. Explain in detail different types of blood cells with its functions.
2. Write in detail the production and importance of dextran.
3. Write a short note on:
    (a) Collection and storage of blood and blood products.
    (b) Blood groups
    (c) Anticoagulants
    (d) Dried human plasma
    (e) Human fibrinogen
    (f) Human albumin.

(C) Multiple choice questions:
1. Dextrans are produced by the bacterial enzyme _____ isolated from *Leucohostoc mesenteroides*.
   - (a) Dextransucrase
   - (b) Amylase
   - (c) Lipase
   - (d) Protease
2. _____ is a naturally occurring anticoagulant made by the mast cells.
   - (a) Disodium edetate
   - (b) Heparin
   - (c) Citrates
   - (d) None of above

(D) Match the following:

A	B
(a) Factor I	(i) Stuart prower factor
(b) Factor III	(ii) Fibrin stabilizing factor
(c) Factor X	(iii) Tissue factor
(d) Factor XIII	(iv) Fibrinogen

(E) Fill in the blanks:
1. Dextrans are polysaccharides produced by the conversion of _____ into long glucose polymers.
2. The factors involved in blood clotting are Factor I to Factor XIII except _____ .

■■■

CHAPTER 15

SURGICAL DRESSINGS, LIGATURES AND SUTURES

CONTENTS
- INTRODUCTION
- SURGICAL DRESSINGS
  - Wound Dressings
  - Absorbents
  - Bandages
  - Adhesive Tapes
  - Protectives
  - Standards for Surgical Dressings
- LIGATURES AND SUTURES
  - Absorbable Sutures
  - Non-absorbable Sutures
  - Standards of Catgut
- SURGICAL NEEDLES

INTRODUCTION

Surgical dressings is a term applied to a wide range of materials used to cover wounds. The skin is a flexible, water-permeable barrier. If the epidermis and dermis are lost through damage the wound becomes plugged with a blood clot which act as a natural first-aid dressing by stopping further loss of blood and tissue fluids. The skin is then restored by repair of the dermis (production of fibrous and vascular tissue) and migration of epidermal cells. A dressing can have a number of purposes, depending on the type, severity and position of the wound. The main purpose of dressings are to protect the wound from infection, promote healing through granulation and epithelialization, removal of slough and foreign objects, relieve the pain, clotting the blood and absorb the blood, plasma and other fluids exuded from the wound.

Surgical suture is a medical device used to hold body tissues together after an injury or surgery. Sutures are materials used to close the wound and help in healing process. They are commonly used on the skin, internal tissues, organs and blood vessels. Different types of materials can be used to close a wound depending upon the style of wound, location and depth in the body. Ligatures and sutures are commonly made from intestinal tissues of animals and birds, vegetable fibres, human hair, horse and camel hair, synthetic threads and metallic wire. Some materials are absorbed or digested in the tissues of the body and others are insoluble in the body. Surface stitches of non-absorbable materials used to seal the wound are removed after healing. 'Ligature' and 'suture' are the terms often used in the same sense. A ligature is a thread used for tying off a blood vessel and suture is used for sewing various tissues of the body by using needle. Surgical dressing and sutures are required to meet specific requirement of the USP for many characteristics.

SURGICAL DRESSINGS

A dressing is an adjunct used by a person for application to a wound to promote healing. Over the last two decades, a large number of new dressings has become available for the treatment of wounds. However, there is still no single dressing suitable for the management of all types of wounds. Many new dressings are designed to manage chronic wounds. It is still difficult to treat because of change in physiology of chronic wounds. Ideal dressing should have the following properties:

(i) Sterile or capable of being sterilized by conventional method.
(ii) Smooth surface and satisfactory tensile strength.
(iii) Inexpensive and porous to water vapour exuded from wound.
(iv) Unaffected by industrial fluids such as oils, detergents or any other chemicals.
(v) Impervious to microorganisms and other fluids from outside.
(vi) Capable of absorbing excess secretions from wound.
(vii) Free from substances that cause skin allergy, tissue reactions or a hypersensitivity response.
(viii) Constant physical properties under conditions of storage and use.

Wound Dressings

Primary wound dressings are designed to be placed next to a wound surface and are usually reinforced by materials of various types to absorb the wound secretions. Dressings are classified into different categories such as:

(i) Based on function in the wound e.g. absorbent, adherence, occlusive etc.
(ii) Physical form of the dressing e.g. film, foam, gel etc.
(iii) Type of material used to produce the dressing e.g. alginate, silicone, collagen etc.

Primary wound dressings are therapeutic or protective coverings applied directly to wounds or lesions on the skin. Secondary dressings are materials that serve a therapeutic or protective function and that are needed to secure a primary dressing. Common types of dressings are summarized in Table 15.1.

Table 15.1: Characteristics and applications of the common types of dressings

Types of dressings	Characteristics	Applications
Gauze dressings.	Inexpensive and absorbent. Need frequent changing. Stick to wound causing pain and damage.	Normal or highly exuding wounds. Apply creams, ointments with antimicrobial agents. Use for infected and necrotic wounds.
Semi-permeable adhesive films.	Sterile and non-absorbent. Permeable to water vapour and gases.	Not applicable for infected wounds and fragile skin. Applicable to later stages of wound healing while little exudate and flexible areas such as the elbows, knees and sacral areas.
Foam dressings.	Absorbent and allow gaseous exchange. Impermeable to water and microorganisms. Good thermal insulation.	Primary wound dressings for absorption and secondary wound dressings for wounds with packing. Used for low to moderately exuding wounds.
Alginate dressings.	Absorbent and protective. Easy to remove without pain. Form hydrophilic gel on contact with wound exudate.	Moderate to heavily exuding wounds. Applicable for infected wounds but not for dry wounds. Haemostasis.
Hydrogel dressings	Absorbent and non-adherent. Inexpensive and need to be changed frequently.	Cleansing of dry and necrotic wounds. Maintain a balanced wound hydration through controlled evaporation.
Hydrocolloid dressings.	Absorbent and impermeable to water vapour and air. Create moist environment and adhere to wet and dry wounds.	Suitable for light to moderately exuding non-infected wounds. Cleansing for a sloughy or necrotic wounds.

Traditional wound dressings, such as natural or synthetic bandages, cotton wool, lint and gauzes have been used for treatment of wound as primary or secondary dressings. Gauze and cotton tissue is composed of a tubular cotton gauze wrap surrounding a layer of absorbent cotton wool. It is used to absorb exudate and applied over a primary wound dressing to avoid contaminating the wound with cellulose fibres. Gauze dressings are made from woven and non-woven fibres of cotton, rayon, polyester or a combination of these fibres. Sterile gauze pads are used for packing open wounds to absorb fluid and exudate. The fibres in the dressing act as a filter, drawing fluid away from the wound. Gauze impregnated with soft paraffin is occlusive and easier to remove from the skin. Silver and povidone iodine are added into some dressings as antimicrobial agents to prevent infection. Debriding agents (saline) are incorporated to prevent maceration.

Semi-permeable adhesive film dressings are made from polyurethane, coated on one side with hypoallergenic acrylic adhesives. These dressings are non-absorbent and permeable to water vapour and gases. It maintains a moist wound healing environment, promoting the formation of granulation tissue and autolysis of necrotic tissue. However, they are not suitable for use on infected wounds or heavily exuding wounds. These dressings are sometimes difficult to handle and apply as they tend to wrinkle on removal from their packs. Semi-permeable dressings are available in different size, thickness, vapour permeability, adhesiveness and extensibility.

Foam dressings are in the form of sheets of polymer foam made up of polyurethane. Some foam dressings have additional wound contact layers to avoid adherence when the wound is dry and an occlusive polymeric backing layer to prevent excess fluid loss and microbial contamination. Foam dressings are superior to film dressings because it maintain moist environment, absorbent and provide good thermal insulation. Foam dressings are considered medically necessary when used on full thickness wounds (stage III or IV ulcers) with moderate to heavy exudate. They are used as primary wound dressings for absorption and insulation and as secondary dressings for wounds with packing.

Alginate dressings are produced from the calcium and sodium salts of alginic acid. They are highly absorbent and are used for moderate to heavily exuding wounds. The are available as dry woven, fibrous mats and sheets. The dressings interact with wound fluid and blood to form a protective film of gel that maintains non-adherent moist healing environment. The gelling properties of individual dressings depend on both the relative concentrations and arrangements of the mannuronic and guluronic monomers. Alginate dressings are easy to remove by lifting the partially gelled sheet off the wound or by rinsing the gel away with water. The dressings are not suitable for dry wounds or those covered with hard necrotic tissue.

Hydrogel dressings are mainly amorphous composed of insoluble hydrophilic polymers such as polyvinyl pyrrolidone or polyacylamide in the form of gel. They are available in the form of amorphous hydrogels, saturated gauzes or hydrogel sheets. Amorphous hydrogels may be supplied in tubes, spray bottles or foil packs. The gel is applied directly to the wound and it covered with a secondary dressing. Exudate is absorbed into the gel while moisture evaporates through the secondary dressing. Saturated gauzes are impregnated with amorphous hydrogel for use to fill the dead space in deeper wounds. Hydrogel sheets are produced from cross linked polymers which physically entrap water to form a solid sheet.

The amorphous hydrogels and impregnated gauzes are used as primary dressings whereas the hydrogel sheets may be used as primary or secondary dressings. Hydrogel dressings provide a moist healing environment that promotes granulation and reepithelialization of wounds. They are suitable for cleansing of dry or necrotic wounds.

Hydrocolloid dressings are prepared from colloidal gel forming materials such as carboxymethyl cellulose, gelatin, pectin, alginate, elastomers and adhesives. They are available in various sizes and shapes including powders or pastes. They are commonly applied to a carrier as thin waterproof polyurethane film or foam sheet. Different types of hydrocolloid dressings are available on the basis of their physical characteristics such as thickness, conformability, moisture vapour permeability and fluid retention. These dressings are useful for acute and chronic wounds as they adhere to dry and moist sites. They do not cause tissue damage or pain on application or removal. They are used for light to moderately exuding wounds including pressure sores, leg ulcers, minor burns and traumatic injuries. Some dressings are not suitable for heavily exuding or infected wounds, as they support the growth of anaerobic bacteria.

Absorbents:

Absorbent Cotton

Absorbent cotton wool consists of epidermal trichomes from the seeds of cultivated species of Gossypium. Absorbent cotton is prepared from the raw cotton fiber by a series of processes which remove the natural waxes and all impurities. It is available as rolls or small balls. Cotton balls can be prepared by hand or special machines. Machine-made balls are firm, compact and uniform in size and shape. The large size balls are made for obstetrical uses and changing perineal pads. The medium cotton ball is useful for applying antiseptics, cleansing the skin and in the nursery where manifold uses are apparent. The small cotton ball is used for skin cleansing before injections.

The raw cotton fiber, mechanically cleaned of dirt and carded into layers, has been used for paddings and coverings of unbroken surfaces. This form is available under the name of 'nonabsorbent cotton'. It is also frequently used as cotton plugs in the bacteriological laboratory. Nonabsorbent bleached cotton is prepared by modified bleaching process has to retained water-repellent natural oils and waxes. This cotton is easily identified by its silky feel and it is well adapted to padding, packing and dressings over traumatized areas. It is also used as nonabsorbent backing on sanitary napkins and drainage dressings.

Absorbent cotton easily absorbs water and retain the water for long period. The high absorbency of cotton wool makes it an excellent material for absorbing wound exudates and cleansing, swabbing and medicating wounds. Water retention coefficient is defined as the number of grams of water absorbed per gram of dressing. However, its absorbency may be reduced considerably by prolonged storage, by exposure to heat and by medication.

The absorbency of surgical cotton is measured using apparatus consisting of dry cylindrical copper wire basket 8.0 cm high and 5.0 cm in diameter. The wire used for construction of basket is about 0.4 mm in diameter, the mesh is 1.5 cm to 2.0 cm wide and the mass of basket is 2.7 ± 0.3g. Weight the basket to the nearest centigram (m_1). Take the cotton (5g) from five different places in the product to be examined and weigh the filled basket to the nearest centigram (m_2). Fill a beaker (12 cm in diameter) to a depth of 10 cm with water. Measure the time for the basket to sink below the surface of the water (not more than 10 s). After the sinking time, remove the basket from the water and it to drain for 30 s. Transfer the basket to a tared beaker (m_3) and weigh to the nearest centigram (m_4). The water holding capacity per gram of absorbent cotton is calculated by following equation.

$$\frac{m_4 - (m_2 + m_3)}{m_2 - m_1}$$

The results are the average of 3 tests. Water holding capacity should not be less than 23.0 g of water per gram.

The official standards for the absorbent cotton wool as per requirements of B.P.C. are as follows:

(i) It must satisfy an absorbency test.

(ii) It must free from surface active agents, colouring matter and optical whiteners.

(iii) The average fibre length must not less than 10 mm. Short fibre length wool is less resilient and more dusty.

(iv) It must not contain more neps than the European Pharmacopoeia standard. Neps are small knots on fibre caused by uneven growth or formed during processing.

(v) The quality of fibres should be the same throughout the use and storage.

(vi) The fibres should be well carded, clean white and free from leaf, seed coat, thread, fibre dust and foreign matter.

Surgical gauzes:

Surgical gauzes are provide an absorbent material of sufficient tensile strength for surgical dressings. The raw cotton fiber is mechanically cleaned and twisted into a thread and in turn, woven into a open mesh cloth. This cloth is non-absorbent, grey in appearance. It is bleached white and rendered absorbent. Gauze is classified according to its mesh or number of threads per inch. Pads, compresses and dressings are made from surgical gauze.

Filmated gauze is a folded absorbent gauze with a thin, even film of cotton or rayon distributed over each layer. It possesses quick absorption and unusual softness. Antiseptic ore mediated surgical gauze is used with antibiotics and other therapeutic agents. Iodoform gauze is used as packing or drainage material which contains 5% iodoform.

Non-woven surgical sponges are suitable alternatives to woven cotton gauze for use in wound cleaning, wound dressing and tissue handling sponges. They typically offer greater absorbent capacity than cotton gauze sponges. Gauze pads or gauze sponges or gauze swabs are folded squares of surgical gauze. The edges are so folded that each size may be unfolded to larger sizes without exposing out edges or loose threads. The number of layers (ply) and the dimensions of the pad vary according to use but the common sizes are 5, 7.5 and 10 cm square, available in 8, 12, 16 or 32 ply. Small gauze pads are a convenient size for swabbing and are often used during surgery. Pads of all sizes are used as wound dressings and for packing wounds.

X-ray detectable gauze pads are similar to all gauze pads but attached to distinctively coloured X-ray detectable strand containing not less than 55% of barium sulphate or other non-toxic material of comparable X-ray opacity. They are non toxic, soft and nonabrasive. They remain permanently detectable because they do not deteriorate in the body. Ray-Tec X-Ray detectable sponges contain a nonabrasive vinyl plastic monofilament which gives a characteristic pattern in the X-ray.

Composite absorbent dressings have been developed for specific purposes consisting of layers of absorbent gauze or non-woven fabrics. These dressings have gauze or non-woven fabric surfaces with fillers of cotton, rayon or absorbent tissue. Dressing combines are designed to provide warmth and protective. They absorb large quantities of fluid that may drain from an incision or wound. They may also incorporate a nonabsorbent layer of cotton or plastic film to prevent spread of fluid.

Abdominal packs, tape pads, stitched pads, gauze mops, laparotomy sponges etc, are used to form a nonabrasive wall that prevent abdominal or other organs from escaping into the field of operation and to maintain body temperature. Sanitary napkins known as V-pads, obstetrical pads, perineal pads, maternity pads are used in gynecological, obstetrical or maternity cases. Napkins which have repellent tissue on the back surfaces because of their greater fluid-holding capacity. Eye pads are used to cover the eye and protecting the eyebrow when taped. These pads are made using non-woven fabric and sealed in individual sterile envelopes. Nursing pads are designed in a contour shape to fit comfortably under the nursing brassiere.

Bandages:

The function of bandages is to hold dressings in place to provide pressure or support. They may be classified as elastic, non-elastic, impregnated and adhesive (Fig. 15.1)

Elastic Bandages

Crepe bandage is the best example of elastic bandage. It is an elastic fabric of plain weave in which the warp threads are of cotton and wool, and the weft threads are of cotton. The wool content is not less than 33 percent. The elasticity makes the crepe bandage especially serviceable in bandaging or light support to sprains, varicose veins, strains etc. It conforms closely to the skin or joint surfaces, lies flat and secure. There bandages are useful for correctional purposes and as a compression bandage. Cotton crepe bandage is similar to crepe bandage but the warp is of cotton and the weft is of cotton or rayon. In cotton stretch bandage, both warp and weft are cotton. This bandage is used to secure and protect dressings.

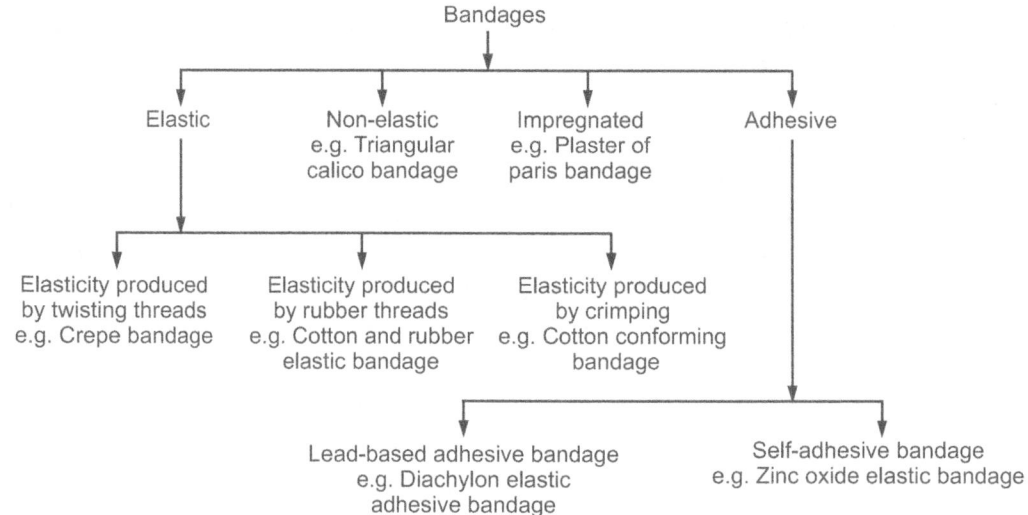

Fig. 15.1: Types of Bandages

Cotton and rubber elastic bandage has a cotton weft but the warp contains rubber threads. Cotton and rubber elastic net bandage is elastic in both warp and weft.

Cotton conforming bandage made from two plies of specially processed, high quality cotton gauze folded to the center and this imparts elasticity to both warp and weft. The sides of the fabric are folded into the centre to avoid frayed edges and produce a thicker more absorbent layer. This type of bandage is easy to use and apply to protect and secure dressings. It readily conforms to all body contours without the necessity of twisting. High bulk bandage is made of multiple layers of crimped cotton gauze.. The high bulk of this bandage type is designed to provide padding protection in wound dressings.

Non-Elastic Bandages

Triangular bandages are non-elastic bandages and usually made by cutting a square of bleached muslin diagonally from corner to corner, forming two right triangles of equal size and shape. They are used in first-aid work for head dressings, binders, arm slings and as temporary splints for broken bones. Cambric bandage or open-wave bandage is a cotton cloth of plain weave in which the weft is heavier than the warp. This bandage is commonly used as first aid and its heavy weft gives additional protection and improves the grip between layers. It is used to secure and protect dressings, and for support and immobilization. Domette bandage is a union fabric and its warp is cotton and the weft is wool. They are used for orthopedic purposes where high wool content provides warmth and additional support.

Impregnated Bandages

Plaster of paris bandage is a cotton cloth of leno weave impregnated with dried calcium sulphate and adhesives such as methycellulose. This bandage is thoroughly moistened with good quality water and applied to the limb or body. It is used for the immobilization and splinting of fractures and construction of body supports. Zinc paste bandage is an open-wove bandage impregnated with a paste containing zinc oxide. It is used to support and prevent swelling of fractured limbs after removing plaster and treat ulcers, varicose eczema and oedema of the legs. Zinc oxide and ichthammol bandage contains zinc oxide, coar tar or ichthammol & it is used for chronic skin disorders such as eczemas and leg ulcers.

Adhesive Bandages

Adhesive bandages are more suitable than paste bandages for treating ambulant patients. It is elastic in nature provides excellent support for the affected region, aided by the adhesive mass which holds the bandage firmly in affected place. Elastic diachylon bandage consists of an elastic cloth spread evenly with diachylon and suitable adhesives. Diachylon is a mixture of lead soaps of higher fatty acids obtained by reacting lead monoxide with vegetable oils. It is used for the treatment of chronic leg ulcers in ambulant patients and for support of varicose veins.

Self adhesive bandages are prepared by spreading a self-adhesive mass, either as a hot melt or in solution in an organic solvent, on a supporting materials. These self adhesive mass contains cohesive substances, plasticizers, resins, fillers, antioxidants, chelating agents and preservatives. Medicaments or drugs may be incorporated in the mass before spreading. Zinc oxide elastic adhesive bandage consists of an elastic cloth spread evenly with a self-adhesive mass containing zinc oxide. This bandage is used for support, compression and secure dressings.

Adhesive Tapes:

Surgical adhesive tapes are available in different forms, varying both in the type of backing and in the formulation of the adhesive mass according to specific needs and requirements. The adhesive tapes are classified as acrylate adhesive and rubber based adhesive. Acrylate adhesives on a non-woven or fabric backing have been widely used as surgical tapes. Acrylate adhesives combine the proper balance of tack and long term adhesion. They are non-occlusive and do not cause over hydration in the stratum corneum. Traumatic response to surgical tapes is substantially minimized when tapes are constructed to allow normal skin moisture to pass through adhesive and backing material. Hypoallergenic surgical tapes with acrylate adhesive are available with a variety of porous backing materials. Rayon taffeta cloth backing provides a high strength tape well suited for affixing heavy dressings. Lighter dressing applications can be accomplished with lower strength, economical paper backed surgical tapes.

Rubber based adhesives or surgical adhesive tapes are the cloth backed and plastic-backed rubber adhesives. These are used mainly where heavy support and a high level of adhesion are required. Rubber based adhesive tape masses are composed of an elastomer, modified rosin, antioxidants, plasticizers, fillers and colouring agents.

Protectives:

Protectives are plastic sheeting and waxed or plastic coated paper to prevent escape of moisture or heat from dressing or compress and to protect clothing or bed linens. Rubber sheeting is a rubber-coated cloth, waterproof and flexible for use as a covering for bedding.

Film dressing system helps to protect the wound site because it is impervious to liquid water and bacteria. Acrylate adhesive coated on a transparent, moisture vapour permeable plastic film applied directly onto a wound surface represents a new approach for dressing selected wounds. Film dressings are not recommended for infected or profusely exudative wounds.

Standards for Surgical Dressings:

Many surgical dressings are hygroscopic in nature, hence, standard tests such as counts, weights and tensile strength are performed under atmospheric conditions. Some tests are mentioned on dressing (Table 15.2), that should confirm before use.

Table 15.2: Specic tests shows properties of dressings

Test	Example
Absorbency	Absorbent cotton wool, absorbent gauze, regenerated cellulose, absorbent lint.
Adhesiveness	Zinc oxide self-adhesive plaster.
Elasticity	Elastic bandages, elastic adhesive, cotton stretch bandage, crepe bandage.
Waterproofners	Self-adhesive plasters (waterproof types).
Water-vapour permeability	Self-adhesive plasters (perforated plastic and microporous types.

The B.P.C has given standards for dressings in relevant parts of the codex including the appendix. The following standards are most desirable to ensure uformity in different samples of surgical dressings.

The count of the yarn: The TEX (unit of count of a yarn) count is the weight in grams of one kilometer of yarn. The count is the number of hanks of specified length (e.g. 840 yards for cotton) in one pound and it measure the fineness. The cotton yarns used in the wrap and weft of cotton and rubber elastic bandage B.P.C must not be finer than 13.4 tex (44 s) and 11.8 tex (50 s) respectively.

The number of threads per specified length of warp and weft: This standard indicates whether the fabric has an open or close texture.

The weight of a specified area: This test detects excess of fillers. Impregnated fabrics are freed from impregnating material or fillers before the test.

Foreign matter: Foreign matter must not exceed 1 percent in gauzes, muslin, tissues and elastic bandages while added foreign matter as fillers, antiseptics or wetting agents. Certain dressings, limit for foreign matter is higher because these dressings are not used in direct contact with wounds and some additives are necessary to produce a fabric suitable for its purpose.

Tensile Strength: Dressing fabrics are tested for tensile strength e.g. Belladonna plaster, salicylic acid plaster. The load required to break the fabric dressing is measured in form of tensile strength.

Extensibility: This test is applied to plastic self-adhesive plasters and plastic wound dressings. Plastic film must be capable of extension to fit body contours and respond to movements.

Packaging: Packaging materials used for dressings must be strong enough to withstand normal handling. All dressings must be stored in well closed containers. Zinc paste bandages require a well-sealed container because it contains hygroscopic or volatile ingredients. Absorbent cotton wool and absorbent guaze are not packed in waxy paper because it reduces their absorbency. Some of dressings must double wrapped to minimize loss of the volatile ingredients e.g. capsicum dressings. Double wrapping is also essential for sterile dressings. Both wrappers must be applied and sealed before sterilization and they should not be readily permeable to microorganisms.

Storage: Surgical dressings should be stored in a cool, dry, well-ventilated place. Wound dressings and adhesive bandages should be kept in dry place, protected from contaminants, at a temperature between 15°C to 20°C.

LIGATURES AND SUTURES

Ligatures and sutures are threads or fibres specially prepared and sterilized for use in surgery. Ligature is used for typing off a blood vessel and suture is used for sewing various tissues e.g. skin, muscle, peritoneum etc. Hence a needle is always used for a suture (sewing) but not for a ligature. Still the terms 'ligature' and 'suture' are often used in the same sense and they are prepared by same material. Ligatures and sutures are made from intestinal tissues and tendons of a large assortment of animals and birds, thread spun from vegetable fibres, human hair, horse and camel hair, synthetic threads etc. The ideal properties of ligatures and sutures are as follows:

- They must non-irritant and sterile.
- The gauze should be fine.
- They must be non-allergic and non-carcinogenic.
- Their tensile strength must be adequate for sewing the tissues.
- The time of absorption of absorbable ligatures and sutures should be known.
- Easy to prepare and sterilize without any loss.

Ligatures and sutures are classified into two major groups as absorbable sutures and non-absorbable sutures (Fig. 15.2).

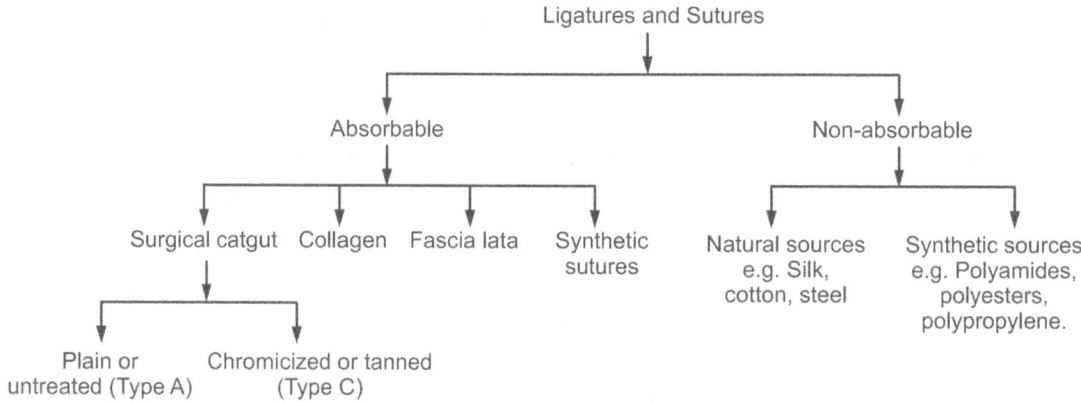

Fig. 15.2: Types of Ligatures and Sutures.

Absorbable Sutures:

Absorbable sutures are absorbed by the tissues during the healing process of wounds. These absorbable sutures are digested or broken down by living mammalian tissue. Absorbable sutures include catgut, collagen, fascia lata and synthetic sutures.

Surgical Catgut: Two types of surgical catgut are described in the USP as Type A (plain) and Type C (medium treatment) on basis of their resistance to absorptive action by tissue enzymes. Plain catgut is absorbed within 2 to 8 days, depending upon the size (00 - 5). Number 00 absorbs in two days and number 0 in four days, so they are used for tissues which heal quickly e.g. superficial ligatures. Number 1 absorbs in six days and is used to tie off muscle bleeders and for sewing muscle. Chromicized or tanned (Type C) catgut are treated with a salt of either chromic or tannic acid and prepared in sterile tubes. This material resists absorption longer than plain catgut upto 10 to 20 days. Numbers 00 and 0 are used on mucous membrane and small tendons and numbers 3 to 5 for tying off larger organs such as lungs and kidneys.

Sterilized surgical catgut is a sterile strand prepared from collagen derived from healthy mammals usually sheep or cattle. The most widely used sources are the submucosal layer of the small intestine of a sheep or lambs and serosal layer of an intestine of a cattle. The intestine is removed from the freshly killed animal and cleaned to remove faecal matter. The submucosal layer is separated mechanically, which is then split longitudinally into ribbons. The ribbons may be tanned or hardened by soaking in solutions of chromic salts. This causes delay in the absorption of the gut in the body. The ribbons are tied at the ends in groups of two, three or more, depending on the gauge of thread to be prepared. The number of twists used in spinning the thread must be carefully controlled to ensure a uniform product of good tensile strength. Drying is done in an atmosphere conditioned with regard to temperature and humidity. The final dried catgut is known at this stage as raw catgut and is usually between 3 and 5 m long. Finishing is smoothing process, in which the strings are rubbed against an abrasive surface to produce a small and uniform string. Quality of surgical gut is depends on finishing process. The gauge of the strings is carefully checked and should show uniformity between strings of the same batch. These strands are cut into appropriate length and sterilized. The sterile catgut is placed in glass bottles or flexible containers such as aluminum foil or plastic films. The container must label containing the length of the strand, the gauge number, type of strand, tensile strength etc. The label on the box must state the name and percentage of any bactericide in the fluid in which the sutures are immersed. Sterilized surgical catgut should be protected from light and stored in a cool place.

Sterilization of Catgut: The catgut may be sterilized by thermal, chemical or ionising radiations. Dehydration of catgut is necessary before its thermal sterilization, otherwise moisture / causes hydrolysis of collagen into gelatin. The heat resistant glass tubes containing anhydrous catgut is sterilized by autoclave filled with anhydrous fluid at 160 °C. The sterilization tubes are filled aseptically with sterile tubing fluid. Absorbable catgut is further classified as boilable catgut and non-boilable catgut, depending on the nature of tubing fluid. Boilable catgut is placed in glass tubes with strands immersed in a water-free high boiling tubing fluid such as toluene or xylol. Before opening the tube, the external surface of the tubes is sterilized by autoclaving. It produces stiff catgut and hence before its use, it requires soaking for few minutes in methylated spirit or in sterile saline solution to make it pliable. Due to such properties of boilable suture, this technique is no longer used. The present method of packaging catgut provides sutures ready for use as removed from the packet (non-boilable). The non-boilable tubes are filled with alcohol containing a small quantity of water. Such system does not allow sterilization by heat. The water in tube maintains catgut pliable and ready to use. The external surface of the tube is sterilized by washing with a germicide solution before opening.

Chemical sterilization by using 5% formaldehyde solution produces hard sutures with reduced tensile strength. Hydrogen peroxide is effectively sterilize catgut but it converts catgut in poor quality. Glutaraldehyde is only active in sodium bicarbonate buffered solutions and it retains sporicidal activity for two weeks. Iodine is the suitable chemical for large scale commercial sterilizing of catgut. Ethyl iodide and methyl bromide in alcohol and mixtures of iodine and iodine trichloride have also been used. Ethylene oxide is also used as a sterilizing agent in the gaseous form or in solution. It is an explosive gas and is usually supplied mixed with carbon dioxide or freon. Care must be taken for limit of residual ethylene oxide in the suture.

Radiation sterilization is most commonly used method of sterilization for sutures. Catgut packed in aluminium tubes is exposed to gamma radiation (CO_{60}). The recognized sterilizing dose for sutures is 2.5 megarad. The method has the advantage that sterilization is effected in the final sealed container.

Collagen: Collagen is available from a large number of sources. It is the major constituent of skin, tendon, ligament, etc. The acidic solution of collagen prepared from hides or tendons which can be extruded into a coagulating solution and the resulting fibres oriented by stretching. The filaments can either be spun or rolled to make up the required sizes of strand. Reconstituted collagen is produced mainly in the finer sizes 0.5, 1 and 2 for ophthalmic surgery.

Fascia Lata: This is obtained from ox fascia and it is used as heavy suture for hernia repair, urethral slings, etc. It is usually attached firmly to a strong structure by means of a non-absorbable suture. Fascia lata is supplied in the form of sterile strips approx. ½ inch wide and 8 inch long and also inch sheets about 3×5 inch.

Synthetic Sutures: Synthetic absorbable sutures have high tensile strength, holds knot very well, have simple hydrolysis and minimum tissue reaction. Polymers such as polyglycolic acid (Dexon), polyglactic (vicryl) and polydixanone (PDS) have been shown to possess properties which make them suitable for many surgical procedures. The first two polyesters mentioned are melt-extruded into multifilament yarns which are then braided into various sizes of sutures and the latter is monofilament. Synthetic sutures do not get absorbed by enzymatic reaction but undergo complete breaking by hydrolysis.

Non-Absorbable Sutures

Non-absorbable sutures are resistant to the action of living mammalian tissues. They remain unchanged and encapsulated in fibrous tissue for many years. The non-absorbable sutures used in seiving skin are removed after healing of wound. These suture consists of natural and synthetic non-absorbable suture materials.

Natural (non-synthetic) non-absorbable sutures

Silk is an important non-absorbable suture obtained from silk worm. The braided silk has compact structure and strength. Silk sutures are easily handled and well tolerated by body tissue. It becomes encapsulated and remains permanently in the tissues. Silk sutures are widely used in surgical procedures of eye, brain, gastrointestinal tract and blood vessels. It has been also used for wound which is not infected. Infected microorganisms may be carried in the interstices of braided suture and thus escape phagocytosis, causing chronic suture infection. Silk is sterilized either by autoclaving, radiation or ethylene oxide sterilization. Autoclaving technique causes a certain loss in its tensile strength.

Cotton and linen sutures derived from cellulose are among the oldest method. These sutures are twisted from fiber staple and have moderately high tensile strength. These sutures are desirable because of their handling properties and low order of tissue reactivity. These sutures undergo degradation with time, hence, they are not used where strength must be maintained for long periods. The metal sutures are useful where great strength is required, mainly in joint or chest surgery. Stainless steel, ferous alloy has been used in the form of wire sutures, fixation plates and screws. It is supplied for surgical purposes in three forms as monofilament, twisted and plaited or braided. It is mainly used for orthopedic, plastic surgery and for repair of tendons.

Synthetic non-absorbable sutures

Synthetic non-absorbable sutures are strong and water resistant. Nylon is synthetic polyamide available in the form of monofilament and multifilament. It is obtained from the condensation of adipic acid and hexamethylenediamine or from condensing caprolactam.

Polyamides and suture materials are produced by an extrusion process. The bulk of the material used in surgery is produced in the form of monofilament.

Polyester suture is prepared by melt-extruding polyethylene terephthalate into fine filaments which are then braided into the various sizes of sutures. The tensile strength of braided polyester suture is superior to nylon and braided silk. Polyester sutures contain no wax or other additives. It remains unaffected in body and has excellent knot holding properties. Polyester sutures are available in the natural colour to enhance visibility in the surgical field. The polypropylene suture is smooth and easily removable from tissue. It withstand moist heat sterilization and have a very low tissue reactivity.

Standards of Catgut

- **Length:** The length of catgut is measured without stretching immediately after removal of the strand from its container. The length must be not less than 90% of the length stated in monograph or label and does not exceed 350 mm.

- **Diameter:** Perform the test for 5 sutures by using suitable instrument capable of measuring with an accuracy of at least 0.002 mm and having a circular pressor foot 10 – 15 mm in diameter. The pressor foot and the moving parts attached to it are weighted so as to apply a total load of 100 ± 10 g to the suture being tested. Measure the diameter of a suture less than 90 cm in length at 3 points evenly spaced along the suture. The average of readings are calculated and not less than two-thirds of the readings taken on each suture are within the limits given in Table 15.3 for the gauge number concerned.

Table 15.3: Diameters and breaking loads

Gauge number	Diameter in range (mm)	Breaking load (Newton's)
0.1	0.010 – 0.019	---
0.5	0.050 – 0.069	0.40
1	0.100 – 0.149	1.8
2	0.200 – 0.249	7.5
3	0.300 – 0.349	12.5
4	0.400 – 0.499	27.5
5	0.500 – 0.599	38.0
6	0.600 – 0.699	45.0
7	0.700 – 0.799	60.0
8	0.800 – 0.899	70.0

- **Tensile Strength (Minimum breaking load):** The tensile strength is determined over a simple knot formed by placing one end of a suture held in the right hand over the other end held in the left hand, passing one end over the suture to form the loop (Fig. 15.3). Perform the test on 5 sutures having length greater than 75 cm by pulling the knot tight using a suitable tensilometer. The apparatus has two clamp for holding the catgut, one of which is mobile and is driven at a constant rate of 30 cm/min. The length of catgut between the clamps is 12.5 to 20 cm and the knot is midway between the clamps. If the catgut breaks in a clamp or within 1 cm of it, the result is discarded and the test repeated on the another catgut or suture. The standard suture results should be in the range as given in Table 15.3. The strands are tested within 15 min of removal from their container in a temperature between 16 and 21°C at relative humidity between 60 and 80.

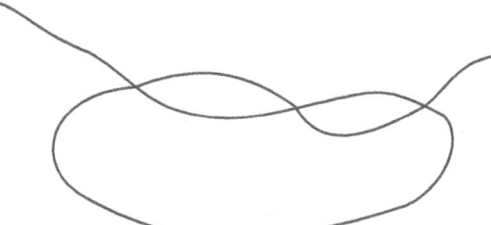

Fig. 15.3: Simple knot of sutures

- **Sterility Testing:** Test for sterility is recommended for all sterile surgical dressings and devices by IP 2007. The test must be carried out under aseptic conditions designed to avoid accidental contamination of the product during testing. Minimum number of items recommended to be tested in relation to the number of items in the batch is given in Table 15.4. The media for sterility test (ATM / FTM / SCDM) is designed to detect the presence of aerobic and anaerobic microorganisms.

Membrane filtration (Method A) and direct inoculation (Method B) methods are used for sterility testing of surgical devices. Quality of sample from each container to be tested is given in Table 15.5.

Table 15.4: Number of item in the batch recommended for sterility testing

Number of items in the batch	Minimum number of items recommended to be tested
Catgut, surgical sutures and other sterile medical devices for use.	2 percent or 5 packages whichever is greater, upto a maximum of 20 packages.
Not more than 100 packages.	10 percent or 4 packages, whichever is greater.
More than 100 but not more than 500 packages.	10 packages.
More than 500 packages.	2 percent or 20 packages, whichever is less.

Table 15.5: Minimum quantity to be tested from each container

Surgical devices	Minimum quantity to be used for each culture medium
Sutures and other individually packed single use material.	The whole device or material, cut into pieces or disassembled.
Surgical dressings / cotton / gauze (in packages).	100 mg per package.
Catgut and other surgical sutures for veterinary use.	3 sections of a strand (each 30 cm long).
Absorbent cotton.	Not less than 1 g from one portion.

- **Packaging:** The surgical catgut is packed in glass tubes sealed by fusion of the glass or in other suitable containers. Glass tubes are ideal method of packaging surgical sutures. They are transparent, inert and impermeable. Flexible packages based on aluminium foil or plastic films are also used in the past few years as a packaging materials. The label on the container must state the length of the strand and the gauge number. The strand is plain, hardened or chromicized. The name and percentage of bactericide in the fluid in which the sutures are immersed is also stated on label.
- **Storage:** Sterilized surgical catgut should be protected from light and stored in a dry / cool place. Sterile catgut sutures are presented in individual sachets that maintain sterility and use of the sutures in aseptic conditions.

The catheters where the inside lumen and outside surface are required to be sterile, either cut them into pieces such that the medium is in contact with the entire lumen or full the lumen with medium. Then immerse the intact unit and proceed by membrane filtration. For direct inoculation, aseptically remove two or more portions of 100 to 500 mg each from the innermost part of the sample. From single use materials, aseptically remove the entire article and immerse the portions or article in each medium (FTM / ATM and SCDM).

If after an incubation period of 14 days, no growth of microorganism is found in any tube, the sample passes the sterility test. If growth of microorganisms is found in any tube, the sample does not comply with the test for sterility. If test was invalid for causes unrelated to the preparation under examination then repeat the test with the same number of units as in the original test.

SURGICAL NEEDLES

Surgical sutures are threaded on needles for suturing or sewing. These are several sizes and shapes of surgical needles. The choice of sutures and needles are depends on location of the lesion, thickness of the skin, and the amount of tension exerted on the wound. The needles selected for sewing is depends on type of surgery such as arterial, intestinal, ophthalmic, plastic or general purpose. There are several shapes of surgical needles such as straight, ¼ circle, 3/8 circle, ½ circle, 5/8 circle, compound curve, half curved (ski) and half curved at both ends of a straight segment (canoe). The ski and canoe needle design allows curved needles to be straight enough to be used in laparoscopic surgery.

Surgical needles are two types as traumatic needles and atraumatic needles with sutures. Traumatic needles are with eyes or holes which are supplied to the hospital separate from their suture thread. This type of suture rips the tissue to a certain extent, when passing through the tissues. Atraumatic needles with sutures comprise an eyeless needle attached to a specific length of suture thread. Suitable eyeless needles on catgut and other materials are now available to meet most of the demands of the modern surgeon. It is also used for fine surgery such as plastic and eye work.

QUESTIONS

(A) Short answer questions:
1. Write ideal properties of surgical dressings.
2. Explain in short surgical gauzes.
3. Write the ideal properties of ligatures and sutures.

(B) Long answer questions:
1. Explain in detail different types of wound dressings.
2. Explain in detail different types of Bandages.
3. Write a note on:
   (a) Absorbent cotton (b) Surgical catgut
   (c) Non-absorbable sutures (d) Surgical needles
4. Explain different standard tests for surgical dressings.
5. Explain the standards of catgut.

(C) Multiple choice questions:
1. Absorbent cotton wool consists of epidermal trichomes from the seeds of cultivated species of _____.
   (a) Papaver (b) Gossypium
   (c) Rawulfia (d) Mycobacterium
2. Two types of surgical catgut are described in the USP as Type A and _____.
   (a) Type B (b) Type C
   (c) Type AB (d) Type BC

CHAPTER 16
ENZYME TECHNOLOGY

CONTENTS
    INTRODUCTION
        Sources and applications of enzymes
        Properties of enzymes
    FACTORS AFFECTING ENZYME KINETICS
    ENZYME IMMOBILIZATION
        Methods of immobilization
        Applications of immobilization
    IMMOBILIZATION OF BACTERIAL AND PLANT CELL
    IMPORTANT ENZYMES
        Amylases, Penicillinase, Streptokinase, Streptodornase, Hyaluronidase, Proteases

INTRODUCTION

Enzyme technology is the technology associated with the use of enzymes as tools in industry, pharmaceuticals, agriculture or medicine. Enzymes are soluble, amorphous, colloidal, proteineous, bioactive organic catalyst produced by living cells. They are proteins, composed of one polypeptide (amino acid chain) or more associated polypeptide chains. The catalytic activity of enzymes depend on the L-α-amino acid sequence and peptide bonds constituting the protein molecule. Primary, secondary, tertiary and quaternary structures of enzyme proteins are necessary for their catalytic activity. Enzymes are called holoenzyme composed of protein (apoenzyme), non-protein (coenzyme) and metal. Protein part of enzyme is attached to non-protein part by covalent or non-covalent bond. When coenzyme is attached to apoenzyme tightly and permanently then it is called as prosthetic group. Enzymes have molecular weights ranging from about 12,000 to over one million.

Enzymes are mainly classified as extracellular enzymes (exoenzyme) and intracellular enzymes (endoenzyme). Exoenzymes are secreted outside the cell such as cellulose, polyglucturonase, pectinmethylesterase etc. Endoenzymes are secreted within the cell such as invertase, uric oxidase, asparaginase etc. Endoenzymes are isolated by breaking the cells by means of a homogenizer or a bead mill and extracting them through the biochemical processes.

Sources and applications of enzymes:

Enzymes are mainly obtained from living cells from plants, animals and microorganisms (Table 16.1). Mitochondria, granular microsome, lysosome and ribosome are major sources for enzymes in plant and animal cells. Animal gland is source for hydrolyzing enzymes used as digestive aids. The pancreas is source of trypsinogen (23%) and chymotrypsinogen (10 to 14%). Pancreatin contains several enzymes such as amylase, protease etc. The selection of the sources for enzyme is dependent on specificity, activation, inhibition, pH, thermostability, availability and cost. The extraction of enzymes from plant and animal sources are simple as compared to microbial sources. Microbial sources are capable of producing a wide variety of enzymes from bacteria and fungi. The enzyme concentration in these cells is dependent on environmental conditions and genetic manipulations. Microbial cells require short fermentation times, inexpensive media and simple screening procedures.

Table 16.1: Sources and applications of enzymes

Source	Name of enzyme	Source of enzyme	Applications
Plant	Proteases	Pineapple, papaya	Inflammation gastritis
	Amylolytic	Wheat, potatoes, beans, soybeans	Production of glucose syrup
	α or β Amylase	Seeds	Paper, textile industries
Animal	Lipase	Pancreatic gland	Food and oil industry
	Chymotrypsin (protease)	Bovine pancreas	Inflammation
	Plasmin (protease)	Plasminogen	Thrombotic disorders
	Pepsin	Animal intestine	Digestion
	Glucose oxidase	Liver	Digestive aid
	Urokinase(protease)	Human urine	Thromboembolic diseases
	Hyaluronidase	Animal *testes*	Local anesthesia
Bacteria	α-Amylase	*Bacillus* spp.	Paper, textile, baking industries
	β-Amylase,	*Bacillus cereus*	Paper, textile, baking industries
	Streptokinase	*Streptococcus* spp.	Thromboembolic diseases
	Urokinase (protease)	*Bacillus fastidiosus*	Thromboembolic diseases
	Proteinase	*Escherichia coli, Bacillus subtilis*	Genetics, rDNA technology
	Penicillin acylase	*Bacillus megaterium*	Production of semi-synthetic penicillin
	Glucose isomerase	*Bacillus coagulans, Streptomyces* sp.,	Preparation of fructose
	Dextran sucrase	*Leuconostoc mesenteroides*	Production of dextran

contd. ...

Source	Name of enzyme	Source of enzyme	Applications
Fungi	α-Amylase, proteinase	*Aspergillus oryzae*	Paper, textile and baking
	Catalase, lactase, amyloglucosidase	*Aspergillus niger*	Cytotoxic agent
	Cellulase	*Trichoderma reesi, Penicillium funiculsosum*	Polymer degradation in detergents
	Dextranase	*Penicillium* sp.	Dental plaque
	Glucoamylase	*Aspergillus niger, Rhizopus* sp.	Production of maltose syrup
	Invertase	*Saccharomyces* sp.	Sugar industry
	Lactase	*Aspergillus niger, Kluveromyces fragilis*	Milk and ice-cream industry
	Lipase	*Candida lipoytica Rhizopus delemar*	Food industry

Properties of enzymes:

Enzymes are characterized by many biophysical properties.

- Enzymes are made up of protein or associated with a non-protein part. Macromolecules including proteins are species specific.
- Enzyme activity and stability may be influenced by temperature, pH and other external factors. Most of the enzymes act best between 20 to 35°C. Stability of enzyme is also increased by presence of their substrate and presence of ions. Change in pH, ionic strength or other interactions mainly causes conformational changes in the enzyme molecules, leading to loss of activity.
- Enzymes obtained from different sources show difference in responses to a given activator or inhibitor. Cobalt activates β-galactosidase isolated from bacteria and inhibits it when obtained from fungi.
- Enzymes act as catalysts and influence the speed of chemical reaction. It has ability to catalyze one specific reaction and most of the reactions catalyzed by enzymes are reversible.

FACTORS AFFECTING ENZYME KINETICS

Enzyme kinetics is the study of the chemical reactions that are catalyzed by enzymes with a focus on their reaction rates. The study of an enzyme's kinetics reveals its role in metabolism, catalytic mechanism, controlled activity and effect of drug on enzymes. The contact between the enzyme and substrate is the most essential pre-requisite for enzyme activity. The rate at which an enzyme works is influenced by several factors e.g. concentration of enzyme, substrate concentration, temperature, pH, time, concentration of reaction products, effect of activators and presence of inhibitors.

Concentration of enzyme:

The velocity of the reaction is more when the concentration of the enzyme increases. (Fig. 16.1). This property of enzyme is made use in determining the activities of serum enzymes for diagnosis of diseases.

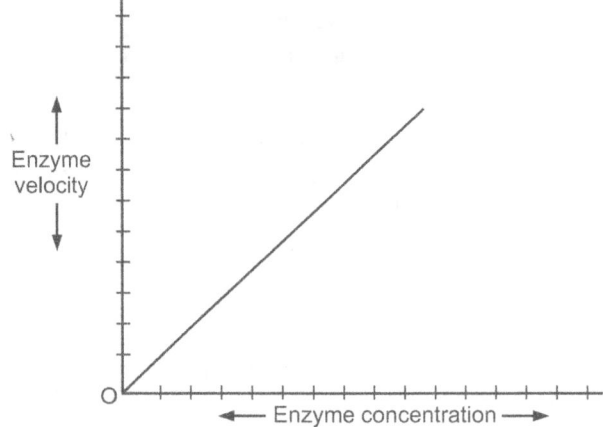

Fig. 16.1: Effect of enzyme concentration on enzyme activity

Substrate concentration:

Increase in the substrate concentration gradually increases the velocity of enzyme reaction. Further increase in substrate concentration do not increase the velocity of enzyme reaction because enzyme active sites are saturated with substrate. Hence, the shape of the curve that relates activity to substrate concentration is hyperbolic (Fig. 16.2)

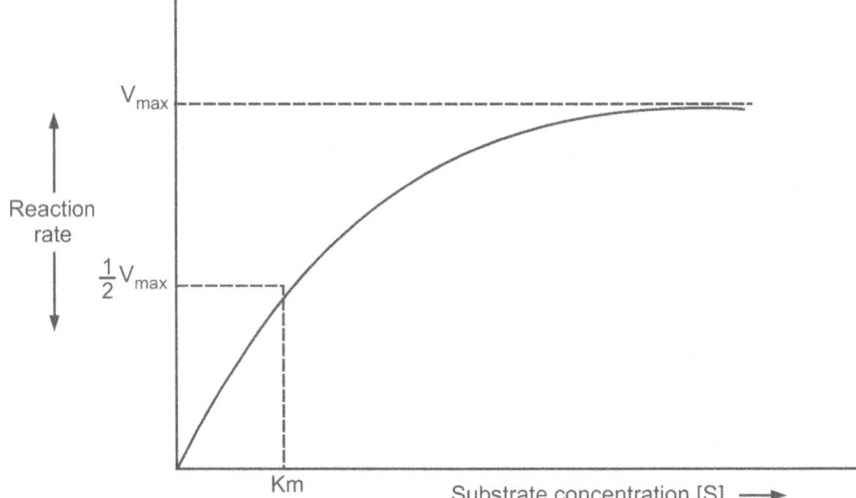

Fig. 16.2: Effect of substrate concentration on the initial velocity of an enzyme-catalyzed reaction

The relationship between substrate and enzyme concentration was proposed by **Victor Henri** (1903) that the combination of an enzyme with its substrate molecule to form an ES complex is a necessary step in enzymatic catalysis. This concept was expanded into a general theory of enzyme action by **Leonor Michaelis** and **Maud Menten** (1913). It postulated that substrate and enzyme are in fast equilibrium with their complex, which then dissociates to yield product and free enzyme.

$$E + S \underset{K_{-1}}{\overset{K_1}{\rightleftharpoons}} ES \xrightarrow{K_2} E + P \qquad \ldots(1)$$

K_1, K_{-1}, K_2 are the rate constants for the individual steps.

The rate of product formation $\frac{d[P]}{dt}$ is referred as the reaction rate (v). The rate of product formation is dependent on the conversion rate constant (K_2) and the concentration of enzyme that is bound to substrate [ES]. The concentration of enzyme that is bound to substrate [ES] is expressed mainly in terms of the known parameters of the system.

$$[ES] = \frac{K_1 [E][S]}{K_{-1} + K_2} \qquad \ldots(2)$$

The Michaelis – Menten constant (K_m) is given by the formula:

$$K_m = \frac{K_{-1} + K_2}{K_1} \qquad \ldots(3)$$

Rearrange the equation (2).

$$[ES] = \frac{[E][S]}{K_m} \qquad \ldots(4)$$

The total concentration of enzyme [E_o] is the sum of the free enzyme in solution [E] and enzyme is bound to the substrate [ES].

$$[E_o] = [E] + [ES] \qquad \ldots(5)$$
$$[E] = [E_o] - [ES] \qquad \ldots(6)$$

Using equation (6), the bound enzyme concentration (4) can be written as:

$$[ES] = \frac{([E_o] - [ES])[S]}{K_m} \qquad \ldots(7)$$

Rearrange the above equation

$$[ES]\frac{K_m}{[S]} = [E_o] - [ES]$$

$$[ES] + [ES]\frac{K_m}{[S]} = [E_o]$$

$$[ES]\left(1 + \frac{K_m}{[S]}\right) = [E_o]$$

$$[ES][E_o] = \frac{1}{1 + \frac{K_m}{[S]}} \qquad \ldots(8)$$

The reaction rate (V) is:

$$V = \frac{d[P]}{dt} = K_2 [ES] \quad \ldots (9)$$

Substituting (8) in (9)

$$\frac{d[P]}{dt} = K_2 [E_o] \frac{1}{1 + \frac{K_m}{[S]}}$$

$$= K_2 [E_o] \frac{1}{\frac{[S] + K_m}{[S]}}$$

$$= K_2 [E_o] \frac{[S]}{K_m + [S]}$$

Here, $\quad V_{max} = K_2 [E_o] \quad \ldots (10)$

The Michaelis-Menten equation is expressed as:

$$V = \frac{V_{max} [S]}{K_m + [S]} \quad \ldots (11)$$

where,
- V = Initial rate of production of the product
- V_{max} = Maximum initial rate of production of the product
- [S] = Substrate concentration
- K_m = Michaelis-Menten rate constant

The Michaelis-Menten constant is defined as the substrate concentration to produce half-maximum velocity in an enzyme catalyzed reaction. It indicates that half of the enzyme molecules are bound with the substrate molecules when the substrate concentration equals the K_m value. A low K_m value indicates a strong affinity between enzyme and substrate, whereas a high K_m value reflects the weak affinity between them.

The Michaelis-Menten equation can be optimized by linear regression and non-linear regression methods. The Michaelis-Menten equation (11) can be algebraically transformed into other forms that are more useful in graphical processing of experimental data. One common transformation is derived simply by taking the reciprocal of both sides of the Michaelis-Menten equation.

$$\frac{1}{V} = \frac{K_m + [S]}{V_{max} [S]} \quad \ldots (12)$$

Separating the components of the numerator as the right side of equation gives:

$$\frac{1}{V} = \frac{K_m}{V_{max} [S]} + \frac{[S]}{V_{max} [S]}$$

$$\frac{1}{V} = \left(\frac{K_m}{V_{max}}\right) \frac{1}{[S]} + \frac{1}{V_{max}} \quad \ldots (13)$$

This form of the Michaelis-Menten equation is called Lineweaver-Burk equation. Michaelis-Menten kinetics is also called 'steady-state kinetics'.

Equation (13) is the equation for a straight line, y = ax + b, where $y = \frac{1}{V}$ and $x = \frac{1}{[S]}$. A plot of $\left(\frac{1}{V}\right)$ verses $\left(\frac{1}{[S]}\right)$ yields a slope $\frac{K_m}{V_{max}}$ and an intercept $\frac{1}{V_{max}}$. Such a plot is called a double reciprocal or Lineweaver-Burk plot (Fig. 16.3). The double-reciprocal plot of enzyme reaction rates is very useful in distinguishing between certain types of enzymatic reaction mechanisms and in analyzing enzyme inhibition.

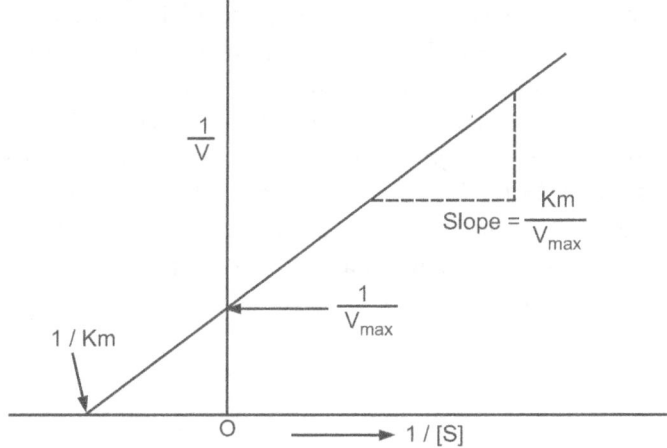

Fig. 16.3: Double reciprocal or Lineweaver-Burk plot

Effect of temperature:

Chemical reactions, both catalyzed and non-catalyzed proceed at a faster rate as the reaction temperature is increased. The optimum temperature for most of enzymes is between 40 to 45°C (Fig. 16.4). However, a few enzymes such as venom phosphokinases, muscle adenylate kinase are active even at 100°C. The increase in the rate below optimal temperature results from the increased kinetic energy of the reacting molecules. As the temperature is raised still further, the kinetic energy of the enzyme molecules becomes so

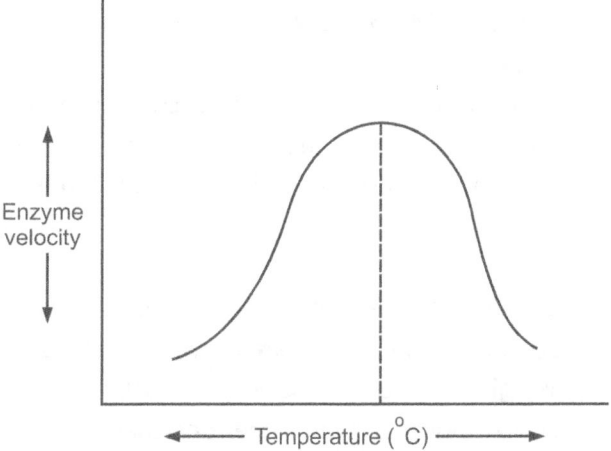

Fig. 16.4: Effect of temperature on enzyme activity

high that hold the enzyme in catalytically active form because it breaks the secondary bonds. However, simultaneously there is a loss of secondary and tertiary structures and a parallel loss of biological activity. The temperature coefficient or Q_{10} is the factor by which the rate of a biological process increases for a 10°C increase in temperature. The velocity of many biological reactions roughly doubles with a 10°C rise in temperature (Q_{10} = 2).

Effect of hydrogen ion concentration or pH:

The rate of almost all enzyme – catalyzed reactions exhibits a significant dependence on hydrogen ion concentration. Most of the enzymes of higher organisms show optimum activity around neutral pH 6 to 8 (Fig. 16.5). Some enzymes such as pepsin, acid phosphatase and alkaline phosphatase shows optimum activity at pH 1 to 2, 4 to 5 and 10 to 11 respectively. The relationship of activity to hydrogen ion concentration reflects the balance between enzyme denaturation at high or low pH and effects on the charged state of the enzyme, the substrates or both. The most common charged groups are the negative carboxylate groups and the positively charged groups of protonated amines. Loss or gain of critical charged groups will adversely affect substrate binding and which retard catalysis.

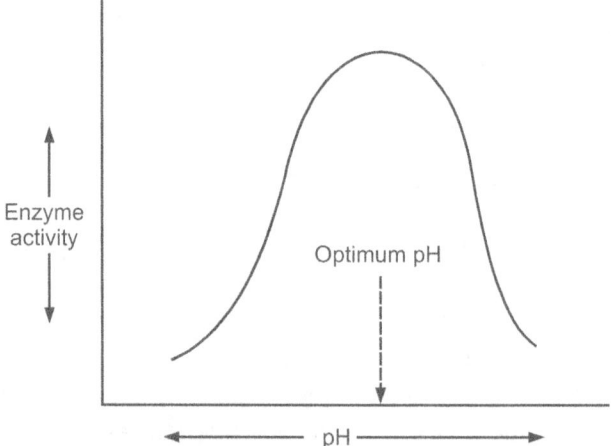

Fig. 16.5: Effect of pH on enzyme activity

Concentration of reaction products:

The accumulation of reaction products generally decreases the enzyme velocity. Some enzymes, the products combine with the active site of enzyme and form a loose complex and inhibit the enzyme activity. In the living system, this type of inhibition is generally prevented by a quick removal of products formed.

Effect of activators:

Many ions and molecules have the capacity to activate some enzymes. Metal ions such as Mg^{++}, Mn^{++}, Zn^{++}, Ca^{++}, Co^{++}, Cu^{++}, Na^+, K^+ etc. are activators of a number of enzymes. Many reducing agents (cysteine, glutathione) act as enzyme activators of enzyme containing sulfhydryl groups. Enzyme themselves activate other enzymes or proenzymes. Enterokinase activates trypsinogen to form active trypsin.

ENZYME IMMOBILIZATION

Enzyme immobilization is a process in which 'enzymes are physically confined, or localized in a certain defined region of space with retention of their catalytic activities' and which can be used repeatedly and continuously. It is the process wherein an enzyme or cell makes use of safe carrier phase for stealth and safe homing. The use of enzymes in industrial applications is limited because most of the enzymes are relatively unstable and high cost of isolation, purification and recovery of active enzymes from the reaction mixtures after the completion of catalytic process. Hence, enzymes must be immobilized on the surface of some solid support or it can convert a continuous flow of substrate to product without being lost. The first commercial application of immobilized enzyme technology was realised in 1969 in Japan with the use of *Aspergillus oryzae* amino acylase for the industrial production of L-amino acids. The advantage of immobilized enzymes are as follows.

- The immobilization process can lead to increased activity and stability of the enzyme molecules.
- They are physically confined during a continuous catalytic process.
- Immobilized enzymes are easily recovered from the reaction mixture and reused. Hence, process is more economic.
- They can be operated continuously and can be readily controlled.
- Enzyme immobilization process avoids the contamination in products and increases enzyme: substrate ratio.
- The products can be easily separated.

Methods of enzyme immobilization:

Enzyme immobilization methods are classified as surface immobilization and within surface immobilization (Fig. 16.6). These methods depend upon physical relationship of the catalyst to the matrix (carrier).

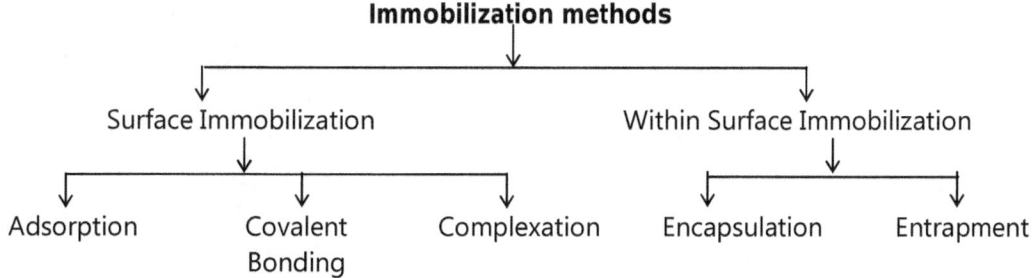

Fig. 16.6: Methods of enzyme immobilization

The major components of an immobilized enzyme are the enzyme, the matrix and the mode of interaction of the enzyme with the carrier. The selected matrix must enhance the operational stability of the immobilized enzyme purification. The carriers used for enzyme immobilization are porous or nonporous materials with organic (natural or synthetic) or inorganic nature. An ideal carrier matrix should be inert, cost effective, stable, high regidity, regenerability, large surface area, more permeability, suitable shape and highly resistance to microbial attack.

Adsorption: Adsorption is the most economical and simple method to immobilize enzymes by adsorbing them on to charged or neutral surfaces of inert substrate. Various kinds of supports are used for adsorption such as aluminium oxide, charcoal, starch, modified sepharose, cellulose derivatives, glass and ion exchange resins. The adsorption of an enzyme is dependent on the experimental variables such as pH, ionic strength, temperature, nature of solvent and concentration of enzyme and adsorbent. The surface of the support involves weak binding forces between protein and adsorbent such as hydrogen bonds, van der waals forces and ionic or hydrophobic interactions (Fig. 16.7).

The process of adsorption of an enzyme is performed by mixing the enzyme and polymer support in a stirred reactor or by percolating the enzyme through a packed bed, tube or membrane. The quantity of enzyme adsorbed to a solid support is dependent on the enzyme concentration exposed to the unit surface of carrier during the immobilization process. Time and temperature are important parameters in adsorption of enzymes with porous carrier. The disadvantage of adsorption is that the binding forces between the enzyme and the support are weak. Hence, adsorbed enzymes are liable to desorption during the utilization. The desorption of the protein is dependent on changes in temperature, pH and ionic strength. The various enzymes that may be immobilized by adsorption on respective carrier matrix are given in Table 16.2.

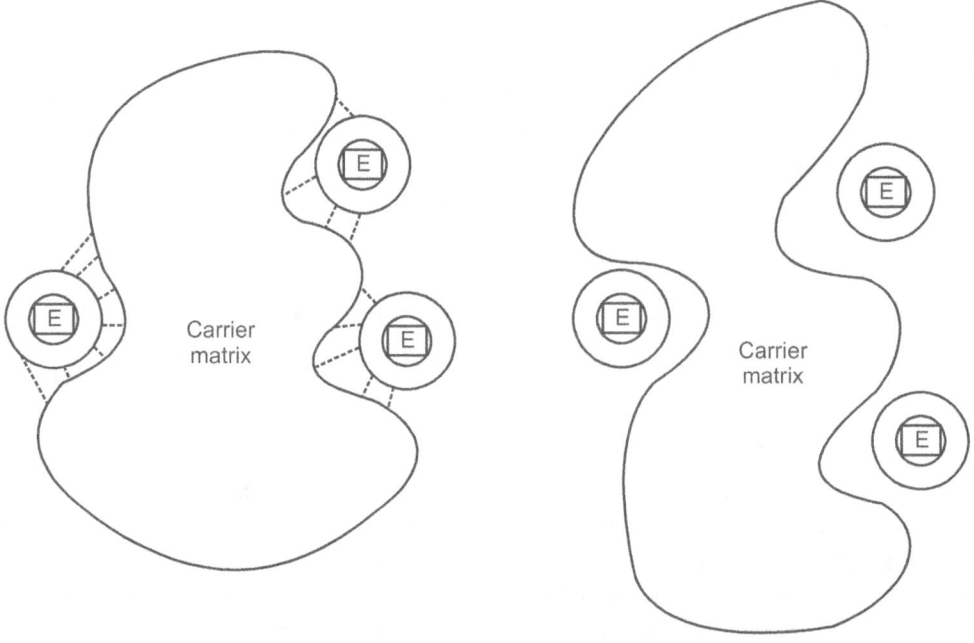

(a) Van der Waals forces   **(b) Hydrogen bonding**

Fig. 16.7: Enzyme immobilization by adsorption

Table 16.2: Enzymes immobilized by adsorption

Enzymes	Carrier matrix
α - Amylase	Calcium phosphate
Catalase	Charcoal
Invertase	Charcoal, DEAE – sephadex
Subtilisin	Cellulose
Aminoglycosidase	Agarose gel, DEAE – sephadex
Glucose oxidase	Cellophane

Covalent bonding: Covalent bond is formed between the chemical groups of enzyme and chemical groups on surface of carrier (Fig. 16.8). Covalent bonding has an advantage of an attachment not reversed by pH, ionic strength or substrate. The active site of an enzyme may be blocked through the chemical reaction and the enzyme rendered inactive. Adsorption of enzymes to the carrier matrices is quite easy and convenient by covalent bonding.

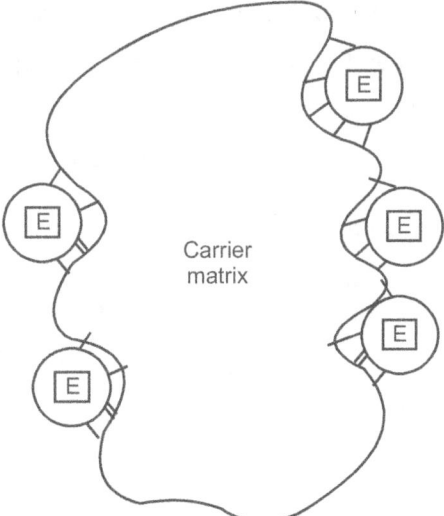

Fig. 16.8: Covalent bonding

The formation of covalent bond usually takes place particularly with the side chains of amino acids present in the enzyme. The various groups are sulphide, sulphahydril, oxide, amino, carboxyl, hydroxyl, ammonium, imino, amide, methylthiol, guanidyl, imidazole and phenol ring. Different methods of covalent bonding are classified as follows.

(i) **Diazotation:** This reaction involves bonding between the amino group of the support e.g. aminobenzyl cellulose, amino derivatives of polystyrene, aminosilanised porous glass and a tyrosyl or histidyl group of the enzyme. The amino functional moiety containing support material is converted to the corresponding diazonium chloride salt by treating with a mixture of sodium nitrate and diluted hydrochloric acid. (Fig. 16.9)

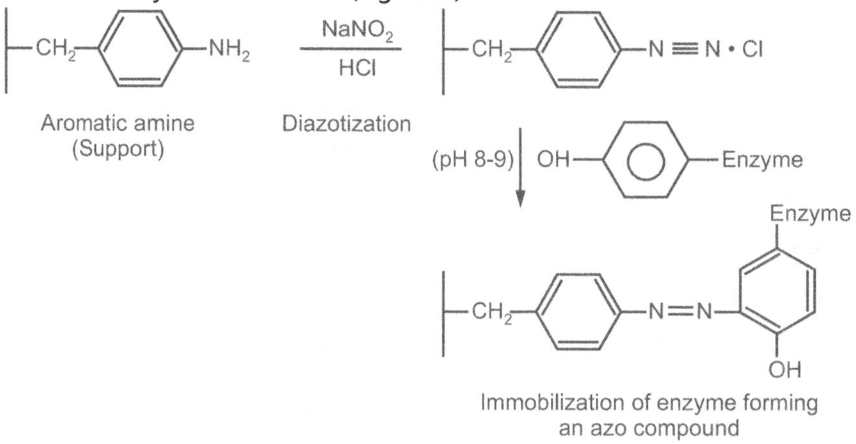

Fig. 16.9: Immobilization of enzyme forming an azo compound

(ii) **Formation of peptide bond:** The reaction occurs between the amino or carboxyl groups of the support and the carboxyl or amino groups of the enzymes. Acyl azide derivatives react with the enzyme protein involving predominantly the primary amino groups of enzyme to form the peptide bond (Fig. 16.10)

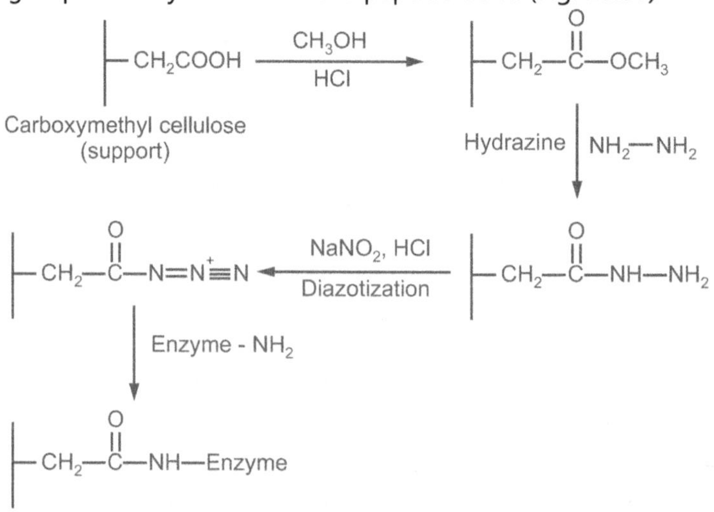

Fig. 16.10: Immobilization of enzyme using CMC support by peptide bond formation

(iii) **Group activation:** In this method, cyanogen bromide (Fig. 16.11) is applied to a support containing glycol groups e.g. cellulose, sephadex, sepharose etc.

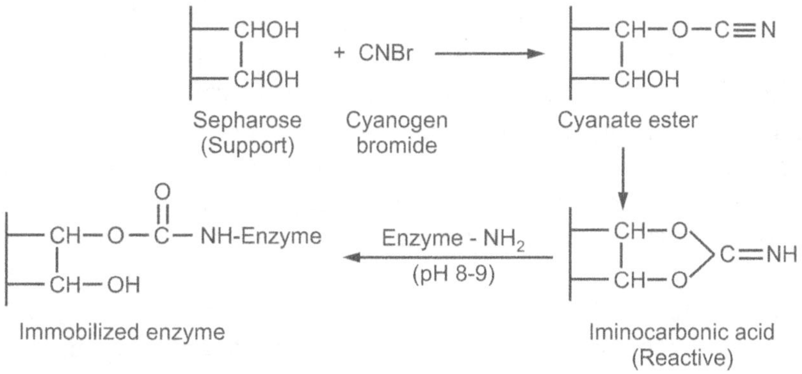

$$\begin{array}{c}\substack{\text{—CHOH}\\|\\\text{—CHOH}}\end{array} + \text{CNBr} \longrightarrow \begin{array}{c}\substack{\text{—CH—O—C}\equiv\text{N}\\|\\\text{—CHOH}}\end{array}$$

Sepharose (Support)   Cyanogen bromide   Cyanate ester

$$\begin{array}{c}\substack{\text{—CH—O—C(=O)—NH-Enzyme}\\|\\\text{—CH—OH}}\end{array} \xleftarrow[\text{(pH 8-9)}]{\text{Enzyme - NH}_2} \begin{array}{c}\substack{\text{—CH—O}\\|\\\text{—CH—O}}\end{array}\!\!\!\!>\!\!\text{C}=\text{NH}$$

Immobilized enzyme   Iminocarbonic acid (Reactive)

Fig. 16.11: Immobilization of enzyme by cyanogen bromide activation

(iv) **Polyfunctional reagents:** In this method, a bifunctional or a multifunctional reagent such as glutaraldehyde (Fig. 16.12) is used to create bonding between the amino group of the support and the amino groups of the enzyme. Some of enzymes immobilized by covalent bonding are given in Table 16.3.

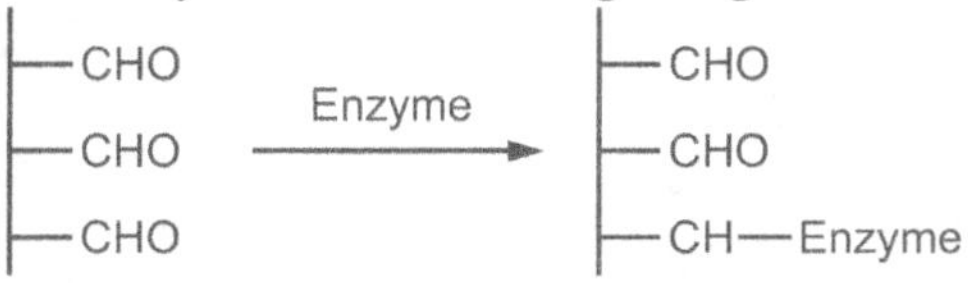

$$\begin{array}{c}\substack{\text{—CHO}\\\text{—CHO}\\\text{—CHO}}\end{array} \xrightarrow{\text{Enzyme}} \begin{array}{c}\substack{\text{—CHO}\\\text{—CHO}\\\text{—CH—Enzyme}}\end{array}$$

Fig. 16.12: Immobilization of enzyme by activation of bifunctional agent

Table 16.3: Enzymes immobilized by covalent bonding

Enzyme	Carrier matrix	Binding agent/Reaction
α-Amylase	DEAE – cellulose (cellulose – 2-(diethylamino) ethyl ether)	Direct coupling
Amyloglucosidase	DEAE – cellulose	Cyanuric chloride
Cellulose	Polyurethane	Isocyanate
Glucose isomerase	Polyurethane	Isocyanate
Glucose oxidase	Porous glass	Isothiocyanate
Pectinase	Polyurethane	Isothiocyanate
Pronase	Carbodiimide activation	CM-sephadex

Complexation or chelation: This method is based on the chelating properties of the transition metals, which can be employed to couple enzymes. Immobilized enzymes are prepared using transition metal compounds (e.g. titanium, zirconium metal salts) for the activation of the surface of organic carriers or using the corresponding hydrous metal oxides. The metals like Co (II), Cu (II), Mn (II), tin (II) (IV), Zn (II), chromium (II), zirchonium (IV) are converted into metal oxides and in the presence of enzyme it gives metal oxide enzyme. The interaction of the transition metal compounds with biopolymers are occur as follows.

Titanium metal + chloride ion = octahedral co-ordination = ligand + cellulose = glycosidic linkage = titanium chloride – cellulose. Cellulose contains vicinal dio groups which are not involved in glycosidic linkage hence available for free chelation by transition metals.

Encapsulation: Enzymes are immobilized within microcapsules prepared from organic polymers. The membrane encloses the enzyme and remain semipermeable to the substrate and the products. The method of encapsulation is cheap and simple. It provides large surface area to enzyme to contact with the substrate and several enzymes can be immobilized in single step.

Encapsulation technique is not applicable for high molecular weight substrates. During the process of immobilization, enzymes may be inactivated or may be leaked through microcapsule. Enzyme immobilization by encapsulation and microenapsulation is shown in Fig. 16.13.

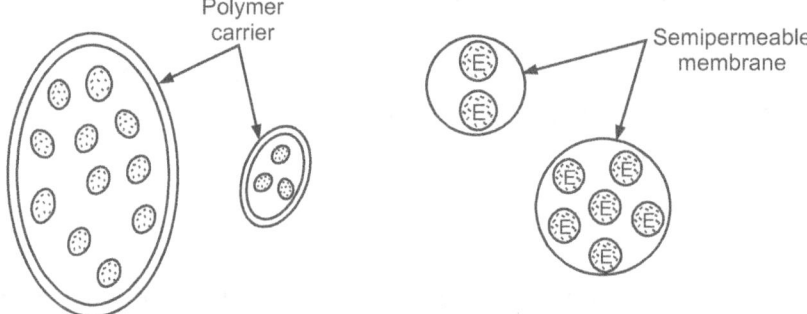

(a) Encapsulation (b) Microencapsulation or membrane confinement
Fig. 16.13: Enzyme immobilization techniques

The methods used for microencapsulation of enzymes are classified as (i) Phase separation method, (ii) Interfacial polymerization method, (iii) Liquid drying method and (iv) Liquid-surfactant-membrane method.

Many enzymes are microencapsulated by the process of phase separation method, which is based on coacervation. Aqueous enzyme solution is first emulsified in a organic solvent (water insoluble) containing the polymer and then to the organic phase containing aqueous microdroplets. Another organic solvent is slowly added in which the polymer is insoluble. The polymer is concentrated and membranes are formed around the microdroplets of the aqueous enzyme solution. Interfacial polymerization method is also similar to the phase separation method. In interfacial polymerization method, aqueous solution of the enzyme and a hydrophilic monomer are emulsified in a water immiscible organic solvent. In this emulsion, the hydrophilic monomer is added with stirring. These two monomers polymerize at the interface between the aqueous and organic solvent phases in the emulsion and forms a semipermeable membrane of the copolymer in which the enzyme in the aqueous phase is enclosed.

In liquid-drying method, the enzyme solution is emulsified in an organic solvent with a boiling point lower than that of water containing the membrane forming polymers and using an oil-soluble surfactant. The emulsion containing aqueous enzyme microdroplets is then dispersed in an aqueous medium with protective colloidal substances and secondary emulsion is formed. The final microencapsulated enzyme is obtained by removing the organic solvent. In liquid-surfactant-membrane method, the enzyme emulsion is prepared in two steps. First, the aqueous enzyme solution is emulsified in the organic phase at high shear stresses. The stability of the microdroplets is attained by adding suitable surfactants to the organic phase. In the second step the stable emulsion is injected into the outer continuous aqueous phase.

Entrapment: Immobilization of enzyme molecules can be performed by the physical entrapping of the enzyme inside a polymer matrix, gel or fibres (Fig. 16.14). Entrapment is based on coupling enzymes to the lattice of a polymer matrix or enclosing them in semipermeable membrane. It prevents the release of proteins while allowing the diffusion of substrates and products.

Gels can be formed by polymerization in which covalent bonds are formed by use of prepolymers with very little change in covalent bonds. Enzymes are dispersed or dissolved into an aqueous buffer containing acrylamide and bis acrylate as a cross linker. Pore size and mechanical strength of gel is dependent on concentration of acrylamide.

In the process of inclusion in fibres, the mixture containing the polymer and the enzyme is extruded to have the enzyme trapped in fibre format. Penicillin acylase is immobilized by entrapment in the micro cavities of synthetic fibres.

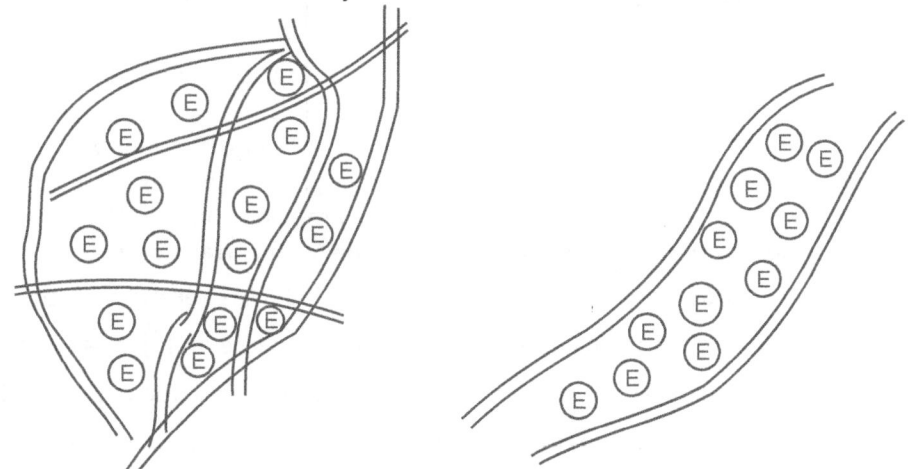

(a) Entrapment in gels (b) Entrapment in fibres

Fig. 16.14: Enzyme immobilization by entrapment

Applications of immobilization:

Immobilized enzymes and cells are commonly used in industrial processes, analytical techniques, secondary metabolic production, drug targeting, designing of bioreactors, bio-environmental modification etc. In 1969, Tanabe Seiyaku Co. were the first developed immobilized aminoacylase for the continuous production of L-amino acids from acyl-DL-amino acids. Immobilized enzymes have wide applications in the following areas.

Industrial processes

Immobilized biocatalysts are used for production of antibiotics, steroids and amino acids in pharmaceutical industries. Immobilized penicillin acylase has been used in the production of semisynthetic penicillin's through deacylation of penicillin G to 6-amino penicillianic acid (6-APA) using macroreticular ion exchange resin as supports. Cephalosporin amidase obtained from different microorganisms can be immobilized by various methods and are used for production of various cephalosporin derivatives. Macrolide antibiotic tylosin and the nucleoside peptide antibiotic nikkomycin are produced using living cells of *Streptomyces* spp. immobilized with calcium alginate.

Microbial cells containing systems of cofactors are immobilized and employed for large-scale steroid transformations. The synthesis of hydrocortisone and prednisolone from cortexolone is obtained by immobilizing the biocatalyst by entrapment with polyacrylamide. (Fig. 16.15)

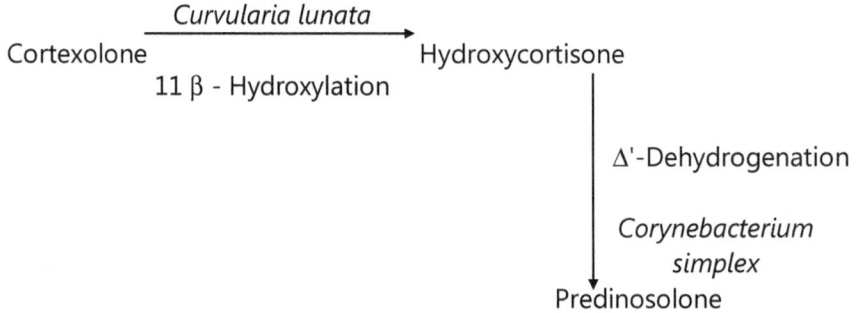

Fig. 16.15: Production of predinosolone from cortexolone

Sugar and sugar syrups prepared by enzyme technology has received much attention from food industry. Fructose manufactured by using glucoamylase and glucose isomerase is being produced on a large scale to replace sucrose as a sweetening agent. Aminoacylase is used for the continuous optical resolution of DL-amino acids and is isolated from *Aspergillus oryzae*. Enzyme is obtained by ionic binding of DEAE-sephedex covalent binding to iodoacetyl cellulose and entrapment of polyacrylamide gel. DL-Acylamino acid is asymmetrically hydrolyzed by enzyme aminoacylase and it produces L-amino acid and unhydrolyzed D-acylamino acid. L-alanine is produced from L-aspartic acid by using *Pseudomonas dacunhae* cells (L-aspartate 4-decarboxylase) which are immobilized with k-carrageenam. Immobilized biocatalysts used for chemical transformations in the pharmaceutical industries are shown in Table 16.4.

Table 16.4: Immobilized biocatalysts used for chemical transformations

Compounds	Microbial cells	Enzyme	Matrix for Immobilization
1. Antibiotics			
Ampicillin	*Bacillus megaterium*	Penicillin amidase	DEAE-cellulose
Penicillin G	*Penicillium chrysogenum*	Multi-enzymes	Polyacrylamide, calcium alginate
Cephalexin	*Achromobater* sp.	Cephalosporin amidase	DEAE-cellulose
Bacitracin	*Bacillus* sp.	Multi-enzymes	Polyacrylamide
Tylosin	*Streptomyces* sp.	Multi-enzymes	Calcium alginate
2. Steroids			
Prednisolone	*Arthrobacter simplex*	Complete cell	Photo-crosslinkable resin, calcium alginate
Hydrocortisone	*Curvularia lunata*	Complete cell	Photo-crosslinkable resin, polyacrylamide
3. Amino Acids			
L-Alanine	*Pseudomonas dacunhae*	L-aspartate 4-decarboxylase	Carrageenam
L-Arginine	*Serratia marcescens*	Multi-enzymes	Carrageenam
L-Glutamic acid	*Brevibacterium flavum*	Multi-enzymes	Collagen
D-α-Phenylglycine	*Bacillus* sp.	Hydantoinase	Polyacrylamide
L-Tryptophan	*Escherichia coli.*	Tryptophan synthase β-tyrosinase	Polyacrylamide
L-Tyrosine	*Erwinia herbicola*		Collagen and glutaraldehyde
4. Organic Acids			
Acetic acid	*Acetobacter aceti*	Multi-enzymes	Porous ceramic
Citric acid	*Aspergillus niger*	Multi-enzymes	Calcium alginate
Gluconic acid	*Aspergillus niger*	Glucose oxidase	Calcium alginate
Lactic acid	*Lactobacillus casei*	Multi-enzymes	Polyacrylamide
2-Ketogluconic acid	*Serratia marcescens*	Multi-enzymes	Collagen
L-Malic acid	*Brevibacterium flavum*	Fumarase	Carrageenam

Analytical applications:

Enzymes are commonly used in medical diagnosis, industrial monitoring programs and analysis of specific reactions. Determination of organic and inorganic compounds in biologicals fluids is important in clinical analysis. Most of analysis of these compounds are performed by enzyme catalyzed reactions. Enzyme electrodes or biosensors are probes capable of generating an electrical potential as a result of a reaction catalysed by an immobilized enzyme. The first enzyme electrode to be reported was the glucose-sensitive electrode (Fig. 16.16). The enzyme glucose oxidase was immobilized in a polyacrylamide gel around a platinum oxygen electrode. When a solution of glucose is brought into contact with electrode, glucose and oxygen diffuses into an enzyme layer and are converted into gluconolactone and hydrogen peroxide lowering the oxygen concentration. The principle involved is the removal of oxygen from solution at a rate dependent upon the concentration of glucose present. The response of biosensor is measured in terms of substrate used or product form. Different biosensors are used for estimation of compounds (Table 16.5) such as glucose, lactic acid, alcohol, glutamic acid, vitamin B1, nicotinic acid, urea, penicillin, nystatin etc. are easily analysed by using enzyme electrodes.

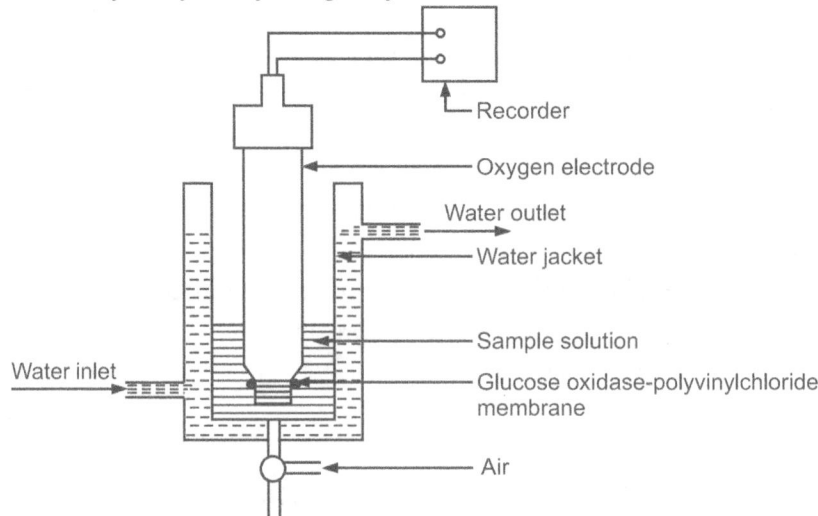

Fig. 16.16: Enzyme electrode for determination of glucose

Biosensors are composed of a bifunctional material and a transducer and it is applied to analytical fields, clinical analysis and food industry. Microbial sensors have been developed and applied to the measurement of biological compounds. Microbial sensors are based on either the change the respiration or the amount of produced metabolites as the result of assimilation of substrates by microorganisms.

Table 16.5: Electrochemical devices used for estimation of compounds

Electrochemical Devices	Sensor	Enzyme	Immobilization
1. Oxygen electrode	Glucose	Glucose oxidase	Covalent
	Ethanol	Alcohol oxidase	Crosslinked
	Uric acid	Uricase	Crosslinked
	Inosine	Nucleoside phosphorylase	Covalent
	Monoamine	Monoamine oxidase	Entrapment
	L-Alginine	Alginine decarboxylase	Crosslinked
2. Ammonia gas electrode	L-Amino acid	L-Amino acid oxidase	Covalent
	L-Asparagine	Asparaginase	Entrapment
	Urea	Urease	Crosslinked
	Nitrite	Nitrite reductase	Crosslinked
	L-Methionine	Methionine ammonia lyase	Crosslinked
3. CO_2 gas electrode	L-Tyrosine	L-Tyrosine decarboxylase	Adsorption
4. pH electrode	Penicillin	Penicillinase	Entrapment
	Neutral lipid	Lipase	Covalent
5. Platinum electrode	Cholesterol	Cholesterol esterase	Covalent
	Phospholipid	Phospholipase	Covalent

Immunoadsorption techniques:

Enzyme-linked immunosorbent assay (ELISA) is widely used for detection of antigens and antibodies. This technique involves immobilization of antigen or antibody on to a microtiter plate. The excess antigen or antibody used for coating is washed off. The counter antibody linked with an enzyme is added and allowed to react with the immobilized antigen or antibody. A substrate specific for the enzyme is then added and colour produced is used for detection of antigen and antibody.

Protein A and G are generally immobilized on agarose or sephadex and used as affinity chromatography medium a typical immobilized protein complex or conjugation. The matrix based on an immobilized mannan binding protein support is most effective for purifying mouse IgM from ascites. Mannan binding protein is usually immobilized on agarose bead and used in affinity chromatography. Radioallergosorbent (Rast) test is based on absorption of IgE antibody by immobilized antigens and subsequently the degree of binding is determined.

Therapeutic applications:

Preparation of immobilized enzymes such as streptokinase, urokinase, fibrinolysis in microgranules of sephadex can be effectively used for the treatment of thromboses and thromboemboli of any vessels. Urea-urease modulated system suggests the interesting possibility of using immobilized enzymes to alter local pH and consequently to change the pH sensitive polymer erosion rates. Enzymes, adsorbents or other material can be incorporated together with target enzyme into the artificial cells. The simple artificial organs are designed and constructed using the principle of artificial cells e.g. artificial liver, artificial kidney, blood detoxifier etc. Artificial cells containing multienzyme systems are used for the sequential conversion of substrates into products. Immobilized enzymes are also recommended in replacement therapy needed in hereditary enzyme-deficiency conditions.

IMMOBILIZATION OF BACTERIAL AND PLANT CELL

Immobilized individual enzymes can be successfully used for single-step reactions. They are not suitable for multienzyme reactions and for the reactions requiring cofactors. The whole cells or cellular organelles can be immobilized to serve as multienzyme systems. Immobilized cells rather than enzymes are sometimes preferred even for single reactions, due to cost factor in isolating enzymes. Stability of the desired enzyme is normally improved by retaining its natural environment during immobilization and subsequent operation. Purification of several enzymes is avoided and cell compartmentation with optimal spatial location of the enzymes remains intact. Cofactor regeneration sites are not disturbed so that overall structural integrity of the catalytic complex is retained. In several cases, bound cell systems are much more tolerant to perturbations in the environment (e.g. ionic strength, pH, temperature) and are less sensitive to toxic substances as compared to immobilized enzymes. With a large increase in enzyme loading in immobilized enzyme systems, catalytic activity decreases due to protein-protein interaction. Catalytic activity is not decreased even at very high microbial loading in immobilized cell systems.

Enzymatic activity may be lost in non-growing cells. Hence, it is necessary to supply the immobilized cells with a nutrient medium to keep the cells viable. Many enzymes active in a whole cell might lead to unwanted side reactions. The viability of the cells can be preserved by mild immobilization and there cells are mainly useful for fermentations. Immobilized non-viable cells are also preferred over the enzymes or even the viable cells because of the costly isolation and purification processes. Immobilized microorganisms and their applications are given in Table 16.6.

Table 16.6: Immobilized cells and their applications

Immobilized microorganism	Applications
Anthrobacter simplex	Synthesis of prednisolone from hydrocortisone
Bacteria and yeast species	In biosensors.
Escherichia coli.	Production of L-tryptophan from indole and serine.
Humicola species	Conversion of rifamycin 'B' to rifamycin 'S'.
Pseudomonas chlororaphis	Production of acrylamide from acrylonitrile.
Saccharomyces cerevisiae	Hydrolysis of sucrose.
Zymomonas mobilis	Production of sorbitol and gluconic acid from glucose and fructose.

The techniques employed for immobilization of cells are almost the same as that used for immobilization of enzymes with appropriate modifications. Immobilization methods for microbial and animal cells are classified as:

1. Immobilization of cells within an inert substratum involving the entrapment of cells in one gel matrix or their combinations.
2. Adsorption of cells to an inert substratum such as charged microspheres or glass beads.
3. Cells are adsorbed to an inert substratum such as gel via biological macromolecules like lectins.
4. Cells are covalently bonded to an inert substratum such as carboxymethyl cellulose.

Entrapment is the most widely used technique for immobilization of whole cells particularly for viable cell preparations. Animal cells are most commonly immobilized by the adsorption of cells to an inert substratum such as charged microspheres or glass beads. Animal cells secrete proteins which permit their adhesion to glass or other smooth surfaces. These surfaces are electrically charged, it allows their immobilization on oppositely charged particles. The difference with the plant cell is that the plant cell plasmalemma is enclosed in a polysaccharide cell wall which in general prevent the use of this method. Most of the techniques reported for the immobilization of plant cells involves embedding the cells in a polymeric matrix. Some of the examples of immobilizing plant cells, protoplasts and chloroplasts are given in Table 16.7. The greatest potential of the technique is in their utility in the large-scale production of secondary metabolites either by replacing immobilized enzymes or microbes as catalysts in biotransformation reactions. Immobilization might increase the capacity for long-term storage or transport of cells and protoplasts.

Table 16.7: Examples of immobilizing plant cells

Plant species	Cell type	Immobilized substratum
Cannabia sativa	Cells	Calcium alginate
Catharanthus roseus	Cells	Calcium alginate
Capsicum frutescens	Cells	Reticulate polyurethane
Digitalis lanata	Cells	Calcium alginate
Datura innoxia	Cells	Matting, Calcium alginate
Daucus carota	Protoplast	Agarose + lectins
Mucuna pruriens	Cells	Calcium alginate
Papaver somniferum	Cells	Calcium alginate
Spinacia oleracea	Chloroplast	Calcium alginate

IMPORTANT ENZYMES

Enzymes used in industry are isolated from microorganisms, plants and animals. Enzymes are commercially produced by semisolid culture method and submerged culture. In semisolid culture method, enzyme producing culture is grown on the surface of a suitable semisolid substrate supplemented with specific nutrients. Now-a-days submerged culture methods are widely used in the production of enzymes. The fermentation equipment used is the same as in the manufacture of antibiotics. Microbial enzymes produced by fermentation include amylases, proteases, catalase, penicillinase, streptokinase etc.

Amylases:

Amylolytic enzymes are widely distributed in bacteria and fungi. Amylases are mainly used for production of sweetners for the food industry e.g. glucose syrup, fructose syrup. Dextrins are prepared by the hydrolysis of starch with amylases. The amylases are used commercially for the preparation of sizing agents and removal of starch sizing from woven cloth. It is also used in preparation of starch sizing pastes for use in paper coatings and liquefaction of heavy starch pastes which form during steps in the manufacture of corn and chocolate syrups. These amylases can be employed as a replacement for malt for starch hydrolysis in the brewing industry. Amylases are characterized by their ability to hydrolyze 1, 4 glucosidic linkages in polysaccharides e.g. starch, glucogen etc. They are mainly classified as α-amylases and β-amylases.

α-Amylases, 1, 4-α-glucanglucanohydrolyases are endoenzymes, responsible for affecting the cleavage of the substrate strategically positioned in the interior of the molecule. They attack all the linkages between glucose units in the starch molecule. A large number of bacterial species are used for production of α-amylases such as *Bacillus subtilis, B. cereus, B. licheniformis, B. amyloliquefaciens, Lactobacillus* sp., *Pseudomonas saccharophila, Arthrobacter* sp., *Escherichia* sp., *Thermononospora* sp. etc. Selected strains of *Bacillus subtilis* are mainly preferred for industrial scale production of amylase. Fungal α-amylases for commercial purposes are derived from *Aspergillus oryzae*. Different species of *Aspergillus, Candida, Cephalosporium, Penicillium* and *Rhizopus* are used for production of highly specific α-amylase. Bacterial α-amylase is produced only by submerged culture method. The media employed are generally based on the use of natural raw materials including certain growth factors such as trace elements, vitamins and amino acids. A careful balance of carbohydrate and nitrogen ingredients of the medium is most important. It is necessary to maintain the pH near neutrality and incubation temperature 30 to 40°C of the fermentation medium for 3 to 5 days. After fermentation, culture is filtered or centrifuged to separate the cells. Amylase can be precipitated from aqueous solution by the addition of cold acetone, ethanol, isopropanol or ammonium sulfate. It is purified by dialysis and chromatographic techniques. Fungal α-amylase was originally and is still produced in significant amounts in solid substrate culture.

The β-amylases, α-1, 4-glycanmalthodrolases hydrolyze starch and other amyloses by splitting off maltose molecules until the action is blocked by the occurrence of either 1, 3 linkages or branch points. The residual molecule is then called a limit dextrin. β-Amylases are mainly belong to plant origin however, certain specific microorganisms produce this enzyme such as *Bacillus polymyxa, Bacillus cereus, Streptomyces* sp., *Pseudomonas* sp. and *Rhizopus* species.

Penicillinase:

Penicillinase is a bacterial extracellular enzyme produced from *Bacillus* species, *Staphylococcus* species and members of the coliform group of bacteria. The enzyme penicillinase inactivates penicillin by the process of hydrolysis and converts to penicilloic acid (Fig. 16.17).

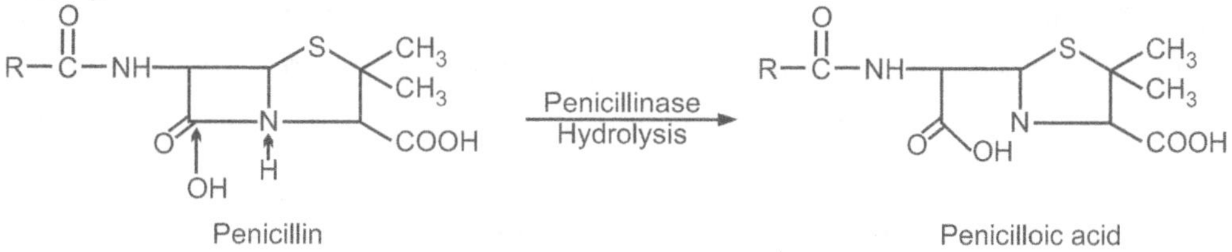

Fig. 16.17: Hydrolysis of penicillin by penicillinase

The enzyme penicillin amidase is normally produced by fungal species such as *Penicillium, Aspergillus* and *Mucor*. Penicillinase is divided into two major classes based on their activity such as penicillin amidase or penicillin acylase and β-lactamase or penicillinase. The enzyme penicillin amidase is specific on attacking the acyl group attached to the basic nucleus i.e. 6-amino-penicillanic acid. This enzyme is more specific with penicillin 'V' and 'K'. The enzyme β-lactamase acts on the basic nucleus itself. It breaks the β-lactam bond and produce penicilloic acid. This enzyme is more specific with penicillin G and penicillin X.

Streptokinase:

Streptokinase is a proteolytic extracellular enzyme derived from the culture of β-hemolytic *Streptococcus* species. It is mainly capable of converting plasminogen to plasmin. It is used extensively as a fibrinolytic agent to help for the specific removal of fibrin thrombi from arteries. It is also recommended for the management and control of myocardial infarction (AMI) in adults to bring about various therapeutic benefits. Streptokinase is antigenic due to its bacterial origin and may bind to antibodies and non-specific inhibitors. The immune response shown by streptokinase affects the alteration of urokinase.

It is given intravenously as soon as possible after the onset of a heart attack to dissolve clots in the arteries of the heart wall. This reduces the amount of damage to the heart muscle. Streptokinase is a bacterial product so the body will build-up an immunity to it. This medication should not be used again after four days from the first administration, as it may not be effective and can also cause an allergic reaction. Overdose of streptokinase or (tPA) can be treated with aminocaproic acid.

Streptodornase:

Streptodornase enzyme produced by certain strains of haemolytic streptococci. Streptodornase is mainly obtained from *Streptococcus haemolyticus* that affords depolymerization of polymerized deoxyribonucles proteins. It is used extensively in conjunction with streptokinase as desloughing agent to cleanse ulcers and promote the healing process progressively.

Hyaluronidase:

The hyaluronidases are a family of enzymes that degrade hyaluronic acid. Hyaluronidase catalyzes the random hydrolysis of 1, 4-linakges between 2-acetamido-2-deoxy-b-D-glucose and D-glucose residues in hyaluronate.

Some bacterial species such as *Staphylococcus aureus, Streptococcus pyogenes* and *Clostridium perfringens* produce hyaluronidase as a means for greater mobility through the body's tissues and as an antigenic disguise that prevents their being recognized by phagocytes of the immune system.

Hyaluronidases are used in medicine in conjunction with other drugs in order to increase their dispersion and delivery. The most common application is in ophthalmic surgery, in which it is used in combination with local anesthetics.

Proteases:

Complex mixtures of true proteinases and peptidases are usually called proteases. Microbial proteases can be divided into three groups based upon the pH range in which their activity is higher, namely acid, neutral or alkaline proteases. Proteolytic enzymes are produced by various bacteria such as *Bacillus, Pseudomonas, Clostridium, Proteus* and *Serratia* species and fungi such as *Aspergillus niger, Aspergillus oryzae, Aspergillus flavus, Penicillium roquefortii* and *Mucor pusillus*. However, the enzymes associated with these microorganisms are actually mixtures of proteinases and peptidases. Proteinases are excreted to the fermentation medium during growth while the peptidases are liberated only on autolysis of the cells.

Proteases are used on a large scale in detergent, food and leather industries. The enzymes cause adequate alterations in the hides to provide a finer grain and texture, greater pliability and better general quality. Proteases also find usage in the textile industry to afford proteinaceous sizing. In the silk industry, proteases help in the liberation of the silk fibers from the naturally occurring proteinaceous material wherein they are actually imbedded. Proteases are also employed as a meat tenderizer e.g. papain. Proteases are used in brewing industry, film industry, waste-disposal management and manufacture of protein hydrolyzates. They are the active ingredient in spot-remover preparations for removing food spots in the dry-cleaning industry. Industrial production of microbial proteases is carried out by cultivation of the microorganisms in the submerged fermentation for the bacteria. However, fungi usually give higher yields when cultured on solid media. Most of the microorganisms excrete more than one kind of protease. The type of proteolytic enzyme formed may depend on the composition of the medium.

QUESTIONS

(A) Short answer questions:
  (a) What is enzyme technology? Explain.
  (b) Write advantages and disadvantages of immobilization of enzymes using entrapment.
  (c) Write different properties of enzymes.
  (d) Explain in short methods used for microencapsulation of enzymes.
  (e) Explain the role of following:
    (i) Penicillinase
    (ii) Proteases

(B) Long answer questions:
  1. Explain in short different applications of enzyme immobilization.
  2. Explain in detail methods for enzyme immobilization.
  3. Discuss in short 'factors affecting enzyme kinetics'.
  4. Write note on:
     (a) Michaelis – Menten equation.
     (b) Amylases
     (c) Immobilization of bacterial and plant cell
     (d) Streptokinase

(C) Multiple choice questions:
  1. The synthesis of hydrocortisone and prednisolone from cortexolone is obtained by immobilizing the biocatalyst by entrapment with _____
     (a) Starch
     (b) Acacia
     (c) Calcium alginate
     (d) Polyacrylamide
  2. _____ is the method of covalent bonding.
     (a) Adsorption
     (b) Diazotation
     (c) Phase separation
     (d) Polymerization
  3. _____ precipitation method, enzymes are recovered from fermentation broth.
     (a) Ammonium chloride
     (b) Ammonium oxalase
     (c) Ammonium nitrate
     (c) Ammonium sulfate
  4. _____ enzyme is used for saccharification of starch.
     (a) Amylase
     (b) Invertase
     (c) Protease
     (d) Xylanase
  5. Which value is required for enzyme action?
     (a) Low K_M
     (b) Constant K_M
     (c) High K_M
     (d) None of above

(D) Match the following:

A	B
(a) Adsorption	(i) Reaction used to produce bonds between enzyme molecules
(b) Entrapment	(ii) Reaction not require to produce bonding between enzyme and support
(c) Cross-linking	(iii) Reaction used to polymerize support material
(d) Direct covalent linking	(iv) Reaction used to produce high energy bonding between enzyme and support

(E) Fill in the blanks:

1. The enzyme _____ inactivate penicillin by the process of hydrolysis and convert to penicilloic acid.
2. _____ is act as a fibrinolytic agent to help for the specific removal of fibrin thrombi from arteries.

■■■

CHAPTER 17
PLANT TISSUE CULTURE

CONTENTS
    INTRODUCTION
    LABORATORY REQUIREMENTS
    CULTURE MEDIA
    CELLULAR TOTIPOTENCY
    TYPES OF CULTURES
        Callus, Suspension, Meristem, Root-tip,
        Hairy root, Haploid, Protoplast
    PROTOPLAST FUSION AND SOMATIC HYBRIDIZATION
    PRESERVATION OF PLANT CELLS – CRYOPRESERVATION

INTRODUCTION

Plant tissue culture is the technique of growing plant cells, tissues or organs in an artificially prepared nutrient medium under aseptic conditions. Plant tissue culture is common term used for cell, tissue, organ, protoplast or whole plant cultures grown under aseptic conditions. The term 'cell culture' refers to the growth of any cell such as microbes, plants or animals and term 'tissue culture' refers to the cultivation of a plant or mammalian tissues in a nutrient medium.

During the last two decades plant cell and tissue culture have developed rapidly. Plant tissue culture is a major biotechnological tool in horticulture, agriculture and pharmaceutical industry. Plant biotechnology has affected all avenues of human life. Genetic engineering has provided the technology with which plants can be genetically modified to increase the yield or to produce bioactive secondary metabolites. Plants can be modified by manipulating plant's own genes or by introducing genes from unrelated plants and other organisms such as bacteria, actinomycetes, fungi and viruses. Genetic engineering have shown the way of increasing food production and modification of plants for active molecules. Plant tissue culture is commonly used for biosynthesis of secondary metabolites and it also provides raw materials to pharmaceutical and cosmetic industries (Table 17.1). Plants are important source of raw materials for the production of paper, fabrics, dyes, oils, medicines, chemicals etc.

Table 17.1: Secondary metabolites produced by plant tissue culture

Source	Metabolite	Applications / Use
Atropa belladona	Atropine	Anticholinergic
Cinchona ledgeriana	Quinine	Antimalarial, Bitter tonic
Cinchona ledgeriana	Quinidine	Antihypertensive
Digitalis lanata	Digoxin	Cardiac tonic
Digitalis purpurea	Digitoxine	Cardiovascular
Datura metel	Scopolamine	Anticholinergic
Catharanthus roseus	Vincristine	Anticancer
Jasminum officinalis	Jasmine	Perfume
Hyoscyamus niger	Hyoscyamine	Anticholinergic
Papaver somniferum	Codeine	Analgesic, Antitussive
Pilocarpus jaborandi	Pilocarpine	Cholinergic
Rawulfia serpentina	Reserpine	Hypotensive
Thaumatococcus danielli	Thaumatin	Sweetener (Non-nutritive)
Datura innoxia	Tropane	Anticholinergic
Carica papaya	Papain	Proteolytic enzyme
Nicotiana tobacum	Nicotine	Anticholinergic
Ipomoea violacea	Indole	Cathartic
Coeffea arabica	Caffeine	CNS stimulant
Cassia angustifolia	Anthraquinones	Purgative

German Botanist **Gottlieb Haberlandt** (1902) developed the concept of in-vitro cultivation for isolated cells of *Tradescantia*. He did not succeed to divide the cells in artificial condition but for his pioneer work he is regarded as father of plant tissue culture. He described the in-vitro cultivation of mesophyll cells of *Lamium purpureum*, epidermal cells of *Ornithogalum* and epidermal hair cells of *Pulmonaria mollissimia*. Identification of auxin (natural growth regulator) and recognition of the importance of B-vitamins in plant growth in the mid-1930's gave a big push in the development of plant tissue culture. Important discoveries made in the plant tissue culture are summarized in Table 17.2.

Table 17.2: Important discoveries in plant tissue culture (PTC)

Researchers	Year	Contributions	Species
Gottlieb Haberlandt	1902	First attempt to isolate plant cells in-vitro on medium	*Tradescantia*
W. J. Robbins and W. Kotte	1922	First to develop a technique for the culture of isolated maize and pea roots	*Zea, Pisum*
Philip R. White	1934	Successful study of growing cultures of tomato root tips	*Lycopersicum*
R. J. Gautheret	1939	First permanent callus culture using vitamin B and auxins	*Daucus*
Philip R. White	1939	Callus culture of tobacco tumour tissue from hybrid of *Nicotiana glauca* and *Nicotiana langsdorffii*	*Nicotiana*
J. Van Overbeck	1941	Used coconut milk for embryo development and callus formation	*Datura*
W. H. Muir	1954	First suspension culture of single cells and cell aggregates	*Nicotiana, Tagetes*
Routien and Nickel	1956	First US patent for the production of metabolites from tissue culture	*Phaseolus*
F. Skoog and C. O. Miller	1957	Importance of auxins / cytokinins in culture media and introduced the concept of hormonal control of organ formation.	*Nicotiana*
Tulecke and Nickel	1959	First report of a large scale culture of plant cells	*Ginkgo*
Vasil and Hildebrandt	1965	Plant regeneration from single cell cultivated in hanging droplet.	*Nicotiana*
S. G. Guha and S. C. Maheshwari	1966	Production of embryos from cultures of pollens and sporogenous tissues of anther	*Datura innoxia*
J. P. Nitsch	1974	Discovered the chromosomal doubling in haploid tissues in the medium	*Datura Nicotiana*
G. Melchers	1978	Production of somatic embryos by using the protoplast fusion technique	*Nicotiana*
Tabata and Fujita	1982	Large scale production of shikonin	*Lithospermum*
K. A. Barton	1983	Demonstrated gene transfer into the protoplast by using plasmid vectors	*Agrobacterium*

LABORATORY REQUIREMENTS

The size of tissue culture laboratory set-up and design depends upon space availability, nature of project, type of research work and available funds. Tissue culture laboratory must have the facilities for:

(i)   Washing and storage of glasswares,
(ii) Preparation and sterilization of nutrient media,
(iii) Aseptic condition for culture and media transfer,
(iv) Controlled environmental conditions for growth of cultures,
(v)   Observation and evaluation of culture, and
(vi) Acclimatization of in-vitro developed plants.

A tissue culture facility requires large quantities of good quality water and provision for waste water disposal. A generator backup must be provided to prevent shut-down of transfer hoods and to avoid change in temperature in the growth room. The laboratory has very few entry sites and sufficient area designated as clean rooms with HEPA filters under positive pressure to avoid airborne contamination. Entry into the clean area must be restricted and researchers must take-off shoes, wash hands, change clothes and wear headgear and slippers. The basic areas (Fig. 17.1) of plant tissue culture laboratory must be separated as unclean (washing room, offices, general store, media preparation room and autoclaving room) and clean area (transfer room and growth room). The important areas for plant tissue culture are listed as follows:

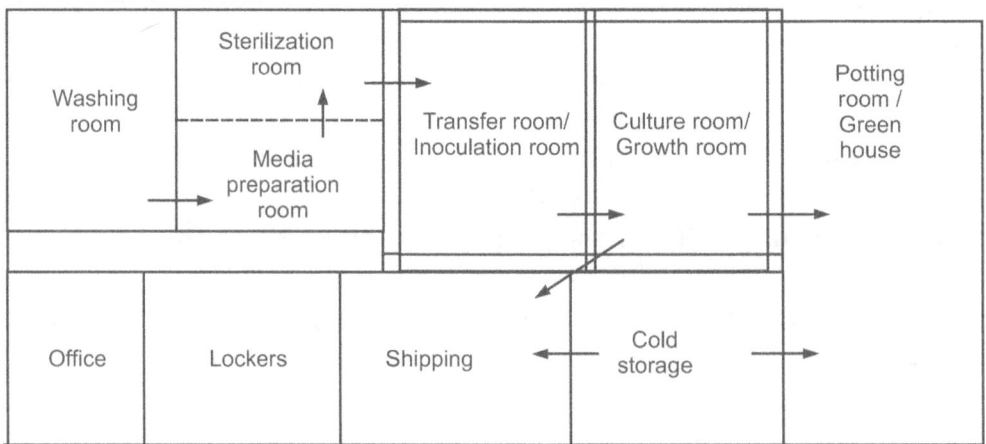

Fig. 17.1: Design of tissue culture laboratory

Washing room:

A separate area is required which should have large sink with provision for hot and cold running water, washing machine, distillation apparatus, drier, clearning brushes etc. It should also have plastic buckets (to soak labware), ovens (to dry labware) and a dust-proof cupboard (to store). A list of equipments, glasswares and chemicals required for tissue culture is given in Table 17.3.

Table 17.3: Requirements for plant tissue culture laboratory

1. **Instruments:** Incubator, autoclave, refrigerator, microscope, hot air oven, centrifuge, shakers shelves, pH-meter, balance, hot plate-cum-magnetic stirrer, water distillation, filtration assembly, vacuum pump, air-conditioner, heater, glass bead sterilizer, laminar-air-flow cabinet.
2. **Tools:** Hemocytometer, forceps, Bunsen burners, fine needles, scalpels, microscope slides, cavity slides, cover-slips, hypodermic syringes, screw-cap bottles, spatula, plastic carboys.
3. **Glasswares:** Volumetric flasks (500 ml, 1 lit. and 2 lit.) measuring cylinders (10, 25, 100, 500 ml and 1 lit.), pipettes (1, 2, 5 and 10 ml), Petri dishes, culture tables, screw-cap bottles, Erlenmeyer flasks (50, 100, 250, 500 ml and 1 lit.), plastic and metallic closures, trays, wire-mesh baskets.
4. **Media, chemicals and others:** Culture media, detergents, surfactant, ethanol, 1N NaOH, 1N HCl, green house.

Media preparation room:

The facilities required for the preparation of culture medium includes benches (for work), hot plates, stirrers, pH meter, waterbath, oven, autoclave, refrigerator, deep freeze, plastic carboys, vaccum pump etc. Refrigerator and deep freeze may be kept in a corridor or another laboratory close to media preparation room. A small weighing chamber for weighing balances may be provided in a dry corner of the media preparation room. [Fig. 17.2 (a)]

Transfer room:

All transfer techniques are carried out under strictly aseptic conditions to avoid any contamination of microorganisms. Laminar air-flow cabinets [Fig. 17.2 (b)] are used for aseptic transfer of tissue cultures. The movement of researchers in transfer room should be minimum. The walls of this room should be smooth and it can be painted with water tolerant paint. Laminar air-flow cabinets and air conditioners should be connected to an emergency source of power.

Culture room:

Largest area of the plant tissue culture laboratory is provided for growth room, where the cultures are incubated on shelves under specific conditions of temperature and light [Fig. 17.2 (c)]. Air conditioners and heater are used to maintain the temperature around 20 to 25°C. Cultures are mainly grown in diffuse light. The source of light for the cultures in racks should be make available with cool-day-light (fluorescent tube lights of 40 watts, 2000 lux). Some space is also used for maintaining cultures under higher light intensities and total darkness. Shakers with temperature and light controls are required for growth of cell suspensions [Fig. 17.2 (d)].

(a) Media preparation and storage room

(b) Laminar air-flow cabinet for transfer of tissue cultures

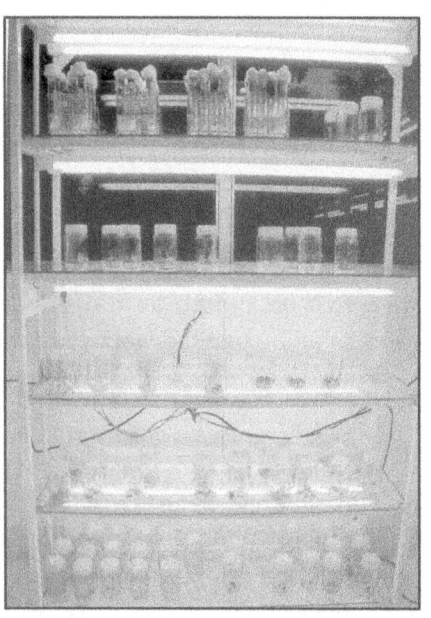

(c) Growth room in PTC laboratory

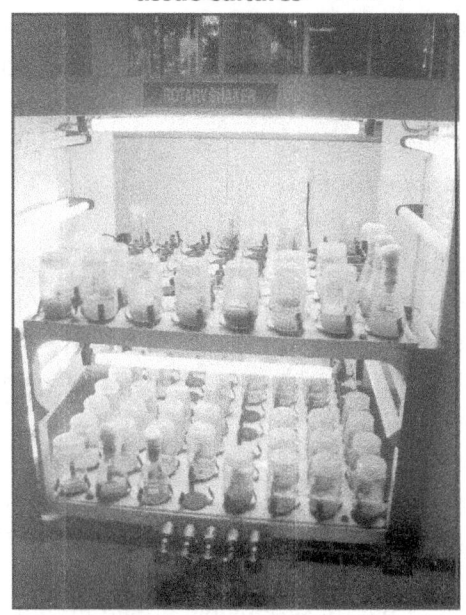

(d) Shaker for growth of cell suspensions

Fig. 17.2: Plant tissue culture laboratory

The tissue culture laboratory should have a green house or glass house or plastic house or potting room attached to it (Fig. 17.3).

Fig. 17.3: Green house for plant tissue culture

CULTURE MEDIA

The plant cells and tissues require a proper medium for their growth and development. The success in plant tissue culture technology depends on development of the culture media. The nutrient media for plant tissue culture is well defined mixture of inorganic salts and carbon sources like sucrose and glucose. Different parts of plant tissues may require different growth factors. **Gautherete** medium (1942), **Hildebrandt** medium (1946), **Nitsch** medium (1953), **Heller** medium (1953), **Murashige** and **Skoog** (1962), White medium (1963), **Eriksson** (1965), **Gamborg** medium (1968), **Nagata** and **Takebe** medium (1971), **Llyod** and **McCown** (1981) and **Raj Bhansali** (1990) are common media used for growth of plant cells. Composition of some nutrient media are given in Table 17.4. **Murashige-Skoog** (MS) medium is widely used for plant tissue culture. This medium is effective for growth promotion of both monocotyledons and dicotyledons.

In the preparation of media, usually a series of stock solutions are prepared (microelements, vitamins etc.) and stored in the freezer. Macronutrients, micronutrients, vitamins and growth hormones are dissolved separately and mixed in final container to make volume. The pH of solution is adjusted to 5.6 to 5.8 with 0.1M NaOH solution or 0.1M HCl solution. If solid medium is desired, agar is added and the solution is heated by stirring until agar is dissolved. The medium is transferred into the desired culture vessels and sterilized by autoclaving at 15 psi (121°C) for 20 minutes. Thermolabile components like vitamins, some carbohydrates, growth regulators and plant extracts are conveniently sterilized by filtration (0.22 μm pore size membrane filter) and then added aseptically to the sterile liquid medium.

Table 17.4: Composition of some nutrient medium required for plant tissue culture

Constituents (mg/lit.)	White medium	Murashige-Skoog medium (MS)	Eriksson medium (ER)	Gamborg medium (B₅)
1. Macronutrients				
KNO₃	80	1900	1900	2500
NH₄NO₃	–	1650	1200	–
CaCl₂·2H₂O	–	440	440	150
MgSO₄·7H₂O	750	370	370	250
(NH₄)₂SO₄	–	–	–	134
Ca(NO₃)₂·4H₂O	300	–	–	–
Na₂SO₄	200	–	–	–
NaH₂PO₂·H₂O	19	–	–	150
KCl	65	–	–	–
2. Micronutrients				
MnSO₄·4H₂O	5	22.3	2.3	–
MnSO₄·H₂O	–	–	–	10
KI	0.75	0.83	–	0.75
H₃BO₃	1.5	6.2	0.63	3
ZnSO₄·7H₂O	3	8.6	–	2
Na₂MoO₄·2H₂O	–	0.25	0.025	0.25
MoO₃	0.001	–	–	–
CuSO₄·5H₂O	0.01	0.025	0.0025	0.025
CoCl₂·6H₂O	–	0.025	0.0025	0.025
FeSO₄·7H₂O	–	27.8	27.8	27.8
Na₂EDTA·2H₂O	–	37.3	37.3	–
Fe₂(SO₄)₃	2.5	–	–	–
ZnNa₂·EDTA	–	–	15	–
3. Vitamins				
Glycine	3	2	2	–
Nicotinic acid	0.05	0.5	0.5	1
Pyridoxine-HCl	0.01	0.5	0.5	1
Thiamine-HCl	0.01	0.1	0.5	10
4. Cytokinin				
Inositol	–	100	–	100
Kinetin	–	0.04 to 10	0.02	0.1
Indole acetic acid (IAA)	–	1 to 30	–	–
5. Carbon source				
Sucrose	20,000	30,000	40,000	20,000

Media components:

Main components present in plant tissue culture are inorganic nutrients, organic supplements, growth regulators, antibiotics, carbon sources, gelling agent etc. The use of these components in plant tissue culture media is given in Table 17.5.

Inorganic nutrients: Inorganic nutrients are commonly required for plant growth. These include macronutrients (e.g. nitrogen, potassium, calcium, magnesium, phosphorus and sulphur) in the form of salts in large amounts and micronutrients (e.g. copper, zinc, manganese, iron, chloride, boron etc.) in small amounts. Nitrogen is one of main element in plant tissue culture media. It is a constituent of proteins, amino acids, hormones and chlorophyll. Potassium is required for normal cell division and for synthesis of proteins and chlorophyll. Phosphorus also plays major role in cell division as well as in storage and transfer of energy in plants. The majority of the microelements are required in trace quantities for the growth of plant cells.

Organic Supplements: Organic supplements are the main source of carbon and energy and it includes vitamins, amino acids and organic extracts. Vitamins are required to catalyse the enzyme system of the plant cells. The most widely used vitamins are thiamine (vitamin B_1), niacin (vitamin B_3), pyridoxine (vitamin B_6) riboflavin (vitamin B_2), biotin (vitamin H) and cyanocobalamin (vitamin B_{12}). Plant tissue culture media are commonly supplemented with amino acids like L-asparaginase, L-arginine, L-glutamine, L-glycine, L-cysteine, casein hydrolysate etc. Amino acids may be directly utilized by the plant cells or may serve as a nitrogen source. PTC media also contains complex nutritive mixtures including yeast extract, malt extract, potato extract, coconut milk, fruit juices, corn milk etc.

Growth regulators: It is necessary to add one or more growth substances in plant tissue culture media such as auxins, cytokinins, gibberellins and abscisic acid. An auxin is required for the induction of cell division and root initiation in cultured tissues. The auxins commonly used in tissue culture are indole-3-acetic acid (IAA), naphthalene acetic acid (NAA), indole-3-butyric acid (IBA), dichlorophenoxy acetic acid (2, 4-D), naphthoxy acetic acid (NOA), 4-chlorophenoxy acetic acid (4-CPA), trichlorophenoxy acetic acid (2, 4, 5-T) and 4-amino 3, 5, 6-trichloropicolinic acid (Picloram). The cytokinins are adenine derivatives inducing cell division, modification of apical dominance, short differentiation and somatic embryogenesis e.g. 6-furfuryl aminopurine (kinetin), 6-benzyl adenine (BA), 6-benzyl aminopurine (BAP), 2-isopentenyl adenine (2iPA), zeatin etc. The gibberellins are infrequently used in plant tissue cultures but GA_3 is used in meristem culture. It is prepared by dissolving in water and filter sterilized. Abscisic acid (ABA) is used in embryo culture and embryogenesis.

Carbon source: Sucrose, D-glucose, glycerol and myoinositol are the main sources of carbon in PTC media. Sugars also represent the major osmotic component of the medium.

Table 17.5: Uses of components in plant tissue culture media

Types	Constituents	Uses
Inorganic nutrients	Nitrogen	Growth of plants
	Phosphorus	Cell division, photosynthesis
	Potassium	Cell division, synthesis of proteins, nitrate reduction
	Calcium	Maintain integrity of the membrane
	Magnesium	Co-factor for many enzyme reactions
Organic supplements	Thiamine	Biosynthesis of amino acids and co-factor in carbohydrate metabolism
	Vitamin E	Anti-oxidant
	Vitamin C	Prevent blackening during explant isolation
	Vitamin D	Growth regulator
	L-Arginine	Facilitate rooting
	L-Serine	In haploid embryos induction in microspore cultures
	L-Cysteine	Controls phenol leaching from explant tissues
	L-Tyrosine	Important role in shoot initiation
	L-Asparagine, L-Glutamine	Somatic embryogenesis
Growth regulators	Auxins	Cell division and root initiation in cultured tissues.
	Cytokinins	Promote cell division, organogenesis, shoot proliferation, somatic embryogenesis
	Gibberellins	Plant regeneration and elongation in meristem culture
	Abscisic acid	Normal growth and development of somatic embryos
Carbon source	Sucrose	Differentiation of xylem and phloem elements in cultured cells, metabolic activity, growth of some tissues.
Gelling agents	Agar	Solidifying agent for preparation of media.

Gelling or solidifying agents: Agar, gelatin, agarose and gelrite (gellan gum) are used in plant tissue culture media as gelling agents. Agar is most commonly used gelling agent obtained from red algae (*Gelidium amansii*). Agar is used at varying concentrations from 0.8 to 1.2%.

The various fungicides and bactericides (antibiotics) are used in PTC media to avoid contamination. Media may be provided with antibiotics like streptomycin or kanamycin but generally antibiotics are not recommended as they retard cell growth.

CELLULAR TOTIPOTENCY

Cellular totipotency is the genetic potential of a plant cell to grow and develop a multicellular entire plant. The basis of plant tissue culture is to grow large number of cells in culture medium under sterile environments. The cells in culture media may produce an unorganized proliferative mass of the cells is known as callus tissue. The cells that form callus culture are totipotent. Totipotency of the cell is manifested through the process of differentiation. In this process, hormones play important role with appropriate concentration ratio of auxin and cytokinin. When the ratio of cytokinin to auxin is higher, only shoots are developed (caulogenesis) and when the ratio is lower, only roots are formed (rhizogenesis). In isolated cell culture, some single cells develop somatic embryos (embryoids) to develop complete plantlet called embryogenesis (Fig. 17.4). The cells of some callus mass differentiate into vascular elements like xylem and phloem without forming embryoids or any plant organs called cytodifferentiation or histogenesis. This indicates that the totipotent cells may express themselves in different way on the basis of manipulation and differentiation process.

Callus culture contains large number of totipotent cells but formation of specific part of plant is depends on the expression of totipotency. The expression of totipotency may be manipulated by adding specific nutrients in the medium. Diagrammatic representation of cellular totipotency is shown in Fig. 17.5. The totipotentiality of somatic cells has been exploited in vegetative propagation of many medicinal and agriculturally important plant species. Cellular totipotency is highly important in plant tissue culture for somatic hybridization, mutation and genetic modification of plants. Many plant tissue culture techniques are performed for exploitation of totipotency of plant cells.

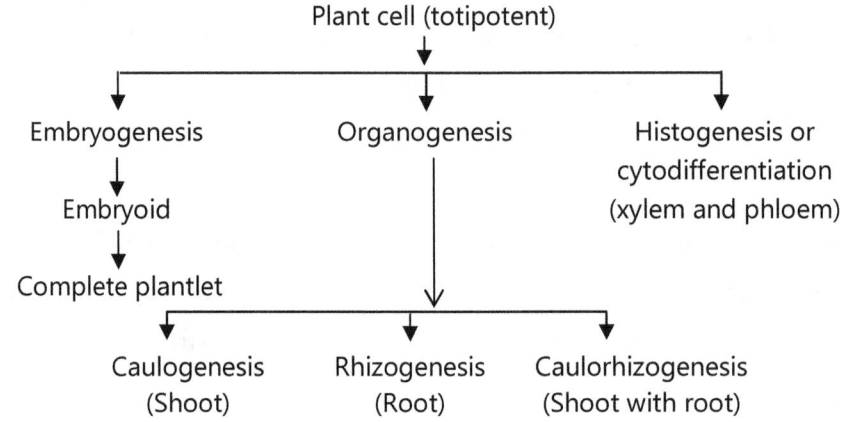

Fig. 17.4: Cytodifferentiation of totipotent cell

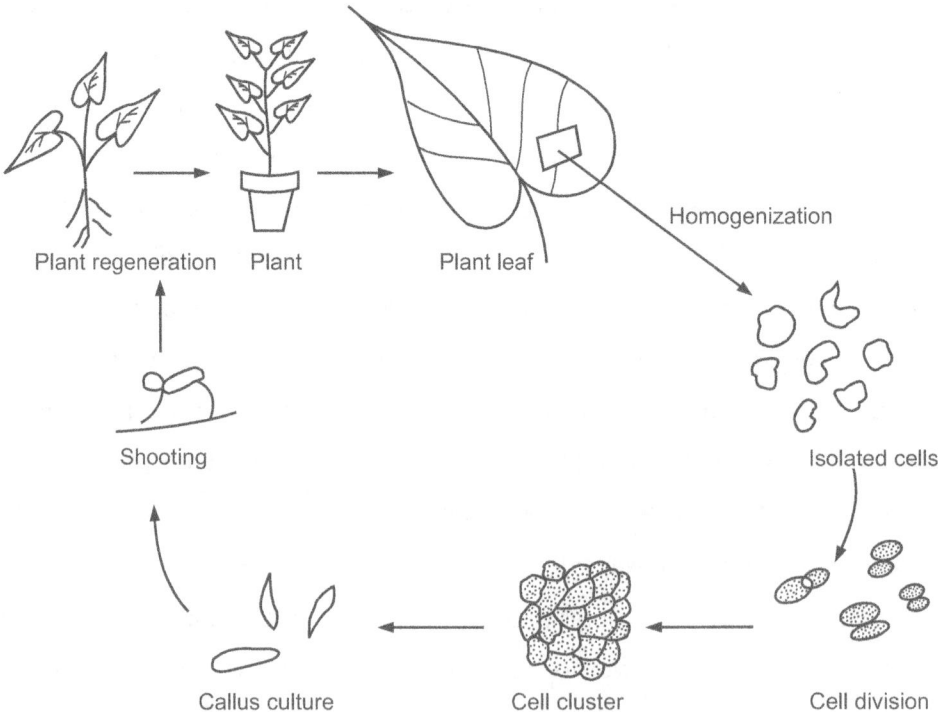

Fig. 17.5: Representation of cellular totipotency

TYPES OF CULTURES

Different techniques are used for in-vitro cultivation of plant cells, tissues and organs. These techniques are classified in Fig. 17.6. The application of plant tissue culture techniques are dependent on the regeneration of plants from cells and tissues in culture. Various plant explants mainly used in PTC are shown in Fig. 17.7. Growth curve of plant cell culture are to a great extent similar to microorganisms.

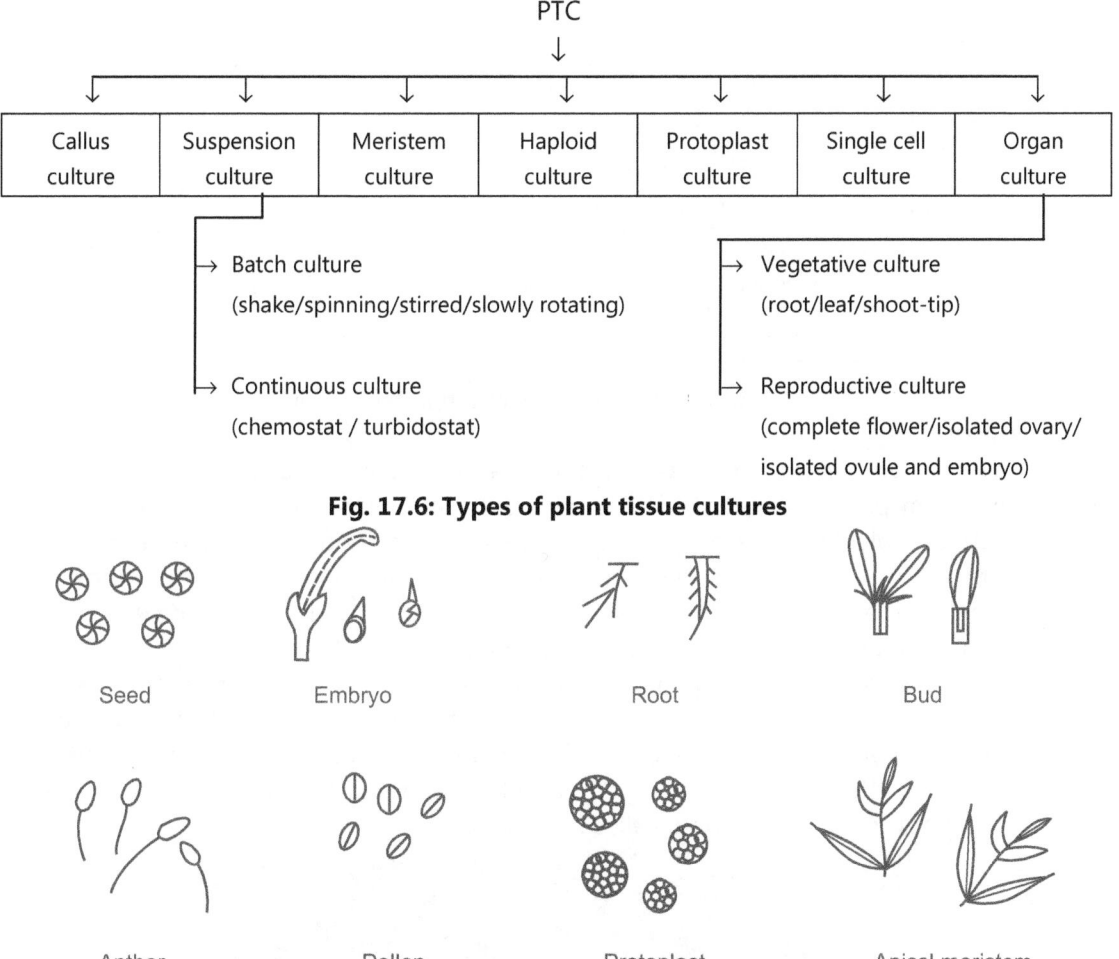

Fig. 17.6: Types of plant tissue cultures

Fig. 17.7: Plant explants used in plant tissue culture

The various stages of plant growth are classified as lag phase, exponential phase, linear phase, progressive deceleration phase, stationary phase and senescent phase (Fig. 17.8). Cell cultures are maintained by routine transfer of cells in early stationary phase to a fresh medium. Incubation period from culture initiation to stationary phase depends on initial cells density, lag phase period, growth rate and medium constitution. Several techniques are used for measurement of culture growth such as cell counting, packed cell volume (PCV, pellet/1ml), cell fresh weight (g/ml), cell dry weight (g/ml), nutrient uptake, cell viability, biochemical activity, cell turbidity etc.

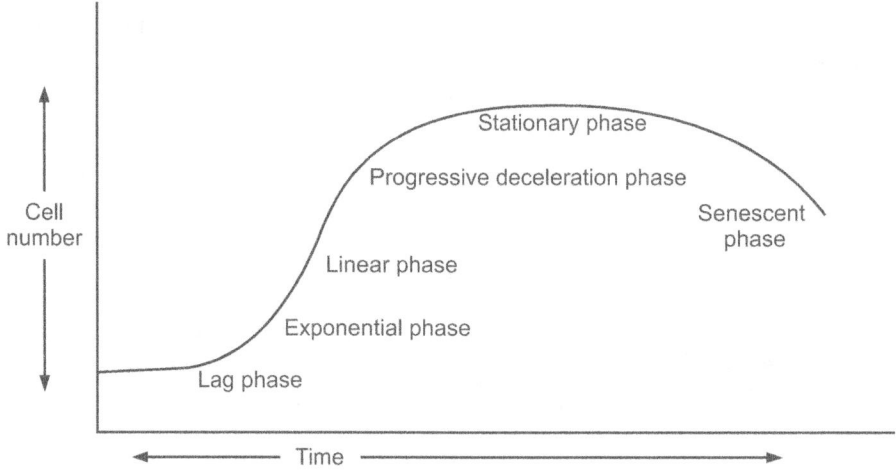

Fig. 17.8: Growth curve pattern in batch culture

Callus culture:

A callus is an amorphous mass of thin walled undifferentiated parenchyma cells developing from proliferating cells of the parent tissue. Callus is developed form various types of organ explants such as shoot buds, apical meristem, nodal regions, root segments, floral parts, pollen tissues etc. Callus formation depends on source of explant, nutritional composition and environmental factors. Callus is formed through three developmental stages such as induction, cell division and differentiation (Fig. 17.9). Callus is formed in-vivo as a result of infection by microorganisms from wounds at the cut edge of a stem or a root. The formation of callus is controlled by the endogenous growth hormones such as auxins and cytokinins. In-vitro callus formation on the explant of the parent tissue can be induced by incorporating the plant growth regulators into the nutrient medium. Murashige and Skoog medium is commonly used for callus formation.

Fig. 17.9: Callus culture

Explant (2 to 4 mm sterile segment) separated from a stem or root is transferred into nutrient medium and incubated at 25 to 28°C for 12 to 24 hrs. Nutrient medium containing auxins induces cell division and upper surface of explant is covered by callus. The callus is transferred to fresh medium (subculture) after every fourth or sixth week. Compact mass of callus (2 to 4 cm in diameter) is aseptically cut into small pieces (5 to 10 mm in diameter) and each piece is transferred on fresh solid or liquid medium. Callus is induced to undergo organogenesis and/or embryogenesis and generate whole plant. Callus culture is preserved at low temperature for long period. Maize, cherry and tobacco callus cultures produce certain organ specific antigens which are proteinous in nature. Root callus cultures of *Ruta graveoleus* synthesize essential oil components.

Suspension culture:

Suspension culture is a type of culture in which cells or small aggregates of cells multiply while suspended in agitated liquid medium. It is also called as cell suspension culture or cell culture. The plant cells in agitated liquid media has been reported by **Caplin** and **Steward** (1949), **Muir** (1954), **Nickel** (1956), and **Steward** and **Shantz** (1956).

Cell suspension is prepared by transferring a fragement of callus (0.5 to 1 gm) to the liquid medium which is continuously agitated on a moving rotary shaker. The movement of the nutrient medium provides vital aeration of the medium to sustain cell respiration and to separate callus tissue. Friable callus tissue is an ideal material for the dispersion of cells in culture medium. The dispersion of cells may be increased by adding more amount of auxins or adding small amount of cellulase and pectinase enzymes in the culture medium. The selection of the culture media is dependent on growth rate. The growth curve for a typical cell suspension culture consists of lag phase, exponential phase, linear phase and stationary phase (Fig. 17.8). The cells in cell suspension culture grow by cell division and the number of cells increases. Sucrose is the most common sugar used as a carbon source for growth of cells. The cell suspension is passed through a nylon mesh to remove the larger pieces of callus tissue. The filtrate containing small cell aggregates and single cell is transferred into fresh liquid medium (Fig. 17.10). Cell suspensions are diluted by using new flasks of culture medium. Cell aggregates may be transferred from liquid medium to solid medium to grow as a callus. It is possible to generate callus on solid medium from single suspension cells. By the technique, a whole plant may be regenerated from a single cell.

Cell suspension cultures are mainly classified into two types as: batch culture and continuous culture. The cell material or inoculum grows in a finite volume of agitated liquid medium is called batch culture. It is subdivided into shake culture, stirred culture, spinning culture and slowly rotating culture. In continuous culture system, liquid medium is continuously replaced by the fresh medium to stabilize the physiological states of the growing cells. In this method, nutrient depletion does not occur due to continuous flow of nutrient medium. Continuous culture system is divided into two types such as chemostats and turbidostats.

Cell cultures have many advantages over the callus cultures as the suspension can be easily pipetted and separated. Cell cultures are less heterogeneous and easily cultured up to two liters. It can be manipulated for preparation of metabolic products by adding precursors. Suspension culture is important for obtaining single cell clones by plating cell suspension on agar plates. It is also used for induction of somatic embryos and shoots. Genetic transformation and in vitro mutagenesis may be studied by the use of cell cultures. Cell cultures are also used for production of secondary metabolites, such as alkaloids, glycosides etc.

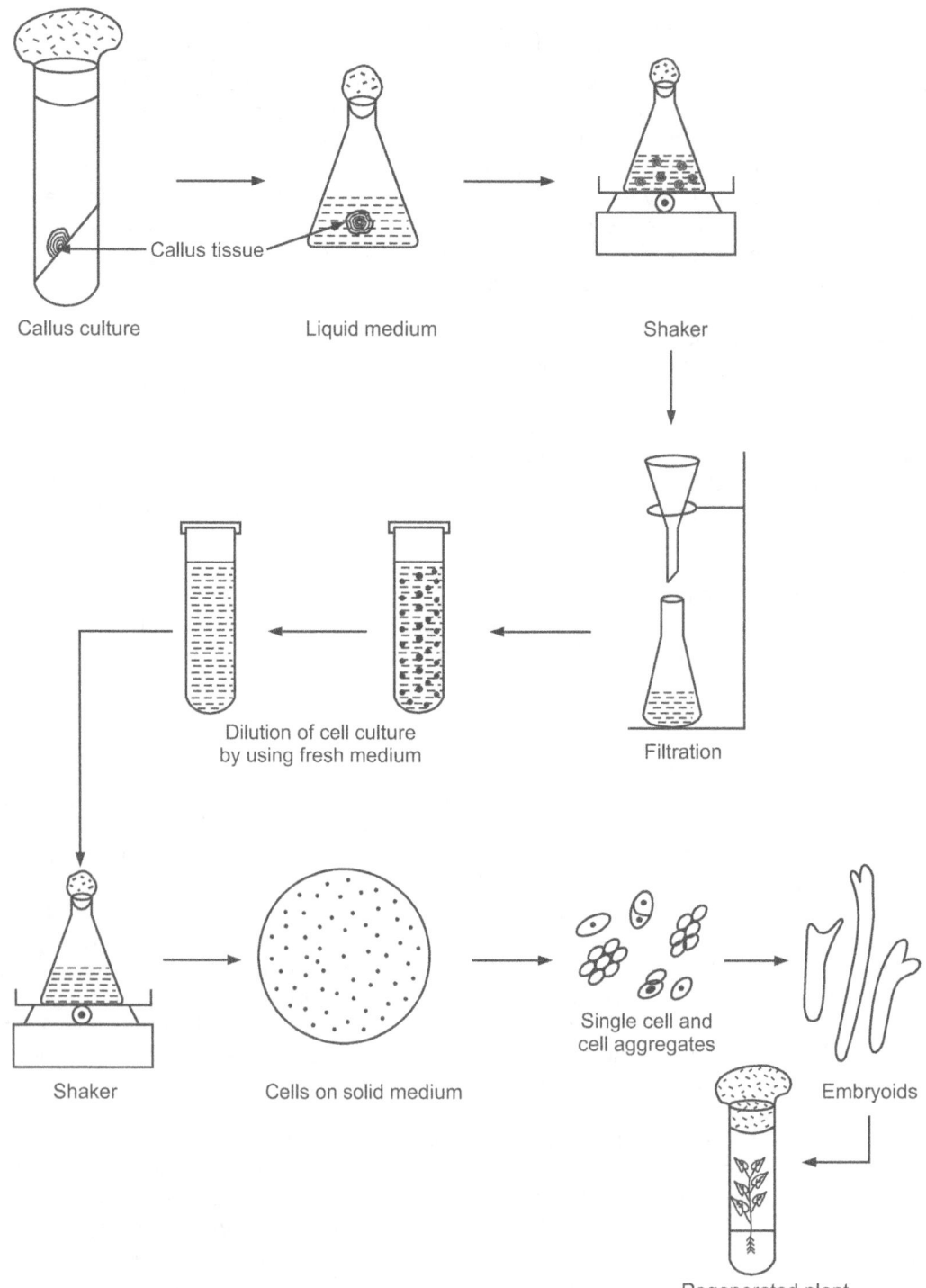

Fig. 17.10: Cell suspension culture and regeneration of plants

Meristem culture:

Meristem is the mass of undifferentiated parenchyma cells found at the extreme tip of the shoot and not stems. They have the totipotency to regenerate into plantlets. Meristem culture (Fig. 17.11) is a method in which shoot apices with a few primordial leaves are grown in vitro. This method is also known as apical tip culture or shoots tip culture. Shoot tip culture may be described as the culture of terminal (0.1 to 1.0 mm) portion of a shoot comprising the meristem (0.05 to 0.1 mm) together with primordial and developing leaves and adjacent stem tissue.

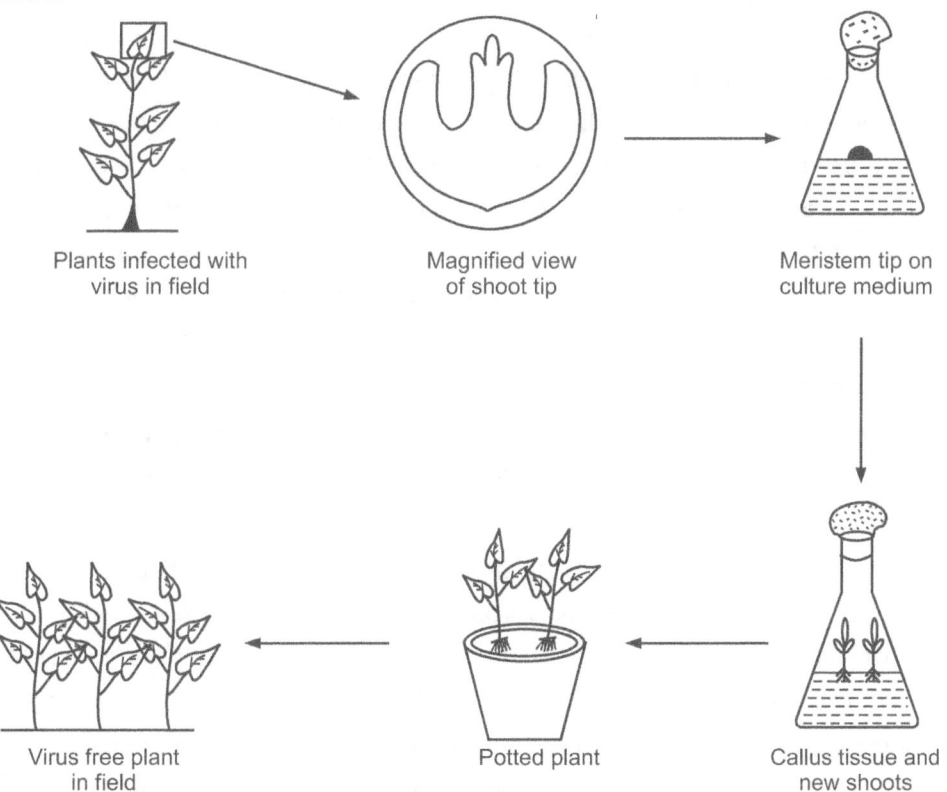

Fig. 17.11: Shoot tip or meristem culture

Shoot apices is isolated from young twigs from a healthy plant and sterilize by using sodium hypochlorite solution. The explants are rinsed by using sterile distilled water and transferred into sterile Petri plate. Leaves are removed from shoot apices and the apex cut with the help of scalpel. The excised shoot tips and meristem is cultured aseptically on solid medium or paper bridges dipping into liquid medium. Incubate the culture under 16 hrs light at 25 to 27°C. Leafy shoot or multiple shoots are obtained from single shoot tip or meristem. Roots are developed and then transfer into hormone free medium. The plantlets formed by this technique are transferred to pots containing compost. Explants size, temperature condition and composition of nutrient media are the important factors for the meristem culture. The smaller the size of the initial explant greater are the chances of virus elimination. Cytokinins (e.g. –BAP) in the nutrient medium plays a major role in the development of a leafy shoot or multiple shoots from meristem or shoot tip. NAA (naphthalene acetic acid) is the most effective auxin used in shoot tip culture.

The main application of the meristem culture technique is to obtain virus free plants. Pathogen free stock (viral, bacterial or fungal) can be easily prepared for the propagation even from the infected donor plants. The terminal region of the shoot meristem is used as culture which is free from pathogens. This technique combined with heat treatment or chemical treatment has proved to be very effective in virus eradication. Meristem culture is successfully used for the production of virus free plants of potatoes, orchids, pineapple, cymbidiums, strawberry, carnation and sugarcane. This technique is also employed for eliminating seed borne viruses from cowpea, bean and soybean. Meristem culture of many plant species may be used for micropropagation. Shoot tip cultures are usually acceptable for international transport as they comply with quarantine requirements and regulations.

Root and hairy root cultures:

Root is generally cultured in liquid medium and it has many advantages over solid media. Root culture gives informations about infection by *Rhizobium* and nodulation, nutritional requirements and physiological activities.

Plants regenerated from hairy roots usually possess an abnormal phenotype. In-vitro production of secondary plant products from hairy roots has been observed for the same spectrum of compounds as with non transformed roots. Treatment of hairy root of *Nicotiana tobacum* with elicitors derived from *Botrytis fabae* lead to increase synthesis of nicotine.

Hairy root culture has been obtained by the genetic transformation of plant tissue by the pathogenic soil bacterium, *Agrobacterium rhizogenes*. The infection of dicotyledons plants by *A. rhizogenes* causes roots to proliferate rapidly at the infection site. The integration of a portion of Ri (root inducing) plasmid into plant genome are responsible for phenotypic changes. Normal roots of dicotyledonous plants are transformed into hairy roots by the infection of *A. rhizogenes*. Hairy roots are characterized by high degree of lateral branching, profusion of root hairs and absence of geotropism.

The explant material is inoculated with a suspension of *A. rhizogenes* for development of hairy root cultures. Transformation may be induced on aseptic plants grown from seeds or on leaves, leaf discs or stem segments from green house plants. In some species, hairy roots may appear directly at the site of inoculation.

Hairy root cultures are mainly applicable for the production of root derived metabolites from dicotyledonous plants. Atropine, hyoscyamine, tropane, solasidine compounds are produced by hairy root cultures.

Haploid culture:

Anther or the pollen grains of different species have been used to obtain large number of haploid plants. Hence, this culture technique is also called anther and pollen culture. Anther culture is a technique by which the developing anthers are separated aseptically from unopened flower bud and are cultured on a nutrient medium where the microspores within the anther develop into callus tissue or embryoids that give rise to haploid plantlets either through organogenesis or embryogenesis. Pollen culture is a technique in which pollen grains are sequeezed at aseptically from the intact anther and then cultured on nutrient medium where the microspores develop into haploid embryoids or callus tissue that give rise to haploid plantlets. Haploid plants have single complete set of chromosomes that in turn may be useful for the improvement of many crop plants. Haploid plants are very useful in direct screening of recessive mutation in plants and development of homozygous diploid plants following chromosome doubling of haploid plant cells.

The successful isolation of haploid plants from anther and pollen are dependent on development of anthers, physiological status of the donor plant, nutrient medium and pretreatment. The anther and pollen culture has established that pollens at the uninucleate stage, just before the first mitosis or during mitosis are most suitable for the induction of haploids. Anther or flower bud may be stored at low temperature (5 to 10°C) for induction of haploids. Activated charcoal and iron in the medium also plays a very important role for the induction of haploids. Coconut milk, potato extract and growth regulators (auxin and cytokinin) are also used in anther and pollen culture. Colchicine treatment is given for duplication of chromosome to obtain homozygous diploid plants from haploid culture. Preparation of haploid plants from anther and pollen culture techniques are given in Fig. 17.12.

Anther and pollen cultures are important for the development of mutants and also useful material for studying somatic cell genetics. Haploids prepared from anther and pollen culture are useful in cytogenetic studies. Haploid culture is also useful for plant breeding crop improvement. Homozygous diploid plants can be used as pure lines in breeding programme.

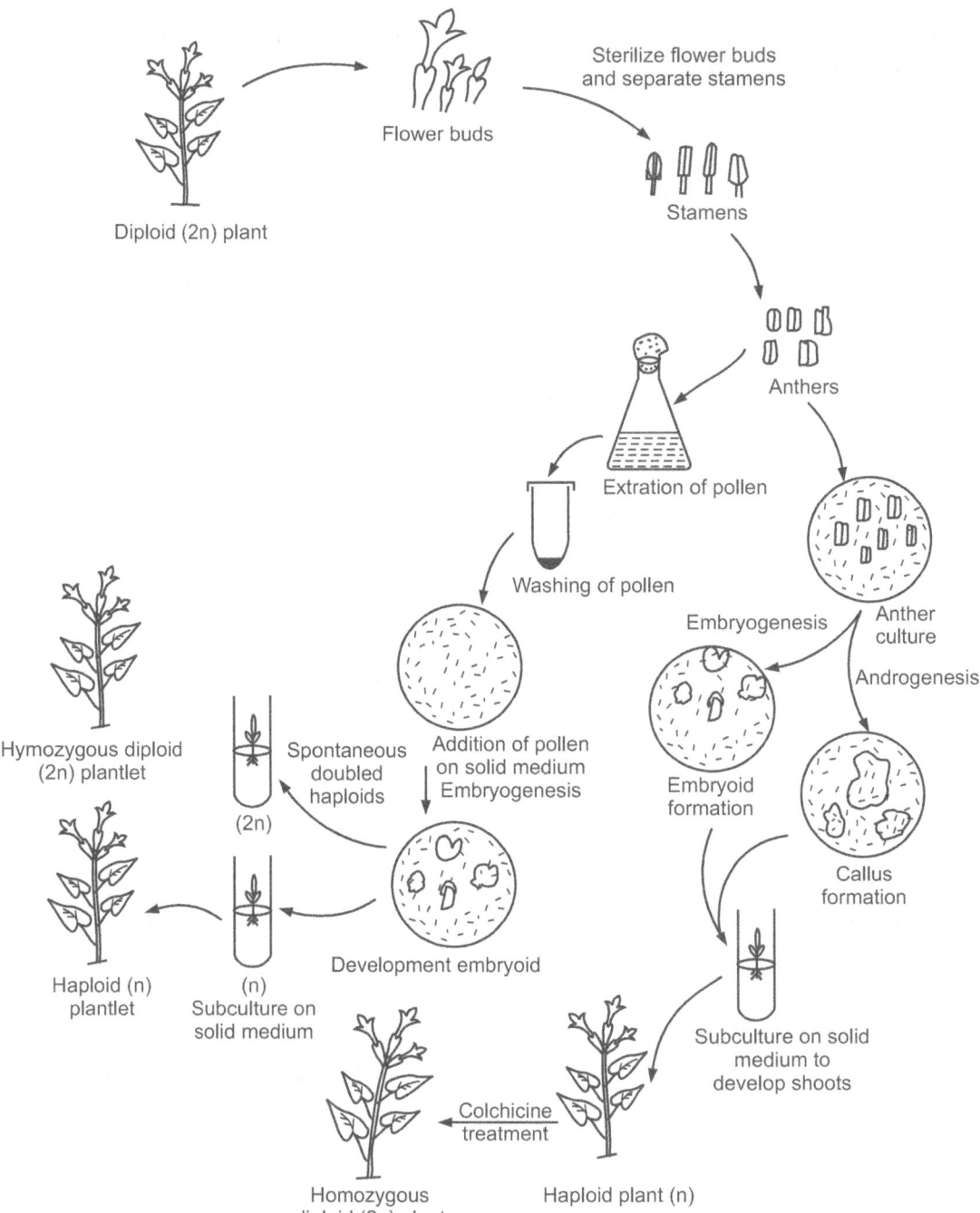

Fig. 17.12: Production of haploid and diploid plants from anther and pollen culture

Protoplast culture:

Plant cells from which the cell wall has been removed are called protoplast. Protoplast is the biologically active cell containing all the normal cell organelles except cell wall. The nucleus present in protoplast expresses totipotency to regenerate plants. The cell wall of a plant cell is removed by the treatment of enzymes like cellulose, pectinase, hemicellulase, pectin glycosidase, zymolase etc.

Protoplasts can be isolated from almost all parts of plants such as roots, leaves, fruits, stems, pollens, root nodules, tubers, callus tissues etc. Callus tissue and cell suspension cultures are frequently used as sources of protoplasts. Mature leaves or any part of plants are collected from healthy plants which are washed in tap water and sterilized by sodium hypochlorite solution. The stripped surface of leaf is kept in mannitol solution for 2 to 3 hours to allow plasmolysis of cells. Protoplasts are usually isolated by mechanically slicing of plant tissues or by treating tissues with cell wall degrading enzymes in solutions which contain osmotic stabilizers to preserve the structure and viability of the protoplasts. In the mechanical method, removal of cell wall is facilitated by the aid of needles, forceps and scissors. Enzymatic method is most often used in isolation of protoplasts from various plant parts. The enzyme solution containing protoplasts are filtered with a nylon mesh (45 μm) and filtrate is centrifuged. The supernatant is decanted off and the protoplasts are washed three times with mannitol. Flotation technique may be used for protoplast systems containing excessive amounts of debris especially for leaf mesophyll derived protoplast. The protoplasts are finally cleaned with 20 to 25% sucrose solution. Plant protoplasts are mainly observed under the light and fluorescence microscope. Absence of birefringence and spherical shape indicates the complete removal of the cell wall. Protoplast viability can be determined by using fluorescein diacetate (FDA). Viable protoplasts emit green/yellow fluorescent while the nonviable protoplasts remain unchanged. Dead protoplasts are also converted to red colour in the presence of phenosafranine (0.01%) dye. The number of protoplasts present in suspension can be counted using a modified haemocytomerter.

Protoplasts are cultured in liquid media or placed on nutrient agar in Petri plates. The nutritional requirements of protoplasts and cell suspension cultures are almost similar. Protoplast culture media consist of carbon sources, vitamins, organic nitrogen, inorganic nutrients, osmotic stabilizers and growth hormones. The protoplast solution (10^5 protoplast / ml) is poured in nutrient medium in Petri dishes and incubated at 25°C in the dim white light. The protoplasts regenerate a cell wall, undergo cell division and form callus (Fig. 17.13). Murashige and Skoog (MS) medium is commonly used for protoplast culture. The callus can subcultured to develop mature plants. Plant species regenerated from protoplasts are *Capsicum annum, Beta valgaris, Cucumis sativus, Rosa* sp. etc.

The isolated protoplasts are used for ultrastructural studies, transformation assessments and physiological investigations. The somatic protoplasts are fused with one anther to form somatic hybrids which are having new characters as compare to parents. The protoplast cultures are used for genetic modification to exploit from crop improvement in agriculture.

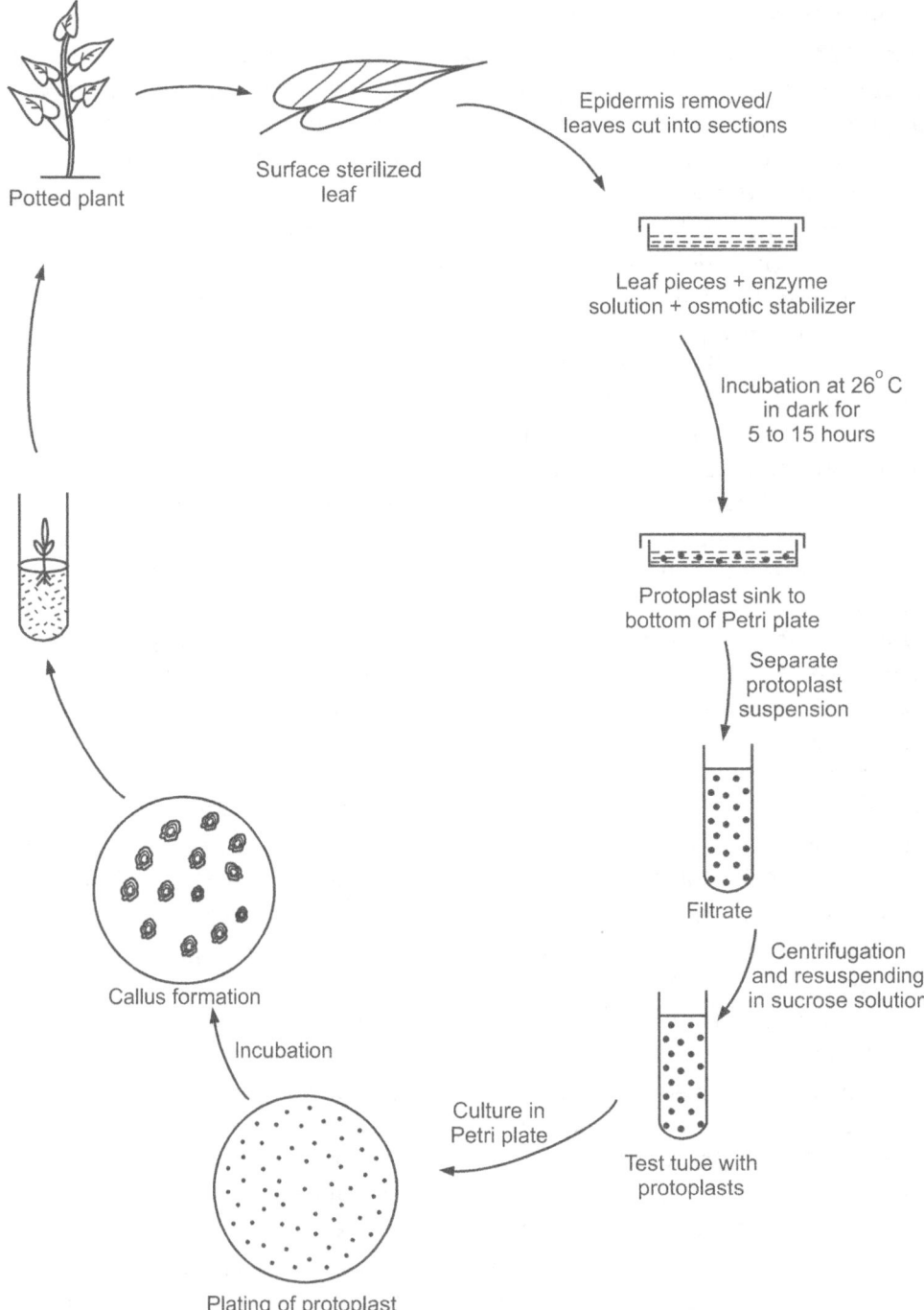

Fig. 17.13: Steps used in the isolation, culture and regeneration of plants from leaf protoplast

PROTOPLAST FUSION AND SOMATIC HYBRIDIZATION

Protoplast fusion has opened up a novel approach to raising new hybrids. Sexual hybridization in higher plants is a valuable tool for the conventional plant breeding to improve cultivated crops. The in vitro fusion of plant protoplasts derived from somatic cells which differ genetically is called somatic cell hybridization. Protoplasts from different species of plants can be fused when protoplasts come into contact with other protoplasts. Protoplasts may be fused by spontaneous fusion or induced fusion (Fig. 17.14).

Protoplasts during isolation often fuse spontaneously is called spontaneous fusion. During enzymatic degradation, some of the protoplasts come in physical contact to bring about the spontaneous fusion among the similar parenteral protoplasts. It is found that protoplasts from adjoining cells fuse through their plasmodesmata to form a multinucleate protoplast and it is strictly intraspecific. Mechanical fusion is performed by contact of protoplasts by micropipettes or micromanipulators. This kind of fusion is not dependent upon the presence of fusion inducing agent.

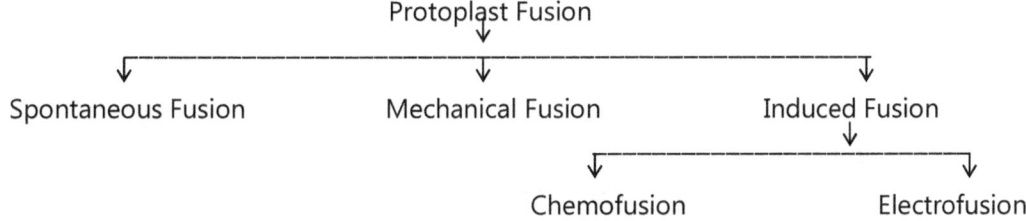

Fig. 17.14: Types of protoplast fusion

Fusion of isolated protoplasts from different sources with the help of fusion inducing chemical agents is known as induced fusion. The chemical fusion can be done with the help of sodium nitrate ($NaNO_3$), calcium ions (Ca^{++}), polyethylene glycol (PEG) etc. This method can bring together both intraspecific and interspecific protoplasts. The inducing agent is called fusogen. Several chemicals like polyvinyl alcohol, dextran sulphate, lysozyme, glycerol, dimethyl sulphoxide, poly-D-lysine have been used as fusogens. Polyethylene glycol (PEG) is the most commonly employed fusogen in conjunction with alkaline pH and high calcium concentrations. Chemical fusogens cause the isolated protoplasts to adhere to one another and leads to tight agglutination (Fig. 17.15). The adhesion of protoplasts are mainly occur due to attraction of protoplasts or due to reduction of negative charges of protoplast. Electric fusion mediated protoplast fusion has many advantages over chemical fusion. Electric fusion technique does not require any chemicals that are often toxic to the cells. Electrofusion may achieve a high yield (20%) as compare to chemical fusion (1%). Electrofusion method is simple, rapid, synchronous and more easily controlled. The protoplasts are brought close by agglutination and then the cell membranes are perturbed by an electrical shock to promote membrane fusion. This technique of fusion is called dielectrophoresis. Dielectrophoresis polarizes the cells so that each protoplast has a positive and negative area. The positive ends and the negative ends of protoplast are drawn closer to obtain the 'pearl chains' of protoplasts prior to fusion.

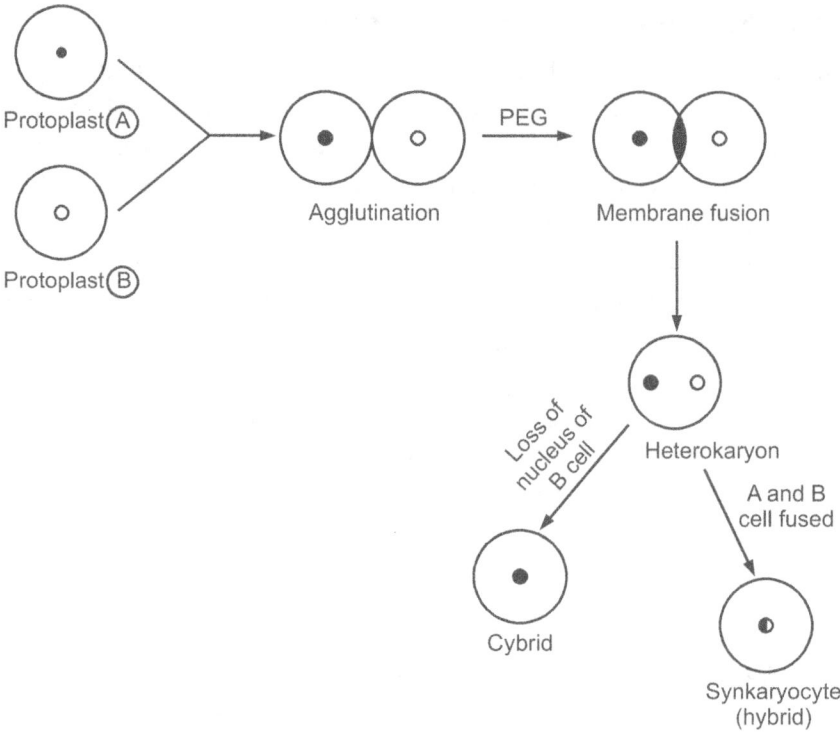

Fig. 17.15: Stages in protoplast fusion

Fusion of cytoplasm of two protoplasts form a coalescence of cytoplasms. The nuclei of two protoplasts may or may not fuse together even after fusion of cytoplasms. The binucleate cells are known as heterocyte or heterokaryon. When nuclei are fused the cells are known as hybrid and when only cytoplasms fuse and genetic information from one of the two nuclei is lost is known as cybrid (heteroplast or cytoplasmic hybrid). The production of hybrid is called hybridization and production of cybrid is called cybridisation. Somatic hybridization of plants involves protoplast isolation, protoplast fusion, regeneration of plants and analysis of regenerated plants (Fig. 17.16). Purified protoplasts are isolated from two different plants or tissue sources and then treated with fusion agents to form hybrid cell lines. Heterokaryones (hybrids) homokaryones and unfused protoplasts are obtained by fusion treatment. Hybrid cells are different from other cells and they are totipotent. Selection methods used for fused products is dependent on physical and biological properties of fused cells. Heterokaryons or true hybrid protoplast or synkaryons that develop in a selective medium can be isolated by dilution plating or micromanipulation. Drug sensitivity and resistance test, fluorescent antibodies and biochemical method are used for selection of hybrids.

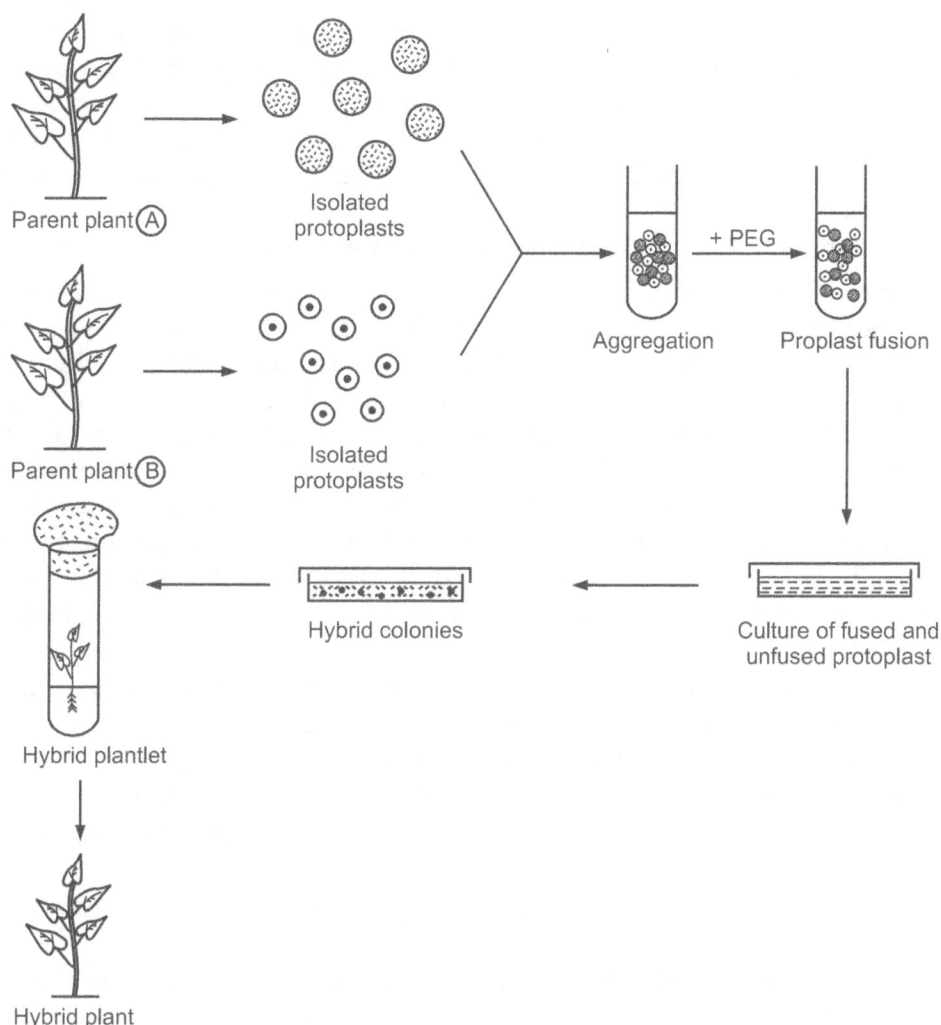

Fig. 17.16: Protoplast fusion and regeneration of somatic hybrid plants

Somatic cell hybridization plays important role in plant biotechnology. Protoplast fusion provides a technique of combining the different genomes of different species, with the potential of overcoming sexual incompatibility barrier between plants. Protoplast fusion product can give information about compatibility or incompatibility of the nuclei or cytoplasm. Genetic transformation of single cell has been accomplished by co-cultivating protoplasts with *Agrobacterium tumifaciens* or by direct DNA transfer. This methods can be used to create plants with improved characteristics as well as increased insect and disease resistant. By protoplast fusion, it is possible to transfer some useful genes such as disease resistance, rapid growth rate, protein quality etc. Genetic variation can be induced through protoplast fusion in vegetatively reproducing plants. Interspecific and intergeneric hybrids are useful in the creation of novel and superplants hybrid production. Interspecific protoplast fusion have been successfully used in the transfer of atrazine resistance from *Sotanum nigrum* to *Lycopersicum esculentum*. Somatic hybridization has been used for examination of both virus replication cycles and the functions encoded by virus genomes. There are some limitations of protoplast fusion and somatic hybridization. The percentage of fusion product is very low and there is no any standardized method for hybrid identification, selection and isolation. Elimination of chromosomes from the hybrid cell is another limitation of somatic cell hybridization.

PRESERVATION OF PLANT CELLS: CRYOPRESERVATION

Most of the plants are stored in the form of seeds or as growing plants. Some seeds may not retain their originality or fail to develop into plants. Plant tissue culture technique is used to overcome this problem by using identical clones. The plant materials are easily stored in a minimal medium with low light intensity and low temperature to reduce growth rate and maintain totipotency of plant tissue. Many plant tissues or cells can be stored in a limited area and this type of storage is called germplasm storage. Germplasm is stored in the form of seeds, shoot tips, buds, roots, protoplasts etc and sub cultured at regular intervals of one year. The germplasm in the growing stage is used for storage by addition of chemical retardants or by reducing the temperature or by decreasing oxygen concentration. Storage at low temperature using nitrogen i.e. cryopreservation is the most effective method for preservation of plant tissues.

Cryopreservation is defined as the nonlethal preservation and storage of living biological cells at low temperatures in a frozen state. e.g. deep freezers (− 80°C), vapour phase nitrogen (−150°C) or liquid nitrogen (− 196°C). This method is important for short or long term preservation of small explants such as apical meristem, mutant cell strains and organized structures such as embryo, anthers, cotyledons etc. The main advantages of this method are as follows.

(i) Less space is required for the preservation of large number of clonally multiplied plants.
(ii) Plants are easily maintained free from pathogens, pests, viruses and other natural hazards.
(iii) The clonal plant materials are easily transferred from nation to nation because these plant materials are free from pathogens.
(iv) The plants are stored as nucleus stock and it is may propagate larger number of plants rapidly, when required.

The main disadvantages of cryopreservation are as follows.

(i) This method is not applicable to vegetatively propagated crops e.g. Ipomoea, potato etc.
(ii) Cost for maintaining a large proportion of the available genotypes of crop plants is high.
(iii) It may cause damage to cells during freezing and thawing which may be caused by ice crystals formed inside the cells and by cell dehydration.
(iv) Cell dehydration and protoplast shrinkage during slow thawing may cause cell destruction owing to irreversible contraction of the plasmalemma.

Healthy plants are used for collection of tissues for cryopreservation. The ability of explant to survive at low temperature is influenced by morphological and physiological condition of the plant material, prior to freezing. Organized structures such as shoot pieces, embryos, young plantlets etc are preferred for cryopreservation. Cryoprotectants are generally added to the freezing mixtures to protect cells from toxic effect and to prevent the formation of large ice crystals inside the cells. Cryoprotectants are a heterogeneous group of compounds which include polyethylene glycol (PEG), polyethylene oxide (PEO), dimethyl sulfoxide (DMSO), glycerin, sugars, alcohols, glycols, polyvinyl pyrrolidone (PVP), proline, dextran, glycerine, sucrose, hydroxystarch etc. Complex mixtures of these compounds are more effective than single compound e.g. DMSO + glycerol + sucrose. Dimethyl sulfoxide (DMSO), sucrose, glycerol and proline are most frequently used cryoprotectants. DMSO is most superior as compare to others due to its low moleculer weight, easily miscible, rapidly permeable and easily washable nature. Desiccation of cells prior to freezing excludes the need for cryoprotectants and also simplifies the cryopreservation process. Disicated cells are survive by direct immersion in liquid nitrogen. Ice formation during cryopreservation is avoided through vitrification. Vitrification is the process in which a concentrated aqueous solution cooled to low temperature directly solidifies into an amorphous glassy state without crystallization. The plant tissues to be preserved is added in culture medium and treated with a cryoprotectant. This plant material is transferred to sterile cryovials or ampoules containing cryoprotectant (5 to 10%) and closed with a screw cap. The cryopreservation of plant cell culture and eventual regeneration are shown in Fig. 17.17.

The sample is frozen by slow freezing, rapid freezing or stepwise freezing. Slow cooling method, the material is freezing at a cooling rate of 0.1 to 10°C/min from 0 to –100°C and then transferred in liquid nitrogen. Meristems of potato and strawberry are successfully cryopreserved by slow freezing performed by using computer-controlled freezers. In rapid freezing, the cryovials are directly put into liquid nitrogen which causes rapid cooling. Dry ice (CO_2) may be used in place of liquid nitrogen (LN) to prevents ice crystals (ultra cooling). Desiccation or vitrification pretreatment with ultra-rapid cooling is most effective method for cryopreservation. In stepwise or pre-freezing method, the cells are cooled gradually (1°C/min) or step wise (5°C/min) to get temperature between –20 to –50°C. After 30 minutes, cells are rapidly cooled in liquid nitrogen to get –196°C. The storage temperature (–100 to –200°C) for frozen cells is used to avoid all metabolic activity and prevents biochemical injury. The short term storage may be done at –80 to –100°C. Long term storage can be done at –196°C in liquid nitrogen refrigerator.

Cryopreserved plant tissues can be returned to a temperature suitable for growth is also critical as the initial freezing. Thawing process is used for releasing the vials containing cultures from the frozen stage to elevate temperature between 35 to 40°C. Thawing is performed quickly but without overheating. Slow warming may be responsible for damage of cells by ice crystal formation. Cell viability test can be done by using FDA staining and growth measurements. Cryopreservation process can be evaluated on the basis of morphological, physiological, biochemical and genetic studies of the cryopreserved plant materials.

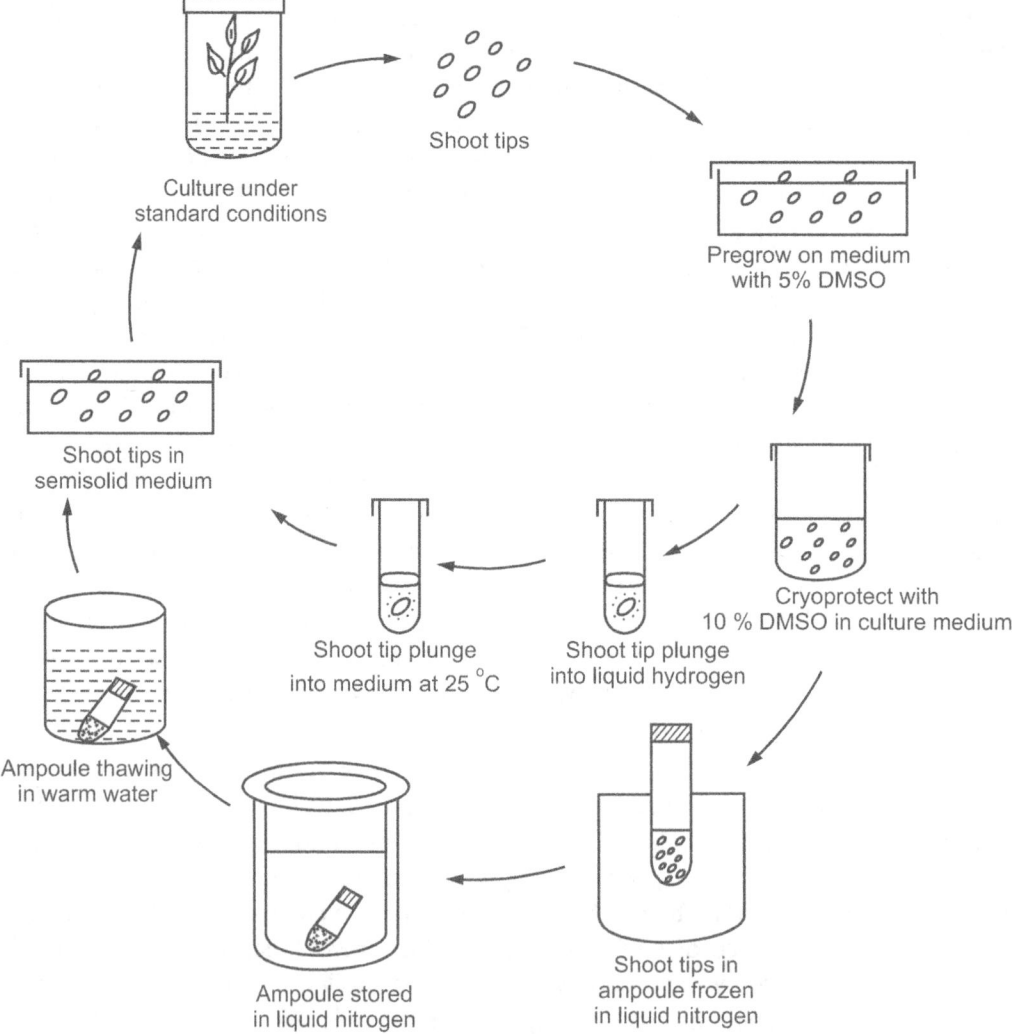

Fig. 17.17: Steps of cryopreservation of shoot tips

QUESTIONS

(A) Short answer questions:

1. What is meristem culture? Write the difference between meristem culture and shoot tip culture.
2. Write advantages of suspension culture over callus culture.
3. What are the advantages of protoplast fusion over traditional methods of sexual hybridization?
4. What is cybrid? Write its significance.

5. What is explant? How callus is induced from it?
6. Explain in short:
   (a) Callus culture
   (b) Fusogens
   (c) Cryoprotectants

(B) Long answer questions:
1. Write short note on:
   (a) Cellular totipotency
   (b) Cryopreservation
   (c) Hairy root culture
2. What is protoplast fusion? Write the procedure and mechanisms of protoplast fusion. Discuss the importance of protoplast fusion and somatic hybridization.
3. Write in detail requirements for establishing a tissue culture laboratory.
4. Explain the method of preparation, formulation and nutritional component of culture media used in plant biotechnology.
5. Write the method of isolation of protoplasts from plant cells. Write the applications of protoplast culture.
6. What is haploid? How will you prepare haploid plant from anther and pollen culture?

(C) Multiple choice questions:
1. _____ is mainly used for cell division and root initiation in cultured tissues.
   (a) Gibberellins   (b) Cytokinins
   (c) Absisic acid   (d) Auxins
2. Protoplast viability can be determined by using _____ dye.
   (a) Fluorescein diacetate (b) Safranin
   (b) Crystal violet   (d) Congo red
3. _____ medium is commonly used for protoplast culture.
   (a) NT   (b) MS
   (c) ER   (d) B_5
4. _____ is most commonly used fusogen in conjunction with alkaline pH and high calcium concentrations.
   (a) PEG   (b) $NaNO_3$
   (c) PVA   (d) DMSO
5. _____ is most superior cryoprotectant used in cryopreservation.
   (a) PEG   (b) $NaNO_3$
   (c) PVA   (d) DMSO
6. What is the term used to define the capacity of the cell to give rise to the whole plant?
   (a) Plant tissue culture (b) Xenoplantation
   (c) Totipotency   (d) Protoplast.

7. Plants in natural conditions are:
   - (a) Autotropic
   - (b) phototrophic
   - (c) Exotropic
   - (d) None of the above
8. Which of the following hormone is generally responsible for shoot formation?
   - (a) Abscisic acid
   - (b) Gibberelic acid
   - (c) Indole acetic acid
   - (d) Kinetin
9. _____ triggers the synthesis of secondary metabolites in plants.
   - (a) Auxins
   - (b) Gibberellins
   - (c) Inhibitors
   - (d) Elicitors
10. Fe-EDTA in plant tissue culture media acts as _____.
    - (a) Surfactant
    - (b) Solidifying agent
    - (c) Buffer
    - (d) Chelating agent
11. An essential ingredient in the general preparation of plant tissue culture media is _____.
    - (a) Glucose
    - (b) Pyridoxine HCl
    - (c) Gibberlin G_1
    - (d) Naphthalene acetic acid

(D) Match the following:

1.

	A		B
(a)	*Cinchona ledgeriana*	(i)	Codeine
(b)	*Catharanthus roseus*	(ii)	Reserpine
(c)	*Papaver somniferum*	(iii)	Vincristine
(d)	*Rawulfia serpentina*	(iv)	Quinine

2.

	A		B
(a)	Abscisic acid	(i)	Auxin
(b)	NAA	(ii)	Gibberlin
(c)	GA_3	(iii)	Cytokinin
(d)	6-Furfuryl aminopurine	(iv)	Growth inhibitor

(E) Fill in the blanks:
1. Gene transfer into the protoplast by using plasmid vectors are demonstrated by **K. A. Barton** in 1983 by using _____ species.
2. Some single cell develops somatic embryos and then develop complete plantlet called _____.
3. _____ is the most common sugar used as a carbon source for growth of cells.
4. Hormones in plant tissue culture medium is added in ppm quantities. 1 ppm is equal to _____.
5. The pathogen of plant roots that is used as a cloning host is _____.

CHAPTER 18
TRANSGENIC PLANTS

CONTENTS

INTRODUCTION

METHODS OF GENE TRANSFER

    Indirect gene transfer (vector mediated)

    Direct gene transfer

APPLICATIONS OF TRANSGENIC PLANTS

    Production of pharmaceuticals

    Agricultural or horticultural uses

INTRODUCTION

The change in the genome of an organism by introduction of one or a few specific genes is referred as genetic transformation. The plants obtained through genetic engineering contain a gene usually from an unrelated organism, such genes are called transgenes and the plants containing transgenes are called as transgenic plants. These plants are the plants that carry the stably integrated foreign genes. These plants may also be called transformed plants. A number of transgenic plants carrying genes for traits of economic importance have been released for commercial cultivation. Transgenic plants can be produced by various techniques of gene transfer. Gene transfer techniques are mainly depends on natural plant vectors as well as vectorless systems, which include directed physical and chemical methods for delivering foreign DNA into plant cells.

The development of transgenic plants is the outcome of an integrated application of recombinant DNA technology, gene transfer methods and tissue culture techniques. Genetically modified plants can be manipulated to act as bioreactors to produce wide range of biologically important compounds such as secondary metabolites, carbohydrates, lipids, proteins etc. Metabolic engineering of transgenic plants is gaining importance in recent years as an alternative to animals and microorganisms for the isolation of biologically active compounds. The main aim of transgenics is to improve the crops with the desired traits.

METHOD OF GENE TRANSFER

Transgenic plants can be produced by two methods:
- Indirect gene transfer (vector mediated)
  - (a) Bacterial vectors
  - (b) Viral vectors

- Direct gene transfer
  (a) Chemical treatment
  (b) Electroporation or electrical treatment
  (c) Lipofection or liposomes
  (d) Microinjection
  (e) Macroinjection
  (f) Particle gun delivery or Ballistic method
  (g) Pollen transformation
  (h) Fibre-mediated gene transfer.

These gene transfer methods are described as follows:

Indirect gene transfer or vector mediated gene transfer

Crown gall and hairy roots diseases of higher plants are caused by soil borne Gram-negative bacteria, *Agrobacterium tumefaciens* and *Agrobacterium rhizogenes*, respectively. A. tumefaciens has ability to infect dicotyledonous plants at wound site occurring neoplastic growth called crown gall tumour. The bacterial genes are able to replicate along with the plant genome and synthesis a special class of compounds, called opines. This has occurred due to the presence of Ti (tumour inducing) plasmid in *Agrobacterium tumefaciens* which induces tumour after integration into plant host genome. There are six types of opines produced by Ti-plasmids such as octopine, nopaline, mannopine, argopine, argocinopine and leucopine. This Ti-plasmid can be used as vector to transform plant cell (Fig. 18.1). The Ti-plasmid is made up of 2,00,000 nucleotide pairs of which only a 23,000 nucleotide pairs are introduced into the host cell. T-DNA region and virulence region in the Ti-plasmid are essential for agrobacterium mediated transformation.

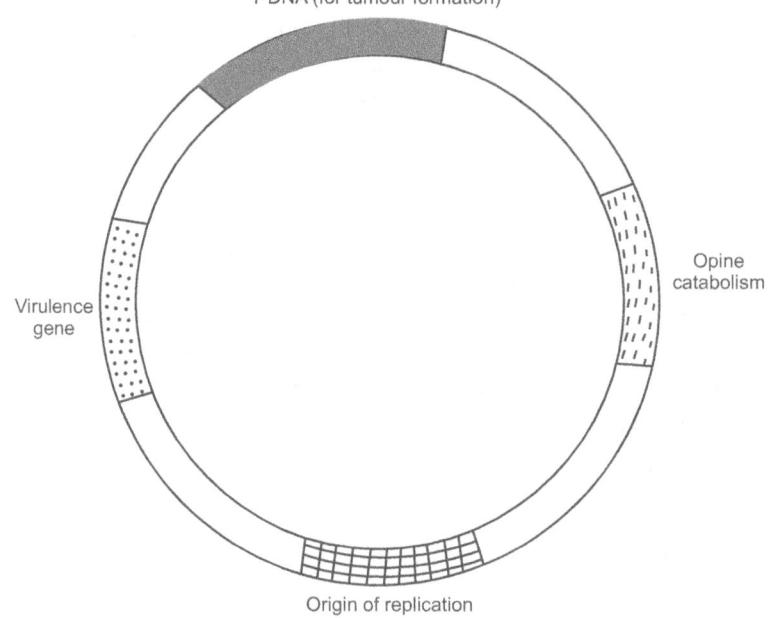

Fig. 18.1: Structure of Ti-plasmid

The T-DNA (Fig. 18.2) is bordered on both sides of 25 base pairs (bp) direct repeated sequences of nucleotides. The T-DNA border sequences are the only elements of the plasmid required in cis for T-DNA transfer to the plant genome. It carries genes for the synthesis of opines and phytohormones and it is easily transferred and integrated into host genome during the infection. An onc region consist of three genes (tmr, tms1, tms2) which are responsible for the synthesis of phytohormones IAA (an auxin) and isopentyladenosine 5' monophosphate (a cytokinin). The OS region is responsible for synthesis of unusual amino acids or sugars called opines e.g. octopine, nopaline, lysopine etc.

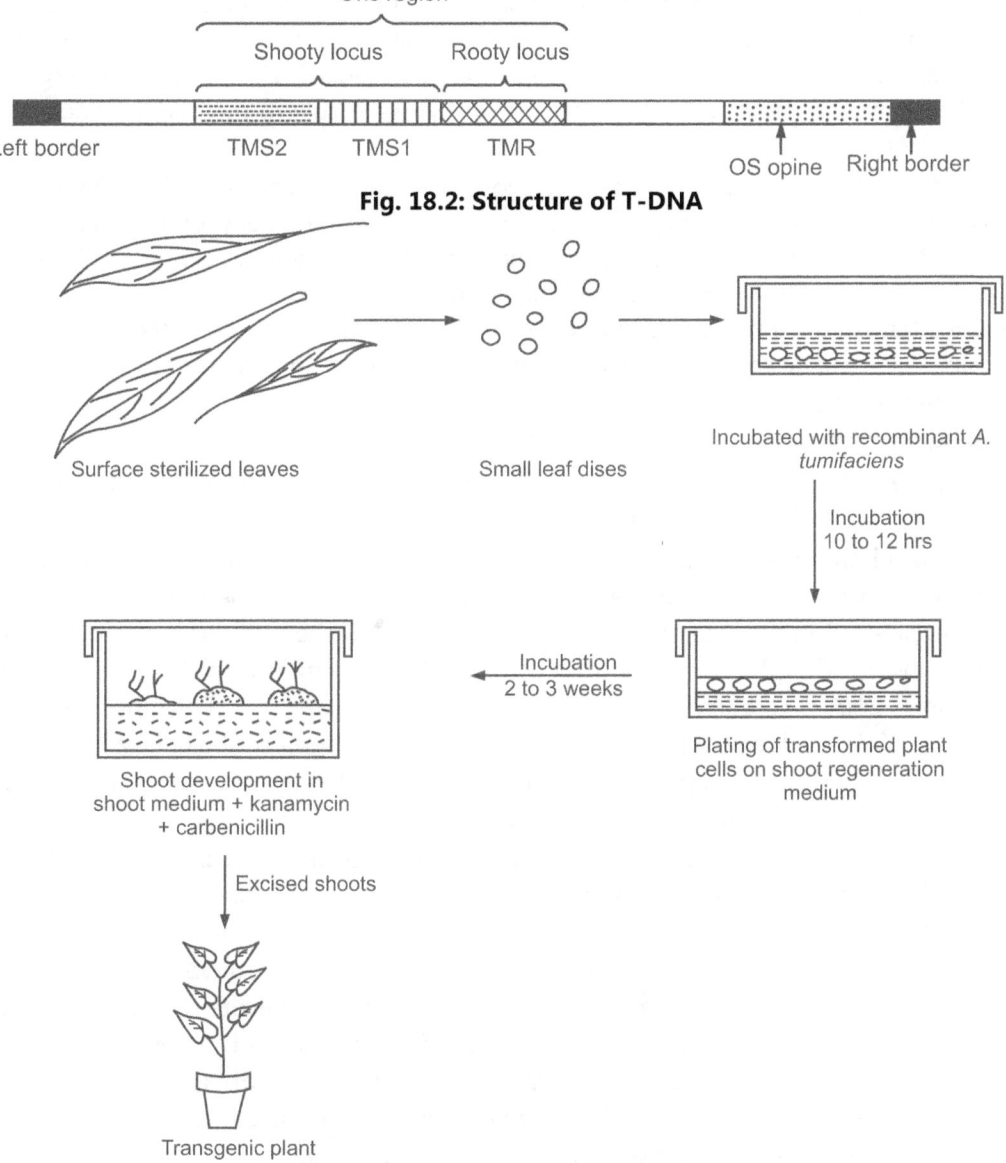

Fig. 18.2: Structure of T-DNA

Fig. 18.3: *Agrobacterium* mediated gene transfer

Agrobacterium containing the vector can be used in a number of ways to produce transgenic plants. Foreign DNA is inserted into the plasmid vectors and transferred into agrobacterium. Most transgenic plants are produced by co-cultivation method. This method is easy, more reproducible and shows stable integration and expression of foreign genes. The explants used for inoculation with *Agrobacterium* are protoplasts, tissue slices, whole organ sections, callus cell clumps, suspension cultured cells etc. Surface sterilized explants are incubated with bacteria for 24 to 48 hours so that the cut surface of the explant is able to interact with the bacteria. The bacterial cell number and composition of medium may vary with the bacterial strain and plant host. The explants are transferred aseptically to a selection medium containing antibiotics such as carbenicillin, cefotaxime, vancomycin etc. Untransformed cells are unable to grow in this modified media while the transformed cells grow and form callus. The callus are further grown by tissue culture method to regenerate transgenic plants.

The leaf *Agrobacterium* culture, acetosyringone released by plant cells includes the vir genes which brings about transfer of recombinant T-DNA into many of the plant cells. The T-DNA is integrated into the plant genomes and the transgene is expressed. The leaf discs are transferred (Fig. 18.3) on regeneration medium containing kanamycin and carbencillin. Kanamycin antibiotic does not allowed to grow untransformed plant cells while carbencillin kills *Agrobacterium* cells. The shoots are separated and transferred into soil for growth of transgenic plants.

Direct gene transfer

Direct gene transfer is the technique in which the DNA is inserted into plant cells without the involvement of any biological agent.

- **(a) Chemical treatment:** Many chemicals such as polyethylene glycol (PEG), polyvinyl alcohol (PVA), calcium phosphate, polyamines etc. enhances the uptake of DNA by protoplasts. Polyethylene glycol (PEG) is most effective chemical for DNA uptake into protoplasts. The plant protoplasts are suspended in a transformation medium and plasmid DNA is carefully added into the protoplast suspension. Polyethylene glycol (15 to 20%) is added in resulting solution and pH is adjusted to 8.0. Protoplasts are treated with $MgCl_2$ to improve rate of transformation. Finally, protoplasts are washed and then plated in Petri plate for growth.

- **(b) Electroporation or electrical treatment:** The introduction of DNA into the cells by exposing them for very short period to high voltage electrical pulses (1500 to 2000 V cm^{-1}) which perhaps induced transient pores in the plasma lemma is called electroporation. Plant cell protoplasts are suspended in a suitable ionic solution containing recombinant plasmid DNA. The electroporation mixture is then exposed to the chosen voltage – pulses combination for the desired number of cycles. Protoplasts are then cultured in suitable culture media to obtain new transgenic plants. Transformation frequencies may be enhanced by a heat stock to protoplasts, use of carrier DNA and addition of PEG during electroporation.

(c) **Lipofection or liposomes:** Introduction of DNA into cells via liposomes is known as lipofection. Liposomes are small, microsopic lipid molecules produced by dispersing phospholipids in aqueous phase. DNAs are entrapped into liposomes and they are induced to fuse with protoplast using devices like PEG (Fig. 18.4). In this method, nucleic acids are stable due to encapsulation in liposomes. Liposome technique is also used in the gene transfer for the production of transgenic animals.

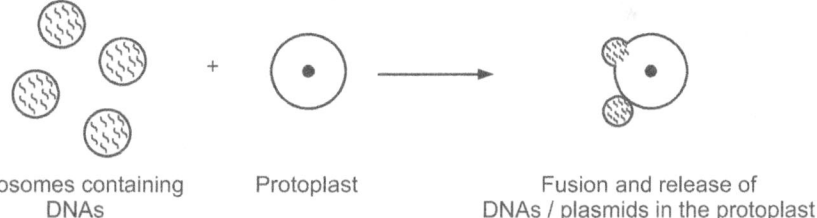

Liposomes containing   Protoplast   Fusion and release of
DNAs   DNAs / plasmids in the protoplast

Fig. 18.4: Gene transfer by lipofection

(d) **Microinjection:** In this method, the DNA solution is injected directly inside the cell using capillary glass micropipettes with the help of micromanipulators of a microinjection set of apparatus. The cells or protoplasts are immobilized on a solid support such as agarose and the DNA is injected into the nucleus or cytoplasm. (Fig. 18.5)

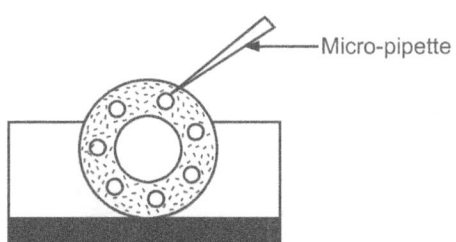

Fig. 18.5: Microinjection by agarose method

(e) **Macroinjection:** The injection of plasmid DNA into the lumen of developing inflorescence using a hypodermic syringe is called macroinjection. A marker gene is successfully macroinjected into the stem below the immature floral meristem, so as to reach the sporogenous tissue leading to production of transgenic plants.

(f) **Particle gun delivery or Ballistic method:** Tungsten or gold particles coated with genetically engineered DNA are used for transformation into plant cells with high velocity. The particles penetrate the cell wall and liberate the DNA, leading to the transformation of individual cells of the explant. Particle acceleration is achieved by using pressurized helium gas or electrostatic energy released by a droplet of water exposed to a high voltage. Helium pressurized device contains gas acceleration tube, rupture disc, stopping screen, macroparticles (DNA-coated) and target cells (Fig. 18.6). These components are enclosed in a chamber to enable for the creation of partial vacuum which facilitates particle acceleration. Helium gas is released in the acceleration tube after creation of partial vacuum and it break the rapture disc. This generates helium shock waves which accelerates the macroprojectile to which DNA coated microprojectiles are attached. The macroprojectile (macrocarrier) is adequately retained by a stopping screen while the microprojectiles (microparticles) pass this screen and embedded into the target tissue cells.

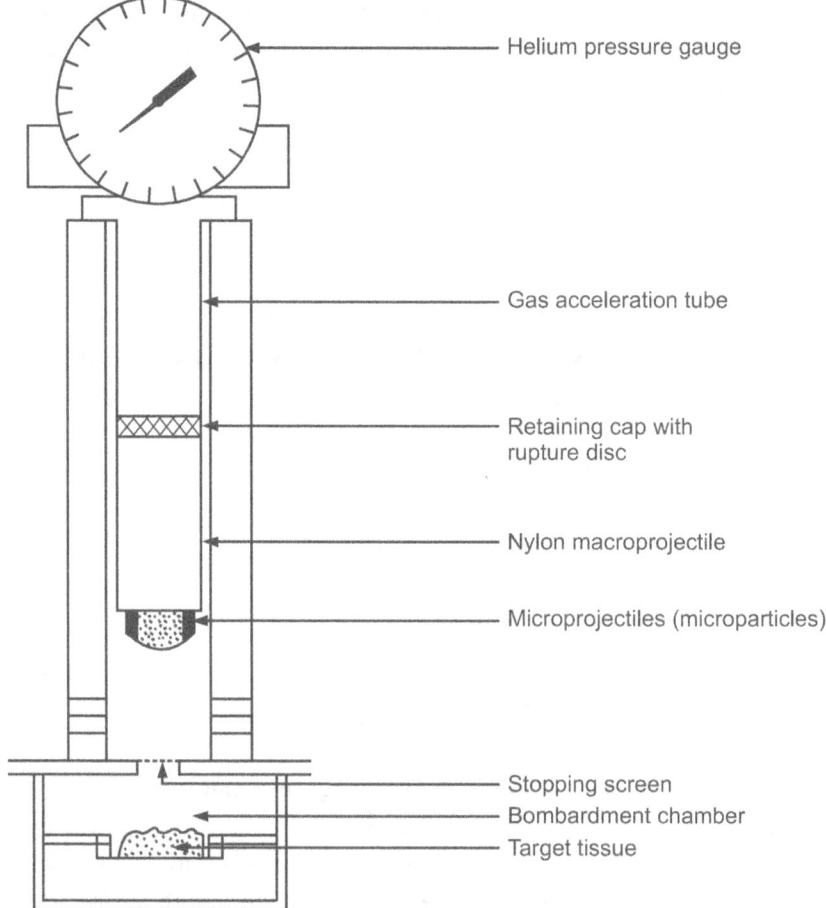

Fig. 18.6: Particle gun delivery by Ballistic method

(g) Pollen transformation: In this method, gene transfer is occurs by simply allowing DNA to soak in pollen grains just prior to their actual usage for pollination.

(h) Fibre-mediated gene transfer: In fibre-mediated gene transfer, DNA is delivered into the cell to cytoplasm and nucleus by silicon-carbide fibres (0.6 μm diameter, 10-50 μm length). The suspension culture cells are mixed with plasmid DNA having *gus* gene along with silicon-carbide fibres. The mixture is thoroughly mixed in a vortex mixer and the cells are estimated for their transient *gus* gene expression. This method is similar to microinjection. It is successfully used for maize and tobacco with cell cultures.

When plant cells are transformed by any of the transformation method, it is necessary to isolate the transformed cells. There are certain selectable marker genes present in vectors that facilitate the selection process. A selectable marker gene is introduced into the plat transformation vectors and a suitable selecting agent is added to the culture medium which favours the growth of only transformed cells (Table 18.1). The compounds (e.g. antibiotics, herbicides) that inhibit the growth but does not kill the wild type cells is preferred as a selecting agent in plant transformation. The reporter or scorable gene is also inserted into the transformation vector which allows for the detection of transformed cells or plants e.g. chloramphenicol acetyl transferase (*CAT*) gene, luciferase (*lux*) gene, β-galactosidase (*lac Z*) gene, β-glucuronidase (*GUS*) gene etc. The screening markers are mainly derived from bacterial genes coding for an enzyme that is readily detectable through the use of chromogenic, fluorigenic, photon emitting or radioactive substrates.

Table 18.1: Selectable marker genes used in plant transformation

Class	Selective agent	Marker gene	Enzyme encoded
Antibiotics	Bleomycin	*ble*	Unknown enzyme
	Streptomycin	*spt*	Streptomycin phosphotransferase
	Gentamycin	*gat*	Gentamycin acetyl transferase
	Methotrexate, trimethoprim	*dhfr*	Dihydrofolate reductase
	Hygromycin B	*hpt*	Hygromycin phosphotransferase
Herbicides	Bromoxynil	*bnl*	Bromoxynil nitrilase
	Chlorsulfuron, imidazolinones	*als*	Mutant forms of acetolactate synthase
	Phosphinothricin (Bialaphos)	*bar*	Phosphinothricin acetyltransferase
	Glyphosate	*aro A*	5-Enolpyruvate shikimate-3-phosphate (EPSP) - synthase

APPLICATIONS OF TRANSGENIC PLANTS

Plant genetic engineering has made possible the transfer of genes across all taxonomic barriers. Genes from bacteria, fungi, insects, viruses and even mammals have been introduced into plants. The different transgenic varieties are developed by recombinant DNA technology such as tomato, cotton, maize, potatoes, soyabean, oilseed rape, tobacco, corn, papaya, melon, cucumber, rice etc.

The production of homologous high quality plant material for pharmaceutical purpose requires the use of genetically defined plant material with adequate phytochemical and agrochemical characters. Medicinal plant breeding aims at the development and supply of such plant material to the growers and the pharmaceutical industry. The transgenic plants are developed to produce high degree of tolerance or resistance to pests and diseases. The different applications of transgenic plants are described as follows:

Production of pharmaceuticals

The pharmaceutical products can be manufactured by transgenic plants are antigens, antibodies, starch, oligopeptides, proteins, cyclodextrins, polymers, alkaloids, vitamins etc.

Hepatitis B surface antigen (HBsAg) in transgenic plants was made by **Arntzen** and associates. Antigens such as CT-B, LT-B, capsid protein, surface antigen, malaria epitope, rabies virus Drg 24 antigen are produced from transgenic plants of potato and tobacco. **Arntzen** and coworkers expressed hepatitis B surface antigen in tobacco to produce immunologically active ingredients via genetic engineering of plants. Various proteins such as serum albumin, human α-interferon, human erythropoietin, murine IgG and IgA immunoglobulins have been successfully expressed in plants. Antigens and antibodies expressed in plants can be administered orally or by parenteral route. The plants are capable of producing vaccines in large quantities at low cost. Transgenic potato tubers are used for the preparation of cyclodextrins (CDs). Genetic transformation and selection in the kanamycin-containing medium have resulted in transgenic *A. belladonna* plants which produce alkaloids and phenolics. 'Vitamin A' is synthesized from carotenoid which is precusor of vitamin A. Genetically engineered rice is prepared by introducing three genes associated with biosynthesis of carotenoid. The transgenic rice was rich in pro-vitamin A. The seeds of transgenic rice is yellow in colour due to pro-vitamin A, the rice is commonly known as golden rice. Different enzymes produced by transformed plants are shown in Table 18.2.

Table 18.2: Enzymes produced by transformed plants

Enzyme	Plant	Origin of gene
α-Amylase	Tobacco	*B. licheniformis*
β (1, 3-1, 4) Glucanase	Tobacco	*R. flavefaciens*
β (1, 3-1, 4) Glucanase	Barley	*B. macerans/B. amyloliquefaciens*
β (1, 4) Xylanase	Tobacco	*C. thermocellum / R. flavefaciens*
Phytase	Tobacco/soyabean	*A. niger*

Transgenic plants are used by biotechnology industries as 'bioreactor' for preparation of chemicals and pharmaceutical compounds.

Agricultural or horticultural uses

The production of new plant strains with improved resistance to infectious diseases is another major goal of plant breeders.

Virus resistant transgenic plants: Viruses are responsible for several diseases to plants causing considerable losses in agricultural products. There are three approaches for developing genetically engineered resistance in plants such as: (i) expression of the virus-coat protein (CP) gene, (ii) expression of satellite RNAs and (iii) Use of antisense viral RNA. Coat protein-mediated resistance (CPMR) is the most favoured strategy to make virus-resistant plants. Virus-resistance transgenics have been developed by introducing either CP gene or replicate gene encoding sequences.

Protection against fungal and bacterial pathogens may be obtained by transferring a fungal or bacterial gene for virulence into the target plants. The success depends on the type of strains, plant species, controlled glasshouse conditions and natural field conditions.

Insect-resistant transgenic plants: Insects are serious pests of agricultural products in the field and during storage. Insects belonging to the orders Coleoptera, Lepidoptera and Diptera are the most serious plant pests. Bacillus thuringiensis (*Bt*), a Gram-positive soil bacterium has been employed as an insecticide. The insecticidal toxin of *B. thuringiensis* has been classified into cry I, cry II, cry III and cry IV based on insecticidal activities.

The *Bt* gene is isolated and introduced into Ti-DNA plasmid of *Agrobacterium tumifaciens*. The genetically modified *A. tumifaciens* is allowed to infect the desired plant. The first group to report success in producing insect resistant plants by inserting *Bt* gene was Belgian biotech company. The *Bt* gene inserted into tobacco plants produced enough of the endotoxin to kill *Manduca sexta* larva attempting to feed on their leaves. Many transgenic crops having *cry* gene are developed. e.g. cotton, maize, potato, tobacco, rice, soyabean, brinjal, cabbage, corn etc. Transgenic cotton containing *Bt* gene is introduced in India by Maharashtra Hybrid Seeds Co. (MAHYCO), Jalna.

Herbicide-resistant transgenic plants: Herbicides are used in agriculture for killing the unwanted plants (weeds). Weeds compete with crop plants for nutrients, moisture and light and cause considerable decline in the yields. Herbicides such as chlorsulfuron, imazapur, DL-phosphinothricin, bromoxynil are effective for broad spectrum weed control. They act by inactivating target proteins or enzymes present in plants. They are non-selective and kill the crop plants also. Genes coding for herbicide sensitive proteins have been isolated from plants and used to produce several herbicide resistant transgenic crop plants.

A herbicide resistant gene for EPSPS (5-enolpyruvate – shikimate – 3 – phosphate – synthase) is isolated from plants resistant to glyphosate (Roundup herbicide). The resistant gene for EPSPS is transferred to petunia plants and transgenic petunia is developed which is resistant to glyphosate. Roundup tolerance in transgenic tobacco plants has been introduced by using other EPSPS genes along with chloroplast transit peptide sequence.

QUESTIONS

(A) Short answer questions:
1. What is lipofection?
2. Explain the gene transfer method by electroporation.

(B) Long answer questions:
1. Write short note on:
    (a) Gene transfer by Ballistic method
    (b) Application of transgenic plants
2. Explain in detail *Agrobacterium* mediated gene transfer

(C) Multiple choice questions:

1. Transgenic plant which is now cultivated in India is _____ .
   - (a) Bt. cotton
   - (b) Jowar
   - (c) Banana
   - (c) Grape

2. _____ is most effective chemical for DNA uptake into protoplasts.
   - (a) Polyethylene glycol
   - (b) $NaNO_3$
   - (c) DMSO
   - (d) Indole acetic acid

CHAPTER 19

ANIMAL TISSUE CULTURE

CONTENTS
    INTRODUCTION
    ANIMAL TISSUE CULTURE MEDIA
        Natural Media
        Artificial Media
    TYPES OF ANIMAL CELL CULTURE
        Primary Cell Culture
        Organ Culture
        Cell Lines
    TRANSGENIC ANIMALS
        Transgenic Process
        Applications of Transgenic Animals

INTRODUCTION

The animal cell culture is a technique in which cells or tissue are obtained from animals, grown and maintained in a suitable medium. Animal tissue culture is divided as organ culture (organotypic) and cell culture (histotypic). In organ culture, whole embryonic organ or small tissue fragments are cultured in-vitro in such a manner that they retain their some or all of the histological features. Cell culture is derived from dispersed cells taken from original tissue, from a primary culture or from cell line or cell strain by enzymatic or mechanical disaggregation. The culture produced by the cell or tissue taken from an organism is called as primary culture. The sequence of culture obtained from the first subcultivation of the primary culture is called 'cell line'. Primary cultures are heterogeneous and slow growing. The animal cells can grow only to a limited generations and it require controlled physiochemical environment (O_2, CO_2, pH, temperature, osmotic pressure etc.) and defined physiological conditions.

The first attempt to grow animal cells in culture is attributed to **Ross Harrison** in 1907. He was able to cultivate frog embryonic nerve cells using the hanging drop technique. The discovery of antibiotics in the late 1940's led to the development of improved cell culture techniques by reducing microbial contamination. During this period, many human carcinoma cell lines (HeLa cell line) were isolated and grown in culture. **Wilmut** and co-workers successfully produced a transgenic sheep named **Dolly** through nuclear transfer technique.

ANIMAL TISSUE CULTURE MEDIA

Design of animal tissue culture media is more difficult than that of microorganisms and plant cultures. Animal cell culture media (Fig. 19.1) are used to support the survival as well as growth by synthesizing certain chemical constituents from inorganic substances. It is classified as natural and artificial or synthesized media. Selection of media is dependent on type of cells and main objective of culture.

Fig. 19.1: Animal cell culture media

Natural media:

This media are obtained from natural sources such as plasma clots or coagulans, biological fluid and tissue extracts.

Plasma clots or coagulans are available commercially as liquid plasma in silicone ampoules or lyophilized plasma. Biological fluids are obtained in the form of serum from human blood, placental cord blood, horse blood, calf blood or in the form of biological fluids such as amniotic fluid, ascitic fluid, coconut water, insect haemolymph serum, aqueous humor from eye, culture filtrate etc.

Blood plasma: Blood plasma provides a nutritive substrate and a supporting structure for many types of cultures. It protects the cells and tissues from excessive traumatic damage during subculture and also used for conditioning the surface of glass for better attachment of cells. Plasma from the chicken is preferred to mammalian plasma because it form a clear and solid coagulum even when diluted several times. The plasma is obtained by centrifugation of whole blood before coagulation. The tissue is then placed in plasma and coagulation encouraged by addition of a small amount of tissue extract or thrombin. This is require for a solid support to continue growth and activity for the cells in the culture.

Blood serum: Blood serum (fibrinogen free plasma) with or without other nutritive substances is used in animal tissue culture. It is liquid exuded from coagulating blood and is filtered through Millipore filters. The sera used in tissue culture are calf (bovine), fetal bovine, horse and human serum. Calf and fetal bovine serum are most widely used in animal cell culture. Human serum is sometimes used in conjunction with some human cell lines but it is necessary to screen for viruses such as HIV and hepatitis B. Blood serum is highly complex mixture of plasma proteins, peptides, lipids, carbohydrates, hormones, enzymes and minerals.

The chicken serum is prepared by the coagulation of fluid plasma. The plasma is coagulated by adding embryo tissue extract or equivalent amount of thrombin. The tubes are incubated for several hours at 37°C. The coagulated plasma is broken up into fragments and then serum is separated by centrifugation. The mammalian blood is kept at room temperature for an hour for the coagulation. The clot is removed by a glass rod and then centrifuged at 3000 rpm for 30 minutes and the mammalian serum is separated.

Tissue extracts used in animal cell culture includes embryo, spleen, liver, bone marrow, leukocyte etc. Chick embryo extract is most commonly used and substituted by mixture of amino acids. Chick embryo extract is prepared from 10 to 12 days old embryos. The embryos are isolated from the egg and then mixed by using homogenizer with measured quantity of balanced salt solutions (e.g. 2 ml/embryo). The crude extract is fractionated to give fractions of either high or low molecular weight. The low molecular weight fraction promoted cell proliferation while the high molecular weight fraction promoted pigment and cartilage cell differentiation. It is centrifuged and again diluted 10 to 15 times. It has been dried from the frozen state and stored.

Artificial media:

Synthetic or artificial media are prepared by adding organic and inorganic nutrients, vitamins, salts, serum proteins, carbohydrates, O_2 and CO_2 gas phases. Different types of synthetic media are prepared for a variety of cells and tissues to be cultured e.g. Minimal essential medium (MEM), CMRL 1066, RPMI 1640, Ham's F 12 Fischers etc. Synthetic media are classified into two types as serum containing media and serum free media.

Serum containing media: In animal cell culture media, 5 to 20% serum is added in many serum free medium. Serum is the source of basic nutrients, provides several hormones (cortisone, testosterone, insulin), growth factors (platelet desired growth factors, PDGF, fibroblast growth factor) and proteins like fibronectin, albumin and transferrin. It also provides minerals (Na, K, Fe, Zn etc.), protease inhibitors and acts as buffer. It binds and neutralizes different toxins. Serum is important source of all nutrients still it has many disadvantages.

- Serum is most expensive ingredient in the culture media.
- It increases difficulties and cost of down stream processing.
- It varius from batch to batch because it is not chemically defined. Changing serum batches requires extensive testing to ensure the replacement is similar or close to previous batches.
- Some growth factors may be inadequate and may not be supplemented.
- Supply of serum is less due to spread of disease among the cattle or drought in the cattle rearing areas.
- Serum is source of contamination of viruses, mycoplasma, prions etc.

Serum free media: Serum free media are developed to overcome the limitations of serum. It has the ability to make the medium more selective for a particular cell type. The overgrowth by stromal fibroblasts can be reduced effectively in breast and skin cultures by using MCDB 170 and 153, melanocytes can be cultivated in the absence of fibroblasts and keratinocytes. Serum variability and toxicity is avoided by replacing serum. Down stream processes and bioassays are easy in absence of serum. Serum free media also have many disadvantages in routine use.

- Growth is slow in serum free media and only for few generations.
- Purity of reagents and more control about pH and temperature of media is require in serum free media.
- The availability of properly controlled serum free media is quite limited, hence preparation of this media require more time in laboratory.
- Most of the media are specific to one cell type and laboratories face problems in maintaining cell lines of several different origins.

Fig. 19.2: CO_2 Incubator for growth of cell lines

Physicochemical studies are also important for growth of different cell lines. The optimal temperature for cell culture is dependent on the body temperature of the animal from which the cells are obtained. The temperature recommended for most human and warm blooded animal cell lines is 37°C. Osmolality between 260 m Osm/kg and 320 m Osm/kg are quite acceptable for most cell lines. Most cultured cells have a fairly wide tolerance for osmotic pressure. Buffers are incorporated into the medium to stabilize the pH. Exogenous CO_2 may be required to some cell lines to prevent the total loss of dissolved CO_2 and bicarbonate from the medium. Cell lines incubated in CO_2 incubator for growth is shown in Fig. 19.2. Each media is prepared by the addition of biocarbonate and CO_2 tension for achieving the correct pH and Osmolality. Most cell lines grow well at pH 7.4 phenol red (red at pH 7.4) is commonly used as an indicator for detection of pH. Most of cells require oxygen for respiration in vivo and it is major constituent of the gas phase. The viscosity of the culture medium is influenced by the serum content. Cell damage is avoided mainly by increasing the viscosity of the medium with carboxymethyl cellulose (CMC) or polyvinyl pyrrolidone. Balanced salt solution (BSS) is composed of inorganic salts and it is used as a diluent for concentrates of amino acids and vitamins to make complete media.

TYPES OF ANIMAL CELL CULTURE

Animal cell cultures are classified as primary cell culture, organ culture, tissue culture and cell lines.

Primary cell culture:

A piece of tissue from the organism is usually quite complex and it contains connective tissue cells, variety of blood cells and reticuloendothelial cells. The first cell suspension is isolated and then inoculated into a new culture vessel along with fresh medium, such culture is called primary cell culture or primary cell line. Primary cell line is more suitable for vaccine production because it minimizes the probability of in-vitro transformation of cells to malignancy. Three stages are used for isolation of primary cell culture such as (i) isolation of the tissue (ii) disaggregation of tissue and (iii) seeding the culture into the culture vessel. All stages are performed in laminar bench to avoid contamination (Fig. 19.3).

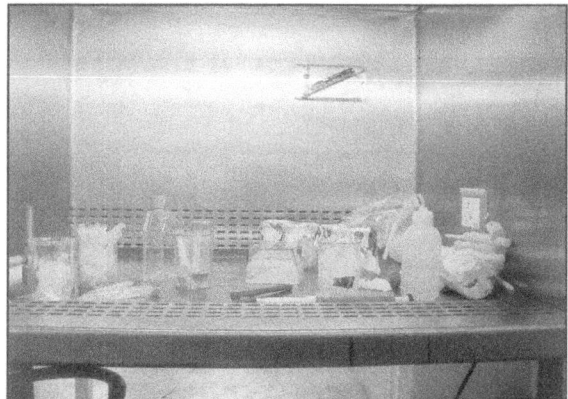

Fig. 19.3: Laminar bench used for isolation and disaggregation of tissue

   (i)   Isolation of the tissue: The explant from an excised portion of the body of an animal is used for the culture of animal cells in a suitable nutrient medium. The major explant tissues are collected (Fig. 19.4) from laboratory animals like mice, rabbit, guinea pig etc. Mouse embryos are a convenient source of cells for undifferentiated fibroblastic cultures. The explants from humans such as smooth muscle cells, alveolar cells, macrophages, leukocytes etc are isolated and cultured in simulated media. Organ from which cells are to be isolated are surface sterilized with 70% alcohol and then removed aseptically. Excised tissues from the explant source are immediately transferred in sterile nutrient medium or a well balanced salt solution (BSS) containing antibiotics. The tissues isolate from explant is either stored in freeze or used immediately.

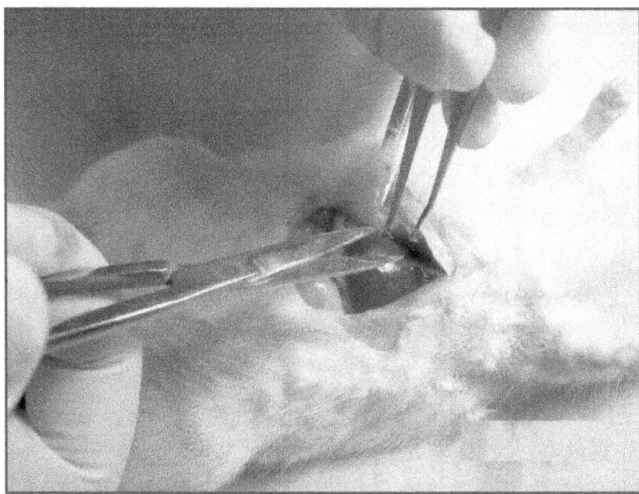

Fig. 19.4: Collection of explant tissues for cell lines

(ii) Disaggregation of tissue: A primary cell culture is obtained by disaggregating the tissue mechanically, enzymatically or by use of chelating agent (Fig. 19.5)

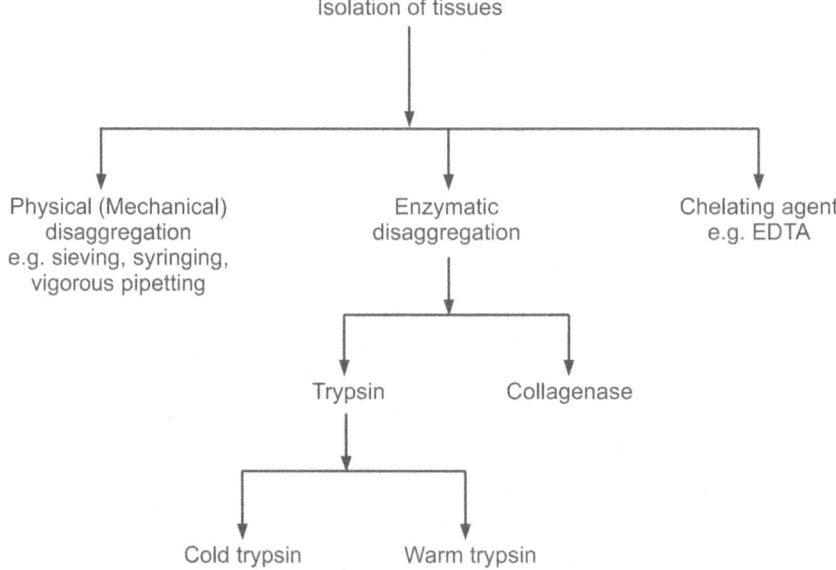

Fig. 19.5: Techniques for tissue disaggregation

Mechanical or physical disaggregation: The physical disaggregation is force based method in which the tissue is carefully sliced and then exposed for sieving. The tissues may be forced through a syringe and needle or repeatedly pipetted. Sieving is most important method where tissues are forced through gradually reduced mesh sieves. The cells are counted by hemocytometer and transferred into medium to get the suspension of cells (10^4 cells/ml). This method gives a cell suspension more quickly than enzymatic disaggregation but may cause mechanical damage.

Enzymatic disaggregation: The enzymes used in enzymatic disaggregation are trypsin, mucase, pronase, collagenase, papain, pancreatin elastase etc. This method is labour intensive and involves damage of cells. Code trypsin and collagenase enzymes are commonly used in tissue disaggregation.

The process of treatment of the tissues with trypsin is called as trypsinization. It is classified as warm trypsinization and cold trypsinization. In warm trypsinization, the tissue sample is chopped into 2 to 3 pieces and then transferred into conical flask containing 100 ml warm trypsin (36.5°C). The contents are mixed for 4 hours and then dissociated cells are collected at every 30 minutes. The process may be repeated by adding fresh trypsin and incubating the contents. The dissociated cells are counted by using haemocytometer and pooled in the medium containing serum for growth. In cold trypsinization, the tissue sample is chopped similar to warm trypsinization. The whole contents are washed by using BSS and then transferred in glass vial which is placed on ice for soaking with trypsin for 4 to 5 hours. Trypsin is removed and tissues are incubated at 36.5°C for 20 to 30 minutes. Serum (10 ml) is added in vials and cells are dispersed by repeated pipetting. The cell are counted, adjusted the cell density (10^4 cell/ml) and incubated for growth.

The disaggregation by trypsin may damage some epithelial cells or it becomes ineffective for fibrous connective tissue. Collagenase has more effective and simple method for disaggregation of normal and malignant tissues. Extracellular matrix often contains collagen mainly in connective tissues and muscles. Hence, collagenase has been first choice for the treatment to tissues. Biopsy tissues are mainly disaggregated in BSS containing antibiotics. All chopped tissues are washed and then transferred in complete medium containing collagenase. The cells are separated by centrifugation and cultured in the medium for the growth.

Chelating agents: Chelating agents are mainly used for preparation of cell suspensions from established cultures. Calcium and magnesium ions are treated with chelating agents (e.g. EDTA) which are require for epithelium tissues for its integrity.

   (iii) Seeding the culture into the culture vessel: The dissociated (primary) cells grow well when seeded on culture plates (Fig. 19.6) at high density.

Fig. 19.6: Culture vessel (T-25 culture flask)

Most of the cells require support of substrate for the growth. These cells are called anchorage dependent (adherent) cells and it grows as monolayer. Some cells do not require substrate called anchorage independent (suspension culture) cells. The adherent cells can be obtained from organs (e.g. liver, kidney etc) which are fixed at a place. These cells have positive surface charge except neuron and muscle cells. Anchorage dependent cells may grow well by adhering to negatively charged surface. Substrates used for growth of such cells are glass (coverslip, slide, test tubes, plates or flasks), plastic and metals (stainless steel, titanium etc). The anchorage independent cells or suspension cells are generally cultivated in liquid medium and they do not attach to the surface of the vessel. It is classified into batch culture, feed batch culture, perfusion culture, semi-continuous culture and continuous flow culture.

Organ culture:

Organ can be cultured in-vitro for normal development and to avoid damage of tissue. Media used for growing organ cultures are similar to tissue culture. Growing embryonic organ culture is easy than the normal organs isolated from animals. Plasma clot or watch glass method, agar gel method, raft method, grid method etc are mainly used for organ culture.

Plasma clot or watch glass method: Explant is cultured on suitably prepared plasma clot kept in watch glass. Plasma clot is prepared by mixing 15 drops of plasma with five drops of embryo extract. The watch glass is placed over a pad of cotton wool contained in a Petri dish (Fig. 19.7). The cotton wool is kept moist to prevent evaporation in the dish. Plate is closed with lid, sealed with paraffin wax, incubated at 37.5°C and fresh clots have been provided every 2 to 4 days. The method is modified by using raft of lens paper or rayon net which is used to place the tissue. The movement of the raft allows for easy transfer of tissue, feeding of culture and replacement of media.

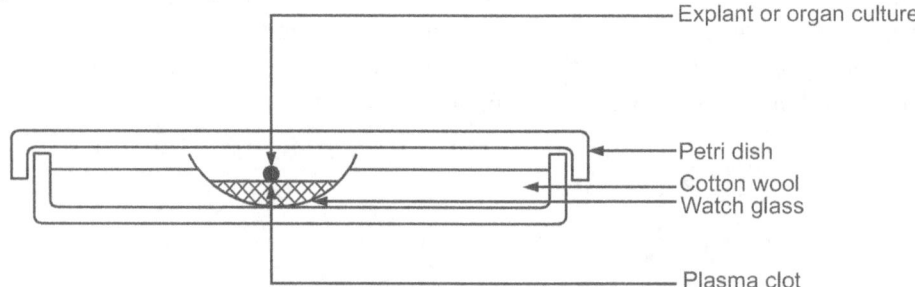

Fig. 19.7: Plasma clot method of organ culture

Agar gel method: Medium containing all nutrients are solidified by using 1% agar and then kept in embryological watch glass. Defined media with or without serum are also used to give mechanical support for organ culture. Embryonic organ or explant is transferred on surface of agar (Fig. 19.8), sealed with paraffin wax and subcultured into fresh agar gels after 5 to 6 days.

The different explantation techniques are used for cultivation of pieces of fresh tissues isolated from the organism such as slide culture, carrel flask culture, roller test tube culture etc. These techniques are modified and also use for embryo and organ culture.

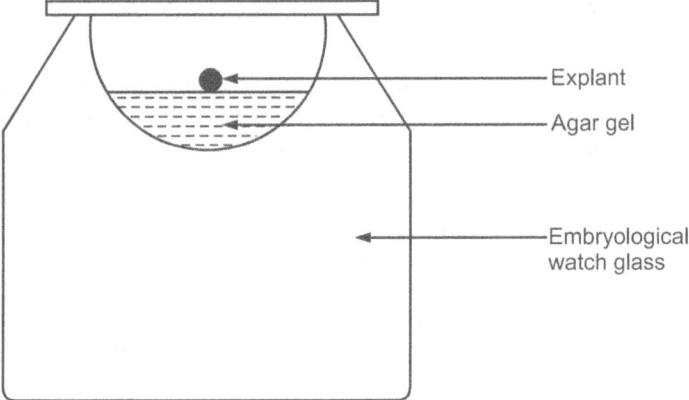

Fig. 19.8: Agar gel method of organ culture

Cell Lines

The primary culture may not be viable for a long time because the cells utilizes all nutrients of the medium. Hence, the cells are diluted with fresh medium and passed into fresh culture flask for maintaining the viability of cells. When primary culture is subcultured or transferred into fresh medium then it is called cell line (Fig. 19.9).

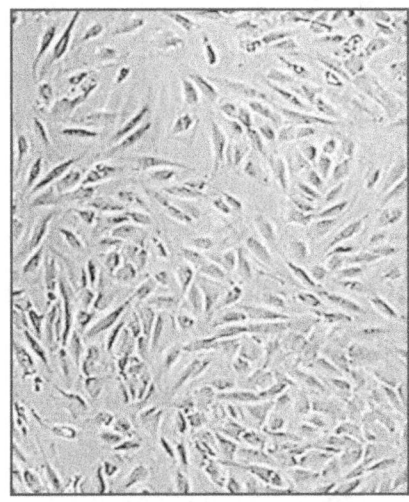
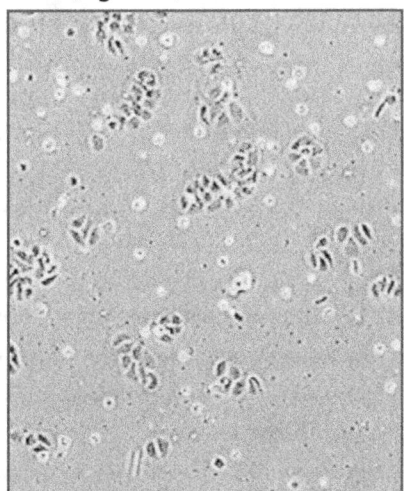

(a) Magnification (10 ×)   (b) Magnification (4 ×)

Fig. 19.9: Animal cell lines

Subculturing is required on fresh medium at regular intervals for growth as cell line. The first subculture gives rise to a secondary culture and so on. Number of times that the culture has been subcultured is called passage number and the number of doublings that the cell population has undergone is called generation number. Some cells of secondary cell cultures are transformed spontaneously or chemically. Such cell line or strain have the capacity for infinite survival (immortal). These cells are called continuous cell lines, cancerous cell lines or established cell lines or immortal cell lines. Continuous cell line may be discontinued by the effect of mutation, chemical or viruses. This concept of change in continuous cell line is called 'in-vitro transformation'.

Cell lines are classified as finite cell lines and continuous cell lines (Table 19.1). Finite cell lines can grow only for limited number of cell generations and it form monolayer. These are slow growing cells and they require 24 to 96 hours for one generation. The cell lines are anchorage dependent and they are invariably euploid. High serum concentration is required for growth of finite cell lines and they have low cloning efficiency. Established cell lines are obtained from transformed cell lines or cancerous cells.

Table 19.1: Types of cell lines

Cell lines	Source	Age	Ploidy	Morphology
Finite cell line				
IMR – 90 / WI – 38/ MRC – 9/ MRC – 5	Human lung	Embryonic	Diploid	Fibroblast
Continuous cell line				
HeLa/He La-S3	Human cervix	Adult	Aneuploid	Epithelial
LS/L·929/S·180	Mouse	Adult	Aneuploid	Fibroblast
P-388D1	Mouse	Adult	Aneuploid	Lymphocytic
EB – 3	Human blood	Juvenile	Diploid	Lymphocytic
3T3 – A31 / 3T3 – L1	Mouse	Embryonic	Aneuploid	Fibroblast
CHO – K1	Chinese hamster ovary	Adult	Diploid	Fibroblast
HT – 29	Human colon	Adult	Aneuploid	Epithelial

These continuous cells lines have following characteristics:
- They have short generation time i.e. 12 to 24 hours.
- Existence of altered ploidy i.e. heteroploidy or aneuploidy due to altered chromosome number.
- They grow has monolayer or suspension culture.
- Cloning efficiency is high and they grow well in low concentration of serum also.
- Cell lines are anchorage independent.

TRANSGENIC ANIMALS

Transgenesis is a new technology for altering the characteristics of animals by directly changing the genetic material. It has been gaining application among biotechnologists since the development of transgenic 'super mice' in 1982 and the development of the first mice to produce a human drug (tissue plasminogen activator) in 1987. Transgenic sheeps and goats are being used to produce recombinant proteins secreted in milk. In pharmaceutical development, transgenic animals and plants may be used as 'bioreactors' for chemical production. The transgene is introduced into a fertilized ovum or cells of an early stage embryo by microinjection, manipulation of embryonic stem cells or using retroviral vectors.

Transgenic process:

The first step in developing a transgenic organism is to identify, prepare and purify the DNA coding of the particular trait desired. The transgene contains not only the gene of interest, but a promoter sequence which controls the gene's function. The purity of the DNA construct is important in order to avoid toxic effect on the embryo. Transgenes can be introduced into animals by three methods. Each involves gene transfer into a fertilized ovum or into cells of an early stage embryo. Modified embryos are them implanted into the uterus of a host animal where they develop into genetically modified offspring.

Microinjection: The microinjection method was first documented in 1966. This is most commonly used method to produce genetically modified animals. In this method, eggs are harvested from superovulated animals and fertilized in-vitro. A microtube is used to hold the fertilized egg and an extremely fine needle used to inject DNA directly into the nucleus (Fig. 19.10). The embryo is then implanted in the uterus of a surrogate mother. After birth, the animals are tested to determine if they have the transgene and corresponding desired traits. This method is commonly used to produce transgenic fish, insects, birds and mammals.

Retroviral vectors: Retroviruses can be used to infect cell of an early stage embryo prior to implantation. Viruses are effective vectors for DNA, however, transgene size is limited to 8 to 10 kilobases. The offspring are chimeric and transmission only occurs if the retrovirus integrates into some of the germ cells. Embryos that carry the transgene can be frozen and stored for implantation.

Embryonic stem cell: Embryonic stem (ES) cells are pluripotent cells isolated from inner cells mass of early embryos. Embryonic stem cells can be genetically modified in the laboratory and incorporated into blastocysts for implantation. Embryonic transfer is then conducted resulting in the production of a chimeric animal (Fig. 19.11). In production of chimeric mouse, the ES cells of black mouse intermingle with that of albino. The microinjected embryo is transplanted into the uterus of a surrogate mother. The progeny born has black and white skin colour. Such mouse was called chimera or chimeric mouse. Transgenic mice that carry a knockout gene is called knockout mice. Now it is possible to select and knockout (remove) a gene and make genetic modifications in the embryonic cells and mouse. These animals are particularly useful in the study of genetic control of the developmental process.

Recently it has become possible to extend the nuclear transplantation procedure, originally carried out in amphibians to mammals. The first mammal to be cloned in this way was 'Dolly'. **Ian Wilmut** and his colleagues at Roslin Institute, Edinburgh, Scotland developed first mammalian clone 'Dolly' in 1996. 'Dolly' is the first transgenic lamb to be produced by nuclear transfer. She was produced from foetal fibroblast cells that were modified by the addition of the human gene coding for blood clotting factor IX together with a marker gene.

Nuclear transfer has been used successfully in cloning several mammalian species including sheep, mice, cattle, cats and monkeys.

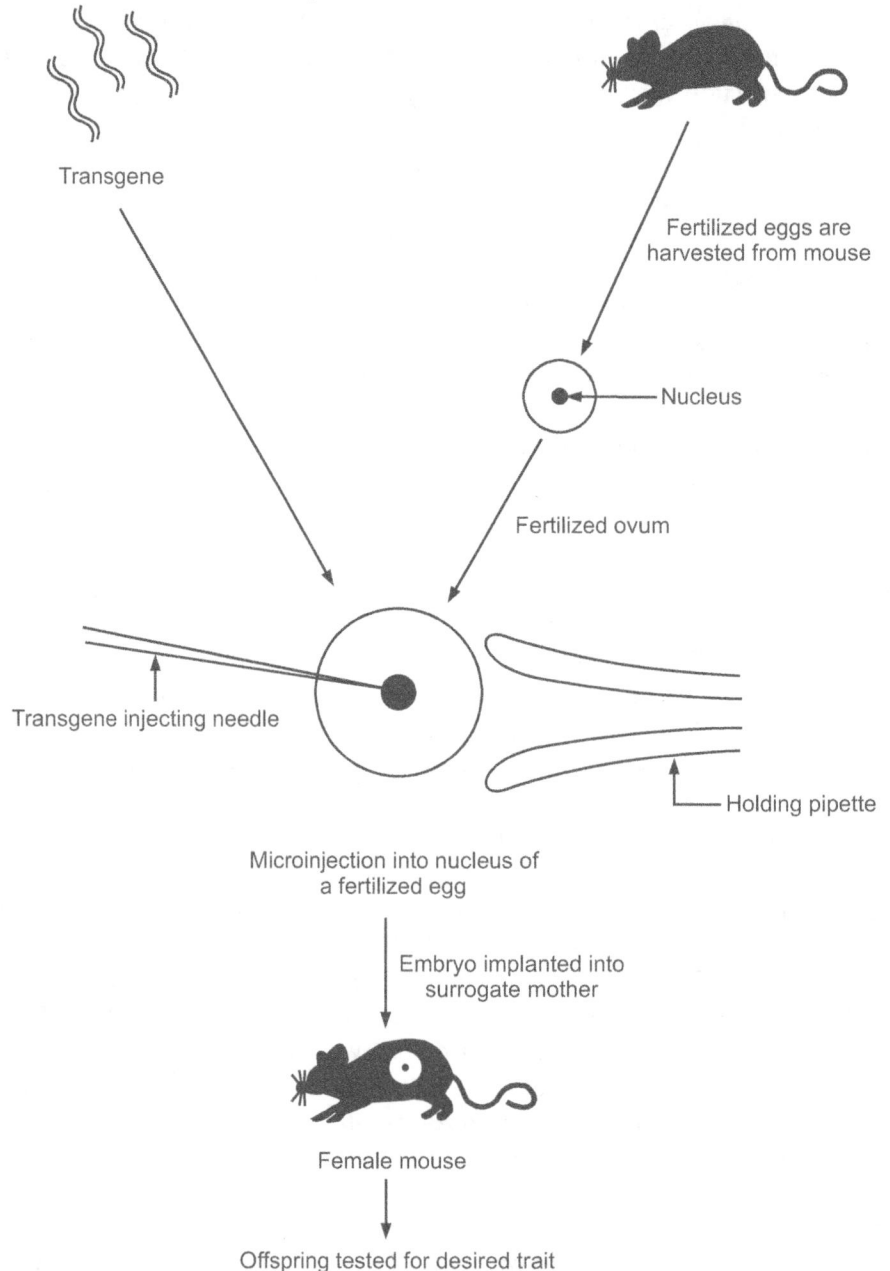

Fig. 19.10: Gene transfer by microinjection

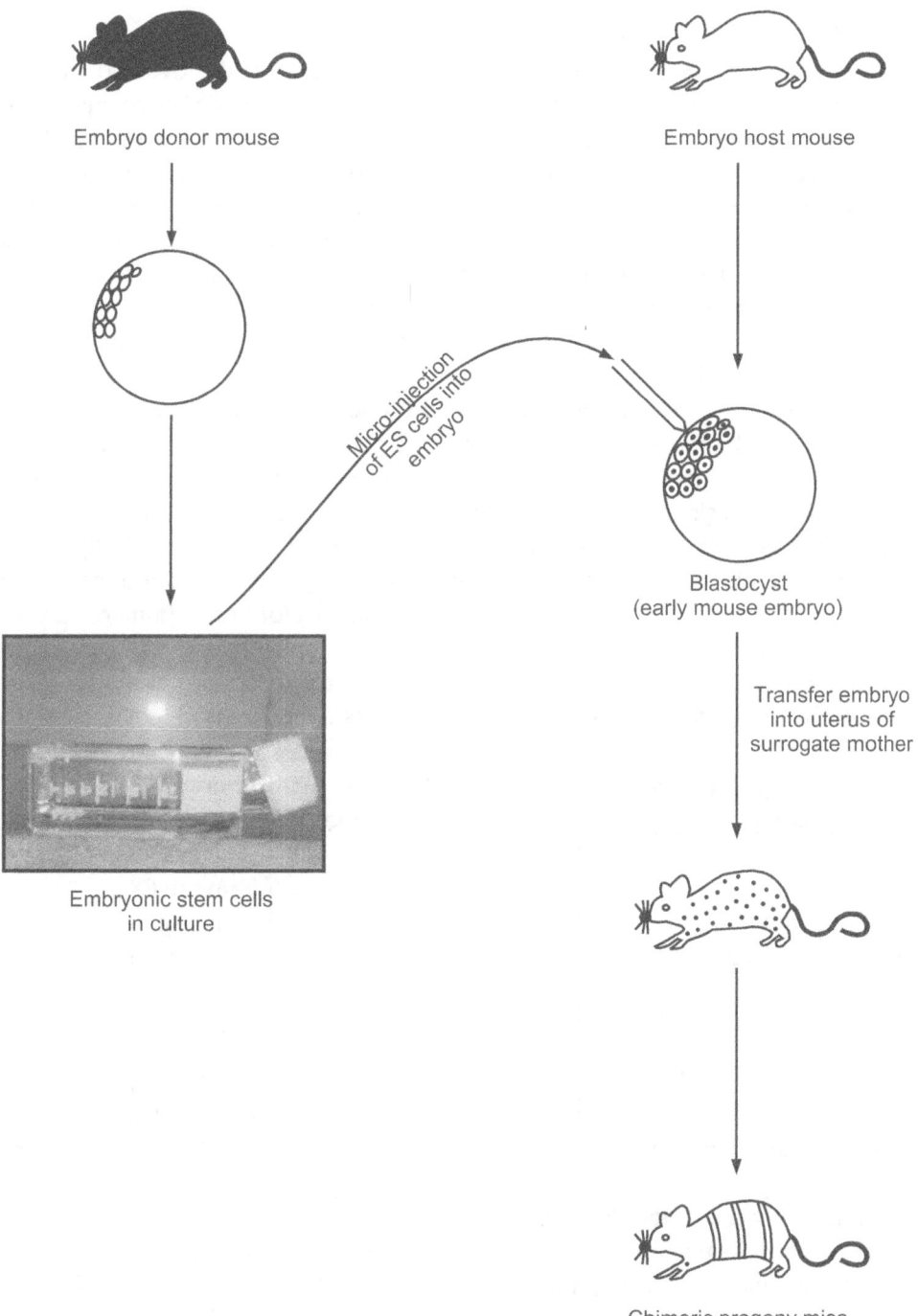

Fig. 19.11: Production of chimeric mouse by embryonic stem cell transplantation

Applications of transgenic animals:

The animal production industry is gradually reaching towards revolution due to the development of genetic map, knowledge of expression of genes and techniques for large propagation. Transgenic animals are used as tools in research and for the production of recombinant proteins. The main applications of transgenic animals are described as follows:

Studying gene function: Transgenic expression is not only used to breed animals which have specific traits but also to breed animals that are lacking specific genes. This technique is called as knockout or gene targeting. Transgenic technology was perfected using mice in the early 1980s. Knockout mice which lack functional forms of specific genes are produced which provide information about the function of the knocked out gene. This technique allows scientists to target specific genes for inactivation and mutagenesis.

Molecular pharming or pharmaceutical production: Transgenic sheep, goat and cattle are bring used as 'bioreactors' to produce important human proteins in milk. Milk is produced in large quantities and can be collected without harm to the animals. Livestock are used to produce medicines and nutraceuticals. A transgenic animals mainly produce the desired drug at high levels without endangering its own health and pass its ability to produce the drug at high levels to its offspring. Proteins commonly produced from transgenic animal includes the blood clotting protein Factor IX, lactoferrin, human protein C, alpha–1–antitrypsin etc. Drugs developed in transgenic animals are listed in Table 19.2. Human drugs purified from animal milk or blood are likely to require exceptional levels of safety testing before animal and human health concerns are addressed to the satisfaction of consumers.

Table 19.2: Drug developed in transgenic animals

Drug	Transgenic animal	Use
Factors VIII, IX	Sheep	Blood clotting factor, hemophilia
Alpha-1-antitrypsin (AAT)	Sheep	Emphysema
Tissue plasminogen activator (tPA)	Goat	Treatment for blood clots.
Lactoferrin	Cow	Infant formula additive
Human protein C	Pig	Anticoagulant
Hemoglobin	Pig	Blood substitute
Cystic fibrosis transmembrane (CFTR)	Sheep, mouse	Treatment for blood clots.

Biomedical research model: Transgenic animals can be created which simulate human diseases in which defective genes play a major role. Human mutant genes are inserted into mice and other animals, causing them to suffer from human diseases. Such transgenic animals are used as a disease model for investigations into the development of the particular disease and medicine to prevent it. These animal models facilitate the identification of chemically induced mutations, gene expression and are instrumental in identifying signal transduction pathways and hormonal factors that modulate the activity of genes. Transgenic animals are used as model for diseases such as cancer, autoimmune diseases, diabetes, cardiovascular, Alzheimer's disease, neurological diseases, AIDS, cystic fibrosis, hypercholesterolemia etc. Transgenics are also important research tools for studying environmental pollutants, bone marrow, germinal cell mutations and target organ susceptibility.

The mouse is most widely used animal model in transgenic research. The genetic makeup of the mouse resembles that of humans, rapid reproduction rates and relative ease of genetic manipulation are the important characteristics for animal model mainly observe in mice. Rat, sheep, cow, goat and pigs are commonly used as research models and for production of protein based pharmaceuticals.

Transgenic animals in agriculture: Transgenic pigs bearings a human metallothionein promoter/porcine growth–hormone gene construct showed significant improvements in economically important traits such as growth rate, feed conversion and body fat/muscle ratio. Transgenic sheep carrying a keratin–IGF–I construct showed that expression in the skin and the amount of clear fleece is about 6 to 7% greater in transgenic than in non–transgenic animals.

Dairy production is an attractive field for targeted genetic modification. It is possible to produce milk with a modified lipid composition by modulating the enzymes involved in lipid metabolism or to increase curd and cheese production by enhancing expression of the casein gene family in the mammary gland. Transgenic applications used in animals to enhance disease resistance includes the transfer of major histocompatibility - complex genes, T–cell receptor genes and immunoglobulin genes. Transgenic constructs bearing the immunoglobulin - A (I_gA) gene have successfully introduced into pigs, sheep and mice in an attempt to increase resistance against infections.

Transgenic animals are playing major role in the drug development process and the potential benefits to human and animal health.

QUESTIONS

(A) Short answer questions:
1. Write advantages and disadvantages of:
    (i) Serum-free media
    (ii) Enzymatic disaggregation
    (iii) Natural media for ATC.
2. Write the difference between:
    (i) Finite cell line and continuous cell line.
    (ii) Plasma clot method and agar gel method.
    (iii) Blood plasma and blood serum.
3. Write the method of preparation of:
    (i) Chicken serum
    (ii) Mammalian serum
    (iii) Primary cell culture

4. Explain the followings:
   (i) Established cell lines
   (ii) BSS

(B) Long answer questions:
1. Explain in detail different methods used for disaggregation of animal tissue.
2. Write a note on:
   (a) Transgenic animals
   (b) Animal tissue culture media
   (c) Organ culture
3. What are transgenic animals? Explain in detail different applications of transgenic animals.

(C) Multiple choice questions:
1. **Wilmut** and co-workers successfully produced a transgenic sheep named _____ through nuclear transfer technique.
   (a) Polly   (b) Dolly
   (c) Tally   (d) Sally
2. _____ cells are pluripotent cells isolated from inner cells mass of early embryos.
   (a) Retroviral   (b) Blood
   (c) Embryonic stem   (d) Fibroblast

(D) Match the following:

(A)		(B)	
(a)	CMRL – 1066	(i)	Natural media
(b)	IMR – 90	(ii)	Continuous cell line
(c)	HeLa – S3	(iii)	Finite cell line
(d)	Coagulants	(iv)	Artificial media

(E) Fill in the blanks:
1. _____ extract is most commonly used for growth of animal cells and its substituted by mixture of amino acids.
2. The first transgenic animal, Dolly, was developed using nuclear transfer of _____ cells.

■■■

CHAPTER 20
BIOTECHOLOGY AND ETHICS

CONTENTS
    INTRODUCTION
    BIOTECH PRODUCTS AND ITS SAFETY
    INTELLECTUAL PROPERTY RIGHT (IPR) AND PROTECTION (IPP)
    IN-VITRO FERTILIZATION (IVF) IN HUMANS
        Infertilities in Humans
        Human Artificial Insemination
        In-Vitro Fertilization and Embryo Transfer

INTRODUCTION

Recent advances in biotechnology and their applications are most frequently associated with controversies. Ethical, Legal and Social Implications (ELSI) of biotechnology broadly covers the relationship between biotechnology and society with particular reference to ethical and legal aspects. The recent development in biotechnology deals with genetic manipulations of bacteria, actinomycetes, fungi, viruses, plants, birds and animals. The developments in this area are beneficial to the fied of healthcare, pharmaceuticals, agriculture and environmental management. Biotechnological developments are widely accepted for benefits of humans but it should not cause problems of safety to people and create unacceptable social, moral and ethical issues.

The release of genetically manipulated organisms into the environment has been a controversial issue. This is due to the fact that living GEOs proliferate, disperse and sometimes may transfer their DNA into other organisms and create new species. This may lead to serve environmental damage. The transgenic plants and animals are used genetically modified foods. Some social and environmental groups are against the consumption of genetically modified foods. The transgenic plants such as cotton, corn, soybean and potato are approved for cultivation in USA. However, some countries does not allow Bt-plants in their field e.g. Philippines (Bt-rice), France (Bt-cotton) etc. A majority of transgenic animals are used for medical purposes but the major problem of transgenic animals comes from animal activists. The most series hazard associated with recombinant DNA technology is the construction of harmful biological agents for use as biological weapons. Many countries are concerned about the possible use of gene manipulations for military purposes.

The recombinant products designed for human healthcare are easily acceptable by the society such as insulin, vaccines, interferons, tissue plasminogen activator etc. The main objective of biotechnological research is for the benefit of human beings. Now-a-days, main research in biotechnology is focused on genetic testing, genetic portfolios and human gene therapy. The elucidation of the entire human genome sequence and identification of genes are possible by recent developments in genetics. It is possible to have individual genetic portfolios that will diagnose future health complications such as risk of cancer, heart disease etc. This development in genetics may have certain problems with regard to marriages and insurances. There is not much controversy over gene therapy because it is used for medical disorders. However, the gene therapy must be under a close supervision to satisfy medical, legal, ethical and safety implications, besides addressing the public concerns. Embryonic stem cell research technology may be used for treating diseases with cell therapy. There are many ethical and legal issues involved in embryonic stem cell research.

BIOTECH PRODUCTS AND ITS SAFETY

Biotechnological discoveries in the areas of pharmaceuticals, agriculture and healthcare have raised many ethical issues for biotech products. Most of the countries have environmental regulations that ban the deliberate release of genetically engineered microorganisms (GMMs). These microorganisms may be responsible to spread the disease in the society or to change the ecological balance in the environment. The International Centre for Genetic Engineering and Biotechnology (ICGEB) has also played an important role in biosafety. The ICGEB has provided an on-line bibliographic data base on biosafety and risk assessment for the environmental release of genetically modified organisms (GMOs). This database is easily accessible through the website of ICGEB and it also provides information on biosafety to its member states. India has instituted the Recombinant DNA Advisory Committee located in the Department of Biotechnology (DBT), under the Government of India. This committee mainly formulates and updates the biosafety guidelines, guides and advises the institutional biosafety committees. The main areas for safety aspects in biotechnology are as follows:

- Highly pathogenic organisms (natural and modified) to infects humans, animals and plants.
- Development of antibiotic resistant microorganisms.
- Transgene instability and unpredictable gene expression.
- Change in nutritional value and loss of biodiversity in agriculture.
- Disposal of spent microbial biomass and purification of effluents from biotechnological processes.
- Transfer of gene and generation of new line viruses by recombination.
- Contamination, infection or mutation of process strains.

Recombinant DNA technology enables humans to combine DNA sequences from different sources to create functional DNA molecules with novel properties. The recombinant DNA techniques initially raised concerns in the scientific community and remain a public concern even today. A living modified organisms means any living organisms that contains a novel combination of genetic material obtained through the use of modern biotechnology. The National Institute of Health (NIH, USA) has developed guidelines for recombinant DNA research with a view to specify the practices for constructing and handling of recombinant DNA molecules. Recombinant DNA experiments are performed after approval from NIH or any other agency.

In India, DBT has evolved 'the recombinant DNA safety guidelines' to exercise powers through the Environmental protection Act, 1986 for the manufacture, use, storage, export and import of hazardous microorganisms or genetically engineered organisms. These guidelines are being implemented through the institutional biosafety committees (IBSCs) which monitor the research activity at institutional level, the review committee on genetic manipulation which allows the risky research activities in the laboratories and the genetic engineering approval committee (GEAC) which permits large scale use of GMOs at commercial level.

INTELLECTUAL PROPERTY RIGHT (IPR) AND PROTECTION (IPP)

Pharmaceutical biotechnology has played a significant role in processing, designing and production of commercial products utilizable in many area of the society as agriculture, medical, health care industry and environment. Intellectual property right (IPR) usually refers to laws that protect inventions that are new and have use for society. Inventions are protected in different ways such as patents, copyrights, trade secrets and trademarks, designs etc. Patent is a special right to the inventor that has been granted by the respective government through legislation for trading new articles. Patent consists three parts as grant, specifications and claims. The grant is filled at the patent office which is not published. It is a signed document that represents actually the agreement which solely grants patent right to the inventor. The specification and claims are published as a single document which is made public at a minimum charge from the patent office. US-FDA has regulatory purview pertaining to the patented pharmaceuticals before allowing them for actual use. The environment protection agency of the USA working under the jurisdiction of Federal Insecticide, Fungicide and Rodenticide Act permits the release of genetically engineered microbial pesticides. In India, Department of Biotechnology (DBT) has formulated the recombinant DNA safety guidelines to exercise powers conferred through Environmental Protection Act, 1986. The genetic engineering approval committee (GEAC) of the Ministry of Environment and Forest has the powers to allow large scale use of genetically engineered microbes (GEMs).

The application of a patent is prepared with a specific, clear, concise title with novelty of product or process. The inventors must decide first that the patent is to be filed at national or international office. A patent attorney is appointed for the legal aspects of the patent and then the patent is filed in the office of the controller of patents. The patent comes into enforcement after getting the grant. Steps envolved in patent process are given in Fig. 20.1. The patent is in the form of letter which contains the name of inventor, the name of patentee, a description of patent and the relevant claims.

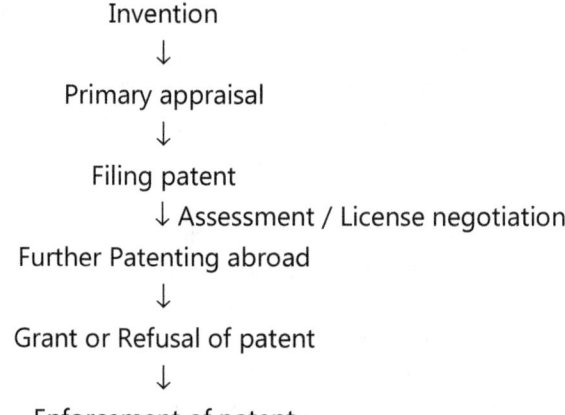

Fig. 20.1: Steps involved in patent process

The copyright protection is nothing but a kind of expression of ideas. In copyrights of books, the authors, editors, publishers or both publisher and author/editor have the provision of copyrights. The materials/contents of the book can not be reproduced without the prior written permission from the legal copyright holders. Biotechnological derived materials subject to copyright includes photomicrographs, database of DNA sequences and any published forms. Trade secrets refers to the 'private proprietary information' which benefits the owners. The trade secrets in the area of biotechnology may essentially comprise of several parameters such as cell lines, hybridization conditions, processing, designing, consumer's list etc. The trade mark is an identification symbol which is used in the course of trade to enable the public to distinguish on trader's goods from the similar goods of the other traders. e.g. KODAK-photography goods, IBM computers, RAYMONDS-suiting materials etc. Multinational companies spend large amount of money to maintain their trademarks throughtout the world.

A genetically engineered strain of the *Pseudomonas* called superbug was the first microorganism to be patented by US government. In 1990, the US government allowed to **Dr. Anand Mohan Chakrabarty** to treat oil spill by using this species. In 1988, the patent was issued to genetically engineered mouse 'oncomouse' in USA and UK which is the first patent for 'live form'. This transgenic mouse carries a gene that makes it susceptible to tumor formation. Similarly, genetically engineered *E. coli* in which human genes for insulin, growth hormone, tPA etc. have been patented in the USA. Insect-resistant tobacco and bollworm-resistant cotton have been granted patents. Patenting of DNA sequences and genes in the human genome projects has become a controversial and debatable issue. So far, patents have not been granted for genes because genes are natural and inherent biological functional units of all individuals.

IN-VITRO FERTILIZATION (IVF) IN HUMANS

Assisted Reproductive Technology (ART) in humans in one of the greatest advances in the reproduction of humans. When the union between sperm and egg cell occurs outside the body in a culture vessel by maintaining optimum conditions artificially, it is known as in-vitro fertilization. This involves collection of ovum from females and sperms from males and their fusion under appropriate conditions in-vitro. The resulting zygotes may be cultured in-vitro to obtain young embryos, which are implanted in the uterus of healthy females which act as foster mother or surrogate mothers. This technique is called as embryo transplantation. In-vitro fertilization and embryo transfer are being applied to animals for a rapid multiplication of desirable genotypes of animals and in cases of infertility of certain types in humans.

Infertilities in humans:

There is a large number of reasons for developing infertilites in humans. Total count of sperms should be 15 to 20 million per ml in fertile human. When the number of sperms decreases, the person is called oligospermic and the condition as oligospermia. Infertility may be because of total lack or very low concentration of motile sperm. This type of male is called azoospermic and the phenomenon as azoospermia. There are several reasons and types of female infertility.

Tubal infertility: This occurs due to non-functional or damaged fallopian tubes. In-vitro fertilization followed by embryo transfer in uterus has replaced the function of fallopian tubes.

Non-functional or inaccessible ovaries: Some women, possess ovaries that are non-functional or in some cases the ovaries may be totally absent. These females may serve as surrogate mothers. The oocyte has to be obtained from a donor woman and in-vitro fertilized with the husband's sperm.

Non-functional or absent uterus: In some woman, the uterus may be absent or non-functional. In such a case, the oocytes of these women can be fertilized by the husband's sperms and then embryo is transferred into the uterus of surrogate mother for pregnancy and further development.

Idiopathic infertility: Some women may be infertile for unknown reasons which is called as 'idiopathic infertility'. It may be due to abnormal fertilization or failure in fertilization. In-vitro fertilization followed by embryo transfer may be used to treat this infertility.

Human Artificial Insemination:

Human artificial insemination is used as assisted reproductive technology primarily to treat infertility. It is mainly used to enable women without a male partner (single women and lesbians) to become pregnant and to produce children by using sperm provided by a sperm donor. In this case, the woman is the genetic and gestational mother of the child, and the sperm donor is the genetic or biological father of the child.

A sperm sample is provided by the male partner of the woman undergoing artificial insemination. Sperm sample may be used from sperm donor if the woman's partner produces too few motile sperm or he carries a genetic disorder or the woman has no male partner. Sperm is usually obtained through masturbation or a special condom may be used to collect the semen during intercourse. The man providing the sperm is usually advised not to ejaculate for two to three days before providing the sample in order to increase the sperm count.

In intra-uterine insemination (IUI), the sperm must immediately be "washed" in a laboratory and a chemical is added to the sample. The process of "washing" the sperm increases the chances of fertilization and removes any chemicals in the semen that may cause discomfort for the woman. If sperm is provided by a sperm donor through a sperm bank, it is frozen and quarantined for a particular period. The donor is tested before and after production of the sample to ensure that he does not carry a transmissible disease. Sperm samples donated in this method are produced through masturbation by the sperm donor at the sperm bank. Cryoprotectant is added in the sperm to aid the freezing and thawing process. Some chemicals may be added which separate the most active sperm in the sample as well as extending or diluting the sample so that vials for a number of inseminations are produced.

A woman's menstrual cycle is closely observed, by tracking basal body temperature (BBT) and changes in vaginal mucous or using ovulation kits, ultrasounds or blood tests. When an ovum is released, semen provided by the woman's partner or by a donor is inserted into the female's vagina or uterus. Semen is occasionally inserted twice within a 'treatment cycle'. A pregnancy resulting from artificial insemination is no different from any other pregnancy.

The easiest way to inseminate is by intracervical insemination (ICI), where semen is injected high into the cervix with a needle-less syringe. This process most closely replicates the way in which semen is depositied by the penis in the cervix when the male ejaculates during vaginal intercourse. However, more technical procedures may be used which increase the chances of conception. Semen from which certain chemicals have been removed (washed semen) can be injected directly into a woman's uterus in a process called intrauterine insemination (IUI). If the semen is not washed it may elicit uterine cramping, expelling the semen and causing pain, because it content prostaglandins. Intrauterine insemination can be combined with intratubal insemination (ITI), into the Fallopian tube.

Artificial insemination has become a significant issue in recent years, particularly in debates revolving around same sex parenting, single mother parenting and surrogate parenting. Legal issues have arisen in cases where the gestational (and possibly genetic) mother decides to keep the child. Likewise, there have been debates over the rights and obligations of sperm donors.

In-vitro fertilization and embryo transfer:

In-vitro fertilization and embryo transfer is aimed to enable couples suffering from certain types of sterility to have children to their own. This technique deals with the removal of eggs from a women, fertilizing them in the laboratory and then transferring the fertilized eggs (zygotes) into the uterus of women. The different steps involved in the technique are:

(i) Collection of oocytes (ii) Collection of sperms (iii) In-vitro fertilization (iv) Embryo transfer

(i) Collection of oocytes:

Oocytes for in-vitro fertilization are collected from the female, who is interested for child. The sterility of female is due to the absence of ovaries, then the oocytes are collected from donor females. Oocytes are collected at right time of development by monitoring the stimulation of ovary. There are many parameters which are used as indicators for stimulation of ovary that includes rise in the level of luteinising hormone (LH) either in urine or in blood, rise in temperature of body during preovulatory and postovulatory days, changes in cervical mucus and estimation of progesterone and oestrogen. Controlled ovarian hyperstimulation (COH) technique is used in in-vitro fertilization for development of more embryos. The specific drug regimes are used to induce superovulation such as clomiphene citrate (CC), human menopausal gonadotrophin (hMG), follicle stimulating hormone (FSH),CC+ hMG, CC + FSH etc.

Oocytes are recovered by the most convenient and efficient equipment called laproscopy. The follicles are observed by using microscopic equipment and aspirated with the aspirating apparatus. The aspirating apparatus inserted into the abdomen of the female via a suitable tube for collection of oocytes. The oocytes are identified and incubated for 5 to 10 hours depending on maturity of oocytes and follicles. Whittingham's T6 medium, Earl's solution, modified Whitten's medium or modified Ham's F10 medium is used for oocyte culture andin-vitro fertilization.

(ii) **Collection of sperms:**
The semen is collected from husband of female partner or from semen bank. Husband's semen is collected at proper place when required through masturbation, 60-90 minutes prior to insemination. Semen is liquefied and centrifuged. The sperm pellet is resuspended in culture medium and incubated at 37^oC for 30 to 60 minutes. The most active spermatozoa float at surface. Hence, the sample of spermatozoa is used from the surface of the medium for in-vitro fertilization.

(iii) **In-vitro fertilization:**
In-vitro fertilization is performed by adding 10,000 to 50,000 motile sperms in 1 ml of culture medium containing oocytes. The oocytes are examined after 12 to 13 hours for the number of pronuclei and polar bodies, and granulation and shape of the oocyte. A normally fertilized oocyte (zygote) contains two pronuclei and two polar bodies. The abnormal fertilized oocyte contains more than two pronuclei and granulation in cytoplasm. The abnormal embryo is discarded and only normal embryo is used for implantation.

(iv) **Embryo transfer:**
In-vitro fertilized embryos of 1 to 16 cells have been successfully transferred into uterus but the best stage is 2 to 4 cell stage. A prolonged in-vitro culture of embryos reduces their survival rate while younger embryos are sensitive to uterine environment. The success rate may increases by transferring multiple embryos but it may lead to multiple pregnancy.

The embryo is transferred into uterus through cervical canal with the help of a teflon catheter along with 10 ml of tissue culture medium. Embryo transfer must be performed with extreme care to avoid fallopian tube pregnancy or expulsion or embryo from uterine cavity. It is necessary that the female receiving the embryo must be in the correct stage of her menstrual cycle and the female is allowed to take rest for about 5 to 7 hours. Sometimes, a surrogate mother may be used for the embryo transfer.

Human embryos are successfully preserved in the presence of cryoprotectants such as glycerol, dimethyl sulfoxide or 2-propanediol and stored at $-196^\circ C$ under liquid nitrogen. The embryos are thawed, removed cryoprotectants and then transferred at appropriate time. Semen, fertilized eggs and embryos are commonly preserved in assisted reproductive technology.

The bodies produced by using this in-vitro fertilization approach are known as test tube babies. The first test tube baby **Loise Brown** was born in UK on 28th July, 1978. This technique is widely used in all over world to provide the joy of having their own babies to couples suffering infertility. However, many religious, ethical, emotional, social or political issues related to this development may need resolution. Some communities do not approve in-vitro fertilization techniques. Some countries believe the sperm donation as immoral. Children born of donated sperms are considered illegitimate. About unused embryos has an emotional problem. Whether this embryos implanted in surrogate mothers or thrown away. For children born through donated egg or sperm, its social or religious recognition, biological parents and acceptance from the parents are the major issues in in-vitro fertilization technology.

QUESTIONS

(A) Short answer questions:
1. What is oocytes?
2. Write the importance of patenting biotech products.
3. Explain the following: (a) ICGEB (b) GMOs

(B) Long answer questions:
1. Write a note on
   (a) Infertilities in humans
   (b) IPR and IPP of biotech products.
   (c) Safety of biotech products
2. Explain in short in-vitro fertilization and embryo transfer in humans.

(C) Multiple choice questions:
1. A genetically engineered strain of the _____ called superbug was the first microorganism to be patented by US government
   (a) *Pseudomonas*   (b) *Aspergillus*
   (c) *Bacillus*   (d) *Candida*
2. _____ is used for oocyte culture and in-vitro fertilization
   (a) Whittingham's N12 medium   (b) Whittingham's T12 medium
   (c) Whittingham's N6 medium   (d) Whittingham's T6 medium

(D) Fill in the blanks:
1. The _____ protection is nothing but a kind of expression of ideas.
2. Human embryos are successfully preserved in the presence of _____ and stored at $-196^\circ C$ under liquid nitrogen.

■■■

APPENDICES

APPENDIX I – ANSWER KEY

Chapter 1 : Biotechnology - Scope and Importance
- (C) 1 – (a), 2 – (d), 3 – (d), 4 – (b), 5 – (d), 6 – (b)
- (D) (a) – (iii), (b) – (i), (c) – (iv), (d) – (ii)
- (E) 1 – plant tissue culture, 2 – Meseleson and Stahl

Chapter 2 : Development of Industrial Strains
- (C) 1 – (d), 2 – (d), 3 – (d)
- (D) (a) – (iv), (b) – (iii), (c) – (ii), (d) – (i)
- (E) 1 – oceans, 2 – Replica

Chapter 3 : Fermentation Process
- (C) 1 – (c), 2 – (a), 3 – (d), 4 – (b), 5 – (c)
- (D) (a) – (iii), (b) – (i), (c) – (ii), (d) – (iv)
- (E) 1 – *Saccharomyces cervisiae*, 2 – Molasses,

Chapter 4 : Down Stream Process and Biological Waste Treatment
- (C) 1 – (d), 2 – (b), 3 – (c),
- (D) 1 – Chlorine, 2 – *Pseudomonas putida*, 3 – oxygen

Chapter 5 : Production of Pharmaceuticals
- (C) 1 – (C), 2 – (B), 3 – (C), 4 – (B), 5 – (B)
- (D) (a) – (ii), (b) – (iv), (c) – (i), (d) – (iii)
- (E) 1 – *Streptomyces aureofaciens*, 2 – 6-aminopenicillanic acid

Chapter 6 : Microbial Biotransformation
- (C) 1 – (d), 2 – (b), 3 – (a), 4 – (a)
- (D) (a) – (iii), (b) – (i), (c) – (iv), (d) – (ii)
- (E) 1 – prostanoic acid, 2 – penicillin acylase, 3 – *Rhizopus nigricans*

Chapter 7 : Introduction to Genetics
- (C) 1 – (d), 2 – (b), 3 – (b), 4 – (d), 5 – (b), 6 – (a), 7 – (c), 8 – (d), 9 – (b), 10 – (a), 11 – (a)
- (D) a – (iv), b – (iii), c – (ii), d – (i)
- (E) 1 – Transposase 2 – episomes 3 – Watson and Crick 4 – ultraviolet radiation 5 – 20A°

Chapter 8 : DNA Replication, Transcription and Translation
- (C) 1 – (a), 2 – (d), 3 – (a), 4 – (b), 5 – (a)
- (D) (a) – (iv), (b) – (i), (c) – (ii), (d) – (iii)
- (E) 1 – aminoacyl-tRNA, 2 – replication

Chapter 9 : Genetic Recombination (Gene Transfer)
- (C) 1 – (b), 2 – (d), 3 – (d), 4 – (a)
- (D) a – (iv), b – (i), c – (ii), d – (iii)
- (E) 1 – conjugation, 2 – lysogeny, 3 – vector, 4 – prophage.

Chapter 10 : Recombinant DNA Technology (Gene Cloning)
(C) 1 – (a), 2 – (c), 3 – (b), 4 – (a)
(D) (a) – (iv), (b) – (iii), (c) – (ii), (d) – (i)
(E) 1 – *Haemophilus influenzae*, 2 – Shuttle

Chapter 11 : Techniques of Genetic Engineering
(C) 1 – (b), 2 – (c), 3 – (a)
(D) 1 – genomic library, 2 – dideoxynucleotide

Chapter 12 : Blotting Techniques and Gel Electrophoresis
(C) 1 – (a), 2 – (a), 3 – (c)
(D) (a) – (ii), (b) – (i), (c) – (iv), (d) – (iii)
(E) 1 – polyacrylamide, 2 – ethidium bromide, 3 – southern

Chapter 13 : Healthcare Biotechnology
(C) 1 – (b), 2 – (d)
(D) (a) – (iv), (b) – (i), (c) – (ii), (d) – (iii)
(E) 1 – diabetes mellitus, 2 – Somatotropin

Chapter 14 : Blood and Blood Products
(C) 1 – (a), 2 – (b)
(D) (a) – (iv), (b) – (iii), (c) – (i), (d) – (ii)
(E) 1 – Sucrose, 2 – Factor VI

Chapter 15 : Surgical Dressings, Ligatures and Sutures
(C) 1 – (b), 2 – (b)

Chapter 16: Enzyme Technology
(C) 1 – (d), 2 – (b), 3 – (d), 4 – (a), 5 – (a)
(D) (a) – (ii), (b) – (iii), (c) – (i), (d) – (iv)
E) 1 – Penicillinase, 2 – Streptokinase

Chapter 17 : Plant Tissue Culture
(C) 1 – (d), 2 – (a), 3 – (b), 4 – (a), 5 – (d), 6 – (c), 7 – (a), 8 – (d), 9 – (d), 10 – (d), 11 – (d)
(D) 1. (a) – (iv), (b) – (iii), (c) – (i), (d) – (ii)
    2. (a) – (iv), (b) – (i), (c) – (ii), (d) – (iii)
(E) 1 – *Agrobacterium*, 2 – embryogensis, 3 – Sucrose, 4 – 1.0 mg/lit., 5 – *Agrobacterium*

Chapter 18 : Transgenic Plants
(C) 1 – (a), 2 – (a)

Chapter 19: Animal Tissue Culture
(C) 1 – (b), 2 – (c)
(D) (a) – (iv), (b) – (iii), (c) – (ii), (d) – (i)
(E) 1 – Chick embryo, 2 – Mammary

Chapter 20 : Biotechnology and Ethics
(C) 1 – (a), 2 – (d)
(D) 1 – Copyright, 2 – Cryoprotectants

APPENDIX II – BIBLIOGRAPHY

(A) BOOKS

- Anathnarayan R. and Panikar C. K. J., (2000). Textbook of Microbiology, Sixth Edition, Orient Longman.
- Arora D. R., (1999). Textbook of Microbiology, First Edition CBS Publishers and Distributor, New Delhi.
- Baird, R. M., et al. (eds.), (2000). Handbook of Microbiological Quality Control – Pharmaceutical and Medical Devices. Taylor and Francis Inc., London.
- Balasubramanian D. et. al. (eds); (2004). Concepts in Biotechnology, First edition, Universities Press (India) Private Limited.
- Bhatia R. and Ichhpujani R. L., (1994). Essentials of Medical Microbiology, Fifth Edition, Jaypee Brothers, New Delhi.
- Bhojwani S. S. and Razdan M. K. (1996), Plant Tissue Culture, Elsevier, New Delhi.
- British Pharmacopoeia, (1993). London, HMSO.
- Casida L. E., (2000). Industrial Microbiology, New Age International, Delhi.
- Collee J. G. et al., (1996). Mackie and McCartney Practical Medical Microbiology, Fourteenth Edition, Churchill Livingstone Publications, New York.
- Crueger W. and Cruegar A. (2005). Biotechnology, Second Edition, Panima Publishing Corporation, New Delhi.
- Cruickshank R. (ed.), (1965). Medical Microbiology, Eleventh Edition, E. and S. Livingstone Ltd.
- Debnath M. (2005). Tools and Techniques of Biotechnology. First Edition, Pointer Publishers, Jaipur.
- Demain A. L. and Davies J. E. (eds), (1999) Manual of Industrial Microbiology and Biotechnology, Second Edition, ASM Press, Washington, D.C.
- Dubey R. C., (2006). A Text book of Biotechnology, Fourth Edition, S. Chand and Company Ltd.
- Gangal S., (2007). Principles and Practice of Animal Tissue Culture. Universities Press (India) Private Limited, Hyderabad.
- Gupta P. K., (2007). Elements of Biotechnology, First Edition, Rastogi Publications, Meerut.
- Gupte S., (2002). The Short Textbook of Medical Microbiology, Eighth Edition, Jaypee Brothers, New Delhi.
- Hugo W. B. and Russell A. D., (1998). Pharmaceutical Microbiology, Sixth Edition, Backwell Science.
- Ian Freshney R., (2000). Culture of Animal Cells – A manual of basic technique, Fourth Edition, Wiley-Liss Publication.

- Indian Pharmacopoeia, (1996). Govt. of India, Ministry of Health and Family Welfare.
- Ingraham J. L. and Ingraham C. A. (2002). Introduction to Microbiology, Second edition, Thomson Books / Cole.
- Ketchum P. A., (1988). Microbiology- Concepts and Applications, John Wiley and Sons, New York.
- Kokare C. R., (2013), Pharmaceutical Microbiology – Experiments and Techniques, Fourth Edition, Career Publications, Nashik, India.
- Kokare C. R., (2008), Basic Microbiology – For Nursing and Health Science, First Edition, Nirali Prakashan, Pune.
- Kokare C. R., (2013), Pharmaceutical Microbiology – Principles and Applications, Nineth Edition, Nirali Prakashan, Pune.
- Kokare C. R., (2009), Pharmaceutical Biotechnology- Fundamentals and Applications. Second Edition, Nirali Prakashan, Pune
- Kokare C. R., (2011), Pharmaceutical Biotechnology- Experiments and Techniques. First Edition, Nirali Prakashan, Pune
- Kokare C. R. and Kokare S. R. (2013), Research Methodology, First Edition, Nirali Prakashan, Pune (In Press)
- Lachman L. et al., (1987). The Theory and Practice of Industrial Pharmacy, Third Edition, Varghese Publishing House.
- Lorian V. (1986). Antibiotics in Laboratory Medicine. Second Edition, Williams and Wilkins. Co. Baltimore, USA.
- Nelson D. L. and Cox M. M., (2005), Lehninger Principles of Biochemistry, Fourth Edition, W. H. Freeman and Company, New York.
- Patel A. H. (2005). Industrial Microbiology. First Edition, Macmillan India Ltd.
- Pelczar M. J. et al., (1986). Microbiology, Fifth Edition, MaGraw Hill, New York.
- Philopose P. M. (2004). A Textbook of Biotechnology, First Edition, Dominant Pubishers and Distributors, New Delhi.
- Rangari V. D. (2003). Pharmacognosy and Phytochemistry Part II, First Edition, Career Publications, Nashik.
- Rawlins E. A., (ed.), (1992). Bentley's Textbook of Pharmaceutics, Eighth Edition, Bailliere Tindall, London.
- Rehm H. J. and Reed G. (eds.), (1989), Biotechnology, Volume 7b, VCH Publishers.
- Salle A. J., (1974). Fundamental Principles of Bacteriology, Seventh Edition, Tata McGraw-Hill Publishing Company Ltd., New Delhi.

- Sambrook J., Russel D. W., (2001), Molecular Cloning, A laboratory manual, Vol. – I, Third Edition, Cold Spring Harbor Laboratory Press, New York.
- Satyanarayana U (2005). Biotechnology, First Edition , Books and Allied (P) Ltd. Kolkatta.
- Singh B.D. (2005). Biotechnology, Second Edition, Kalyani Publishers, Ludhiana.
- Stanbury P. F. et. al., (1995). Principles of Fermentation Technology, Second Edition. Butterworth-Heinemann.
- Swarbrick J. and Boylan J. C., (1994). Encyclopedia of Pharmaceutical Technology, Vol.9, Marcel Dekker, Inc., New York.
- Talaro K. and Talaro A., (1996). Foundations in Microbiology, Second Edition, Wm C. Brown Publishers, U. S. A.
- Tortora G. J. et al., (1998). Microbiology: An Introduction, Third Edition, Benjamin/ Cummings Publishing, California.
- Vyas S. P. and Dixit V. K. (2003), Pharmaceutical Biotechnology, First Edition, CBS Publishers and Distributors.
- Vyas S. P. and Kohli D.V. (2004), Methods in Biotechnology and Bioengineering. First Edition, CBS Publishers and Distributors, New Delhi.
- Walsh G., (2003), Biopharmaceuticals, Biochemistry and Biotechnology, Second Edition, Antony Rowe Ltd., Great Britain.
- Winfield A. J. and Richards R. M. E. (eds.), (1998). Pharmaceutical Practice, Second Edition, Varghese Publishing House.

(B) JOURNALS

- Athalye M. and Lacey J. (1981). Selective isolation and enumeration of actinomycetes using rifampicin *J. Appl. Bacteriol.* 51 : 289-97.
- Austin B. (1989). A Review : Novel pharmaceutical compounds from marine bacteria. *J. Appl. Bacteriol.* 67 : 461-470.
- Carter K. C. (2006). The genome as a tool for drug discovery and development. *Genomics*, 71-76.
- Chirino A. J. and Mire-sluis A. (2004). Characterizing biological products and assessing comparability following manufacturing changes. *Nature Biotech.*, 22(11), 1383-1389.
- Danzen P. M. et. al. (2005). Productivity in pharmaceutical–biotechnology R and D : the role of experience and alliances. *J. Health Economics*, 24, 317-339.
- Elnifro E. M. et al. (2000). Multiplex PCR : Optimization and application of diagnostic virology. *Clinical Microbiol. Reviews*, 13(4), 559 – 570.
- Florian M. Wurm (2004). Production of recombinant protein therapeutics in cultivated mammalian cells, *Nature Biotech.*, 22 (11), 1393 – 1397.
- Gupta P. K. et. al. (1999). DNA chips, microarrays and genomics. *Curr. Sci.*, 77(7), 875-884.

- Hall W. D. et. al. (2004). The prediction of disease risk in genomic medicine, *EMBO reports*, 5, 22-26.
- Iwai Y. and Omura S. (1982). Culture conditions for screening of new antibiotics. *J. Antibiot.* 35(2): 123-141.
- Jensen P. R. and Fenical W., (1994). Strategies for the discovery of secondary metabolites from marine bacteria : Ecological perspectives. *Annu. Rev. Microbiol.* 48 :559-584.
- Juma C. and Konde V. (2001). Industrial and Environmental application of biotechnology. Paper prepared for the united nations conference on Trade and Development Geneva, Switzerland.
- Kokare C. R. et. al., (2004). Iosolation, characterization and antimicrobial activity of marine halophilic *Actinopolyspora* species from west coast of India. *Curr. Sci.* 58, 283-289.
- Kokare C. R. et. al., (2004). Isolation of bioactive marine actinomycetes from sediments isolated from Goa and Maharashtra coastline (west coast of India). *Indian J. Mar. Sci.*, 33(3), 248-256.
- Kokare C. R. et. al. (2005). Production of acetamide derivatives from marine *Streptomyces* species isolated from west coast of India. *Biosci. Biotech. Research Asia*, 3(2), 307-316.
- Kokare C. R. et. al. (2009). Biofilm : Importance and Applications, *Indian J.* Biotech, 8, 159-168.
- Lai K. M. et. al. (2002). Biotransformation and bioconcentration of steroid estrogens by *Chlorella vulgaris*. *Appl. Environ. Microbiol.* 68(2), 859-864.
- Mulherkar R. (2001). Gene therapy for cancer. *Curr. Sci.*, 81(5), 555-560.
- Palmer D. H. et. al. (2006), Cancer gene-therapy : clinical trials. *Trends in Biotech.*, 24(2), 76-82.
- Perez-Guerra N. et. al. (2003). Main characteristics and applications of solid substrate fermentation. *Electron. J. Environ. Agric. Food chem.*, 2(3), 1-8.
- Plourde R. et. al. (1972). Reduction of the 20-carbonyl group of C-21 steroids by spores of *Fusarium solani* and other microorganisms. *Appl. Microbiol.*, 23(3), 601-612.
- Raimbault M. (1998). General and microbiological aspects of solid substrate fermentation. *Electron J. of Biotech*. 1(3), 174-188.
- Samrat C. et. al. (2009). Isolation and Characterization of novel α-amylase from marine Streptomyces sp. D1. *J. Molecular Catalysis B : Enzymatic*, 58, 17-23.
- Wang D. et. al. (2005). The bioreactor : A powerful tool for large scale culture of animal cells. *Curr. Pharm. Biotech.* 6, 397-403.
- WIlliamson J. et. al. (1985), Microbiological hydroxylation of estradiol : Formation of 2- and 4-hydroxyestradiol by *Aspergillus alliaceus*. *App. Environ. Microbiol*, 49(3), 563-567.

INDEX

A

Absorbable sutures, 15.12
Absorbent cotton, 15.5
Absorbents, 15.5
Accidental contamination, 2.5
Actinomycetes, 2.3
Activated sludge process, 4.7
Activators, 16.8
Adapter, 10.8
Adhesive bandages, 15.9
Adhesive tapes, 15.9
Adsorption, 16.10
Agranulocytes, 14.5
Agrobacterium tumefaciens, 9.9, 18.2
Air-lift, 3.15
Alkaline phosphatase, 10.5
Amide formation, 6.10
Amylases, 16.22
Animal cell culture, 19.1
Antibodies, 1.6
Anticoagulants, 14.8
Applied branches, 1.2
Aromatization, 6.6
Automated DNA sequencing, 11.17
Auxanography, 2.6

B

Bacteriophage vectors, 10.12
Bandages, 15.7
Batch culture, 3.2
Bioinformatics, 1.4, 1.9
Biological waste treatment, 4.6
Biosafety, 20.2
Biosensors, 16.18
Biotech products, 20.2
Biotechnology, 1.1, 1.3, 12.13, 20.1
Blood groups, 14.6
Blood serum, 19.2
Blood, 14.2, 14.5
Blotting techniques, 12.1
Blue biotechnology, 1.4
Bubble-column, 3.16

C

Callus culture, 17.14
cDNA library, 11.9
Cell lines, 19.9
Cellular totipotency, 17.11
Cloning vectors, 10.9
Collagen, 15.14
Colony hybridization, 10.20
Complexation, 16.13
Condensation, 6.12
Conjugation, 9.2
Continuous culture, 3.5
Continuous fermentation, 3.13
Cosmid vectors, 10.14
Covalent bonding, 16.11
Criminal forensic, 1.7
Crowded plate, 2.4
Culture media, 17.7, 19.2
Culture room, 17.5
Cup-plate, 2.9
Cylinder plate, 2.8

D

Decarboxylation, 6.11
Dehydrogenation, 6.5
Dextran, 5.18, 14.18
DNA cloning, 10.1
DNA ligase, 10.6
DNA polymerase, 10.6, 11.13
DNA probes, 12.5
DNA replication, 8.1, 8.3
DNA transfer, 2.13
DNA, 7.1
Dot blotting, 12.4
Downstream processing, 4.2
Drug resistance, 7.19

E

Elastic bandages, 15.7
ELISA, 16.19
Encapsulation, 16.14
Enrichment culture, 2.5
Entrapment, 16.15

Enzymatic disaggregation, 19.7
Enzyme immobilization, 16.9
Enzyme kinetics, 16.3
Enzymes, 16.2
Epoxidation, 6.5
Erythrocytes, 14.3
Esterification, 6.10
Expression vector, 10.18

Fed-batch culture, 3.6
Fermentation media, 3.8
Fermentation, 3.1
Fermenter, 3.11, 3.20
Finger printing, 11.11
Fluctuation test, 7.17
Forms of DNA, 7.6

Gel electrophoresis, 12.6
Gelatin, 14.16
Gene library, 11.16
Gene machine, 11.12
Gene sequencing, 11.14
Gene therapy, 11.18
Gene transcription, 8.9
Gene transfer, 18.1
Genetic engineering, 11.1
Genetic recombination, 9.1
Genomic library, 11.6
Genotypic changes, 7.13
Giant-colony, 2.8
Granulocytes, 14.4
Growth curve, 3.4
Growth phase, 6.2
Growth regulators, 17.10

H

Halogination, 6.10
Haploid culture, 17.19
Homopolymer tails, 10.9
Human albumin, 14.14
Human fibrin foam, 14.13

Human fibrinogen, 14.12
Human gene therapy, 11.18
Human genome project, 1.9
Human insulin, 13.2
Human normal immunoglobulin, 14.13
Human plasma protein fraction, 14.11
Human plasma, 14.10
Human RBCs, 14.9
Human serum, 14.12
Human thrombin, 14.13
Hyaluronidase, 16.24
Hybrid selection, 10.19
Hybridization, 11.5
Hydrolysis, 6.8
Hydroxyethyl starch, 14.16
Hydroxylation, 6.3

Impregnated bandages, 15.8
Indicator dye, 2.6
Inoculum development, 3.6, 5.3
Intellectual property right, 20.3
Interferons, 13.4
Inverse PCR, 12.12
Isolation of cultures, 2.1
Isolation of DNA, 11.3
Isomerisation, 6.10

Laboratory requirements, 17.4
Laminar bench, 19.5
Leukocytes, 14.4
Lineweaver-Burk, 16.7
Linker, 10.8

M

Milestones in biotechnology, 1.4
Molecular markers, 1.7
Monoclonal antibody, 1.7
Media, 2.2
Microbial biostransformation, 6.1
Mutagens, 7.15
Meselson-stahl, 8.2
Mutation, 2.10, 7.13

Non-elastic bandages, 15.8
Non-absorbable sutures, 15.14
Michaelis-Menten, 16.5
Media preparation room, 17.5
Meristem culture, 17.17

N

Nature of DNA, 7.2
Northern blotting, 12.3
Nucleosides, 7.3
Nucleotides, 7.3

O

Organ culture, 19.8
Oxidation pond, 4.8
Oxidation, 6.3

P

Packed bed, 3.17
PAGE, 12.8
pBR 322 plasmid, 10.11
PCR, 12.10
Penicillin, 5.1
Penicillinase, 16.23
Perfluorochemicals, 14.17
PFGE, 12.8
Pharmaceutical biotechnology, 1.2, 1.6
Phenotypic changes, 7.13
Plant tissue culture, 1.8, 17.1
Plasma substitutes, 14.15
Plasmid vectors, 10.10
Plasmids, 7.18
Pneumatic fermenter, 3.17
Polyacrylamide, 12.8
Polyvinylpyrrolidone, 14.16
Post-translation processing, 8.18
Preservation, 17.26
Primary cell culture, 19.5
Primers, 12.10
Proteases, 16.24
Protectives, 15.9
Protoplast culture, 17.21
Protoplast fusion, 9.9, 17.23
Pyharmacogenomics, 1.9

R

rDNA technology, 11.1, 1.6
Red biotechnology, 1.4
Reduction, 6.7
Replica plate, 7.18
Replication fork, 8.5
Restriction enzymes, 10.2
Reverse transcriptase, 10.6, 11.6
RFLP, 11.10
RNA Polymerase, 8.12
Root culture, 17.18
rRNA, 7.10
RT-PCR, 12.12

S

S1 nuclease, 10.5
Secondary screening, 2.6
Semiconservative mode, 7.5, 8.2
Septic tanks, 4.8
Shotgun method, 11.3
Shuttle vector, 10.14
Sigma mode, 8.4
Site-directed mutagenesis, 11.9
Solid state fermentation, 3.19
Somatostatin, 13.6
Somatotropin, 13.4
Southern blotting, 12.2
Spontaneous mutation, 7.16
Sterility testing, 15.16
Steroid, 6.1, 6.7
Strain improvement, 2.10
Streptodornase, 16.23
Streptokinase, 16.23
Streptomyces, 2.7, 5.6
Streptomycin, 5.6
Stroma-free hemoglobin, 14.17
Structure of DNA, 7.4
Submerged fermenter, 3.12
Surgical catgut, 15.12
Surgical dressings, 15.2
Surgical gauzes, 15.6
Surgical needles, 15.18
Suspension culture, 17.15
Synthetic sutures, 15.14

T

Tensile strength, 15.11, 15.16
Tetracycline, 5.10
Theta mode, 8.4
Thrombocytes, 14.5
Transduction, 9.5
Transfection, 10.18
Transfer room, 17.5
Transformation phase, 6.3
Transformation, 10.18, 9.7
Transgenic animals, 19.10
Transgenic plants, 18.7
Translation, 8.13
Tray fermenter, 3.18
Trickling filter, 4.7
tRNA, 7.11
Types of cultures, 17.12
Types of DNA, 7.8
Types of mutation, 7.14

U

U-tube, 9.3

V

Vitamin B_{12}, 5.15
Vitamin B_2, 5.13
White biotechnology, 1.4

W

Watch glass method, 19.8
Western blotting, 12.4
Wound dressings, 15.2

Y

Yeast vector, 10.14
Yeast artificial chromosome, 10.16

NOTES

Publication Offices

Pune Office
1312, Shivaji Nagar, 'Abhyudaya Pragati'
Off. J. M. Road, Pune 411005
Tel: (+91-020) 2551 2336/7/9
Fax: (+91-020) 2551 1379
Email: niralipune@pragationline.com

Mumbai Office
385, S.V.P. Road,
Rasdhara Co-op. Hsg. Society Ltd.
Girgaum, Mumbai 400004
Tel: (+91-022) 2385 6339 / 2386 9976
Fax: (+91-022) 2386 9976
Email: niralimumbai@pragationline.com

Main Distributions

☆ **Dhayari : NIRALI PRAKASHAN**
Sur. No. 28/25, Dhayari-Katraj Road,
Near Pari Company, Pune 411 041.
Tel: (+91-020) 24690204
Fax: (+91-020) 24690316.
Email: dhayari@pragationline.com
bookorder@pragationline.com

☆ **Pune City : NIRALI PRAKASHAN**
119, Budhwar Peth,
Jogeshwari Mandir Lane,
Pune 411 002.
Tel: (+91-020) 2445 2044, 6602 2708
Fax: (+91-020) 2445 1538
Email: nirililocal@pragationline.com

Retail Outlets

Mumbai :
PRAGATI BOOK CORNER
- Indira Niwas,
  111- A, Bhavani Shankar Road,
  Dadar (W) Mumbai 400 028
  Tel: (+91-022) 2422 3526 6662 5254
  Email: niralimumbai@pragationline.com

Pune :
PRAGATI BOOK CENTRE
- 157, Budhwar Peth, Pune 411 002.
  Tel: (+91-020) 2445 8887
  Fax: (+91-020) 6602 2707

- 676/B, Budhwar Peth,
  Opp. Jogeshwari Mandir, Pune 411 002
  Tel: (+91-020) 6601 7784 / 6602 0855
  Email : pbcpune@pragationline.com

- 28/A, Budhwar Peth, Ambar Chamber,
  Appa Balwant Chowk, Pune 411 002
  Tel: (+91-020) 6628 1669 / 2024 0335

- **PBC Book Sellers & Stationers**
  152, Budhwar Peth, Pune 411 002.
  Tel: (+91-020) 2445 2254

Branches

NAGPUR : Pratibha Book Distributors
Lokratna Commercial Complex,
Shop No. 3, First Floor,
Rani Zanshi Square, Sitabuldi,
Nagpur 440 012, Maharashtra,
Tel: (+91-0712) 254 7129

JALGAON : Nirali Prakashan
34, V. V. Golani Market, Navi Peth,
Jalgaon 425 001, Maharashtra,
Tel: (+91-0257) 222 0395

KOLHAPUR : Nirali Prakashan
New Mahadvar Road, Kedarling Plaza,
1st Floor, Opp. IDBI Bank,
Kolhapur 416 012, Maharashtra.
Mob: 9850046155

BANGALORE : Pragati Book House
House No.1, Sanjeevappa Lane,
Avenue Road Cross, Off. Rice Church,
Bangalore 560 002, Karnataka
Tel : (+91-080) 6451 3344 / 6451 3355
Fax : (+91-080) 2332 4437
Mob : 98450 21552 / 98805 82331
Email:bharatsavla@yahoo.com

CHENNAI : Pragati Books
9/1, Montieth Road, Behind Taas Mahal,
Egmore, Chennai 600 008, Tamil Nadu,
Tel: (+91-044) 5518 3535
Mob: 94440 01782

Email: info@pragationline.com   Website: www.pragationline.com

Also find us on www.facebook.com/niralibooks

www.ingramcontent.com/pod-product-compliance
Lightning Source LLC
Chambersburg PA
CBHW081204240426
43669CB00039B/2897